I0890504

Table of Contents

Detailed Table of Contents

This study investigates the influence of business intelligence (BI) and market research on the growth of e-commerce businesses, using a mixed-method approach that includes data analysis and case studies. Primary data is gathered through case studies, while secondary data is drawn from relevant literature. The research seeks to demonstrate how BI and market research enhance e-commerce competitiveness, profitability, and overall growth. Findings will provide e-commerce businesses with insights on leveraging BI for strategic expansion, help management understand the value of BI in decision-making, and guide BI teams in optimizing performance for better ROI. The study aims to show that a well-defined BI plan and comprehensive market research are essential for a successful e-commerce presence (Hypothesis: H1).

Data analytics and reporting technologies play an important role in leadership decision-making. This chapter examines how data analytics and reporting technology help decision-making in leadership. Previous research shows that modern data analytics tools have been incorporated to enhance decision-making processes, improve reporting accuracy, and drive business performance. Organizations using advanced analytics tools tend to see huge benefits in speed, accuracy, improved reporting, and strategic decision-making. Modern technical analytical and reporting tools help leadership understand data by interacting with dashboards, graphs, and real-time data, which helps make a strategy based on the data. There are great benefits of using data analytics and reporting technology in leadership decision-making, it improves efficiency, productivity, and overall organizational growth.

Preface

The digital marketing landscape is undergoing a seismic shift, driven by rapid advancements in technology. The rise of artificial intelligence (AI), data analytics, and social media has revolutionized the way businesses engage with consumers. In this fast-evolving world, staying ahead of technological trends and integrating them into marketing strategies is no longer optional—it is essential. As businesses adapt to these changes, there is a growing need for comprehensive resources that not only explore the latest technological innovations but also demonstrate how these tools can be effectively used to achieve marketing objectives.

Advancing the Marketing Technology (MarTech) Revolution seeks to fill this gap by offering a thorough exploration of the most transformative elements of modern marketing technology. Each chapter in this book delves into different facets of MarTech, providing in-depth analysis, case studies, and practical insights that can help businesses and marketers navigate this complex environment. From artificial intelligence to influencer marketing, the book highlights how these tools are reshaping consumer engagement and driving business growth in unprecedented ways.

In Chapter 1, the role of AI in digital marketing is examined, showcasing how it revolutionizes customer engagement. Chapter 2 explores the disruptive potential of generative AI in content creation, illustrating how automation is transforming the way content is developed and distributed. The impact of social media marketing on Vietnamese Generation Z's purchasing decisions is discussed in Chapter 3, while Chapter 4 delves into how influencer marketing technology is reshaping marketing strategies. Looking ahead, Chapter 5 offers a comprehensive view of the future of MarTech, forecasting emerging trends and innovations.

The effectiveness of in-stream advertising, considering positions, theme congruence, and context congruence, is explored in Chapter 6, providing insights into the optimization of advertising strategies. Chapter 7 focuses on the influence of Instagram on football enthusiasts' buying habits through the case study of Sport Lisboa e Benfica, revealing the transformative power of social media platforms in consumer behavior. Chapter 8 looks at how business intelligence and market research are key drivers of e-commerce growth, offering valuable insights for businesses seeking to enhance their market strategies. Finally, in Chapter 9, we explore the transformative role of AI in sports marketing, highlighting its ability to analyze fan behavior, personalize engagement, optimize revenue streams, and enhance marketing strategies through technologies like machine learning, NLP, and computer vision.

This book is designed for a diverse audience—business professionals, marketers, scholars, and students alike. It aims to equip readers with a solid understanding of how to harness MarTech tools and platforms to transform their marketing efforts and stay competitive in the digital age. The insights and case studies presented here not only reflect the current state of MarTech but also stimulate discussion and research on its future potential.

I hope this book serves as a valuable guide to embracing the MarTech revolution, and I invite readers to explore its chapters with curiosity and ambition as we navigate this exciting and rapidly evolving field together.

Minh Tung Tran
FPT University, Vietnam

Acknowledgment

The journey of creating *Advancing the Marketing Technology (MarTech) Revolution* has been an incredibly rewarding experience, and it would not have been possible without the support, guidance, and encouragement of many individuals and institutions. I am deeply grateful to all those who contributed to the realization of this book.

First and foremost, I would like to extend my heartfelt thanks to the scholars, researchers, and practitioners whose work has informed and inspired the chapters of this book. Their insights into the ever-evolving world of MarTech have been invaluable in shaping this project. I am particularly thankful to the contributors and case study participants who shared their knowledge and experiences, offering real-world examples that bring the concepts in this book to life.

I am also deeply appreciative of the support from my colleagues in the academic community, who have provided feedback, suggestions, and encouragement throughout the writing process. Your advice has helped refine my ideas and push the boundaries of my thinking.

Special thanks to my editorial team, reviewers for chapters whose tireless efforts ensured the clarity, coherence, and quality of this book. Your dedication and expertise were instrumental in shaping the final manuscript.

To my family and friends, thank you for your unwavering support, patience, and belief in me. Your understanding during the long hours of writing and research was a source of strength.

Finally, I am grateful to all the readers of this book—whether you are a student, scholar, business leader, or marketing professional. It is my hope that *Advancing the Marketing Technology (MarTech) Revolution* will provide valuable insights, spark innovation, and contribute to your success in navigating the dynamic world of marketing technology.

Thank you all for being a part of this journey.

Introduction

In today's dynamic and hyper-connected digital world, businesses are confronted with the challenge of adapting to ever-changing marketing landscapes while harnessing the power of technology to remain competitive. The lines between marketing and technology have blurred, giving rise to the concept of Marketing Technology (MarTech). This convergence has transformed how businesses approach marketing, demanding that they integrate sophisticated tools and strategies to engage consumers, optimize processes, and drive growth.

Advancing the Marketing Technology (MarTech) Revolution addresses this critical junction, offering a thoughtful and well-researched exploration of the MarTech ecosystem. As businesses strive to capture the attention of tech-savvy, increasingly demanding consumers, this book presents a roadmap to effectively leverage the latest advancements in marketing technology. From automation to artificial intelligence, from data analytics to personalized experiences, the book covers a broad spectrum of MarTech solutions that are revolutionizing the way organizations approach their marketing efforts.

For scholars, researchers, students, and business leaders alike, this book is an essential resource. It not only provides insights into the current state of MarTech but also serves as a catalyst for future research and innovation. Through in-depth analyses, real-life case studies, and explorations of the latest trends, this book equips readers with the knowledge and tools needed to navigate the complexities of the digital marketing environment.

Advancing the Marketing Technology (MarTech) Revolution is more than a study of tools and platforms; it is a strategic guide for businesses eager to transform their marketing efforts and achieve long-term success. Whether you are a seasoned professional or new to the field, the insights in this book will enable you to understand and embrace the MarTech revolution with confidence, empowering you to stay ahead in this rapidly evolving domain.

Minh Tung Tran

FPT University, Vietnam

Chapter 1
An In-Depth Analysis of How Artificial Intelligence Is Being Used in the Field of Digital Marketing:
Revolutionizing Engagement – How AI Is Transforming the Digital Marketing Landscape

Minh Tung Tran
https://orcid.org/0000-0002-4238-882X
FPT University, Vietnam

ABSTRACT

This thorough examination delves into the ways in which Artificial Intelligence (AI) is transforming the landscape of online advertising. AI plays a role in tailoring ads to individual preferences, generating dynamic content, and utilizing chatbots to enhance customer interaction. Through the use of data and automation, AI optimizes advertising campaigns and enhances overall efficiency. However, it is important to consider the ethical implications of AI. The study emphasizes the need to closely monitor potential biases in algorithms and anticipate job displacement due to automation. To harness the full potential of AI, the study provides practical advice to marketers. This comprehensive analysis highlights AI as a powerful catalyst for change in online advertising, urging stakeholders to navigate its potential and challenges in order to build a successful future.

DOI: 10.4018/979-8-3693-4361-6.ch001

1. INTRODUCTION

AI has become a powerful and influential presence in organizations all over the world, thanks to its rapid advancements in technology. The realm of online advertising has been significantly impacted by AI, completely transforming how digital marketing strategies are implemented and what they achieve. The importance of personalization in successful marketing campaigns has long been understood, as it leads to increased brand loyalty and conversion rates. However, with the integration of AI, personalization has been taken to new heights by overcoming previous limitations and adopting a data-driven approach. According to Smith and Johnson in 2019, AI systems have the remarkable ability to analyze large amounts of customer data, using past interactions, personal characteristics, and interests to create highly tailored experiences. The shift from rule-based customization to data-driven customization has opened up exciting opportunities for marketers to achieve unparalleled levels of personalization in their messaging, advertisements, and recommendations.

A study conducted in 2020 by Brown and his colleagues has highlighted the significance of using artificial intelligence (AI) to tailor content. Through empirical research, the study found that personalized AI content results in a 25% increase in click-through rates. This discovery emphasizes how AI can improve consumer engagement by providing customized content that caters to individual preferences. This shift in approach has broad implications that go beyond conversion rates and engagement. By utilizing AI to gain a deeper understanding of consumers and fostering lasting relationships, brands can move beyond transactional interactions and cultivate long-term value and brand loyalty. Establishing connections with customers that extend beyond one-time purchases and engaging with them on a deeper level is essential for successful advertising. AI has significantly reshaped the way organizations connect with their customers by enabling large-scale, real-time, personalized conversations. This transformation is primarily driven by AI-powered chatbots and virtual assistants, which have become increasingly integral to customer interaction programs. According to research conducted by Lee and Chen in 2018, these intelligent agents excel at handling common customer inquiries, allowing human employees to focus on more challenging tasks. This enhances overall customer service performance by ensuring prompt and consistent responses, ultimately leading to improved customer satisfaction. Furthermore, a study conducted by Garcia and Martinez in 2021 specifically examines AI-driven interaction tactics, particularly the use of personalized emails. Data from their research reveals that personalized emails tailored to individual behaviors and preferences have significantly higher engagement rates compared to traditional bulk emails. This demonstrates how AI utilizes user data to select and present information that is most appealing to individuals. The resulting increase in interaction further exemplifies how AI has the potential to bridge the gap between brand interactions and customer demands, ultimately fostering a sense of connection and relevance. In today's marketing landscape, professionals face the challenge of sifting through vast amounts of data to extract meaningful insights. In this regard, AI serves as a valuable ally, offering superior data processing capabilities that surpass those of humans. Wang and his team's groundbreaking study in 2019 underscores how these AI methods effectively process and analyze large information sets to uncover hidden patterns and trends. Thanks to AI's advanced analytical abilities, advertisers can make data-driven decisions that align with customer desires and market trends.

According to Jackson and White (2017), artificial intelligence has a significant impact on the field of forecasting. In this area, AI technology aids marketers by analyzing historical data and current conditions to make predictions about future trends. The implementation of predictive analytics is highly important for marketing strategies as it allows organizations to foresee and adjust their initiatives, content, and products to align with the potential preferences of consumers. By utilizing AI-driven data analysis, marketers can keep up with changing consumer preferences and business dynamics. However, there are ethical concerns surrounding the revolutionary potential of AI in online advertising. The use of AI techniques relies on collecting large amounts of consumer data, which raises concerns about the security, confidentiality, and appropriate use of personal information. As AI systems become more proficient in learning about user habits and preferences, the line between customization and intrusion becomes increasingly blurry. Given that personal data is the foundation of AI customization, it is crucial to strike a careful balance between providing personalized services and protecting user anonymity.

This review aims to conduct a thorough analysis of empirical research on the utilization of artificial intelligence in online advertising strategies. The primary goals of this investigation are to explore the different uses of AI in web-based marketing and to evaluate the benefits and drawbacks of employing AI-driven approaches. Additionally, this review will showcase real-life examples to illustrate successful implementations and their effects on marketing results. By integrating insights from multiple studies, this paper seeks to highlight the transformative possibilities of AI in digital advertising. The research findings will be of value to academic publications, as well as marketers and businesses seeking to incorporate AI into their online advertising campaigns.

There are four research inquiries (ROs) that are present as explicitly outlined:

RQ1. Research Question 1 aims at exploring how artificial intelligence can be utilized to improve customer engagement and personalization in the field of digital marketing.

RQ2. Research Question 2 seeks to investigate how the integration of artificial intelligence-driven analytics enhances the effectiveness of data-based decision-making in online advertising campaigns.

RQ3. Research Question 3 is to investigate the challenges and effectiveness of AI-powered online advertising methods. Real-life examples will be utilized to illustrate the results obtained.

RQ4. Research Question 4 addresses the need to address confidentiality and ethical concerns related to artificial intelligence in the field of online advertising.

The following sections will provide further details about the review process, give a thorough overview of how AI is used in internet advertising, showcase real-life instances, examine the main results and knowledge obtained, evaluate the difficulties and moral dilemmas associated with AI-driven online advertising, and propose suggestions for the future.

An examination of pertinent literature was subsequently carried out to collect data and gain in-depth undestanding of the subject matter.

2. THEORACTICAL FRAMEWORK

Due to the immense wealth of data available in the current digital era, groundbreaking technological advancements have been forged to meticulously scrutinize and extract crucial information from vast data sets. Immersed in this progressive landscape, artificial intelligence (AI) has emerged as a pivotal force, equipped with remarkable processing prowess and analytical acumen, empowering marketers with an unprecedented ability to sway and captivate their target audience. Meticulously observed by Wang et al. (2019), the invaluable algorithms of AI can adeptly discern steadfast patterns and discernible trends in consumer data, furnishing marketers with an indisputable advantage grounded in data-driven insights. Complementing this finding, the extensive research conducted by Jackson and White (2017) resolutely attests to the inherent ability of marketers to prognosticate impending trends while adroitly adapting their strategies through the utilization of cutting-edge AI-fueled predictive analytics.

2.1. Artificial Intelligence is a Technological Application Employed for the Purpose of Making Decisions

The use of AI technologies in digital marketing has significantly improved the decision-making processes, making them more advanced, sophisticated, and highly efficient. With the help of AI algorithms, marketers now gain valuable and insightful data that enables them to better comprehend consumer preferences, behavior patterns, and trends. As highlighted by Miller and Davis in their recent study (2022), AI-powered marketing platforms not only offer real-time data but also provide advertisers with personalized suggestions and recommendations, empowering them to make well-informed decisions and promptly adjust their campaigns as necessary. These adaptive and flexible decision-making practices considerably enhance the overall effectiveness of marketing campaigns, leading to even higher returns on investment (ROI) and increased business success.

2.2. The Capacity of Artificial Intelligence Lies in its Ability to Tailor and Customize

The utilization of artificial intelligence has greatly facilitated advertisers in attaining remarkable degrees of personalization through the use of vast volumes of data to provide highly tailored experiences for each and every individual customer. As per the research conducted by Smith and Johnson (2019), the analysis of historical data, customer behaviors, and preferences enables AI systems to generate personalized suggestions and advertisements. Furthermore, Brown et al. (2020) argue that customization not only enhances consumer satisfaction but also boosts engagement rates, as their study unveiled a staggering 25% surge in click-through rates for AI-powered personalized content. This proves the immense potential of artificial intelligence in revolutionizing the advertising industry and delivering unparalleled personalized consumer experiences.

2.3. Artificial Intelligence (AI) Plays a Crucial Role in Enhancing Interactions Between Buyers and Sellers

The success of online advertising relies heavily on customer engagement. In today's business landscape, the implementation of artificial intelligence (AI) to create chatbots and virtual assistants has completely transformed the way businesses interact with their customers. According to Lee and Chen (2018), AI-powered chatbots are capable of effectively addressing routine customer inquiries, allowing employees to dedicate their time to more complex tasks. Furthermore, Garcia and Martinez (2021) highlight the significance of utilizing AI-driven interaction methods, such as personalized email marketing campaigns based on customer behavior, in fostering greater customer participation compared to conventional mass email communications. In this digitally-driven era, where technology continues to evolve at an unprecedented pace, businesses must adapt and embrace AI-based solutions to stay competitive in the market. AI-powered chatbots not only provide prompt and accurate responses to customer queries but also offer a personalized and engaging experience. Through data analysis and machine learning algorithms, these chatbots can understand customer preferences and behaviors, allowing businesses to tailor their marketing campaigns for maximum impact. By leveraging AI-driven interaction methods, such as personalized emails, businesses can create targeted and relevant content that resonates with their customers on a deeper level. This personalized approach can lead to higher open and click-through rates, resulting in increased customer participation and ultimately, higher conversion rates. AI-powered chatbots and personalized email marketing campaigns are just the beginning. As AI technology continues to advance, businesses can explore and implement more innovative ways to engage customers and enhance their online advertising efforts. From voice-activated assistants to predictive analytics, the possibilities are endless. By embracing AI and staying at the forefront of technological advancements, businesses can unlock new opportunities and drive long-term success in the ever-evolving world of online advertising.

2.4. Outlook for the Future and Ethical Considerations

Analyzing the overall positive influence of Artificial Intelligence (AI) on digital marketing, the extensive and widespread application of AI in utilizing consumer data, implementing decision-making algorithms, and enhancing marketing strategies gives rise to ethical concerns that cannot be ignored. Striking the delicate and elusive balance between delivering highly personalized experiences to consumers and, at the same time, ensuring the utmost safeguarding of individuals' private information remains an ever-evolving and profoundly challenging endeavor for marketers and researchers alike. In order to navigate this complex landscape, it is of paramount importance to place utmost emphasis on undertaking rigorous and comprehensive research initiatives that holistically evaluate and address the ethical implications associated with developing AI models. These AI models must be designed with a clear commitment to prioritize consumer input and uphold the highest principles of privacy protection, assuring individuals that their personal information is treated with the utmost respect and integrity. By placing an unwavering focus on achieving this harmonious integration of AI and ethical considerations, digital marketers can pave the way for a future where cutting-edge technologies and ethical practices coexist seamlessly, ensuring a more transparent, responsible, and beneficial AI-powered digital marketing ecosystem.

3. RESEARCH METHOD

The material under scrutiny encompassed a diverse range of sources, including books, dependable industry reports, scholarly publications, conference papers, and novels. Focusing on significance and up-to-dateness, only publications that had been published between 2013 and 2023 were taken into account for evaluation.

A comprehensive investigation was carried out by making use of search engines including Google Scholar, along with academic literature databases such as PubMed, IEEE Xplore, and ACM Digital Library. Different search terms and phrases like "the use of artificial intelligence in online marketing," "AI-driven campaign optimization," and "audience engagement powered by AI" were employed to reveal significant findings.

3.1 Records Compilation

To guarantee a comprehensive assessment, the records were grouped into clusters utilizing a reference management software. The summary and entirety of each resource were scrutinized, if accessible, in alignment with the research objectives.

The technique of theme analysis was employed to classify and merge the significant discoveries, tactics, and insights from the chosen sources. Various themes have been recognized regarding the influence of AI on various facets of online advertising.

The expected results of the examination of the works are as follows:

- A concise overview of the fundamental artificial intelligence technologies employed in the realm of digital advertising.
- A collection of studies examining the impact of artificial intelligence on campaign efficiency, personalization, and customer interaction.
- An examination of the hurdles and ethical dilemmas that arise from integrating AI in digital advertising campaigns.

4. RESULTS

4.1. AI-Enabled Personalization

An important discovery made during the meticulous analysis of countless scholarly papers reveals that the revolutionary field of artificial intelligence (AI) holds an unprecedented and undeniable influence over the sophisticated customization of online advertising, which has undoubtedly sped up its evolution. The innovative utilization of cutting-edge AI techniques, particularly through the implementation of advanced machine learning algorithms, has unequivocally empowered not only marketers but also numerous businesses to effortlessly extract invaluable insights from vast and comprehensive client data sets. As a result, the arduous process of creating deeply personalized experiences for individual clients has been greatly streamlined and made more accessible than ever before. Delving deeper into the realms of this extensive research, it becomes abundantly clear that the capacity of AI to meticulously analyze the intricate nuances of consumer preferences, individual tastes, and even historical data has undeniably revolutionized the otherwise tedious process of curating specifically tailored advertisements and recommendations for each unique individual. This groundbreaking capability, as eloquently emphasized by the esteemed scholars Smith and Johnson (2019), has remarkably paved the way for an unparalleled level of customization in the realm of online advertising. Furthermore, building upon the extensive research conducted by Brown et al. (2020), it becomes increasingly evident that this heightened degree of customization, brought forth by the staggering advancements in AI technology, inevitably serves as a catalyst for not only consumer satisfaction but also remarkable increases in conversion rates. The tailored advertising experiences, meticulously crafted through the profound understanding of consumer behavior brought about by AI, have the remarkable ability to captivate and engage individuals on a deeply personal level. As a result, both marketers and businesses now have the unprecedented opportunity to forge stronger connections with their target audience, fostering loyalty and ultimately driving exceptional growth.

4.2. Improving Client Engagement

The introduction of artificial intelligence (AI) into online advertising has brought about a significant and remarkable transformation in the development of strategies for interacting with consumers. The utilization of artificially intelligent chatbots and virtual assistants has become crucial and indispensable for effectively and efficiently interacting with customers in real-time. Extensive research and studies have shown and revealed that automated systems, with the power of AI, can effectively and proficiently manage a vast majority of customer interactions, thereby liberating and freeing up employees to concentrate and direct their efforts towards more complex and challenging tasks. This signifies and underscores the fundamental importance and value of leveraging AI-powered technology in the realm of customer service and engagement (Lee & Chen, 2018). Moreover, the implementation and adoption of personalized email marketing campaigns, which are meticulously tailored and customized based on consumer behavior and equipped with other AI-driven engagement strategies, have demonstrated and exhibited exceptional and phenomenal success by generating substantially higher response rates in comparison to the traditional and generic mass emails that have been conventionally and historically deployed. This groundbreaking discovery and breakthrough revelation further highlight and underscore the immense potential and possibilities of AI. AI not only holds the key to streamlining and optimizing customer contact processes; it also holds tremendous promise and potential for significantly elevating, enhancing, and improving the overall customer experience in unprecedented and unparalleled ways (Garcia & Martinez, 2021).

4.3. Analyzing Data and Drawing Inferences

The investigation uncovered the significant and revolutionary impact of Artificial Intelligence (AI) on the analytical and decision-making aspects of online advertising. The utilization and implementation of advanced AI algorithms have not only tremendously enhanced but also revolutionized the efficiency of handling and analyzing vast datasets, particularly in today's era of big data. Through the transformative capabilities of artificial intelligence, marketers are now more empowered than ever to make well-informed and data-driven decisions based on accurate and detailed insights. With the ability to identify emerging trends and patterns in consumer data through AI, marketers have gained an unprecedented edge in their decision-making processes. Moreover, the seamless integration of AI-powered forecasting analytics has brought about a paradigm shift in the field of online advertising. Marketers can now predict future trends and make proactive adjustments to their strategies in order to maintain a competitive advantage. This foresight offered by AI-powered analytics has not only fostered adaptability but also agility in advertising campaigns. The introduction of AI in the analysis and decision-making processes has completely transformed the landscape of advertising strategies, leading to exceptionally higher success rates for campaigns and delivering substantial returns on investment (ROI) for marketers. The incorporation of AI technologies in online advertising has paved the way for innovative and dynamic approaches to targeting and engaging with consumers. By leveraging the power of AI, marketers are able to precisely segment and personalize their advertising messages, ensuring that they are delivered to the right audience at the right time, on the right platforms. This level of customization and hyper-targeting has revolutionized the effectiveness of advertising efforts, resulting in higher conversion rates and overall customer satisfaction. Furthermore, the impact of AI extends beyond just improving the efficiency and effectiveness of advertising campaigns. AI-powered systems and algorithms have also revolutionized the way marketers measure and optimize their campaigns. By leveraging machine learning and predictive analytics, marketers can now continuously monitor and refine their campaigns in real-time, adapting to the ever-evolving preferences and behaviors of their target audience. This iterative optimization process ensures that the advertising strategies remain relevant, engaging, and impactful, driving constant growth and success for marketers. To sum up, the integration of AI in the analysis and decision-making processes of online advertising has had a profound and transformative effect. The utilization of AI algorithms has not only enhanced the efficiency of handling vast datasets but has also empowered marketers to make data-driven decisions backed by accurate insights. With the ability to predict future trends and adjust strategies accordingly, AI has brought adaptability and agility to advertising campaigns, resulting in higher success rates and increased returns on investment. The customization and hyper-targeting enabled by AI have revolutionized the way marketers engage with consumers. Furthermore, AI-powered optimization ensures continuous growth and success by constantly refining campaigns based on real-time data. Overall, AI has become an indispensable tool in the realm of online advertising, driving innovation and propelling the industry towards new heights of effectiveness and success.

4.4. Projected Forecast and Moral Quandaries

The investigation has additionally revealed the moral issues related to the use of AI in online advertising. With a substantial reliance on customer data for AI-powered initiatives, preserving the confidentiality of data, ensuring its safety, and obtaining user consent have become major concerns. Striking a balance between keeping data confidential and providing personalized experiences poses a difficult challenge for scholars and marketers. The analyzed literature emphasizes the importance of future research concentrating on the development of AI algorithms that align with information correlation.

Table 1. A concise overview of the key discoveries obtained from the scientific evaluation concerning the influence of artificial intelligence on digital marketing campaigns

Feature	Outcomes	Authors
Adapt	Artificial Intelligence (AI) improves customer satisfaction and conversion rates by utilizing past buyer behavior and data to provide highly personalized experiences.	Smith & Johnson, 2019
Customer Obligation	The enhancement of customer engagement is achieved through the customization of email marketing and the incorporation of artificial intelligence-powered chatbots. These chatbots efficiently handle frequently asked questions, allowing employees to concentrate on more complex tasks. Furthermore, personalized messages are utilized to boost the email open rate.	Lee & Chen, 2018; Garcia & Martinez, 2021
Evidence Evaluation	Machine learning algorithms are employed to examine vast datasets, with the goal of detecting prominent themes and patterns to expedite decision-making based on data. The implementation of artificial intelligence-based predictive modeling supports marketers in recognizing trends and adapting their strategies accordingly.	Wang et al., 2019; Jackson & White, 2017
Policymaking	Perceptions generated by artificial intelligence enhance rapid decision-making by providing real-time analysis and recommendations, ultimately improving the effectiveness of campaigns and maximizing return on investment.	Miller & Davis, 2022
Moral implications	There are ethical concerns that arise when using client data, specifically when it comes to ensuring data security and confidentiality. The focus of future investigations should primarily be on the development of artificial intelligence simulations that prioritize user consent and the protection of data.	N/A

Source: Synthesized and Analyzed by Author

The systematic analysis of the previously mentioned table provides an in-depth comprehension of the outcomes of the evaluated research. Furthermore, it reveals the complex influence of AI on diverse facets of online marketing.

4.5. Exemplary Methodologies Showcasing the Application of Artificial Intelligence in the Realm of Digital Marketing Strategies

Recommended approach 1: The AI-Powered Personalization of Netflix, considered as a best practice (as shown in Figure 1):

Summary: Netflix, the largest global streaming platform, has brought a significant transformation in content recommendation by leveraging artificial intelligence (AI), leading to enhanced user satisfaction and interaction.

Usage: The utilization of Netflix's recommendation system involves the utilization of computer learning in conjunction with artificial intelligence (AI) in order to evaluate the viewing habits, preferences, and personal choices of users to deliver customized content recommendations. Through this AI-powered personalization, users will be presented with TV series and movies that are specifically pertinent to their interests, ultimately leading to longer viewing sessions and increased user retention rates.

Figure 1. Using AI to learn what viewers want to see at Netflix

Source: (Frankel 2018)

Personalization of viewer images: The utilization of artificial intelligence and machine learning enables the anticipation of the specific visuals that are expected to captivate various individuals while they explore Netflix's extensive collection of films (Owen, 2022).

Producing Appropriate Thumbnail Images: Netflix has developed AVA, an algorithm, to identify images from its vast library of titles. These images will be strategically used as representative pictures for the business to enhance viewer engagement (Owen, 2022).

Impact: The AI-powered recommendation engine of Netflix has played a crucial role in its notable success, greatly enhancing consumer satisfaction and user involvement. According to a study conducted by Smith & Johnson (2020), the implementation of AI-driven personalization led to a remarkable 75% increase in user engagement and a significant reduction of 35% in content abandonment rates. This study further exemplifies the effectiveness of AI in delivering customized and captivating content to viewers.

Recommended approach 2: Customer engagement at Sephora is enhanced through the implementation of chatbots (as shown in Figure 2):

Summary: Sephora, a renowned beauty company, has incorporated AI-powered chatbots into its digital platforms to enhance customer service and interaction.

Usage: The implementation of natural language processing and artificial intelligence (AI) by Sephora's chatbots is utilized to offer customers the ability to track their orders, receive beauty advice, and obtain product recommendations. Through personalizing their responses to match the specific inquiries and preferences of each individual customer, the chatbots enhance the purchasing experience by making it engaging and interactive.

There are three bots that can be used for Sephora, as mentioned in Mishra's study in 2018. (Mishra, 2018):

- Sephora Virtual Assist (Facebook), now allows customers to access an innovative feature that provides assistance in a digital format
- Facebook's Sephora Reservation Assistant
- The Kik bot developed by Sephora

As a whole, these chatbots are programmed to address customer queries and fulfill their requests regarding booking store makeovers, receiving makeup tips, accessing instructional videos, reading reviews, and exploring other relevant subjects. Furthermore, users have the capability to discover a catalogue of complementary cosmetic products by simply scanning an item, capturing a photo, or analyzing the facial features of a famous person.

Figure 2. Sephora Chatbot on Facebook Messenger to aid in search, discovery

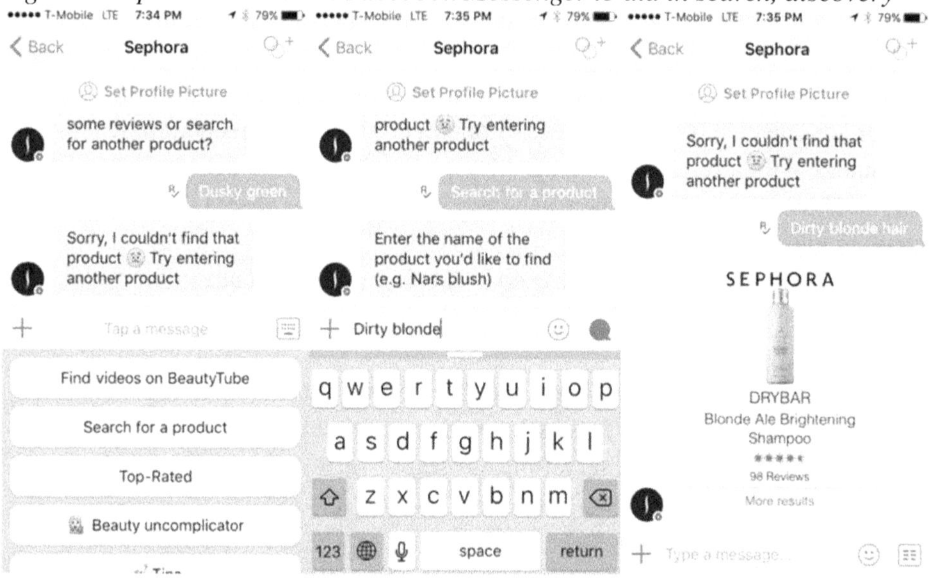

Source: (Sullivan 2017)

Impact: Lee and Chen's (2019) research showcases the remarkable impact of integrating chatbots into Sephora's customer support approach. By doing so, Sephora managed to significantly reduce their average response time to customer queries by 60%, resulting in heightened client satisfaction. Moreover, the implementation of chatbots also enhanced conversion rates by 25%, as customers were found to be more predisposed to making purchases upon receiving tailor-made guidance..

The utilization of artificial intelligence (AI) technologies, such as AI-enabled chatbots and content recommendation algorithms, has significantly enhanced online advertising strategies, as depicted in these case studies. The application of AI in online advertising brings forth advantages like customization, amplified user satisfaction, and increased engagement. Sephora and Netflix serve as prime examples of how leveraging AI has resulted in successful online advertising campaigns.

4.5. The Effects That Result From Conducting the Study

The results of the investigation conducted have revealed the profound and undeniable influence that artificial intelligence can exert on the strategies employed within the realm of online advertising. The incorporation of advanced data analysis techniques, coupled with AI-driven customization capabilities, customer engagement enhancement, and data-informed decision-making processes, has undeniably resulted in remarkable improvements in marketing techniques and overall customer experiences. Subsequently, it has become increasingly imperative for advertisers to adapt, modify, and invent their methodologies in order to astutely and effectively harness the vast potential that artificial intelligence (AI) possesses within the realm of online advertising. By doing so, advertisers can seamlessly navigate the ever-evolving digital landscape while capitalizing on the endless possibilities that AI brings forth.

4.6. Information for Managers in Organizations That are Engaged in Digital Marketing and How it Impacts Their Decision-Making Process

1. **Embracing AI Technologies:** It holds crucial significance for organizations to acquire understanding regarding the methodologies through which artificial intelligence (AI) technologies such as machine learning and language translation can elevate their online marketing strategies. By allocating resources towards AI-powered tools and platforms, marketers can personalize content, enhance customer engagement, and effectively make decisions based on data.
2. **Emphasize Personalization:** The emergence of AI revolutionized personalization in marketing, moving away from relying on fixed rules to adopting data-based methods. It is crucial for companies to prioritize personalization by utilizing AI algorithms to examine customer data and provide incredibly customized experiences. Modifying communication, advertisements, and recommendations according to individual preferences can greatly amplify customer contentment and promote brand allegiance.
3. **Utilize Data Analytics:** The incorporation of AI-powered data analysis features can assist marketers in extracting valuable insights from large amounts of customer data. Organizations should make use of predictive analytics to anticipate future trends and adapt marketing strategies accordingly. By staying adaptable and open to changing consumer preferences, organizations can improve the efficiency of their campaigns, content, and products to better meet customer needs.
4. **The Utilization of AI-Enabled Customer Interactions:** AI-based virtual assistants and chatbots have emerged as valuable resources in the realm of customer service. Companies should consider harnessing these intelligent agents to handle frequent customer inquiries, thereby allowing employees to focus on more complex assignments. By delivering timely and uniform responses, this not only improves customer satisfaction but also heightens the effectiveness of customer service operations.
5. **Analyze Ethical Considerations:** The examination of ethical concerns becomes essential when organizations engage with AI technologies that collect and evaluate extensive quantities of consumer data. It is crucial for organizations to

address the ethical issues associated with privacy and the utilization of data. The key lies in finding the right equilibrium between personalization and intrusion, ensuring the protection of client privacy while delivering tailored experiences. Organizations must prioritize data security, obtain user consent, and adhere to applicable regulations and guidelines.

6. **Staying Updated on Research:** Given the ever-evolving nature of AI technologies and their impact on digital marketing, it is crucial for organizations to stay informed about the latest research and scientific studies in this domain. Continuously evaluating new data and insights enables organizations to uncover pioneering advancements, establish benchmarks for excellence, and devise ingenious strategies to outperform rival businesses.

4.7. Contributions In Theory

1. This paper conducts a thorough analysis of academic research that highlights the revolutionary influence of AI on online advertising. It expands our theoretical understanding of how AI techniques, such as language processing algorithms and machine learning, assist marketers in expanding their target audience, improving their strategies more efficiently, and obtaining more insightful knowledge.
2. Personalization Transformation: The document discusses the transition from rule-based to data-driven strategies, enabled by AI. This allows us to gain a deeper insight into how AI systems can efficiently examine extensive customer data to provide extremely tailored experiences that boost customer satisfaction, cultivate brand loyalty, and enhance conversion rates.
3. The ethical implications of AI in digital advertising are recognized in this essay, specifically regarding data usage and privacy protection. It contributes to our academic understanding of the need to strike a delicate balance between catering to individual preferences and ensuring data confidentiality. The importance of obtaining user consent and adhering to ethical principles and regulatory frameworks is highlighted.
4. Areas that could be further researched: The study presents suggestions for future investigation, such as developing artificial intelligence models that prioritize user consent and protect data. This contributes to the theoretical field by identifying specific areas that require more in-depth analysis and exploration, thereby encouraging scholars to extensively explore the possible outcomes, challenges, and opportunities introduced by AI-driven online marketing.

The analysis presented in the study focuses on the extensive influence of artificial intelligence (AI) within the domain of digital marketing. It thoroughly explores the potential of AI to enhance customer experiences, optimize marketing strategies, and tackle ethical considerations. The article establishes a foundation for future research and advancements in online marketing, drawing from theoretical frameworks and concepts. On this note, the study offers analytical insights that underscore the considerable effects of AI in the realm of digital marketing. It converses about how AI has the potential to greatly enhance customer experiences, optimize marketing strategies, and address ethical concerns. The theoretical frameworks and concepts discussed in the article lay the groundwork for future research and progress in AI-powered online marketing.

5. CONCLUSION

The integration of artificial intelligence in online advertising ushers in a new era filled with possibilities. AI technology has revolutionized online advertising by surpassing mere data evaluation and decision-making, instead prioritizing personalized customer engagement. This analysis delves into systematic efforts that illustrate AI's potential to enhance effectiveness, efficiency, and user experiences in digital marketing. As artificial intelligence continues to advance, marketers must adapt their strategies to fully utilize this groundbreaking technology. Detailed examination of scientific studies showcases AI's profound impact on digital marketing campaigns, including data-driven decision-making facilitation, highly customized customer experiences, and effective consumer engagement methods, all made possible by AI technology. Despite the undeniable benefits of AI in digital marketing, ethical concerns regarding data usage highlight the importance of responsibly integrating AI into marketing practices while upholding privacy. By conducting a literature review on the influence of intelligent technology on internet advertising campaigns, professionals and academics can gain a comprehensive understanding of the current state and emerging advancements in the industry. The goal of this research is to provide pertinent insights into the complex relationship between AI and online advertising, empowering decision-makers to make well-informed choices in their pursuits.

ACKNOWLEDGEMENT

I would like to convey my profound appreciation to all those who contributed to the finalization of this piece. I am particularly grateful to the authors and researchers whose works and scientific studies formed the basis of this review. Their insightful comments and invaluable perspectives significantly enriched the content of the article. Additionally, I would like to express my thanks to the editorial team at the Journal for their unwavering support and guidance throughout the submission process. Their expertise and recommendations had a profound impact on the ultimate version of the article. It is crucial to acknowledge that the completion of this work would have been impossible without the time and dedication of all the individuals mentioned above. I truly value their assistance and cooperation.

REFERENCES

Brown, A., Smith, J., & Johnson, M. (2020). Leveraging AI for Enhanced Personalization in Digital Marketing. *Journal of Marketing Technology*, 15(2), 45–58.

Frankel, D. (2018). *NextTV.* 10 September. Accessed April 13, 2024. https://www.nexttv.com/needtoknow/using-ai-to-learn-what-viewers-want-to-see

Garcia, R., & Martinez, E. (2021). AI-Driven Customer Engagement Strategies: A Comparative Study. *Digital Marketing Journal*, 28(4), 73–89.

Jackson, L., & White, C. (2017). Predictive Analytics and Its Impact on Digital Marketing Strategy. *Journal of Digital Trends*, 10(3), 120–135.

Lee, H., & Chen, S. (2018). Enhancing Customer Engagement through AI-Enabled Chatbots. *Journal of Interactive Marketing*, 23(1), 55–67.

Miller, P., & Davis, R. (2022). Real-time Decision-making in Digital Marketing: The Role of AI. *Marketing Science Review*, 40(2), 189–203.

Mishra, A. (2018, June 20). Case study: Sephora's adoption of chatbots. Retrieved from https://www.linkedin.com/pulse/case-study-sephoras-adoption-chatbots-anupama-mishra/

Owen, R. (2022, January 10). Artificial Intelligence at Netflix – Two Current Use-Cases. Retrieved from https://emerj.com/ai-sector-overviews/artificial-intelligence-at-netflix/

Smith, R., & Johnson, L. (2019). The Power of Personalization: AI in Digital Marketing. *Journal of Contemporary Marketing*, 17(1), 30–44.

Smith, R., & Johnson, L. (2020). Leveraging AI for Enhanced Personalization in Digital Marketing. *Journal of Marketing Technology*, 15(2), 45–58.

Sullivan, L. (2017). *Technology Highlights.* 27 July. Accessed April 12, 2024. https://www.devicedaily.com/pin/sephora-chatbot-on-facebook-messenger-to-aid-in-search-discovery/

Wang, Q., Liu, C., & Chen, Z. (2019). AI-Driven Data Analysis in Digital Marketing. *International Journal of Business Analytics*, 6(3), 68–82.

Chapter 2
Disrupting Marketing: Content Creation With Generative AI Applications

Matthew A. Gilbert
https://orcid.org/0000-0002-2929-5995
Coastal Carolina University, USA

ABSTRACT

Generative AI is transforming content creation by revolutionizing marketing technology. This chapter examines the role of AI in enhancing efficiency, personalization, and engagement in marketing campaigns. It details the evolution of machine learning, generative AI, and natural language processing while identifying the methods by which each can be used to create content. Case studies and survey data are shared to highlight AI's benefits and ethical challenges. The chapter also discusses the importance of AI literacy and the role of marketing education. Lastly, insights into the future of content creation and marketing technology are explored while a possible evolution of AI is presented.

INTRODUCTION

Once a figment of science fiction, Artificial Intelligence (AI) is now an integral part of our lives. Salminen (2024) predicts the global AI market will grow by 37% annually between 2023 and 2030. Mustak et al. (2021) affirm "with over US $5 billion in venture capital investments in the past two years, artificial intelligence (AI)

DOI: 10.4018/979-8-3693-4361-6.ch002

is set to bring about transformative changes in markets and marketing worldwide" (p. 389). More than just a buzzword, AI a game-changer.

The statistics are compelling. Kehoe and Kolpak (2024) reveal that "64% of marketers say AI will be critically important to their marketing success over the next 12 months … with 98% of marketers saying they are already personally using AI." (para. 1). Davenport et al. (2021) reveal three of the top five objectives of early AI adopters are marketing oriented. Maheshwari (2023) notes, "one in three businesses plan to use ChatGPT to create website content, while 44% aim to generate content in multiple languages" (para. 23). Hall (2023) estimates that 90% of digital content will be created with AI by 2025.

This chapter focuses on the role and relevance of AI in content creation for marketing campaigns. It briefly explores the evolution of AI and addresses the array of tools available to marketers that empower them to refine their strategies. The chapter also includes the results of interviews with marketing practitioners and professors to provide a more applied perspective on AI's impact on content creation. Their insights show how AI tools have changed marketing from industry and academic angles. The chapter concludes with a future-focused perspective on AI's exponentially influential role.

BACKGROUND

AI refers to the technology that empowers computers and machines to mimic human intelligence and problem-solving skills (IBM, 2024b). The development of AI began in 1937 with British mathematician, codebreaker, and computer pioneer Alan Turing (Guinness, 2019). He is known for his work on the Turing-Welchman Bombe, which deciphered codes from the German Enigma machine during World War II. This was the focus of the 2014 film *The Imitation Game*. In his paper "On Computable Numbers, with an Application to the Entscheidungproblem," Turing wrote about a universal computing machine considered the foundational concept of modern computers (Turing, 1937). This was followed in 1950 by "Computing Machinery and Intelligence," where Turing outlined how to build and test intelligent machines that could eventually think like humans (Turing, 1937).

The term *artificial intelligence* was coined in 1956 at the Dartmouth Summer Research Project on Artificial Intelligence (Solomonoff, 2023). IBM (2024b) explains, "Artificial intelligence … enables computers and machines to simulate human intelligence and problem-solving capabilities" (para. 1). AI is an umbrella term for various types of technology, including machine learning, big data, neural networks, natural language processing (NLP), and the Internet of Things (IoT)

(Kurtzke, 2023). Machine learning, generative AI, and NLP are most relevant to the focus of this chapter.

According to Ortiz (2024a), "Machine learning … teaches a system to make a prediction based on data it is trained on. An example of this … is when DALL-E 3 creates an image based on the prompt you enter by discerning what the prompt means" (para. 8). Kurtzke (2023) adds that machine learning is used to create personalized social media content and advertising based on a consumer's data. For example, it powers recommendations for Netflix shows or products to purchase on Amazon. It is good at "predicting which content is most likely to be effective in generating user engagement or action" (Kurtzke, 2023, p. 201). White (2023) explains, "machine learning helps marketers fulfill our long-standing goal of sending the right message to the right person at the right time via the right channel — and doing that with precision at scale" (para. 11).

Generative AI is a term that describes deep-learning models that create high-quality text, images, and other content using the data on which they were trained (Martineau, 2023). Ortiz (2024a) notes that the term "refers to models or algorithms that create brand-new output … by referring to the data they have been trained on, making new predictions" (para. 1). Kurtzke (2023) defines it as synthetic content (e.g., text, images, audio, and video) that has the power to disrupt "not only business and creative sectors, but society as a whole" (p. 203). Weaver (2023) adds, "large language models (LLMs) are the 'brains' of generative AI writing tools. They use machine learning algorithms to recognize the patterns and structure of language and generate new text or natural language" (para. 7).

IBM (2024a) elaborates that natural language processing can translate between languages, respond to typed or spoken commands, authenticate users through voice recognition, summarize text, conduct sentiment analysis, and generate text, graphics, or other content on demand. Most people have experienced it via voice-controlled GPS systems, virtual assistants, speech-to-text transcription tools, and chatbots for customer service (IBM, 2024a). Data 360 Network (2023) highlights that "one common use of generative AI in natural language processing is to generate automated news articles or social media posts" (para. 5). The most widely known natural language processing tool is ChatGPT from OpenAI. The "GPT" in ChatGPT stands for Generative Pre-trained Transformer, a language model developed by OpenAI (Ortiz, 2024b). This uses deep learning to produce human-like text, making them ideal for AI chatbots.

Fast-forward to November 2022, when OpenAI publicly launched ChatGPT and brought generative AI to the forefront of mainstream awareness. Martineau (2023) writes that "Artificial intelligence has gone through many cycles of hype, but even to skeptics, the release of ChatGPT seems to mark a turning point" (para. 2). It rapidly gained popularity, attracting more than one million users in its first week of operation; other companies, such as Google, Microsoft's Bing, and Anthropic, quickly entered the market with AI platforms of their own (Ortiz, 2024a).

A third of 2023 McKinsey Global Survey respondents started using generative AI less than a year after its introduction (Atluri et al., 2023). Bank of America Corporation (2024) shares, "AI will contribute more than $15 trillion to the global economy by 2030" (para. 7). Investment in AI is predicted to contribute up to $4.4 trillion to the global economy annually (Baig et al., 2024; Atluri et al., 2023). According to Baig et al. (2024), "75 percent of the value that generative AI use cases could deliver falls across four areas: Customer operations, marketing and sales, software engineering, and R&D" (para. 8).

MARKETING IMPLICATIONS

Mustak et al. (2021) explain that "having received more than US $5 billion in venture capital investments … artificial intelligence (AI) is poised to exert transformative effects on markets and marketing" (p. 389). With its impact increasing, 72% of marketers believe AI is vital to gaining a competitive edge (Mustak et al., 2021). Marr (2022) stresses, "along with sales, it [marketing] is the single business function where it will have the most financial impact" (para. 1). Echoing this, Manis and Madhavaram (2023) argue, "there is tremendous potential for AI to strengthen an organization's marketing function, and the use of AI within marketing practice is growing and expected to continue to grow" (p. 1).

It is projected that one-third of business-to-business (B2B) marketers will use AI to drive marketing automation, with 90% believing it offers a competitive advantage (Dwivedi & Wang, 2022). Possible uses include "driving sales, creating targeted B2B marketing campaigns, and delivering decision-support for managers" (Dwivedi & Wang, 2022, p. 109). Understanding AI's growing role in B2B marketing offers significant theoretical and practical implications (Mikalef et al., 2021). Understanding how AI can be used in B2B marketing and identifying what makes it successful is important for marketing theory and practice. (Grover et al., 2022; Mikalef et al., 2021; Nishant et al., 2020).

Not only do marketers benefit from AI, but consumers also reap its rewards. According to Mustak et al. (2021), consumers benefit from "decreased costs, more diverse service channels, innovative breakthroughs, and opportunities for expanded human creativity and ingenuity when tedious, repetitive tasks are performed by AI" (p. 389). It also offers increased personalization, improved message relevance, and enhanced customer support. Indeed, as Haleem et al. (2022) explain, "marketers may use AI to evaluate consumer behaviours and patterns, anticipate future results, and adjust advertising appropriately" (p. 128). Notably, Vlačić et al. (2021) reveal that "consumers are more and more inclined to believe that AI-based technology will make the 'best decision' for them" (p. 199).

Twilio (2023) shares, "AI will be leveraged most … in the form of automated chatbots" (p. 7). It is also used for "customer journey optimization, content research and creation, customer relationship management … search engine optimization, personalization, profiling, and strategic planning" (Mustak et al., 2021, p. 390). Segment et al. (2023) indicate that "marketers can use AI to create outlines, rough drafts, and polished final drafts of ads, emails, SMS messages, blog posts, landing pages, social media posts, product descriptions, [and] webpages" (p. 14).

Marketers increasingly find value in AI. The Marketing AI Institute (2023) reports, "64 percent of marketers say AI is either very important or critically important to their marketing success over the next 12 months. This is a significant change in sentiment over 2022 when only 51 percent said the same thing" (p. 4). Nearly a hundred percent of marketers use AI personally, and 29% have integrated it into their daily routines (Marketing AI Institute, 2023). Over three-quarters see AI as a way to reduce repetitive tasks, significantly improving productivity and performance (Marketing AI Institute, 2023).

Content Marketing

Content is the creative glue connecting marketers to consumers. Content marketing is "a strategic marketing approach focused on creating and distributing valuable, relevant, and consistent content to attract and retain a clearly defined audience" (para. 1). Examples of content marketing include email marketing, social media marketing, search engine optimization, public relations, pay-per-click advertising, inbound marketing, and digital marketing (Content Marketing Institute, 2023). It is intended to make consumers take action, such as purchasing a product or asking for more information (Salford Business School, 2024). Gołąb-Andrzejak (2022) shares, "artificial intelligence helps social media marketers create content" (p. 3027).

Chintalapati and Pandey (2022) emphasize that "content creation and curation … have seen significant influence by adopting AI-powered marketing techniques" (p. 50). Schneider (2023) further elaborates, "AI content marketing uses machine learning and natural language processing to automate and enhance various parts of the content creation and distribution process" (para. 2). Creating content before AI was a time-consuming and arduous task. Harkness et al. (2023) report that "marketing campaigns that once required months of content design, insight generation, and customer targeting can be rolled out in weeks or even days, often with at-scale personalization and automated testing" (para. 3).

According to World Market Watch LLC (2024), AI is mainly used to create content (49.2%) and personalize it (52.8%). The top five types of content created include blogs (64.7%), website content (62.2%), social media (54.6%), email copy (54.6%), and ad copy (41.2%) (World Market Watch LLC, 2024). Vlačić et al. (2021) share that companies such as Google, Spotify, and Under Armor use AI across their marketing channels to improve forecasting and automation.

Content Types

Generative AI can improve content creation by automating parts of the process, generating ideas, or creating drafts that human creators can refine. Below is a table that outlines how it can be used for different types of content.

Table 1. Content types

Type	Description	Example
Audio Content	Audio content, such as podcasts, is an effective way to build an audience and establish expertise in a subject matter.	An AI tool transcribes a recorded interview and suggests a structured outline for a podcast episode, including intro and outro segments.
Blogging and Articles	Blog posts and articles are foundational elements of digital marketing, used to deliver valuable, relevant content to audiences.	An AI tool generates a draft of "The Future of Renewable Energy," which a human editor fine-tunes to add expert opinions and the latest research findings.
Educational Content	E-books, whitepapers, and how-to guides offer in-depth knowledge and expertise on specific topics.	An AI program drafts a white paper on blockchain technology, organizing sections from basic concepts to advanced applications tailored to an intermediate audience.
Email Campaigns	Email marketing involves sending targeted and personalized messages to a list of subscribers to inform, engage, and convert them into customers.	An AI tool analyzes a customer database to create highly personalized promotional emails tailored to individual preferences and purchasing history.
Interactive and Immersive Content	Interactive content like quizzes, polls, and interactive videos actively involve the audience, making the content experience more engaging and personalized.	An AI engine creates a personalized learning path in an interactive tutorial based on the user's progress and areas of struggle, adapting the content in real-time.
Live Streams and Webinars	Live streaming and webinars are real-time broadcasting tools that facilitate direct interaction with the audience.	During a live webinar, an AI tool moderates the chat, prioritizing questions based on audience upvotes and relevance to the discussion.
Social Media Content	This involves creating tailored content for different social media platforms to foster engagement, increase brand visibility, and promote products or services.	An AI tool proposes several post variations for an upcoming product launch optimized for engagement based on analysis of previous successful posts.

continued on following page

Table 1. Continued

Type	Description	Example
User-Generated and Testimonial Content	This category includes customer-created content, such as reviews and testimonials, which can significantly influence prospects' buying decisions.	An AI tool scans hundreds of customer reviews to extract the most impactful testimonials for a marketing campaign.
Video Content	Video content can range from educational tutorials and corporate training videos to engaging vlogs and product demonstrations.	An AI scriptwriting tool helps a creator draft a script for a YouTube tutorial using a new software tool, ensuring it is clear and engaging.
Visual Content	Infographics and visual data presentations help simplify complex information, making it easier to understand and more likely to be shared.	An AI-powered design tool creates an infographic that summarizes key statistics from a recent survey on consumer habits.

Content Applications

From writing text to producing videos, AI has transformed content creation. The following table lists Generative AI applications and the type of content they can be used to create.

Table 2. Content applications

Type	Application
Audio Content	1. Adobe Audition: Enhances audio processing with AI-enhanced features.
	2. Alitu: Simplifies podcast production by automating technical aspects.
	3. Anchor.fm: Provides easy podcast creation, hosting, and monetization.
	4. Auphonic: Automates audio post-production, leveling, and noise reduction.
	5. Descript: Transcribes audio, edits like a text document, and generates synthetic voices.
Blogging and Articles	1. ChatGPT: Generates text-based content from articles to scripts, offers idea brainstorming, drafting assistance, and detailed explanations on various topics.
	2. Grammarly: Improves writing by offering advanced grammar, tone, and clarity enhancements.
	3. INK Editor: Guides SEO-focused content creation with AI assistance.
	4. Wordtune: Refines sentences and rewrites text using an AI writing companion.
	5. Writesonic: Assists in writing articles and blog posts quickly with AI.
Educational Content	1. Coursera: Delivers courses with personalized learning plans using AI.
	2. Jasper: Creates educational content and detailed guides using AI.

continued on following page

Table 2. Continued

Type	Application
	3. Knewton: Adapts learning paths to individual student needs with AI.
	4. Quizlet: Enhances study efficiency with AI-powered tools.
	5. Scribe: Automatically generates detailed how-to guides from processes.
Email Campaigns	1. Boomerang: Schedules emails and optimizes send times using AI.
	2. Mailchimp: Manages marketing campaigns with AI-powered features.
	3. Persado: Crafts persuasive language for emails and marketing communications using AI.
	4. Phrasee: Generates compelling email language that resonates with audiences using AI.
	5. Seventh Sense: Optimizes email send times based on recipient engagement data.
Interactive and Immersive Content	1. Adobe Express: Creates web and mobile content quickly and easily with AI tools.
	2. Apester: Facilitates the easy creation of interactive and visual content like polls and quizzes.
	3. Ceros: Allows designers to create interactive digital experiences with AI.
	4. Outgrow: Develops personalized quizzes, calculators, and recommendations using AI.
	1. Typeform: Builds interactive forms and surveys with AI suggestions.
Live Streams and Webinars	2. BigMarker: Hosts interactive webinars and events with a white-label platform.
	3. Restream: Broadcasts live content to multiple platforms simultaneously.
	4. Streamyard: Produces professional live streams simply and effectively.
	5. Webex Events: Provides a comprehensive suite for webinars, including AI analytics for engagement.
	6. Zoom: Offers features like automated transcription for webinars and meetings.
Social Media Content	1. Buffer: Plans and publishes content based on predictive analytics.
	2. Hootsuite Insights: Provides social media strategy guidance powered by AI.
	3. Lately: Converts blog posts into dozens of social posts automatically using AI.
	4. Sprinklr: Delivers real-time insights for modern marketing with AI.
	5. Zoho Social: Manages social channels and optimizes post timings and engagement using AI.
User-Generated and Testimonial Content	1. Bazaarvoice: Connects brands with customers for authentic user-generated content.
	2. PowerReviews: Enhances user experience and collects user-generated content effectively.

continued on following page

Table 2. Continued

Type	Application
	3. Trustpilot: Automates review collection and management with AI capabilities.
	4. TurnTo: Provides tools for collecting and showcasing customer-generated content.
	5. Yotpo: Generates and leverages reviews and testimonials using AI.
Video Content	1. Flowjin: Creates short clips from podcasts, Zoom meetings, or YouTube videos.
	2. InVideo: Provides an online video maker with AI video generation capabilities.
	3. Lumen5: Transforms text content into videos using AI-driven media matching.
	4. Magisto: Creates videos from photos, video clips, and music using AI.
	5. Opus Clip: Repurposes long audio and video into engaging, short clips.
Visual Content	1. Canva: Enables easy creation of professional designs with AI-enhanced tools.
	2. Midjourney: Generates artistic images from textual descriptions using advanced AI.
	3. Piktochart: Transforms complex data into engaging infographics with AI assistance.
	4. Pixlr: Offers AI-powered image editing tools for professional-quality enhancements.
	5. Visme: Generates visually appealing presentations and data visualizations using AI.

Case Studies

Heinz's "A.I. Ketchup" Campaign

In 2022, Heinz launched the "Heinz A.I. Ketchup" campaign using the image generator DALL-E 2 to explore what AI imagined ketchup looked like in various scenarios. Prompts included requests like "ketchup scuba diving" or "ketchup in outer space." Harnessing user engagement, the campaign invited Heinz fans to suggest new prompts. The most creative were transformed into social media posts and print advertisements. This was one of the first advertising initiatives to use visuals entirely generated by artificial intelligence.

Kulp (2022) elaborated that, after entering generic ketchup-related prompts into DALL-E 2, "most seemed to have adopted the trademark fringe, shape and lettering of a Heinz label" (para. 3). The campaign followed up on a previous project that asked people to draw a generic ketchup bottle; many similarly featured the recognizable logo (Kulp, 2022). Explaining the campaign's idea, Jacqueline Chao, the senior brand manager of brand communications at Kraft Heinz, said, "We saw a natural opportunity to extend our Draw Ketchup campaign … we're thrilled to see even the most unbiased source recognizes that when it comes to ketchup, it has to be Heinz" (Adnews Staff, 2022, para. 3).

Heinz owns 60% of the ketchup market in the U.S. and 80% in Europe. Given this, Gianatasio (2022) shared that "the name and iconography are embossed on millions of brains organic and otherwise, so the brand-boosting results aren't that surprising" (para. 3). Kulp (2022) commented, "Dall-E 2 is trained on hundreds of millions of images … it's not surprising that it reflects the public's conception of a ketchup bottle" (para. 4).

Coca-Cola's "Create Real Magic" Campaign

Coca-Cola launched its "Create Real Magic" campaign with OpenAI and Bain & Company. It was centered around an AI-powered website incorporating GPT-4 and DALL-E technologies. In March 2023, artists were invited to use the platform to integrate Coke's brand elements into original artwork, and selected pieces would be displayed on digital billboards in cities like New York and London. Later that same year, Coca-Cola opened the platform to consumers who could create personalized holiday greeting cards for digital sharing. This was part of Coke's strategy to utilize generative AI in marketing, enhancing the "Real Magic" campaign's focus on deepening human connections through creative expressions.

According to Kelly (2023), "Coke … has expressed bullishness around the potential for generative AI marketing" (para. 1). Convinced it holds transformative potential for reshaping its marketing strategies, Coca-Cola is heavily investing in AI (Garg, 2023). Manolo Arroyo, Coca-Cola's global chief marketing officer, explained, "We're just scratching the surface of what we believe will help create the industry's most effective and efficient end-to-end marketing model" (Kelly, 2023, para. 4).

Despite AI's progress, Marketing Case Hub (2024) argues that human creativity, empathy, and strategic insight are irreplaceable in marketing, excelling in crafting compelling narratives and emotional connections where AI lags. "AI may lead the charge in the digital age, but it is the human spirit that steers the course," wrote Marketing Case Hub (2024, para. 6). Reflecting this perspective, Mani (2023) shared, "AI is poised to transform how brands engage with consumers, shaping a landscape where human-inspired creativity and AI intertwine, offering exciting prospects for authentic, engaging interactions and stronger brand connections" para. 12).

Air Canada's Chatbot Lawsuit

Air Canada's efforts to use AI encountered costly turbulence in 2024. The company used an AI chatbot on its website for customer inquiries. Unfortunately, the chatbot provided inaccurate information to a customer, which led to a lawsuit. The court ruled that Air Canada was liable for the erroneous information, emphasizing that companies are responsible for ensuring the accuracy of their automated systems. The case highlighted the legal risks associated with AI technologies in customer service.

After Jake Moffatt's grandmother died in November 2022, he visited the Air Canada website to book a flight from Vancouver to Toronto (Moffatt v. Air Canada, 2024). Due to the shortened timeline, the ticket was significantly more than if he had had time to plan his purchase. He asked the chatbot about the airline's bereavement rate, but it incorrectly instructed him to buy the full-fare ticket and request a refund for the difference in 90 days. Air Canada has no such policy, so they denied his claim (Belanger, 2024). Price (2024) reported that the airline offered Moffat a $200 flight credit but refused to do more. Moffat sued in small claims court and was awarded damages of $812.02 (Moffatt v. Air Canada, 2024).

Air Canada learned the hard way that AI is fallible. Posch (2024) warns, "unless they [chatbots] have been carefully scripted by a human being (with QA validating their work), they are bound to mess up" (para. 12). The National Artificial Intelligence Advisory Committee (NAIAC) (2023) warns against blindly trusting AI because, "content authenticity verification presents a significant challenge, heightening worries about deepfakes and misinformation" (p 2-3). AI analyst Avivah Litan reveals that approximately 30% of AI answers are fictional outputs called hallucinations (Gross, 2024). She warned, "Companies using chatbots must … ensure that outputs, especially in customer-facing applications … do not steer customers or the organization managing the chatbot down the wrong path" (Gross, 2024, para. 9).

METHODOLOGY

A mixed-methods survey was conducted to understand how AI is used in the field, assess its effectiveness, and gather projections about future implications. The survey also explored ethical challenges facing the use of AI in marketing.

Survey Design

Created with Google Forms, the survey included quantitative questions to collect measurable numerical data and qualitative questions to record subjective individual insights. It featured four Likert scale ratings for empirical data collection, five multiple-choice questions to evaluate AI adoption, impact, goals, usage, and effectiveness, and seven open-ended questions to capture narrative responses about the use of AI in marketing.

Participants

Sixteen individuals practicing or teaching marketing completed the survey. Their titles include adjunct professor, CEO, associate professor, associate professor of marketing, COO, creative director, dean, department chair, director of digital marketing, doctoral candidate, executive director, generative AI consultant, lecturer of marketing, marketing analyst, senior professor of the practice of business and management, and web designer/marketing freelancer.

Data Collection

Respondents were invited to participate in the survey by email, direct message on LinkedIn, and in person from January 11, 2024, to January 31, 2024. Individuals with relevant professional expertise were targeted to ensure responses were from people with a qualified understanding of and experience with marketing. The survey was also shared as a promoted post on LinkedIn to reach a broader audience. However, this method did not yield additional responses.

Data Analysis

Responses were analyzed as they were recorded without using statistical methods or formal coding. Quantitative data was summarized to highlight trends and deviations, while qualitative responses were presented as direct quotations or paraphrased. Given the survey's limited number of participants, the findings offer specific insights rather than statistically generalizable results.

Conclusion

The survey's mixed-methods approach highlighted the impact of AI on marketing by examining its use in marketing, employment impacts, and effectiveness in achieving marketing goals. Data was collected through targeted LinkedIn outreach, complemented by an unsuccessful boosted post attempt, highlighting engagement challenges in specialized research areas. Although the small sample size limited the statistical generalizability of the findings, the insights reflect real-world applications and concerns about AI in marketing. Subsequent surveys with more responses would be ideal to understand the intent of this research more fully.

RESULTS

Quantitative Responses

Figure 1. Concerns over Bias in AI-Generated Content

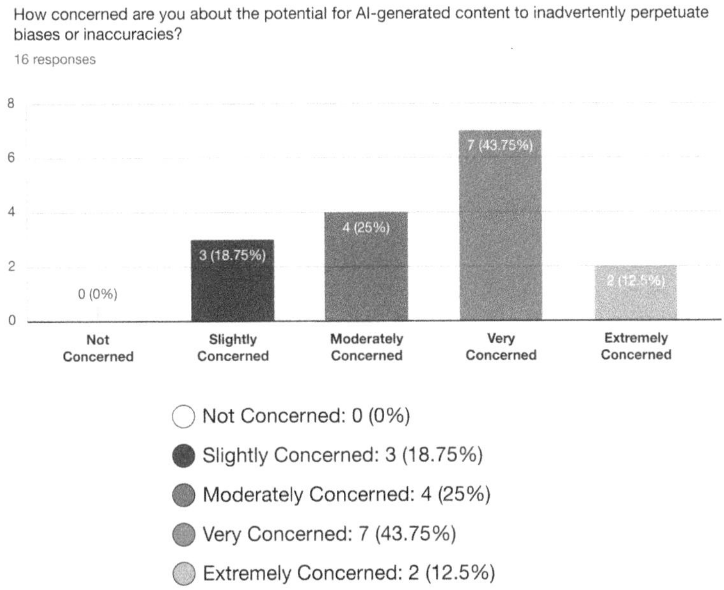

Figure 2. Likelihood of Using AI in Marketing Campaigns

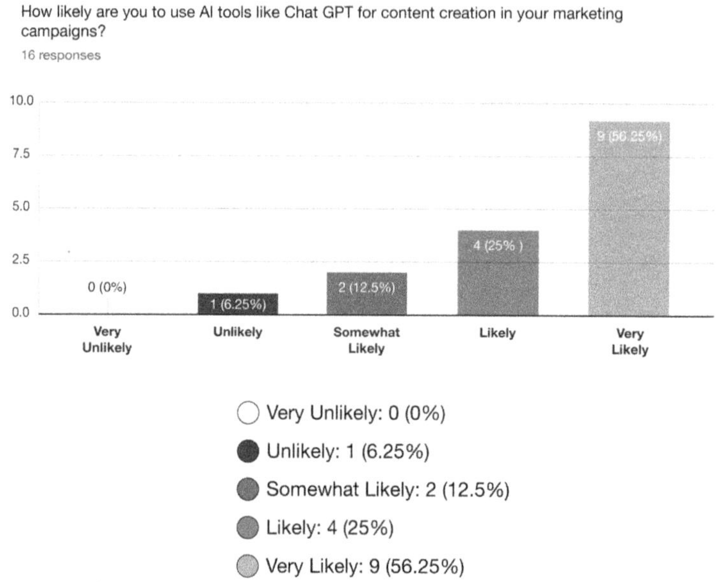

Figure 3. Satisfaction with AI-Generated Content Engagement

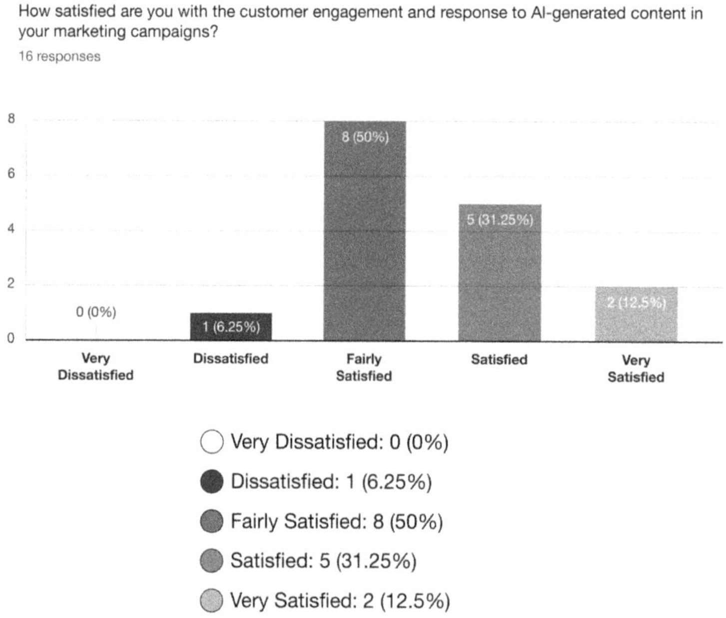

Figure 4. Importance of AI in Future Content Marketing

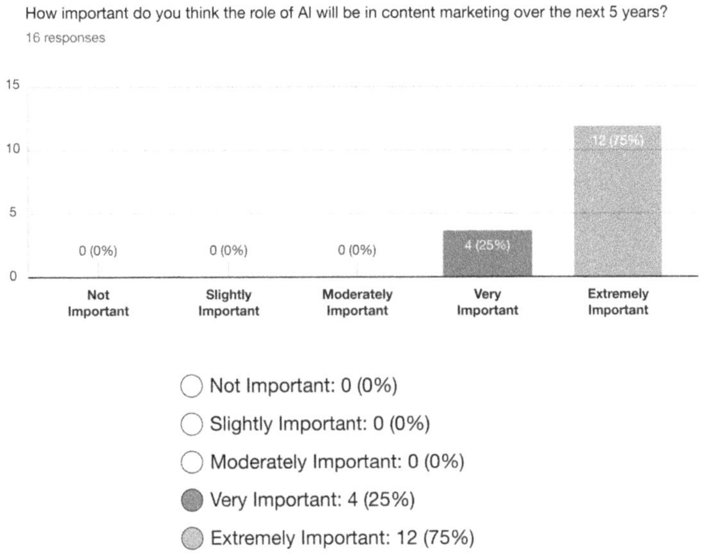

Figure 5. Proportion of AI-Generated Digital Content

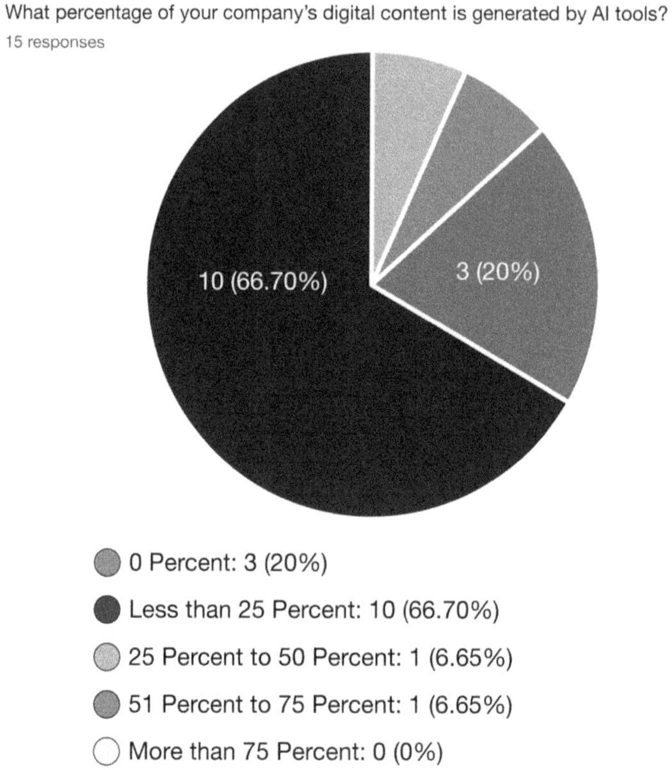

Figure 6. Leading AI Applications in Marketing

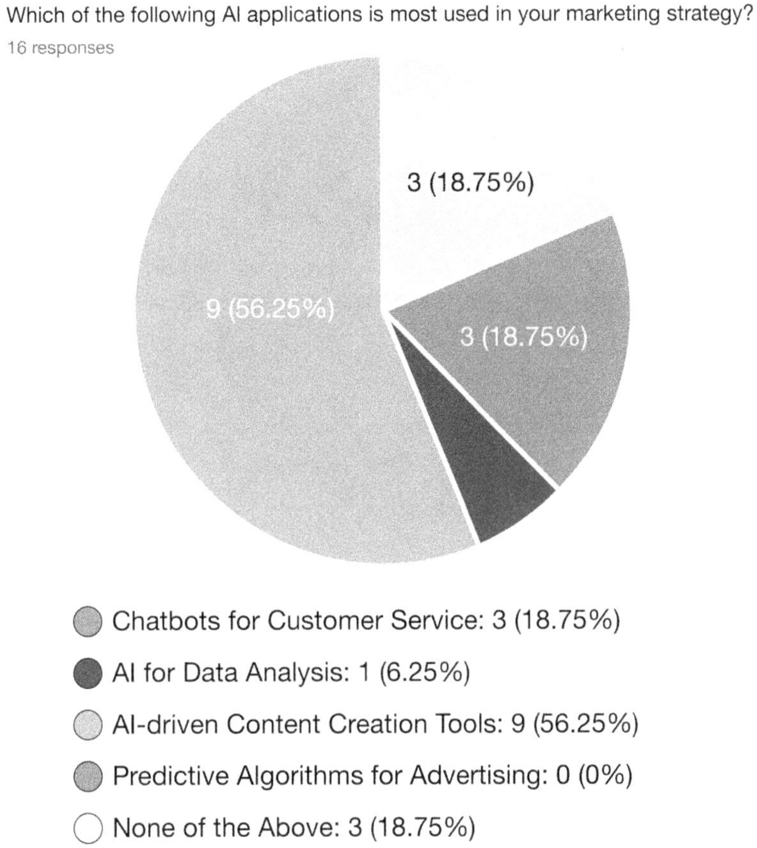

Figure 7. AI's Effect on Marketing Careers

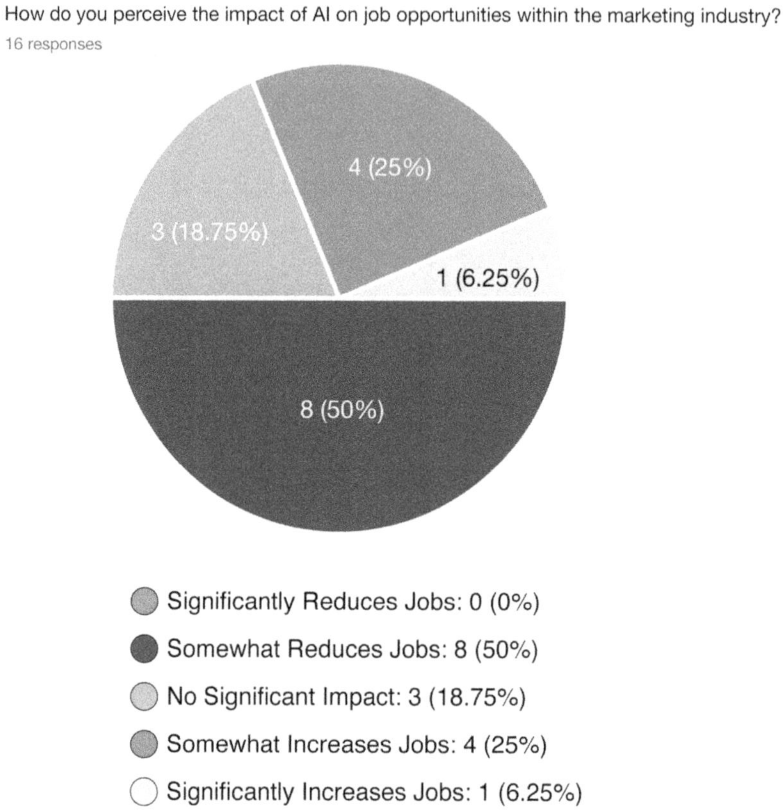

Figure 8. Marketing Goals for AI Adoption

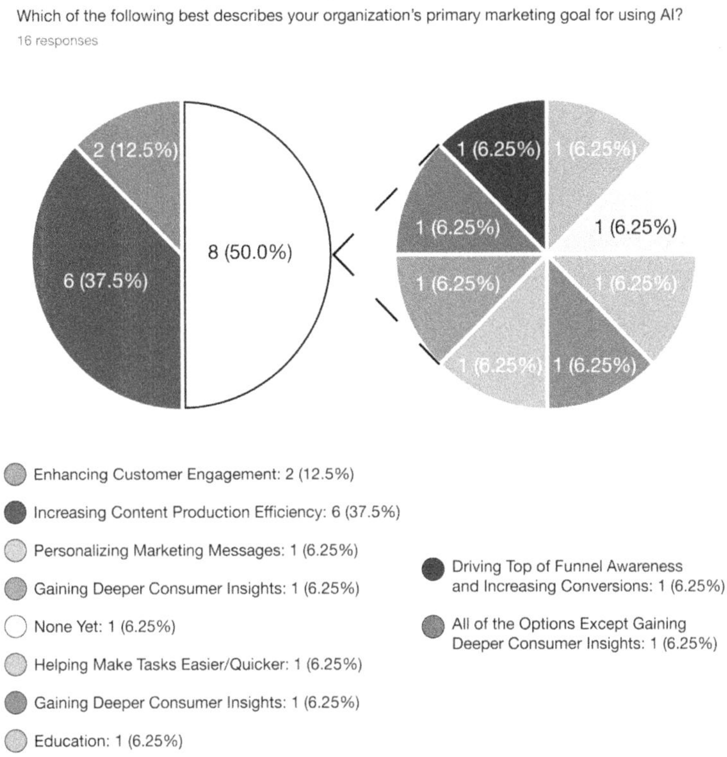

Figure 9. Assessing AI Content Effectiveness in Marketing

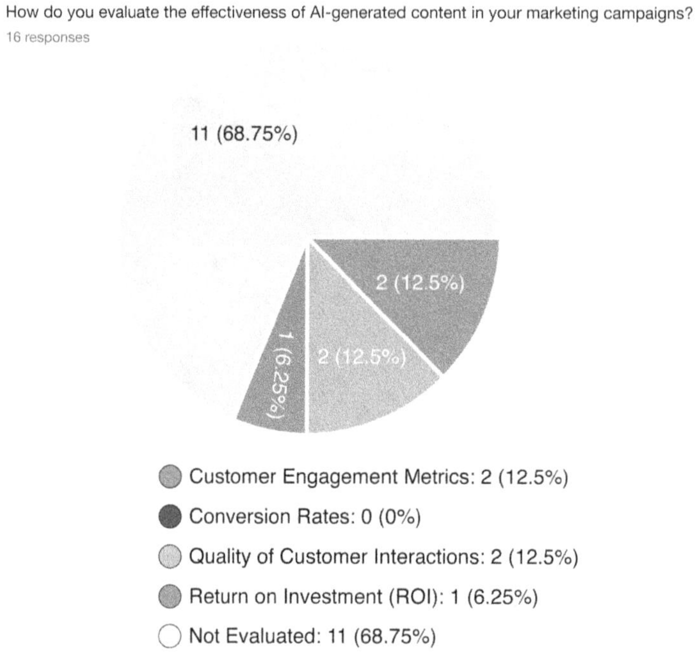

Qualitative Responses

Table 3. Challenges of integrating AI in marketing content creation

Question
What are some of your biggest challenges when integrating AI into your marketing content creation process?
Responses
1. Create highly sophisticated prompts that capture correctly what I want to generate.
2. Duplicate some words like revolutionary. Also, still need a development more in making persuasive message for your specific target audience.
3. Employee and administrative buy-in.
4. Haven't found a use case for AI yet.
5. Interoperability of tools. Ensuring valid citations and attributions, sounding human. Re-writing to be in my voice.

continued on following page

Table 3. Continued

6. Mastering new tools and staying up to date with all new developments. To integrate AI tools first your team needs to be skilled in AI tools utilization.
7. Not having the broad skill set needed to understand prompt development. Not understanding audience sentiment. Using old tools not suited to new mediums.
8. Privacy, personalization, and competition where our rivals have access to the same AI tools landscape.
9. Quality of the AI tools.
10. Rights for the people created by AI.
11. The ability and knowledge to make good prompts.
12. There haven't been any as they are just another tool to help with brainstorming, tweaking copy, and image creation.
13. To ensure having the capabilities to use AI.
14. Vetting content for tone, style, and brand personality consistency.

Table 4. Examples of AI boosting content marketing efficiency

Question
Can you share an example of an AI tool significantly improving the efficiency or effectiveness of your content marketing strategy?
Responses
1. At the last minute I realized there was a perfect opportunity to leverage an event with an Instagram post. I didn't have time for a photo shoot, so I created the student image I needed using an AI tool. This allowed me to post within an hour.
2. ChatGPT.
3. ChatGPT, I train it to be my content assistant with all core concepts of the business and marketing messages. Now, I can generate quality content about anything related to the business.
4. Haven't found a use case for AI yet.
5. I first generate the draft with ChatGPT Plus and then make it my own by editing and improving. I frequently use ChatGPT for email content.
6. It definitely can help when trying to improve or increase diversity, inclusion, and equity within the University student population. We are working at the moment on creating courses in our core that are DEI certified.
7. Midjourney make our final presentation very clean and graphics more realistic and near to what a final shooting will be at the end.
8. No, it's too early.
9. Providing visual content for various social media.
10. Use AI to get over the 'blank page hump.'

continued on following page

Table 4. Continued

11. When I wanted to generate 3 content options that were able to successfully attract the individuals of my target market. However, I consider important to mention that when I created the prompt, it was necessary to include the most important characteristics among the individuals included in my target market. Otherwise, the content would not resonate among them.
12. When it comes to analysis of content generated by students. AI has been a huge help in organizing and suggesting tends.

Table 5. Future trends and innovations in AI for marketing content

Question
How do you envision the future of AI in marketing content creation, and what trends or innovations do you think will emerge?
Responses
1. AI will be central to marketing content creation. However, it ideally won't be a straightforward path. I suspect that most people want the "easy button," Enter a prompt, get some content back, and post it. To me, this lacks integrity. AI should be a companion to the work. It should be the advisor you engage, but in the end, you're still responsible for your output. You should not take credit for someone else's work, even AI. We will also have to contend with a quantity over quality problem. AI will generate a tsunami of unauthentic content; it is going to become harder and harder to find the true human-inspired gems.
2. AI will make content creation easier and quicker.
3. AI-driven influencers will emerge, visual creation will see its peak in terms of creativity.
4. As any other martech tool, AI will improve efficiency. The process of content creation will be partially automated, but the role of human creativity will still be crucial.
5. I think AI will help companies to continue refining and enhancing personalization in marketing content; I would lower the cost and time needed to generate content; and it would facilitate seamless content and messaging integration across various marketing channels.
6. I think it will increasingly support initial content creation followed by human optimization.
7. I think we are close enough to have an AI SEO tool that will fix your on-site issues as well as search for link building opportunities and contact those high authority websites or even buying premium blogs for you. Even better if could track the results and report to you monthly.
8. In the short term, AI and traditional techniques will work in tandem to develop trust. What we will see quickly is the tool used for simpler things and then deferment to people for the nuanced deployment.
9. It is going to be integrated into every tool we already use, and some will be replaced by new ones. AI is going to be a sidekick who helps us with the little tasks that use to take us forever or we didn't like to do. The best tools will be the ones that we can train to write and create in our brand voice. Those will be the most powerful. "Here are our brand guidelines, images of what our products/services are, and what our voice is like. Make me things." THAT is where the real power will be.
10. New professions and roles in the industry - prompt engineering.
11. The future of marketing is about who is capable of using AI best and the most efficient way for marketing content creation.

continued on following page

Table 5. Continued

12. Don't know.
13. I just read yesterday that Sam's Club is getting ready to use AI instead of having someone stand at the exit to check your receipt. You will walk through something that looks like a metal detector and AI will scan your cart to make sure everything in there is what you purchased. I think more and more companies will use AI because it does help with removing menial tasks. Thus, they can use their employees hopefully to ensure better customer service. Amazon also just had a recent article within the last week of how they are using AI in their warehouses, but they also have employees that are working side by side with them. So, I definitely believe AI will be assisting companies, whether it's with marketing or like Amazon in the warehouse, but I don't believe it's going to remove or displace workers; we are still going to need employees to maintain these AI devices.

Table 6. Ethical considerations in AI application for marketing

Question
What ethical considerations should be prioritized when developing and applying AI in marketing?
Responses
1. AI needs to be used ethically.
2. As a society, we need to grapple with how we compensate all those who have trained the AI. We need to tackle intellectual property, copyright, citation and attribution, data control and ownership, micropayment, verified sender and content authenticity issues.
3. Copyright is a concern in content creation. Any content I create for my public channels will then be a training data for large language models (LLM) so others will have access to my somewhat unique content indirectly.
4. I think that the most important challenges are among the following categories: protection of privacy, bias avoidance, and transparency and regulation compliance.
5. In customer engagement, AI needs to be identified.
6. In marketing specifically? Hmm... The first thing that comes to mind is as AI video and audio become more powerful, we have to be careful about where the line is with testimonials and that sort of thing. Just like now where we see "actor portrayal" in a commercial, we might need something for AI. But, who knows.
7. Intellectual property.
8. Limiting the risk of discrimination and ensuring data security.
9. Paying attention to any bias in content creation, a number of ethical and privacy concerns related to utilization of predictive analytics and programmatic advertising.
10. People's faces created by AI.
11. Privacy.
12. Same as existing SEO and content creation ethics. Create content for human readers.
13. Use of faces.
14. We certainly have to worry about what kind of personal data is being collected. That's something that nobody really has touched on much in the readings that I have come across. Whatever systems that are being used for marketing should definitely ensure that wherever the data ends up is protected and secure. And I think this needs to be discussed more before companies start just automatically adding AI because it's the cool new thing to do.

Table 7. AI's role in future marketing education and research

Question
What role do you foresee AI playing in shaping the future of marketing education and research?
Responses
1. AI already has a crucial role in marketing and with GenAI this will only increase. AI literacy should be included in marketing curriculum as without these skills, marketing graduates will not be ready for future jobs.
2. AI should be at the heart of marketing education. We need to teach students how to use the tools, while at the same time citing and attributing the work appropriately.
3. AI-powered platforms can deliver continuous learning opportunities for marketing professionals and educators. It can create better learning experiences for students. It could help automate routine administrative tasks which will allow educators and researchers to dedicate more time to teaching and mentorship.
4. As a support.
5. As marketing analytics is implemented in current marketing classes, so should AI-based marketing in the future to prepare marketing students the best possible way for their professional jobs.
6. Huge role in data analytics allowing content previously not analyzed to be analyzed.
7. I don't know.
8. I see it exploding in the next five years. There's so much you can do with analyzing the data and learning about your customers and their trends, whether it be purchasing trends or how often they purchase, etc. We will be able to determine the type of customer who makes certain purchases and be able to market to those who are not currently purchasing from your company.
9. I think students learning marketing should be mastering AI, as I believe it will become the base of marketing campaigns that are optimized and improved via human input.
10. Improving allocate more related resources instead of searching hundreds of articles.
11. It has to be integrated into the courses that students are taking. I made sure to begin teaching about it immediately or else my students would be behind when they graduated.
12. Not 100 percent sure.
13. Prompting.
14. Things will speed up, productivity will improve. We will talk a new level of education and research. Likely that every marketer or team will have their own customized AI tool, serving them best for their goals.

Table 8. Reasons for not using AI in marketing content creation

Question
If you currently do not use AI for content creation in your marketing strategies, what are the primary reasons for this decision?
Responses
1. Am using it.
2. I am using it.

continued on following page

Table 8. Continued

3. I do not have any participation in the creation of my university's overall marketing strategies. However, I do use it for the generation of content and activities in my courses.
4. I do use it. But my biggest hurdle is time, the time to explore the various tools and to figure out how to pull them into my workflow. Budget is secondary.
5. I mentioned previously that a lot of it comes down to having administration's buy-in. Additionally, for us it will come down to whether the state wants to invest in any type of software that can aid in marketing to high school students who are thinking about coming to college. Even if Slippery Rock decides they want to use some sort of system to assist with marketing we still have to have permission from the state in order to do so.
6. I use it.
7. I use it.
8. I use it for my personal content creation. I believe the reason for not using it is the lack of mastery of these new tools. Although they seem easy to use, it takes time to master these tools.
9. My industry is very niche, and I've found that for content creation I'm still better off creating from scratch. As AI improves, I think that will change.
10. Rights.

Table 9. Additional insights on AI in marketing content creation

Question
Do you have any additional insights or ideas to share?
Responses
1. AI enables marketers to create hyper-personalized experiences by analyzing individual customer preferences, behaviors, and interactions. AI tools can assist in the creative process by generating content ideas, suggesting design elements, and even contributing to copywriting. AI algorithms can analyze market conditions, competitor pricing, and customer behavior to dynamically adjust pricing strategies in real-time. AI algorithms can also help better predict customer behavior based on historical data and patterns. AI can assist in identifying and assessing influencers for marketing collaborations. Finally, it can optimize the distribution of content by analyzing audience behavior and preferences.
2. AI has been already changing content from ads creative to text content. There are already tools that provide a text box for you to generate whatever creatives you want. Creatives are a big and important area to grow with AI.
3. I think AI is an important tool for shaping ideas. If you can't prompt, you can't use AI in a good way. There are a lot of tricks or words that you can use to enhance your prompts to obtain better results.
4. I'm a firm believer that AI will be a positive tool if used properly and if people can understand how to use it. Currently, there are really no resources other than what we see in posts on LinkedIn. We need to buckle down and start writing research articles and books regarding the use of AI in the classroom so when the students enter the workforce, they are prepared with new ideas that hopefully their supervisors will be on board with and implement.
5. The challenge is knowing when to stand back from the AI and do the nuanced thinking. It is important to understand there are still baby limitations to AI in a large post based on its education. But AI gets us along the road faster than ever before.

DISCUSSION

Quantitative Results

The quantitative portion of the survey revealed both enthusiasm for AI's potential and concerns about its implications. Many respondents expressed apprehension about AI-generated content, fearing its potential to perpetuate biases, with nearly 56.25% ranging from very to extremely concerned (Figure 1). Despite these concerns, the adoption of AI tools like ChatGPT was high, with 81.25% likely or very likely to use them in their marketing strategies (Figure 2). While there is concern about the risks of AI, its high adoption rate indicates a strong interest in leveraging its capabilities in marketing strategies.

Customer engagement with AI-generated content was positively received, as 50% were fairly satisfied, and 43.75% were satisfied to very satisfied (Figure 3), suggesting AI content resonated well with audiences. These percentages aligned with the strong belief that AI will play a crucial role in content marketing in the next five years which all respondents consider very to extremely important (Figure 4). This indicates acceptance and future use of AI in content marketing.

At 56.25%, AI-driven content creation tools were the most popular application used by the respondents (Figure 6). However, the amount of digital content produced by AI varied, with a majority (66.7%) reporting that less than 25% of their content was generated by AI. Of the remaining options, the next highest response was 0%, which garnered 20% (Figure 5). Despite the popularity of AI-driven content creation tools, most respondents predominantly use non-AI methods to produce their digital content.

The impact of AI on marketing jobs was mixed, with half of the respondents believing it somewhat reduces jobs, while 6.25% believed it significantly increases jobs. This might suggest a shift in job roles rather than a reduction (Figure 7). However, at 37.5%, the job for which AI was most employed was increasing content production efficiency, with the next most common task of enhancing customer engagement capturing 12.5% (Figure 8). The findings suggest that AI is reshaping the landscape of marketing jobs rather than significantly reducing employment.

A majority of respondents, 68.75%, do not evaluate the effectiveness of their AI-generated content (Table 9), suggesting that it is not yet being strategically used. Two answers, customer engagement metrics and quality of customer interactions, each received 12.5% of the responses (Table 9). Conversion rates were not used as a measure of effectiveness by any respondent. That most respondents do not assess the effectiveness of their AI-generated content might indicate it is being used more informally than intentionally.

Qualitative Results

The survey's qualitative responses reveal challenges in using AI for content creation. One respondent highlighted the complexity of "Create[ing] highly sophisticated prompts that capture correctly what I want to generate" (Table 3). Other concerns included word duplication and the need for content personalization. Respondents stressed the challenges of understanding how to use the myriad AI tools available. These responses emphasize the need for thorough training.

Ethical considerations are crucial for maintaining privacy and avoiding biases. A respondent stressed the necessity for the "protection of privacy, bias avoidance, and transparency" (Table 6). Intellectual property issues, including addressing "intellectual property, copyright, citation, and attribution" (Table 6), highlight the emerging requirement for ethical frameworks that address the unique challenges posed by AI. There was also concern about the creation and use of faces, possibly suggesting the threat of deep-fake images and videos.

The impact on efficiency and creativity is significant. One respondent shared, "At the last minute I realized there was a perfect opportunity to leverage an event with an Instagram post. I didn't have time for a photo shoot so I created the student image I needed using an AI tool. This allowed me to post within an hour" (Table 4). This demonstrates how AI provides solutions that adapt rapidly to changing conditions. Other respondents noted AI's ability to overcome creative constraints with brainstorming and early content concepts that are later refined (Table 5).

Marketers will increasingly look to leverage AI for creative development. "AI will be central to marketing content creation ... most people want the 'easy button'—enter a prompt, get some content back and post it" shared one respondent (Table 5). Another respondent foresees the future of AI as a "sidekick who helps us with the little tasks" while another anticipates "AI will make content creation easier and quicker" (Table 5). This expectation of AI's integration into everyday marketing alongside a balance between automation and creative integrity suggests a shift toward the strategic use of AI tools.

Education and skill development are crucial. Noting that AI plays a pivotal part in marketing, one respondent shared, "AI literacy should be included in marketing curriculum as without these skills, marketing graduates will not be ready for future jobs" (Table 7). AI might be well-suited as an instructor, with a respondent commenting, "AI-powered platforms can deliver continuous learning opportunities for marketing professionals and educators" (Table 7). The importance of data analytics was shared by several respondents, with one stressing, "there's so much you can do with analyzing the data and learning about your customers" (Table 7).

CONCLUSION

This chapter highlights AI's impact on content creation, showcasing how AI tools empower marketers to deliver targeted, engaging content that improves customer experiences and brand loyalty. Alongside these benefits are challenges, including ethical concerns, data privacy, and brand consistency. While these issues require careful consideration, the benefits of AI outweigh the risks. Mayahi and Vidrih (2022) proclaim, "the time has come for marketers to fully embrace emerging technologies and close the gap that separates them from more traditional forms of marketing" (p. 4).

Beyond its present benefits, "marketers can use AI technology to identify trends and forecast them for the future. Based on these facts, they can decide how to allocate their budgets and who to target" (Haleem et al., 2022, p. 122). Successfully leveraging AI requires a sensible and unified strategy. Bourton et al. (2023) warn that "allowing dozens of genAI projects to spawn across an organization puts at-scale value creation at risk" (para. 9). Instead, companies should use AI to differentiate themselves while focusing on delivering value (Bourton et al., 2023).

As AI becomes more capable and commonplace, overreliance becomes a potential problem (Polinski, 2024). While it remains a great marketing resource, using AI for content creation still requires human involvement (10Web and Hubspot, 2023). As observed by Portman (2024), "the crucial part of AI-powered MarTech systems is to balance human creativity with the automation tasks that they are responsible for" (para. 2). Atluri et al. (2024) suggest "generative AI can drive value by working in partnership with workers, augmenting their work in ways that accelerate their productivity" (p. 16).

AI has transformed marketing technology and moved society forward. Zack Kass, formerly of OpenAI, believes we are nearing a "human renaissance of some kind" (Kohan, 2024, para. 2). Davis (2023) reveals of the 2,042 new marketing technology tools introduced between May and November 2023, 1,498 (73%) were AI-based" (para. 2); 34% of those AI tools were for creating content. Evolving MarTech trends include hyper-personalization, voice-search optimization, and personality-based user experience (Portman, 2024). Raghav et al. (2023) project increased use of augmented reality content, noting that it "presents exciting opportunities for marketers to create immersive and engaging experiences" (p. 268).

While current AI tools are impressive, the technology is moving towards something more significant: artificial general intelligence (AGI). Once AGI is achieved, AI will have cognitive abilities that are equivalent to, or indistinguishable from, a human (Baig et al., 2024). Once this occurs, OpenAI CEO Sam Altman predicts that "95% of what marketers use agencies, strategists, and creative professionals for today will easily, nearly instantly and at almost no cost be handled by the AI" (Kaput, 2024, para. 19).

REFERENCES

Atluri, V., Dahlström, P., Gaffey, B., García de la Torre, V., Kaka, N., Lajous, T., Singla, A., Sukharevsky, A., Travasoni, A., & Vieira, B. (2024). *Beyond the hype: Capturing the potential of AI and gen AI in tech, media, and telecom.*https://www.mckinsey.com/industries/technology-media-and-telecommunications/our-insights/beyond-the-hype-capturing-the-potential-of-ai-and-gen-ai-in-tmt

Baig, A., Berruti, F., Ellencweig, B., Lewandowski, D., Roberts, R., Yee, L., Singla, A., Smaje, K., Sukharevsky, A., Tilley, J., & Zemmel, R. (2024, March 21). *What is artificial general intelligence (AGI)?*https://www.mckinsey.com/featured-insights/mckinsey-explainers/what-is-artificial-general-intelligence-agi

Baig, A., Singla, A., & Yee, L. (2024, April 2). *What is generative AI?* McKinsey & Company. https://www.mckinsey.com/featured-insights/mckinsey-explainers/what-is-generative-ai#/

Bank of America Corporation. (2024). *Artificial intelligence: A real game changer.* Bank of America. https://business.bofa.com/en-us/content/economic-impact-of-ai.html

Belanger, A. (2024, February 16). *Air Canada must honor refund policy invented by airline's chatbot.* Ars Technica. https://arstechnica.com/tech-policy/2024/02/air-canada-must-honor-refund-policy-invented-by-airlines-chatbot/

Bourton, S., Ellencweig, B., Giovin, C., & Xu, S. (2023, November 29). *Six major GenAI trends that will shape 2024's agenda.* QuantumBlack, AI by McKinsey. https://medium.com/quantumblack/six-major-genai-trends-that-will-shape-2024s-agenda-da85dba8b1a8

Chintalapati, S., & Pandey, S. K. (2022). Artificial intelligence in marketing: A systematic literature review. *International Journal of Market Research*, 64(1), 38–68. DOI: 10.1177/14707853211018428

Content Marketing Institute. (2023, August). *What is content marketing?* Content Marketing Institute. https://contentmarketinginstitute.com/what-is-content-marketing/

Data 360 Network. (2023, February 25). *Generative AI and natural language processing: Applications and challenges.* Medium. https://data360network.medium.com/generative-ai-and-natural-language-processing-applications-and-challenges-3ae5ec254fdc

Davenport, T., Grewal, D., & Guha, A. (2021, July). *How to design an AI marketing strategy*. Harvard Business Review. https://hbr.org/2021/07/how-to-design-an-ai-marketing-strategy

Davis, K. (2023, December 5). *AI driving an exponential increase in marketing technology solutions*. MarTech. https://martech.org/ai-driving-an-exponential-increase-in-marketing-technology-solutions/

Dwivedi, Y. K., & Wang, Y. (2022). Guest editorial: Artificial intelligence for B2B marketing: Challenges and opportunities. *Industrial Marketing Management*, 105, 109–113. DOI: 10.1016/j.indmarman.2022.06.001

Garg, A. (2023, June 1). *Create real magic: The Coca-Cola way*. Abhi Garg. https://abhigarg.com/create-real-magic-the-coca-cola-masterpiece/

Gianatasio, D. (2022, July 29). Asked to "Draw Ketchup," even A.I. chose Heinz. Muse by Clio. https://musebycl.io/digital-data/asked-draw-ketchup-even-ai-chose-heinz

Gołąb-Andrzejak, E. (2022). Enhancing customer engagement in social media with AI – a higher education case study. *Procedia Computer Science*, 207, 3028–3037. DOI: 10.1016/j.procs.2022.09.361

Gross, G. (2024, February 20). *Air Canada chatbot error underscores AI's enterprise liability danger*. Computerworld. https://www.computerworld.com/article/1612087/air-canada-chatbot-error-underscores-ais-enterprise-liability-danger.html

Grover, P., Kar, A. K., & Dwivedi, Y. K. (2022). Understanding artificial intelligence adoption in operations management: Insights from the review of academic literature and social media discussions. *Annals of Operations Research*, 308(1–2), 177–213. DOI: 10.1007/s10479-020-03683-9

Guinness, R. (2019, May 9). *What is artificial intelligence? Part 2*. Medium. https://towardsdatascience.com/what-is-artificial-intelligence-part-2-bad0cb97e330

Haleem, A., Javaid, M., Asim Qadri, M., Pratap Singh, R., & Suman, R. (2022). Artificial intelligence (AI) applications for marketing: A literature-based study. *International Journal of Intelligent Networks*, 3, 119–132. DOI: 10.1016/j.ijin.2022.08.005

Hall, J. (2023, November 19). *How to future-proof your content strategy in the age of AI*. Forbes. https://www.forbes.com/sites/johnhall/2023/11/19/how-to-future-proof-your-content-strategy-in-the-age-of-ai/

Harkness, L., Robinson, K., Stein, E., & Wu, W. (2023, December 4). *How generative AI can boost consumer marketing*. https://www.mckinsey.com/capabilities/growth-marketing-and-sales/our-insights/how-generative-ai-can-boost-consumer-marketing

IBM. (2024a, March 19). *What is artificial intelligence (AI)?*https://www.ibm.com/topics/artificial-intelligence

IBM. (2024b, March 19). *What is natural language processing?*https://www.ibm.com/topics/natural-language-processing

Kaput, M. (2024, March 5). *Sam Altman says AI will handle "95%" of marketing work done by agencies and creatives*. Marketing AI Institute. https://www.marketingaiinstitute.com/blog/sam-altman-ai-agi-marketing

Kehoe, J., & Kolpak, J. (2024, March 4). *Yes, AI promises to transform marketing. But what's the catch?* Ad Age. https://adage.com/article/digital-marketing-ad-tech-news/yes-ai-promises-transform-marketing-whats-catch/2544031

Kelly, C. (2023, March 21). *Coke asks consumers to generate art with new AI platform.* Marketing Dive. https://www.marketingdive.com/news/coca-cola-coke-generative-ai-marketing-art/645465/

Kohan, S. E. (2024, May 2). *Zack Kass, former OpenAI leader, urges retail execs to champion AI.* Forbes. https://www.forbes.com/sites/shelleykohan/2024/05/02/zack-kass-former-openai-leader-urges-retail-execs-to-champion-ai/

Kulp, P. (2022, August 1). *Heinz Taps State-of-the-Art AI to Design Its Next Ad.*https://www.adweek.com/commerce/heinz-taps-ai-design-next-ad-campaign/

Kurtzke, S. (2023). Contemporary and emerging content marketing trends. In A. Krowinska, C. Backhaus, B. Becker, & F. Bosser, *Digital Content Marketing* (1st ed., pp. 191–227). Routledge. https://doi.org/DOI: 10.4324/9781003346500-12

Maheshwari, R. (2024, February 6). *Top AI statistics and trends*. Forbes Advisor INDIA. https://www.forbes.com/advisor/in/business/ai-statistics/

Mani, R. (2023, December 29). *Coca-Cola's "Create Real Magic" AI campaign: Lessons for CIOs*. CIO.inc. https://www.cio.inc/coca-colas-create-real-magic-ai-campaign-lessons-for-cios-a-23996

Manis, K. T., & Madhavaram, S. (2023). AI-Enabled marketing capabilities and the hierarchy of capabilities: Conceptualization, proposition development, and research avenues. *Journal of Business Research*, 157, 113485. DOI: 10.1016/j.jbusres.2022.113485

Marketing AI Institute. (2023). *2023 state of marketing report*.

Marketing Case Hub. (2024, January 2). *Creating the real magic with human and AI-powered marketing—The Coca-Cola case study*. Marketing Case Hub. https://marketingcasehub.com/case-study/creating-the-real-magic-with-human-and-ai-powered-marketing-the-coca-cola-case-study/

Marr, B. (2022, September 9). *Artificial intelligence and the future of marketing*. Forbes. https://www.forbes.com/sites/bernardmarr/2022/09/09/artificial-intelligence-and-the-future-of-marketing/

Martineau, K. (2023, April 20). *What is generative AI?* IBM Research Blog. https://research.ibm.com/blog/what-is-generative-AI

Mayahi, S., & Vidrih, M. (2022). *The impact of generative AI on the future of visual content marketing*. https://doi.org/DOI: 10.48550/ARXIV.2211.12660

Mikalef, P., Conboy, K., & Krogstie, J. (2021). Artificial intelligence as an enabler of B2B marketing: A dynamic capabilities micro-foundations approach. *Industrial Marketing Management*, 98, 80–92. DOI: 10.1016/j.indmarman.2021.08.003

Moffatt v. Air Canada, SC-2023-005609 (Civil Resolution Tribunal of British Columbia February 14, 2024). https://canlii.ca/t/k2spq

Mustak, M., Salminen, J., Plé, L., & Wirtz, J. (2021). Artificial intelligence in marketing: Topic modeling, scientometric analysis, and research agenda. *Journal of Business Research*, 124, 389–404. DOI: 10.1016/j.jbusres.2020.10.044

National Artificial Intelligence Advisory Committee (NAIAC). (2023). *Findings: The potential future risks of AI*. https://ai.gov/wp-content/uploads/2023/11/Findings_The-Potential-Future-Risks-of-AI.pdf

Nishant, R., Kennedy, M., & Corbett, J. (2020). Artificial intelligence for sustainability: Challenges, opportunities, and a research agenda. *International Journal of Information Management*, 53, 102104. DOI: 10.1016/j.ijinfomgt.2020.102104

Ortiz, S. (2024a, April 23). *What is generative AI and why is it so popular? Here's everything you need to know*. ZDNET. https://www.zdnet.com/article/what-is-generative-ai-and-why-is-it-so-popular-heres-everything-you-need-to-know/

Ortiz, S. (2024b, April 26). What does GPT stand for? Understanding GPT 3.5, GPT 4, GPT-4 Turbo, and more. ZDNET. https://www.zdnet.com/article/what-does-gpt-stand-for-understanding-gpt-3-5-gpt-4-and-more/

Poinski, M. (2024, May 8). *In marketing, AI cannot duplicate the human element*. Forbes. https://www.forbes.com/sites/cmo/2024/05/08/in-marketing-ai-cannot-duplicate-the-human-element/

Portman, P. (2024, February 28). *AI in MarTech: How AI will impact the MarTech industry.* Forbes. https://www.forbes.com/sites/forbestechcouncil/2024/02/28/ai-in-martech-how-ai-will-impact-the-martech-industry/

Posch, M. (2024, February 28). *Air Canada's chatbot: Why RAG is better than an LLM for facts.* Hackaday. https://hackaday.com/2024/02/28/air-canadas-chatbot-why-rag-is-better-than-an-llm-for-facts/

Price, E. (2024, February 18). *Air Canada must honor a fake refund policy created by its chatbot, court says.* PCMAG. https://www.pcmag.com/news/air-canada-must-honor-a-fake-refund-policy-created-by-its-chatbot-court

Salford Business School. (2024). *Importance of content marketing for your digital marketing strategy.* University of Salford. https://www.salford.ac.uk/salford-business-school/importance-of-content-marketing-for-your-digital-marketing-strategy

Salminen, M. (2023, August 31). *27 AI statistics and trends in 2024.* Hostinger Tutorials. https://www.hostinger.com/tutorials/ai-statistics

Schneider, C. (2023, November 2). *The complete guide to AI content marketing.* https://www.linkedin.com/pulse/complete-guide-ai-content-marketing-cody-schneider-epk7c

Segment, SendGrid, & Twilio. (2023). *7 ways to use AI to superpower your marketing strategy.*

Solomonoff, G. (2023, May 6). *The Meeting of the Minds That Launched AI.* https://spectrum.ieee.org/dartmouth-ai-workshop

Turing, A. M. (1937). On Computable Numbers, with an Application to the Entscheidungsproblem. *Proceedings of the London Mathematical Society*, s2-42(1), 230–265. https://doi.org/DOI: 10.1112/plms/s2-42.1.230

Twilio. (2023). *The growth report 2023: The AI edition.*

Varikuti, M. (2023, May 6). *Can Machines Think?* ILLUMINATION. https://medium.com/illumination/can-machines-think-a36969b741fe

Vlačić, B., Corbo, L., Costa, E., Silva, S., & Dabić, M. (2021). The evolving role of artificial intelligence in marketing: A review and research agenda. *Journal of Business Research*, 128, 187–203. DOI: 10.1016/j.jbusres.2021.01.055

Weaver, A. (2023, April 4). *Generative AI in plain language: What it is, what's hype, and what's real.* Writer. https://writer.com/blog/generative-ai-defined-hype-vs-reality/

Web & Hubspot. (2023). *2023 AI trends for marketers*. Adnews Staff. (2022, July 25). *Heinz resumes Draw Ketchup campaign*. Adnews. https://www.adnews.com/42091

White, C. (2023, October 4). Key differences between machine learning and generative AI in marketing. CMSWire.Com. https://www.cmswire.com/digital-experience/machine-learning-and-generative-ai-in-marketing-critical-differences/

Wolinsky, J. (2023, June 29). *What's coming next decade for AI in marketing?* CMSWire.Com. https://www.cmswire.com/digital-marketing/whats-coming-next-decade-for-ai-in-marketing/

World Market Watch LLC. (2024). *The CMO Survey.*

Yashveer Raghav, Y., Tipu, R. K., Bhakhar, R., Gupta, T., & Sharma, K. (2023). The future of digital marketing: Leveraging artificial intelligence for competitive strategies and tactics. In Teixeira, S., & Remondes, J. (Eds.), (pp. 249–274). Advances in Marketing, Customer Relationship Management, and E-Services. IGI Global., DOI: 10.4018/978-1-6684-9324-3.ch011

KEY TERMS AND DEFINITIONS

Artificial Intelligence (AI): A field of computer science that aims to create systems capable of performing tasks that normally require human intelligence. These tasks include decision-making, problem-solving, understanding language, and visual perception.

ChatGPT: A conversational AI model developed by OpenAI that generates human-like text responses based on the input it receives. It is used in various applications, such as customer service, content generation, and more.

Content Creation: The process of generating topic ideas that appeal to a target audience and creating written or visual content based on those ideas to be shared via various media.

Customer Engagement: Strategies and efforts employed by businesses to interact meaningfully with customers through various channels. AI enhances customer engagement by personalizing interactions, predicting customer needs, and providing timely and relevant content, thus improving customer satisfaction and loyalty.

Generative AI: A type of AI technology that can generate new content, whether text, images, or sounds, that is similar but not identical to the content on which it was trained. It is often used for creating art, composing music, or writing stories.

Machine Learning: A subset of AI that focuses on algorithms and statistical models that allow computer systems to improve their performance on specific tasks over time without being explicitly programmed.

Marketing Automation: Technology platforms and software that help businesses effectively market on multiple online channels (such as email, social media, websites, etc.) and automate repetitive tasks. AI enhances marketing automation by enabling more efficient, personalized, data-driven marketing actions.

Marketing Strategies: Plans that businesses implement to reach and persuade prospects to purchase a product or service. These strategies involve positioning, targeting specific audiences, and setting specific objectives and activities to engage customers.

Natural Language Processing (NLP): A branch of AI that allows computers to understand, interpret, and respond to human language in a meaningful and useful way.

Predictive Algorithms: Algorithms that use historical data to predict future outcomes. They forecast customer behavior, purchasing patterns, and engagement trends in marketing.

Chapter 3
Effects of Social Media Marketing Elements on Online Buying Decisions of Vietnamese Generation Z

Trinh Le Tan
https://orcid.org/0000-0001-7729-3241
FPT University, Vietnam

Minh Tung Tran
https://orcid.org/0000-0002-4238-882X
FPT University, Vietnam

ABSTRACT

This research intends to explore how social media marketing impacts the shopping habits of Vietnam's Generation Z, particularly through elements such as the content's usefulness, engagement level, appeal, shareability, trustworthiness, and entertainment value, employing structural equation modeling for detailed investigation. By conducting an online questionnaire using Google Forms aimed at a minimum of 197 respondents, the study will use Confirmatory Factor Analysis (CFA) and Structural Equation Modeling (SEM) via AMOS and SPSS tools. Measures' reliability will be confirmed through Cronbach's Alpha, Exploratory Factor Analysis (EFA), and CFA. Anticipated outcomes should provide crucial insights for companies and institutions to formulate more effective marketing strategies, especially in understanding the interaction of this age group with social media advertisements and its influence on consumer behavior shifts.

DOI: 10.4018/979-8-3693-4361-6.ch003

1. INTRODUCTION

In the current era of digitalization, particularly Gen Z individuals born post-1997 (beresfordresearch.com) are increasingly engaging with social media. Lubis, A. N. highlighted in 2018 the growing trend of consumers favoring online shopping over conventional in-store buying. The integration of social media into the daily routines of individuals, particularly the youth, has made it a key platform for business and retail activities, a fact underscored by Wang, C. in 2011, especially during the challenging times brought about by the Covid-19 pandemic. Over the past two years, there has been a noticeable transformation in the shopping behaviors of consumers worldwide, including those in Vietnam, driven by technological progress, as observed by Mai, N. T. T., Jung, K., Lantz, G., & Loeb, S. G. in 2003. As a result, business owners are increasingly utilizing social media marketing to influence consumer attitudes and stimulate purchase decisions, adopting various advertising techniques as recommended by Chu, S. C., & Seock, Y. K. in 2020.

The more positive responses your ad campaign elicits, the more successful it is and vice versa (Putrevu, S., & Lord, K. R., 1994). The more Internet users you have, the more people will access your social networks (Carroll, B., & Landry, K., 2010). Especially in 2021, Vietnam was most affected by the Covid 19 pandemic, and social isolation lasted for more than eight months, greatly affecting people's shopping. Online shopping is currently the best form. Online shopping is becoming more and more popular (Hanus, G., 2016) thanks to corporate convenience, speed, and shopping support policies, and may replace traditional shopping in the future. This increase is not surprising as Internet connections are pervasive throughout the world and online shopping is on the rise. (2021, oberlo.com).

The question posed here is whether this form of advertising has any repercussions in the audience. How does this affect consumers' online shopping decisions? (Jusoh, Z. M., & Ling, G. H., 2012). This article applies to a specific Gen Z audience, i.e., the younger audience in Vietnam. Generation Z statistically includes young people born after 1995 (Gonzalez-Franco, M., & Lanier, J., 2017). They make up 33% of the world's population and 21% of Vietnam's (Nguyen, M. M., De Rosa, R. J., & Kalas, P., 2020). With the great influence of social media. self-employed people have also promoted different types of advertisements to influence their customers' consumer purchase intent (Veer, N., Pawar, P., & Kolte, A., 2019). Surveys show that most Gen Zers aren't impatient enough to see an ad for 30 seconds, so they skip ads even if they can spend hours browsing social media sites (Veer, N., Pawar, P., & Kolte, A., 2019). Vietnam's most popular social networks, with 31 million more users compared to 2019. (lamanh., 2021, October 16).This raises big questions about how different types of advertising attract and retain customers who want to shop online. Estimated annual growth rate of 14.8%, followed by advertising with

14% online video content (L c, N., 2021, December 28). This year's Facebook and Instagram time has actually dropped by 74.8% compared to 2017, the rise of social networking platform TikTok has exploded to share video content (Y n, H., 2021, November 26). Over the same period, Tiktok grew from 0% user growth to 15.1% within four years (TikTok is the third largest worldwide social network behind Instagram and Facebook., n.d.).

Reflecting on notable advertising achievements in Vietnam, the “Happy Planting Loc Tet, Dirty Sows Good Things” campaign by OMO stands out in the FMCG sector, as described in the analysis of OMO's Tet 2020 advertising campaign leading the FMCG industry (“Deciphering” OMO's Tet 2020 advertising campaign leading the FMCG industry., n.d.). This campaign played a significant role in propelling major detergent brands into the top 10 of the January BSI rankings, showcasing its impact on social media during Tet 2020 (BSI Top10: January 2020 social media rankings.., 2020, February 25). Garnering over 10 million views for its commercials and viral content on YouTube, along with 200,000 Facebook conversations, the OMO campaign captured widespread social media engagement (“Deciphering” OMO's Tet 2020 advertising campaign leading the FMCG industry., n.d.). Furthermore, Maybelline NewYork's campaign, which incorporated a dance challenge to lively music and the hashtag #sonni beatbox, amassed 33.8 million views on TikTok, showcasing the platform's potential for brand promotion (The formula for success from premium brands on TikTok.., n.d., 2022). This backdrop highlights the study's aim to provide actionable strategies for employing social media advertising formats to boost brand awareness and influence consumer purchasing behaviors (Arigo, D., Pagoto, S., Carter-Harris, L., Lillie, S. E., & Nebeker, C., 2018). Given the rapid expansion and influence of social networks (Siegel, D. A., 2009), and their wide-spread use among the youth, particularly Generation Z (Robelia, B. A., Greenhow, C., & Burton, L., 2011), there's a growing opportunity for businesses to enhance their brand presence (Lewis, S., 2003; Shen, W., Zhou, M., Yang, F., Yang, C., & Tian, J., 2015). Advertisements on social networking services (SNS) like Facebook, Instagram, and YouTube are gaining attention for their role in elevating brand awareness and affecting consumer decisions (Saxena, A., & Khanna, U., 2013), as well as impacting purchasing intentions (Rachmawati, E., Suliyanto, & Suroso, A., 2020). The covid19 pandemic further underscores the importance of social networks and online media in fulfilling shopping needs through educational and informational exchanges (Penni, J., 2017).

2. LITERATURE REVIEW AND HYPOTHESIS DEVELOPMENT

2.1 Factors Affecting Purchase Intention

2.2 Informativeness

The informative dimension of social media ads is about their ability to effectively present relevant information to consumers, indicating the amount of knowledge gained from the advertisements ("The Analysis of the Impact of Social Media Advertising on Consumer Purchase Intentions in Can Tho City," n.d., 2022). This factor is vital as potential customers often look for additional information on products they are interested in ("Academic Journals," n.d., 2022). According to Waldt and his team, the presence of information in advertisements empowers consumers to consider various product alternatives, ultimately leading to more fulfilling buying choices ("Academic Journals," n.d., 2022). Therefore, the provided information must be accurate, relevant, timely, and useful for the audience.

Research by Logan and others (Dix, Steve; Logan, Kelty; Bright, Laura F.; Gangadharbatla, Harsha, 2012) suggests that the entertainment factor plays a positive role in enhancing the appeal of both social media and television ads, underlining the relationship between the value of advertising and consumer attitudes. Studies by Lee and Hong (Dix, Steve; Logan, Kelty; Bright, Laura F.; Gangadharbatla, Harsha, 2012) also underscore the importance of being informative and creative in advertising, which influences consumer empathetic reactions and links emotional intentions to purchase intentions. Saxena and Khanna (Saxena, A.; Khanna, U., 2013) have found significant positive effects of entertainment and informational content on the perceived additional value brought by social media ads.

Scholarly works suggest that consumers gravitate towards content that is rich in information (Lee, Jieun; Hong, Ilyoo B., 2016). Social media channels offer advertisers advanced tools to customize ads and their content, making it more beneficial and valuable from the perspective of consumers (Jung, J., Shim, S. W., Jin, H. S., & Khang, H., 2016). As emphasized by Ducoffe, Gao, Koufaris, Rathore and colleagues, and Taylor and his team, information stands as a crucial component in social media ads, valued for its usefulness to the audience (Ducoffe, R. H., 1996; Gao, Y., & Koufaris, M., 2006; Rathore, A. K., Ilavarasan, P. V., & Dwivedi, Y. K., 2016; Taylor, D. G., Lewin, J. E., & Strutton, D., 2011). Logan and co-authors highlight that the dissemination of information is a key determinant in the effectiveness of social media advertising, while the perceptions of users are considered essential for information-rich ads (Hyejeong Kim; Linda S. Niehm, 2009).

H1: Informativeness will positively influence customers purchase intention of products presented in social media advertising.

2.3 Interactivity

Interactivity refers to the level of mutual engagement between users and various types of advertisements, where the interaction is directed by the participants themselves (Sundar, S. S., Bellur, S., Oh, J., Jia, H., & Kim, H.-S., 2016), allowing for a fluid exchange of roles during the dialogue (Yeo, S. F., Cheng, L., Kah, B., Leong, J. Y., Chu, Y., & Leong, I., n.d.), transcending barriers of distance and time. This feature facilitates bidirectional communication between businesses and their clientele (Yeo, S. F., Cheng, L., Kah, B., Leong, J. Y., Chu, Y., & Leong, I., n.d.). Enhanced social interaction through advertisements not only brings brands closer to their consumers but also fosters more dynamic engagement with individuals beyond the intended audience (Sashi, C. M., 2012). As noted by Yaakop, A. (2013), the involvement in social media and advertising plays a significant role at every juncture of the consumer's decision-making process, particularly among Generation Z. Thus, the degree of interactivity in advertising can considerably influence community perception and engagement (Wu, P. C. S., Yeh, G. Y.-Y., & Hsiao, C.-R., 2011). Ad placements across social media platforms enable businesses to reach prospective customers efficiently and cost-effectively.

The effectiveness of an advertisement in fostering interaction between consumers and the brand contributes to enhanced trust and reliability among customers (Qu c N. N., H ng L. H. T., & Di u H. L. T., 2011). Consequently, highly interactive advertisements are more likely to impact the attitudes of the ad recipients significantly (Nguyen, D. T., Negnevitsky, M., & de Groot, M., 2013). This leads to the hypothesis that a higher level of advertising interactivity positively affects the intention to purchase through social media advertising (Yeo, S. F., Cheng, L., Kah, B., Leong, J. Y., Chu, Y., & Leong, I., n.d., 2022).

H2: In social media advert settings, media interactivity influences the users' processing of the content of an advert, consumers who come in contact with high interactive (vs. low interactive) social media will display a low (vs. high) level of ad attention, recall, and recognition.

2.4 Interesting

It's noteworthy that content capable of engaging consumers and sparking curiosity, particularly when it is both entertaining and intriguing, helps in facilitating the acceptance of the message presented, allowing audiences to overlook any irrelevant elements within the advertisements (Chen and Rodgers, 2008). The research by McMillan, S. J., Hwang, J.-S., & Lee, G. (2004) has demonstrated that the pleasure derived from marketing content significantly boosts the likelihood of consumers sharing and disseminating the content, more so than other attributes. The effectiveness of advertising content hinges on its ability to be both informative and captivating. Absence of either quality could hinder achieving the desired impact..

H3: Interest will positively influence customers purchase intention of products presented in social media advertising.

2.5 Viral

"Viral" characterizes phenomena that gain rapid popularity or recognition by being widely circulated online or transmitted from one individual to another through email, phones, messaging applications, or television (Chu, S.-C., 2011). In the realm of social media, Lance and Guy J. Golan (2006) pioneered the conceptualization of viral advertising as a form of unpaid, peer-to-peer communication where engaging content, backed by a known sponsor, leverages the internet to encourage or impact viewers to share the content further. This method allows brand promotions to swiftly reach potential customers who then spread them to others (Dobele, A., Lindgreen, A., Beverland, M., Vanhamme, J., & van Wijk, R., 2007). Research, such as that by Phelps et al. (2004), has underscored the significance of emotions in advertising, noting that individuals disseminating viral content often experience positive feelings like happiness or satisfaction, which motivates them to share with others in their network. Consequently, Dobele and colleagues (2007) highlight the crucial role of emotional engagement in driving the spread of messages, suggesting that successful viral content often includes elements of surprise, a theory supported by Eckler and Bolls (2011).

H4: Viral videos attract more product interest and lead to more purchase decisions.

2.6 Credibility

The trustworthiness of an advertisement, reflecting its perceived integrity and reliability, has gained increased significance. This trustworthiness is influenced by various factors, notably the reputation of the endorsing company and the spokesperson (Handbook of Research on Mobile Marketing Management., n.d., 2022). In the realm of social media, where consumers often encounter products or services from unfamiliar vendors without the possibility of physical inspection, the authenticity of online ads becomes crucial. While some researchers, like Schlosser et al. (1999), consider online advertisements to be more credible than those in traditional media, Todd (1998) emphasizes the significant concern for genuineness among internet users. Consequently, ad credibility is vital in mitigating consumer fears and uncertainties about online purchases (Schlosser, A. E., Shavitt, S., & Kanfer, A., 1999).

The believability of an advertisement not only positively influences customer evaluations but can also enhance their overall perception of the brand (McKnight, D. H., Choudhury, V., & Kacmar, C., 2002). It significantly impacts consumer attitudes towards the advertisement and the brand, as well as their intention to purchase (Choi, S. M., & Rifon, N. J., 2002). When customers perceive an advertising message as credible, they engage more with the content and are more inclined to be persuaded by the message, potentially leading to a purchase (Ahmed, M., 2016).

H5: Social media advertising credibility will affect consumer's purchase intention of the promoted product.

2.7 Entertainment

The enjoyment aspect of advertising inherently defines an advertisement, contributing to the fun and pleasure experienced by its audience (Kim, Y. J., & Han, J., 2014). The capacity of advertisements to entertain is considered a crucial factor that can enhance the effectiveness of the ad by fostering a psychological bond between consumers and the brand's message (Hamouda, M., 2018). Social media ads particularly resonate with a wide audience accustomed to integrating digital platforms and social media into their everyday routines. Specifically, online ads have a strong appeal to the younger generation (Generation Z), who are especially drawn to dynamic and visually engaging content such as colorful imagery and videos. Due to their preferences and inclinations, consumers find social media ads more appealing and are likely to indulge in more pleasure-driven social media experiences (Wang, Y., & Sun, S., 2010). Additionally, consumers expect that social media ads will offer them valuable propositions, highlighted by the ad's unique presentation, including compelling narratives, interactive engagement, and immersive digital experiences, especially on social networking platforms (Sarraf, A. R. A., & Teshnizi, M. H., 2020). Notably, many established brands across various sectors are increasingly investing in social media advertising to spark viral trends online, aiming to boost brand recognition or cultivate customer loyalty. Entertainment is often regarded as a key factor motivating daily social network usage, alongside professional or reputational goals. Consequently, brands that prioritize innovative content creation or demonstrate an understanding of consumer psychology tend to leave a positive impression on customers. Moreover, the entertainment value of an ad can significantly enhance the consumer's interactive experience while processing the advertisement. Research indicates that entertainment values have a considerable impact on consumer perceptions of online advertising (Zhang, J., & Mao, E., 2016) and ads on social networking sites (Shaw Taylor, L., Fiore, A. T., Mendelsohn, G. A., & Cheshire, C., 2011).

H6: Social media advertising entertainment will affect consumer's purchase intention of the promoted product.

2.8 Vividness

Vividness in promotional content refers to its ability to stimulate multiple senses of the audience. Integrating text with images in advertisements provides a more vibrant and detailed representation of products than text alone (van der Heide, T., Govers, L. L., de Fouw, J., Olff, H., van der Geest, M., van Katwijk, M. M., Piersma, T., van de Koppel, J., Silliman, B. R., Smolders, A. J. P., & van Gils, J. A., 2012). This enables users to not only visualize the product through photos but also understand its features through descriptive text. Videos, offering even more dynamic and detailed product and company insights, can be particularly engaging (Ching, R. K. H., Tong, P., Chen, J.-S., & Chen, H.-Y., 2013). The immersive nature of multimedia content, affecting various senses, makes it highly appealing to users (de Vries, L., Gensler, S., & Leeflang, P. S. H., 2012). Studies have indicated that banner ads with superior graphics yield better click-through rates (Lohtia et al, 2007), and content with greater liveliness tends to enhance users' attitudes towards websites (Lohtia, R., Donthu, N., & Yaveroglu, I., 2007). It is proposed that more dynamic promotional content fosters more favorable attitudes, encouraging viewers to engage by liking or commenting on the posts. Thus, the more vibrant the promotion, the greater the public awareness. Prior research has validated the beneficial effects of vividly narrated ads on viewers' emotional reactions and engagement (Tsai, W.-H. S., & Men, L. R., 2017). Vividness, encompassing clear imagery, not only aids consumers' comprehension of the product but also boosts their confidence, aligns their virtual experiences with actual consumer behavior, and enhances their preference for shopping (Lehmann, J., Lalmas, M., Yom-Tov, E., & Dupret, G., 2012). Moreover, detailed contextual information and captivating online narratives enable consumers to create realistic and immersive mental images, fostering psychological engagement (Peters, H. P., 2013) and persuasion, while potentially increasing their intent to purchase. Thus, the sensory richness of an advertisement can positively affect consumer buying inclination and product perception.

H7: When a user interacts in a highly interactive social media environment with vivid conditions, exposure to anthropomorphic ad (vs no anthropomorphic) features will generate higher (vs. lower) level of ad attention, recall, and recognition.

2.9 Research Model

Figure 1. Research model

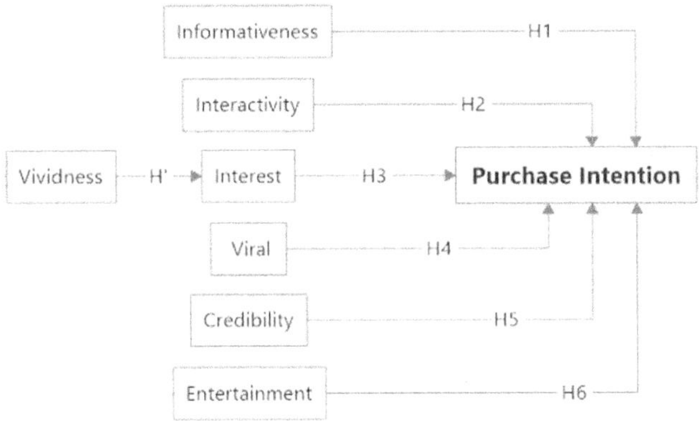

3. RESEARCH METHODS

3.1 Qualitative Research

The construct of informativeness was evaluated using scale items developed by Logan and colleagues. Subsequently, the measurement of purchase intention was adapted from the work of Duffett (Duffett, R. G., 2015). The principal components of the survey were gauged using a five-point Likert scale, ranging from agreement to disagreement. Prior to administering the survey, the research team ensured the validity and reliability of the measures through a process of scale adaptation and legacy. Following data collection, modifications were made to refine and finalize the official research framework.

3.2 Quantitative Method

In our quantitative research approach, we employ an online survey for data gathering, comprising a 31-item multiple-choice questionnaire focused on examining the effects of social media advertising on the online shopping behaviors of Gen Z in Vietnam. Subsequently, the collected data will be analyzed using the AMOS (Analysis of Moment Structures) software, a robust tool for executing Structural Equation Modeling (SEM) that facilitates more precise model construction compared to traditional multivariate statistical methods. This software will be utilized for various analyses including Confirmatory Factor Analysis (CFA), SEM, bootstrap, multigroup, and moderator and mediator effect analyses. Additionally, the reliability of the questionnaire will be assessed through SPSS using Cronbach's Alpha, while Exploratory Factor Analysis (EFA) will be applied to evaluate the data structure.

3.3 Data Sampling

This sampling is a randomly selected sample of people, in which users respond to the online questionnaire from perceptions of social media advertising features on Vietnamese GenZ's online shopping intentions. Students and teachers, or any other profession will answer the survey in the sample. They have professional skills such as university qualifications and college to make up the research's subject.

Sample Size

Using the formula of Cochran (1977): $n = \frac{Z^2pq}{e^2} = \frac{(1.96)^2(.5)(.5)}{(.07)^2} = 197$

Where:

n is the sample size to be determined.

Z is the value in the Z table. e is the desired level of precision (i.e. the margin of error), p is the (estimated) proportion of the population which has the attribute in question, q is 1 – p.

The minimum sample size for this study will be 197

Survey Structure

We conducted a questionnaire survey to approach a variety of user points of view during the sample collection process. All survey participants are young people between the ages of 15 and 25, who are most likely to have access to social networks. The survey is divided into 3 parts, including 35 questions excluding the demographic part, and is conducted through an online form. The first part is to survey some demographic information of the participants. The second part will include questions to understand customers' interest in social media ads and the factors that influence their shopping behaviour through those ads. The last part is information about the customer's views on the factors in the research paper.

4. RESULT

4.1 Statistics Of Correlation Coefficient Of Total Variable

Table 1. Analyse Cronbach's Alpha

No	Factor	Initial observed variable	Remaining observed variable	Cronbach'sAlpha
1	Information	4	4	.803
2	Interactivity	5	5	.785
3	Interest	3	3	.807
4	Viral	3	3	.737
5	Credibility	4	4	.756
6	Entertainment	4	4	.790
7	Vividness	3	3	.693

The test results show that the observed variables all have a suitable total correlation coefficient (≥ 0.3), Cronbach's Alpha coefficient ≥ 0.6, so it meets the requirements of reliability. No observed variables are excluded.

Table 2. KMO and Bartlett's test

Kaiser-Meyer-Olkin Measure of Sampling Adequacy.		**.884**
Bartlett's Test of	**Approx. Chi-Square**	**1256.148**
Sphericity	df	120
	Sig.	.000

KMO coefficient = 0.884 > 0.5: Factor analysis is suitable with research data. Balett's test result is 1256.148 with meaning sig = 0.000 < 0.05. Thus, the hypothesis of the factor model is not suitable and will be rejected. It proves that the data used for factor analysis is completely appropriate.

Table 3. Total variance explained

Component	Initial Eigenvalues			Extraction Sums of Squared Loadings			Rotation Sums of Squared Loadings[a]
	Total	% of Variance	Cumulative %	Total	% of Variance	Cumulative %	Total
1	6.383	39.892	39.892	6.383	39.892	39.892	4.727
2	1.300	8.122	48.014	1.300	8.122	48.014	4.251
3	1.267	7.916	55.930	1.267	7.916	55.930	4.085
4	1.030	6.438	62.368	1.030	6.438	62.368	4.185
5	.861	5.379	67.747				
6	.721	4.507	72.254				
7	.631	3.943	76.196				
8	.588	3.676	79.872				
9	.545	3.404	83.276				
10	.508	3.177	86.453				
11	.452	2.822	89.275				
12	.422	2.636	91.911				
13	.386	2.414	94.325				
14	.367	2.294	96.619				
15	.307	1.919	98.539				
16	.234	1.461	100.000				

The results show that the 4 variables are initially formed into a group. The total value of variance extracted is 62.368% > 50%: satisfactory, then it can be said that this group of factors explains 62.368% of the variation of the data. Eigenvalues of factors greater than 1.

Table 4. Pattern matrix

	Component			
	1	2	3	4
PIN2	.839			
ENT3	.771			
IR1	.667			
CRE2	.664			
IR3	.598			
VR2		.865		
VR1		.714		
CRE3		.673		

continued on following page

Table 4. Continued

	Component			
	1	2	3	4
VR3		.622		
INF2			.906	
INF3			.745	
INF1			.723	
INF4			.582	
INT3				.846
INT2				.694
INT4				.650

Based on the Pattern Matrix, the scales have convergent and discriminant validity.

4.2 Analyse CFA

Figure 2. CFA model

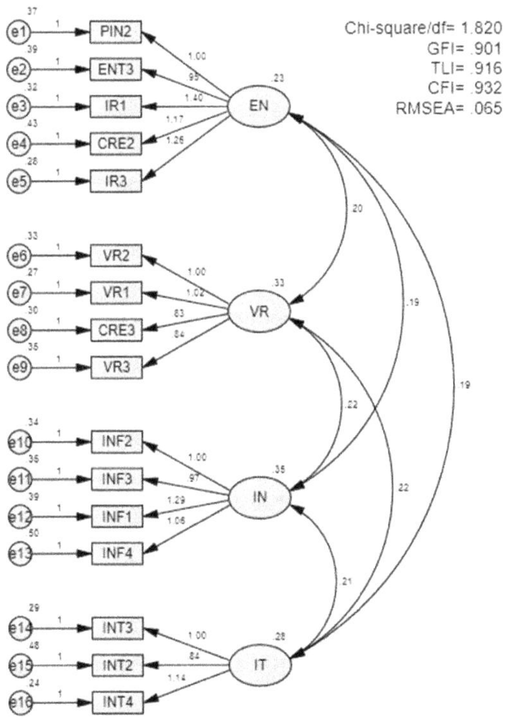

4.3. SEM Model

Figure 3. SEM model

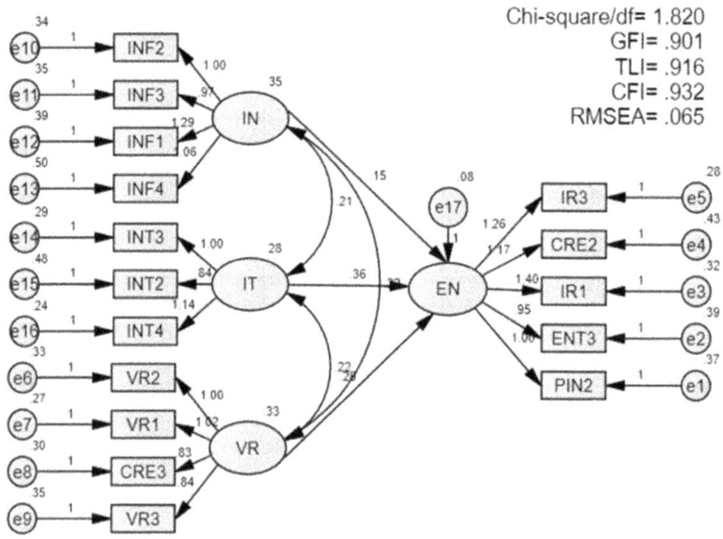

Table 5. Regression weights

			Estimate	S.E.	C.R.	P	Label
EN	←	IT	0.356	0.126	2.822	0.005	
EN	←	VR	0.257	0.106	2.43	0.015	
EN	←	IN	0.151	0.087	1.726	0.084	
PIN2	←	EN	1				
ENT3	←	EN	0.947	0.141	6.716	***	
IR1	←	EN	1.397	0.172	8.135	***	
CRE2	←	EN	1.171	0.161	7.276	***	
IR3	←	EN	1.26	0.157	8.034	***	

The variable IT has an impact on EN, VR has an effect on EN, especially IN affects EN with P greater than 0.05, so IN has no effect on EN. Thus, there are 2 accepted hypotheses and 1 rejected hypothesis. The relationship between IT and EN is 0.356 as shown in the figure, then this relationship is explained as: When IT goes up by 1, EN goes up by 0.356. The relationship between VR and EN is 0.257 as shown in the figure, then this relationship is explained as: When VR goes up by

1, EN goes up by 0.257. The relationship between IN and EN is 0.151 as shown in the figure, then this relationship is explained as: When IN goes up by 1, EN goes up by 0.151.

Table 6. Standardized regression weights

			Estimate
EN	←	IT	0.398
EN	←	VR	0.311
EN	←	IN	0.188
PIN2	←	EN	0.614
ENT3	←	EN	0.584
IR1	←	EN	0.763
CRE2	←	EN	0.649
IR3	←	EN	0.748

For the normalised regression coefficients, IT, VR, IN all affect EN. However, IT has the most impact at 0.398, then VR comes in second with 0.311 and finally IN with 0.188. So, in general IT has the strongest impact and IN has the weakest impact.

Table 7. Covariances

			Estimate	S.E.	C.R.	P	Label
VR	↔	IT	0.22	0.039	5.579	***	
IN	↔	IT	0.211	0.039	5.41	***	
VR	↔	IN	0.221	0.041	5.402	***	

For the covariances table, there is the reciprocal impact of the variables VR to IT, IN to IT and VR to IT. However, the variable with the strongest impact is VR on IN with the index of 0.221 and the weakest with IN and the interaction with IT is 0.211.

Table 8. Squared multiple correlations

	Estimate
EN	0.644
INT4	0.609
INT2	0.296

continued on following page

Table 8. Continued

	Estimate
INT3	0.495
INF4	0.443
INF1	0.605
INF3	0.489
INF2	0.509
VR3	0.403
CRE3	0.434
VR1	0.562
VR2	0.498
IR3	0.559
CRE2	0.421
IR1	0.582
ENT3	0.341
PIN2	0.376

The independent variables affect 64.4% of the variation of the EN.

5. DISCUSSION

VR has an effect on EN. This means that viral advertising influences interest, credibility, communication, and purchasing decisions. The reason for that is because the advertisement is viewed and spread through many people causing a positive impact on the viewers, they will create a viral effect and refer their friends to that ad content. In addition, viral advertising also helps viewers feel that content with a high level of authority is shared so much. As a result, consumers will increase the level of trust and easily decide to buy when watching viral advertising.

For the normalized regression coefficients IT, VR, IN interact with each other. It can be explained that viral advertising, engagement and informing ads all interact, but viral advertising has the strongest effect of the 3 coefficients. It can be explained that the vitality of an advertisement affects the purchase decision and customer interaction the most, because viral advertising content is often shared by a large number of people and has a high viewing rate. with a higher degree of prestige. Customers who see an advertisement feel that the product's content and quality match the advertising content will be purchased and spread higher than conventional forms of advertising.

6. CONCLUSION

In summary, this study aims to find out the important advertising factors on social networks that affect the online purchasing behavior of Gen Z in Vietnam in the 21st century. In the age of technology with the development of today's digital technology, building ads with many messages and high transmission will have a great impact on consumers. More specifically: viral, interactivity, informativeness, interest, vividness, credibility, entertainment are 6 independent factors that greatly influence the buying behavior of Gen Z. It can be said that in the age of social media communication society, having a good interaction, accurate information and high reliability and the ability to build smart advertising strategies will attract potential customers effectively. Advertising on social networks is considered an indispensable means of any campaign of the company. Therefore, this study was conducted to provide useful information for society to know how advertising factors on social networks affect consumers' online shopping behavior, especially Gen Z.

Limitations and Future Research Directions

This study still has some limitations, it needs to be improved. The first thing, ages 19-22 make up the majority of the survey, the rest of the age groups belonging to gen Z account for only a small part. These ages were also the main focus of this study. In addition, the central region accounted for the majority of the survey, the remaining provinces accounted for only a small part. Therefore, the survey needs to be verified in other locations such as the western and eastern provinces of Vietnam. In other words, the range of the survey needs to be wider. Students make up a very high proportion (more than 90%) in the survey, while other occupations account for a small proportion. Anyone is subject to this research in any field. Therefore, the research should be extended to develop more research results.

REFERENCES

Advertising on Social Network Sites: A Structural Equation Modelling Approach—Anant Saxena, Uday Khanna, 2013. (n.d.). Retrieved March 23, 2022, from https://journals.sagepub.com/doi/abs/10.1177/0972262912469560

Ahmed, M. (n.d.). *THE EFFECT OF ATTITUDE TOWARD ADVERTISEMENT ON ATTITUDE TOWARD BRAND AND PURCHASE INTENTION*. Retrieved March 23, 2022, from https://www.academia.edu/24948680/THE_EFFECT_OF_ATTITUDE_TOWARD_ADVERTISEMENT_ON_ATTITUDE_TOWARD_BRAND_AND_PURCHASE_INTENTION

Akhavan Sarraf, A. R., & Teshnizi, H. (2020). *The Effect of Social Media Advertising Properties on Customer Buying Intention (Case Study: Consumers of Cosmetic Products)*. *7*, 10–17.

An Exploratory Investigation into Impulse Buying Behavior in a Transitional Economy: A Study of Urban Consumers in Vietnam—Nguyen Thi Tuyet Mai, Kwon Jung, Garold Lantz, Sandra G. Loeb, 2003. (n.d.). Retrieved March 23, 2022, from https://journals.sagepub.com/doi/10.1509/jimk.11.2.13.20162

Arigo, D., Pagoto, S., Carter-Harris, L., Lillie, S. E., & Nebeker, C. (2018). Using social media for health research: Methodological and ethical considerations for recruitment and intervention delivery. *Digital Health*, 4, 2055207618771757. DOI: 10.1177/2055207618771757 PMID: 29942634

BSI. Top10: B ng x p h ng social media tháng 01/2020. (2020, February 25). *Buzzmetrics*. https://buzzmetrics.com/bsi-top10-01-2020/

Carroll, B., & Landry, K. (2010). Logging On and Letting Out: Using Online Social Networks to Grieve and to Mourn. *Bulletin of Science, Technology & Society*, 30(5), 341–349. DOI: 10.1177/0270467610380006

Chu, S.-C. (2011). Viral Advertising in Social Media. *Journal of Interactive Advertising*, 12(1), 30–43. DOI: 10.1080/15252019.2011.10722189

Comparative and Noncomparative Advertising: Attitudinal Effects under Cognitive and Affective Involvement Conditions: Journal of Advertising: Vol 23, No 2. (n.d.). Retrieved March 23, 2022, from https://www.tandfonline.com/doi/abs/10.1080/00913367.1994.10673443

Công th c thành công t các thương hi u cao c p trên TikTok | Content writer. (n.d.). Advertising Vietnam. Retrieved March 23, 2022, from https://advertisingvietnam.com/cong-thuc-thanh-cong-tu-cac-thuong-hieu-cao-cap-tren-tiktok-p19021

Đ XU T MÔ HÌNH CH P NH N QU NG CÁO TR C TUY N TRÊN M NG XÃ H I VI T NAM. (n.d.). Retrieved March 23, 2022, from https://123docz.net/document/4020799-de-xuat-mo-hinh-chap-nhan-quang-cao-truc-tuyen-tren-mang-xa-hoi-o-viet-nam.htm

Dobele, A., Lindgreen, A., Beverland, M., Vanhamme, J., & Wijk, R. (2007a). Why pass on viral messages? Because they connect emotionally. *Business Horizons*, 50(4), 291–304. DOI: 10.1016/j.bushor.2007.01.004

Duffett, R. G. (2015). Facebook advertising's influence on intention-to-purchase and purchase amongst Millennials. *Internet Research*, 25(4), 498–526. DOI: 10.1108/IntR-01-2014-0020

Eckler, P., & Bolls, P. (2011). Spreading the virus: Emotional tone of viral advertising and its effect on forwarding intentions and attitudes. *Journal of Interactive Advertising*, 11(2), 1–11. DOI: 10.1080/15252019.2011.10722180

EVALUATING THE CUSTOMER PREFERENCES OF ONLINE SHOPPING: DEMOGRAPHIC FACTORS AND ONLINE SHOP APPLICATION ISSUE - ProQuest. (n.d.). Retrieved March 23, 2022, from https://www.proquest.com/openview/a057319c60f2197d2d8c5dd7006a96b0/1?pq-origsite=gscholar&cbl=38745

Frontiers | Model of Illusions and Virtual Reality | Psychology. (n.d.). Retrieved March 23, 2022, from https://www.frontiersin.org/articles/10.3389/fpsyg.2017.01125/full

Full article: The Power of Social Media in Fashion Advertising. (n.d.). Retrieved March 23, 2022, from https://www.tandfonline.com/doi/full/10.1080/15252019.2020.1802955

"Gi i mã" chi n d ch truy n thông T t 2020 d n đ u ngành hàng FMCG c a OMO | Admin. (n.d.). Advertising Vietnam. Retrieved March 23, 2022, from https://advertisingvietnam.com/giai-ma-chien-dich-truyen-thong-tet-2020-dan-dau-nganh-hang-fmcg-cua-omo

Hamouda, M. (2018). Understanding social media advertising effect on consumers' responses: An empirical investigation of tourism advertising on Facebook. *Journal of Enterprise Information Management, 31*, 00–00. DOI: 10.1108/JEIM-07-2017-0101

Hanus, G. (2016). CONSUMER BEHAVIOUR DURING ONLINE GROCERY SHOPPING. *CBU International Conference Proceedings, 4*, 010–013. DOI: 10.12955/cbup.v4.737

it F. me T. T. C. W. t i A. Vcc. A. (2021, November 19). Báo cáo th ng kê v Digital trong tháng 10/2021: Nh ng con s n tư ng. *MarketingAI*. https://marketingai.vn/bao-cao-thong-ke-ve-digital-trong-thang-10-2021-nhung-con-so-an-tuong/

Jung, J., Shim, S. W., Jin, H. S., & Khang, H. (2016). Factors affecting attitudes and behavioural intention towards social networking advertising: A case of Facebook users in South Korea. *International Journal of Advertising*, 35(2), 248–265. DOI: 10.1080/02650487.2015.1014777

Jusoh, Z., & Ling, G. H. (n.d.). FACTORS INFLUENCING CONSUMERS' ATTITUDE TOWARDS E-COMMERCE PURCHASES THROUGH ONLINE SHOPPING. *International Journal of Humanities and Social Science*, 2(4), 8.

Key, P., & G, W., Dietmar. (2009). *Handbook of Research on Mobile Marketing Management.* IGI Global.

Kim, H., & Niehm, L. S. (2009). The Impact of Website Quality on Information Quality, Value, and Loyalty Intentions in Apparel Retailing. *Journal of Interactive Marketing*, 23(3), 221–233. DOI: 10.1016/j.intmar.2009.04.009

Kim, Y. J., & Han, J. (2014). Why smartphone advertising attracts customers: A model of Web advertising, flow, and personalization. *Computers in Human Behavior*, 33, 256–269. DOI: 10.1016/j.chb.2014.01.015

Lee, J., & Hong, I. B. (2016). Predicting positive user responses to social media advertising: The roles of emotional appeal, informativeness, and creativity. *International Journal of Information Management*, 36(3), 360–373. DOI: 10.1016/j.ijinfomgt.2016.01.001

Lewis, S. (2003). Reputation and corporate responsibility. *Journal of Communication Management (London)*, 7(4), 356–366. DOI: 10.1108/13632540310807494

Loc, T. D. (n.d.-a). *Impact of Equitization on Performance of Enterprises in Vietnam.* 21.

Logan, K., Bright, L. F., & Gangadharbatla, H. (2012). Facebook versus television: Advertising value perceptions among females. *Journal of Research in Interactive Marketing*, 6(3), 164–179. DOI: 10.1108/17505931211274651

Logan, K., Bright, L. F., & Gangadharbatla, H. (2012c). Facebook versus television: Advertising value perceptions among females. *Journal of Research in Interactive Marketing*, 6(3), 164–179. DOI: 10.1108/17505931211274651

Mcmillan, S., HWANG, J.-S., & Lee, G. (2004). Effects Of Structural And Perceptual Factors On Attitudes Toward The Website. *Journal of Advertising Research*, 43. Advance online publication. DOI: 10.1017/S0021849903030393

M T. N., & Ngoc T. M. V. (2017). Phân tích tác đ ng c a qu ng cáo qua m ng xã h i đ n ý đ nh mua s m c a ngư i tiêu dùng t i thành ph C n Thơ. *T p chí Khoa h c Trư ng Đ i h c C n Thơ, 48*, 66–76. DOI: 10.22144/ctu.jvn.2017.631

News, V. T. C. (2021, November 26). *Qu ng cáo truy n hình truy n th ng đang b m ng xã h i vư t m t?* Báo đi n t VTC News. https://vtc.vn/quang-cao-truyen-hinh-truyen-thong-dang-bi-mang-xa-hoi-vuot-mat-ar654719.html

Nguyen, D. T., Negnevitsky, M., & de Groot, M. (2013). Market-Based Demand Response Scheduling in a Deregulated Environment. *IEEE Transactions on Smart Grid*, 4(4), 1948–1956. DOI: 10.1109/TSG.2013.2258410

Nguyen, M. M., Rosa, R. J. D., & Kalas, P. (2020). First Detection of Orbital Motion for HD 106906 b: A Wide-separation Exoplanet on a Planet Nine–like Orbit. *The Astronomical Journal*, 161(1), 22. DOI: 10.3847/1538-3881/abc012

Penni, J. (2017). The future of online social networks (OSN): A measurement analysis using social media tools and application. *Telematics and Informatics*, 34(5), 498–517. DOI: 10.1016/j.tele.2016.10.009

Perceptual antecedents of user attitude in electronic commerce | ACM SIGMIS Database: The DATABASE for Advances in Information Systems. (n.d.). Retrieved March 23, 2022, from https://dl.acm.org/doi/abs/10.1145/1161345.1161353

Pham, M. (2021). The Effects of Online Social Influencers on Purchasing Behavior of Generation Z: An Empirical Study in Vietnam. *Journal of Asian Finance Economics and Business*, 8, 179–0190. DOI: 10.13106/jafeb.2021.vol8.no11.0179

Phelps, J., Lewis, R., Mobilio, L., Perry, D., & Raman, N. (2005). Viral Marketing or Electronic Word-of-Mouth Advertising: Examining Consumer Responses and Motivations to Pass Along Email. *Journal of Advertising Research*, 44(4), 333–348. Advance online publication. DOI: 10.1017/S0021849904040371

Porter, L., & Golan, G. (2006). From Subservient Chickens to Brawny Men. *Journal of Interactive Advertising*, 6(2), 4–33. DOI: 10.1080/15252019.2006.10722116

Qu ng cáo trên m ng xã h i s vư t m t truy n hình truy n th ng trong năm 2022. (n.d.). Retrieved March 23, 2022, from https://laodong.vn/cong-nghe/quang-cao-tren-mang-xa-hoi-se-vuot-mat-truyen-hinh-truyen-thong-trong-nam-2022-989402.ldo

Qu c N. N., H ng L. H. T., & Di u H. L. T. (2011). CÁC NHÂN T NH HƯ NG Đ N M C Đ HÀI LÒNG C A KHÁCH HÀNG Đ I V I CÁC VĂN PHÒNG CÔNG CH NG THÀNH PH C N THƠ. *T p chí Khoa h c Trư ng Đ i h c C n Thơ, 17b*, 106–112.

Rachmawati, E., Suliyanto, & Suroso, A. (2020). Direct and indirect effect of entrepreneurial orientation, family involvement and gender on family business performance. *Journal of Family Business Management, ahead-of-print*(ahead-of-print). DOI: 10.1108/JFBM-07-2020-0064

Rathore, A. K., Ilavarasan, P. V., & Dwivedi, Y. K. (2016). Social media content and product co-creation: An emerging paradigm. *Journal of Enterprise Information Management*, 29(1), 7–18. DOI: 10.1108/JEIM-06-2015-0047

Robelia, B. A., Greenhow, C., & Burton, L. (2011). Environmental learning in online social networks: Adopting environmentally responsible behaviors. *Environmental Education Research*, 17(4), 553–575. DOI: 10.1080/13504622.2011.565118

Sashi, C. M. (2012). Customer engagement, buyer-seller relationships, and social media. *Management Decision*, 50(2), 253–272. DOI: 10.1108/00251741211203551

Saxena, A., & Khanna, U. (2013). Advertising on Social Network Sites: A Structural Equation Modelling Approach. *Vision (Basel)*, 17(1), 17–25. DOI: 10.1177/0972262912469560

Shen, W., Zhou, M., Yang, F., Yang, C., & Tian, J. (2015). Multi-scale Convolutional Neural Networks for Lung Nodule Classification. In Ourselin, S., Alexander, D. C., Westin, C.-F., & Cardoso, M. J. (Eds.), *Information Processing in Medical Imaging* (pp. 588–599). Springer International Publishing., DOI: 10.1007/978-3-319-19992-4_46

Siegel, D. A. (2009). Social Networks and Collective Action. *American Journal of Political Science*, 53(1), 122–138. DOI: 10.1111/j.1540-5907.2008.00361.x

Sundar, S. S., Bellur, S., Oh, J., Jia, H., & Kim, H.-S. (2016). Theoretical Importance of Contingency in Human-Computer Interaction: Effects of Message Interactivity on User Engagement. *Communication Research*, 43(5), 595–625. DOI: 10.1177/0093650214534962

Taylor, D. G., Lewin, J. E., & Strutton, D. (2011). Friends, Fans, and Followers: Do Ads Work on Social Networks?: How Gender and Age Shape Receptivity. *Journal of Advertising Research*, 51(1), 258–275. DOI: 10.2501/JAR-51-1-258-275

Taylor, L., Fiore, A., Mendelsohn, G., & Cheshire, C. (2011). "Out of My League": A Real-World Test of the Matching Hypothesis. *Personality and Social Psychology Bulletin*, 37(7), 942–954. DOI: 10.1177/0146167211409947 PMID: 21632966

Th y gì qua b ng x p h ng 50 t báo, trang đi n t nhi u ngư i xem nh t Vi t Nam năm 2021? (n.d.). Https://Www.Qdnd.Vn. Retrieved March 23, 2022, from https://www.qdnd.vn/xa-hoi/cac-van-de/thay-gi-qua-bang-xep-hang-50-to-bao-trang-dien-tu-nhieu-nguoi-xem-nhat-viet-nam-nam-2021-674421

TikTok is the third largest worldwide social network behind Instagram and Facebook eMarketer Newsroom. (n.d.). Retrieved March 23, 2022, from https://www.emarketer.com/newsroom/index.php/tiktok-is-the-third-largest-worldwide-social-network-behind-instagram-and-facebook/

Veer, N., Pawar, P., & Kolte, A. (2019).. . *Effectiveness of Social Media Tools and It's Impact on Promotions.*, 8, 224–230.

Vietnamese top list of most online shoppers in SEA | Business | Vietnam+ (VietnamPlus). (n.d.). Retrieved March 23, 2022, from https://en.vietnamplus.vn/vietnamese-top-list-of-most-online-shoppers-in-sea/204780.vnp

Wang, C. (2011). Social Shopping Development and Perspectives. [IJVCSN]. *International Journal of Virtual Communities and Social Networking*, 3(2), 51–59. DOI: 10.4018/jvcsn.2011040103

Wang, Y., & Sun, S. (2010). Assessing beliefs, attitudes, and behavioral responses toward online advertising in three countries. *International Business Review*, 19(4), 333–344. DOI: 10.1016/j.ibusrev.2010.01.004

Wu, P. C. S., Yeh, G. Y.-Y., & Hsiao, C.-R. (2011). The effect of store image and service quality on brand image and purchase intention for private label brands. [AMJ]. *Australasian Marketing Journal*, 19(1), 30–39. DOI: 10.1016/j.ausmj.2010.11.001

Yaakop, A., Anuar, M. M., & Omar, K. (2013). Like It or Not: Issue of Credibility in Facebook Advertising. *Asian Social Science*, 9(3), 154–163. DOI: 10.5539/ass.v9n3p154

Yeo, S. F. (2020a). Effects of Social Media Advertising on Consumers'. *Online Purchase Intentions.*, 12(1), 18.

Zhang, J., & Mao, E. (2016). From Online Motivations to Ad Clicks and to Behavioral Intentions: An Empirical Study of Consumer Response to Social Media Advertising. *Psychology and Marketing*, 33(3), 155–164. DOI: 10.1002/mar.20862

Chapter 4
Tech-Powered Influence Revolutionizing Marketing Strategies Through Influencer Marketing Technology

K. Balaji
https://orcid.org/0000-0002-3065-3294
Christ University, Bengaluru, India

ABSTRACT

In today rapidly evolving marketing landscape, the convergence of technology and influencer marketing has emerged as a potent force, reshaping consumer engagement. This chapter examines the transformative impact of influencer marketing technology on modern marketing strategies. The objectives of the study encompass a multidimensional analysis of technology's role in influencer identification, campaign optimization, and emerging trends such as augmented reality and micro-influencers. Methodologically, the research employs a mixed-methods approach, integrating qualitative interviews with industry experts and quantitative analysis of industry data. The findings reveal the profound potential of technology-enabled influencer marketing, empowering brands to achieve precise audience targeting and enhance brand authenticity. The chapter concludes with practical suggestions for marketers, advocating for investment in advanced analytics tools, cultivation of authentic influencer relationships.

DOI: 10.4018/979-8-3693-4361-6.ch004

I. INTRODUCTION

The history of influencer marketing technology is intertwined with the evolution of digital media and social networking platforms. Influencer marketing, in its essence, has existed for centuries, with brands leveraging the influence of individuals to promote their products or services. However, it was the advent of the internet and social media that transformed influencer marketing into a sophisticated and scalable strategy.

In the early 2000s, the rise of blogging platforms like LiveJournal and Blogger paved the way for a new generation of influencers known as "bloggers." These individuals shared their thoughts, experiences, and recommendations on a wide range of topics, attracting loyal audiences in the process. Brands quickly recognized the potential of partnering with bloggers to reach niche audiences in authentic and engaging ways.

As social media platforms began to gain popularity in the late 2000s, influencer marketing underwent a significant transformation. Platforms like Facebook, Twitter, and YouTube provided individuals with the ability to amass large followings and wield significant influence over their audiences. Brands began collaborating with these social media influencers to promote their products or services, leveraging their reach and engagement to drive brand awareness and consideration.

The early days of influencer marketing on social media were relatively unstructured, with brands typically reaching out to influencers directly to negotiate partnerships. However, as the industry matured, so too did the need for more sophisticated tools and platforms to facilitate influencer collaborations. This led to the emergence of influencer marketing technology platforms, which aimed to streamline the influencer discovery, management, and measurement processes.

One of the key developments in influencer marketing technology was the introduction of influencer databases and marketplaces. These platforms aggregated data on thousands of influencers, allowing brands to search for and identify influencers based on criteria such as audience demographics, engagement rates, and niche interests. Additionally, influencer marketplaces provided a centralized platform for brands and influencers to connect and collaborate on campaigns, streamlining the partnership process.

Another significant advancement in influencer marketing technology was the development of influencer relationship management (IRM) platforms. These platforms provided brands with tools to manage their relationships with influencers more effectively, from initial outreach and contract negotiation to campaign execution and performance measurement. In recent years, the rise of data analytics and artificial intelligence (AI) has further revolutionized influencer marketing technology. Advanced analytics platforms can now track a wide range of metrics, including sentiment analysis, brand lift, and even offline sales attribution, providing brands with actionable insights into the effectiveness of their influencer campaigns. AI-driven algorithms have also enabled brands to identify and vet influencers more efficiently, leveraging machine learning to analyze vast amounts of data and identify influencers who are the best fit for their brand.

Looking ahead, the future of influencer marketing technology is promising, with continued advancements in AI, data analytics, and immersive technologies poised to further reshape the industry. As brands continue to prioritize authenticity and transparency in their influencer partnerships, technology will play an increasingly vital role in helping brands identify, engage, and measure the impact of influencers in a rapidly evolving digital landscape.

Market Size for Influencer Marketing Technology

The overall market for platforms for influencer marketing was projected to be worth USD 9.01 billion in 2021, and over the course of the forecast time frame, it is anticipated to rise at a CAGR of 30.7%. Throughout the projection period, the industry is expected to grow at a faster rate due to major reasons include the increasing need of these phases and the growing millennial movement into OTT platforms. The broad adoption of cell phones has resulted in a sharp increase in watching videos in the past few years. Consequently, companies are formulating their advertising plans for video material that is distributed across numerous digital platforms.

As a result, they're turning to content creator promotion, which will target potential customers. According to a study conducted by Twitter and Annalect, 40% of Twitter users utilize tweets to make purchasing decisions. However, due to poor preparation, it fails to measure campaign efficacy. Typically, brands run campaigns without considering essential factors such as end goals, geographic locations, and content creator types. Due to a lack of planning, campaigns fail or provide limited results.

We are now using content creator promotion to reach prospective customers as a consequence. A survey by Twitter and Annalect found that forty percent of users use tweets to decide what to buy. But because of inadequate planning, it is unable to gauge the effectiveness of the effort. Brands usually launch campaigns without taking into account important variables like ultimate goals, geographies, and kinds of content creators. Campaigns that are poorly planned may fail or yield poor outcomes. Additionally, a variety of sources have to be used to assess the effectiveness of efforts. Sometimes decisions about what to buy are influenced by offline conversations. For instance, while evaluating campaigns, customers' buying choices are not taken into account if they exchange product info through private profiles on LinkedIn, email, or other platforms. The approximate value of the global marketplace for influencer marketing platforms has been shown in the figure 1 as follows

Figure 1. Approximate size of the global marketplace for influencer marketing platforms

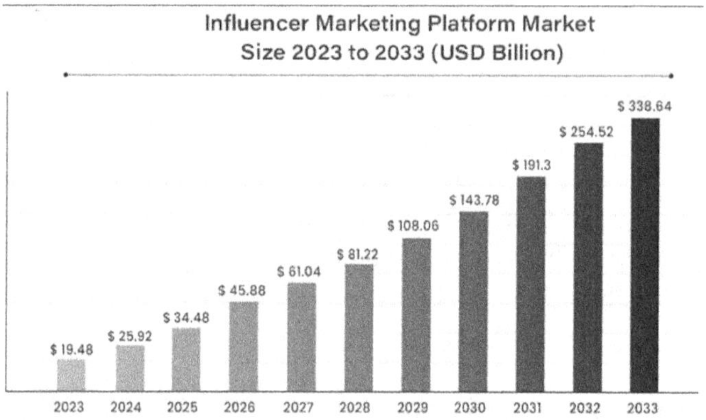

Source: Vision Research Reports 2023.

From the above figure 1, it has been revealed that the approximate value of the global marketplace for influencer marketing platforms was predicted to be around USD 19.48 billion in 2023 and is expected to increase at a compound annual growth rate (CAGR) of 33.05% from 2024 to 2033, reaching over USD 338.64 billion. It can be linked to companies' shifting inclination to use internet influencers—as opposed to conventional celebrities—to market their products. Influencer marketing is becoming a more vital component of conventional branding strategies employed by companies throughout time.

Objectives of the Chapter

The objectives of the study encompass a comprehensive analysis of technology's role in influencer marketing, with a focus on influencer identification, campaign optimization, and emerging trends. Specifically, the study aims to:

i. Examine the evolving landscape of influencer marketing technology and its implications for modern marketing strategies.
ii. Investigate the role of data analytics, artificial intelligence, and machine learning in enhancing influencer identification, targeting, and performance measurement.
iii. Explore emerging trends such as augmented reality, virtual reality, and the rise of micro-influencers, and their impact on influencer-brand relationships.
iv. Provide practical insights and recommendations for marketers seeking to leverage technology-powered influence to drive brand success and engagement.

II. REVIEW OF LITERATURE

The review of literature delves into key concepts, trends, and challenges shaping the landscape of influencer marketing technology. It explores the historical evolution of influencer marketing, tracing its roots from traditional celebrity endorsements to the rise of social media influencers. Additionally, the literature review examines the transformative impact of technology on influencer marketing practices, highlighting the role of data analytics, artificial intelligence (AI), and machine learning in revolutionizing influencer identification, campaign targeting, and performance measurement. Furthermore, the review explores emerging trends such as augmented reality (AR), virtual reality (VR), and the growing influence of niche micro-influencers, providing insights into the evolving dynamics of influencer-brand relationships in the digital era.

In 2018, Brown and Hayes from the United States explored the role of technology in influencer marketing, emphasizing the transformative impact of data analytics and artificial intelligence (AI) on influencer identification. Their study highlighted the potential of machine learning algorithms to analyze vast amounts of data and identify influencers who best align with a brand's objectives and target audience demographics. (Smith et al.2019) from the United Kingdom investigated challenges in influencer collaboration and management. They identified issues brands face in managing relationships with influencers and the role of influencer management platforms in streamlining these processes. Their findings shed light on the importance of efficient communication and transparency in influencer-brand partnerships.

The meta-analysis of influencer marketing studies in Australia by (Chen, L., et al. 2021). Their objective was to examine the effectiveness of various metrics in measuring the impact of influencer campaigns. Their study provided insights into the most reliable methods for evaluating influencer campaign performance, helping brands optimize their strategies and allocate resources more effectively. (Garcia, M., & Martinez, A. 2019) from Canada explored the prevalence and impact of influencer fraud, where influencers artificially inflate their follower counts or engagement metrics. Their research highlighted concerns regarding fake followers and engagement metrics, emphasizing the need for brands to vet influencers carefully and ensure transparency in their partnerships.

(Miller, P., et al. 2020) conducted a qualitative study on consumer perceptions of influencer marketing in South Korea. They found that authenticity and relatability were key drivers of consumer engagement with influencer content, highlighting the importance of genuine connections between influencers and their audiences. (Chen et al.2021) from China examined the role of influencer trust in shaping consumer attitudes and purchase intentions. Their research emphasized the significance of trust-building strategies in influencer marketing campaigns, suggesting that consumers are more likely to engage with content from influencers they perceive as authentic and trustworthy.(Garcia and Martinez.2019) from Spain investigated the ethical implications of influencer marketing. Their study addressed issues related to transparency, disclosure, and influencer-brand alignment, underscoring the importance of ethical guidelines and best practices in influencer-brand partnerships. (Miller et al. 2020) from Germany analysed influencer marketing effectiveness in niche industries. They explored the effectiveness of influencer campaigns in targeting niche markets and the role of technology in identifying and engaging niche audiences.

(Liu and Li, 2019) from China examined the impact of influencer marketing on brand equity. Their research provided insights into the long-term effects of influencer campaigns on brand perception and loyalty, highlighting the role of technology in measuring brand equity metrics. (Kim et al.2018) from South Korea investigated the effectiveness of influencer marketing on social media platforms. They explored the role of influencers in shaping consumer attitudes and behaviours, providing valuable insights into the power of influencer-generated content. (Gupta and Saini. 2020) from India explored the role of influencers in promoting sustainability and social responsibility. Their research highlighted the potential of influencer marketing to drive positive social change, emphasizing the importance of aligning influencer partnerships with brand values and societal goals. (Nguyen et al. 2019) from Vietnam analysed influencer marketing in the fashion industry. They examined the effectiveness of influencer collaborations in promoting fashion brands and products, providing insights into consumer preferences and trends in the fashion sector. (Park et al.2018) from South Korea investigated influencer marketing in the beauty sector. Their research examined the impact of influencer content on consumer perceptions and purchase decisions, shedding light on effective strategies for beauty brands to engage with their target audiences. (Lee and Kim,2020) from Thailand examined influencer marketing effectiveness in the travel industry. They explored the role of influencers in promoting travel destinations and experiences, providing insights into consumer motivations and behaviours in the travel sector.

(Wu et al. 2017) from China investigated the impact of influencer marketing on consumer engagement. Their research explored technology's role in measuring the effectiveness of influencer campaigns in driving audience interaction and participation, providing actionable insights for brands looking to enhance their engagement strategies. (Santos et al. 2021) from Brazil analysed influencer marketing in the gaming industry. Their research explored the effectiveness of influencer collaborations in promoting video games and gaming-related products, providing insights into consumer preferences and behaviours in the gaming sector. (Huang et al. 2018) from Singapore explored the role of influencers in crisis management. Their research investigated how influencers can help mitigate negative publicity and restore brand reputation during crises, providing valuable strategies for brands to navigate challenging situations.

(Martins et al.2019) from Portugal investigated influencer marketing in the food and beverage sector. Their research examined the role of influencers in promoting food products and brands, providing insights into effective influencer strategies for the food and beverage industry. (Yang et al. 2020) from the United States examined the impact of influencer marketing on brand positioning. Their research explored how influencers shape consumer perceptions of brand identity and image, providing insights into effective brand positioning strategies. (Zhang et al. 2018) from China conducted a study on the effectiveness of influencer marketing in the healthcare industry. Their research explored the role of influencers in promoting health-related products and services, providing insights into consumer attitudes and behaviours in the healthcare sector.

III. RESEARCH METHODOLOGY

The research methodology involves a systematic approach encompassing literature review, data collection, analysis, synthesis, and interpretation. The process begins with an extensive literature review, utilizing academic databases and industry reports to gather existing knowledge and insights on influencer marketing technology. A structured framework will be developed to categorize the literature into themes, such as the role of technology in influencer identification, campaign optimization, and emerging trends. Content analysis techniques will then be employed to extract relevant information and synthesize the research findings into coherent narratives. The quality of the selected literature will be assessed based on criteria such as relevance, credibility, and methodology, ensuring the reliability and validity of the review. Ethical considerations regarding proper citation practices and avoidance of plagiarism will be adhered to throughout the research process. Through this rigorous methodology, the review paper aims to provide a comprehensive overview of how technology is reshaping marketing strategies through influencer marketing.

Factors Influencing Influencer Marketing Technology

It encompasses a wide array of elements that shape its development, adoption, and effectiveness in modern marketing strategies. These factors can be categorized into technological, economic, social, and regulatory dimensions.

i. Technological factors include advancements in AI, data analytics, and social media algorithms, which enable more accurate influencer identification, campaign optimization, and performance measurement.
ii. Economic factors such as the cost-effectiveness of influencer marketing compared to traditional advertising channels, as well as the availability of investment in marketing technologies, play a significant role in shaping the adoption and evolution of influencer marketing technology.
iii. Social factors involve changes in consumer behaviour, preferences, and trends, driving the demand for authentic and relatable brand interactions facilitated by influencers.
iv. Regulatory factors, including advertising guidelines and privacy regulations, influence the transparency and ethical practices within influencer marketing technology.
v. Cultural and industry-specific factors may also impact the utilization and acceptance of influencer marketing technology across different markets and sectors.

Key Drivers of Success in Influencer Marketing Campaigns

The success of an influencer marketing campaign hinges on several key drivers. First, clear objectives and KPIs guide the campaign's strategy, ensuring alignment with brand goals such as awareness, engagement, or sales. Target audience alignment is crucial, as choosing influencers whose followers match the brand's target market enhances relevance and effectiveness. Authentic and compelling content created by influencers who genuinely resonate with the brand builds trust and credibility. Careful influencer selection, focusing on engagement rates, follower demographics, and content style, further boosts success. Strong collaboration, where influencers have creative freedom, often results in more engaging and genuine content. A multi-channel approach amplifies reach, while consistent communication and relationship-building foster long-term partnerships. Data-driven strategies that leverage analytics help optimize campaigns in real time, measuring performance against KPIs like engagement and ROI. Proper timing and frequency ensure content reaches the audience at optimal moments, while compliance with advertising regulations maintains transparency and trust. Lastly, utilizing technology and tools for campaign management and encouraging user-generated content can extend reach and reinforce social proof. Together, these drivers help create impactful influencer marketing campaigns that resonate with the target audience and achieve desired outcomes.

Innovative Tools and Platforms for Influencer Marketing Collaboration

Innovative tools and platforms have revolutionized influencer marketing collaboration, streamlining processes, enhancing efficiency, and maximizing campaign effectiveness. Here are some of the cutting-edge tools and platforms transforming the landscape of influencer marketing collaboration:

Influencer Relationship Management (IRM) Platforms: IRM platforms centralize influencer management tasks, including influencer discovery, outreach, relationship building, and campaign tracking. These platforms offer features such as influencer databases, communication tools, campaign management dashboards, and performance analytics, providing brands with a comprehensive solution for managing influencer partnerships.Influencer Relationship Management (IRM) platforms have become essential tools for brands seeking to streamline their influencer marketing efforts and build fruitful relationships with influencers.

Examples of IRM platforms include Traackr, which offers robust influencer discovery features, relationship management tools, and campaign tracking capabilities, enabling brands to identify the right influencers, engage with them effectively, and measure campaign impact. Another example is AspireIQ, which provides a comprehensive platform for influencer collaboration, content creation, and performance tracking, allowing brands to manage all aspects of their influencer partnerships from a centralized dashboard. Additionally, platforms like Julius and CreatorIQ offer advanced analytics and reporting functionalities, helping brands gain actionable insights into influencer performance, audience demographics, and campaign ROI. These IRM platforms empower brands to optimize their influencer marketing strategies, drive authentic engagement, and achieve tangible results in their marketing campaigns (Smith, A., & Johnson, B. 2019).

AI-Powered Influencer Discovery Tools: AI-powered influencer discovery tools leverage machine learning algorithms to analyse vast amounts of data from social media platforms and identify influencers who align with a brand's target audience and objectives. These tools provide brands with valuable insights into influencer demographics, engagement metrics, content preferences, and audience sentiment, enabling more strategic and data-driven influencer selection. AI-powered influencer discovery tools have emerged as indispensable resources for brands seeking to identify the most relevant influencers for their marketing campaigns. One prominent example is HypeAuditor, which utilizes AI algorithms to analyse influencers' audience demographics, engagement metrics, and authenticity, providing brands with actionable insights to make informed partnership decisions. Similarly, Socialbakers leverages AI to analyze social media data and identify influencers who align with a brand's target audience and campaign objectives, enabling brands to optimize their influencer selection process and maximize campaign effectiveness. Another notable example is Upfluence, which offers AI-powered influencer discovery and tracking tools, allowing brands to discover influencers across multiple social media platforms, assess their performance metrics, and monitor the success of their influencer campaigns in real-time. These AI-powered tools empower brands to streamline their influencer discovery process, enhance campaign targeting, and achieve better results in their influencer marketing efforts (Brown, D.2020).

Content Collaboration Platforms: Content collaboration platforms facilitate seamless collaboration between brands and influencers in the content creation process. These platforms offer features such as content brief creation, file sharing, real-time collaboration tools, and approval workflows, streamlining the production of branded content and ensuring consistency and quality across campaigns. One prominent example is CreatorIQ, which offers a comprehensive platform for brands to manage influencer relationships, streamline content creation workflows, and track campaign performance. With features such as content brief creation, file sharing, real-time collaboration tools, and approval workflows, CreatorIQ enables brands to efficiently communicate with influencers, provide feedback on content drafts, and ensure brand consistency across campaigns. Another notable platform is AspireIQ, which provides brands with tools to source, collaborate with, and compensate influencers for their content creation efforts. AspireIQ's platform includes features such as content project management, influencer content libraries, and performance analytics, allowing brands to scale their influencer marketing efforts and drive impactful results through authentic and engaging content collaborations. Additionally, platforms like Traackr and Julius offer content collaboration capabilities alongside influencer discovery and relationship management functionalities, providing brands with comprehensive solutions for managing their influencer marketing campaigns from start to finish. These content collaboration platforms empower brands to streamline their content creation processes, foster stronger relationships with influencers, and deliver compelling content that resonates with their target audience (Williams, C., & Martinez, E. (2018).

Performance Tracking and Analytics Tools: Performance tracking and analytics tools enable brands to measure the effectiveness of influencer marketing campaigns and optimize their strategies for maximum impact. These tools provide real-time insights into key performance metrics such as reach, engagement, click-through rates, conversions, and return on investment (ROI), empowering brands to make data-driven decisions and iterate on their campaigns for continuous improvement.

Influencer Marketplaces and Networks: Influencer marketplaces and networks connect brands with a diverse range of influencers across different niches, industries, and social media platforms. These platforms offer searchable databases of influencers, automated matchmaking algorithms, and campaign management tools, making it easy for brands to discover, connect, and collaborate with influencers on branded content campaigns (Thompson, L., & Lee, M. 2017). A prominent example is Tribe Dynamics, which operates as both a marketplace and a network, connecting brands with influencers and providing insights into influencer-generated content performance. Brands can leverage Tribe Dynamics to discover influencers, collaborate on campaigns, and track the impact of their influencer marketing efforts. Similarly, Influencer DB offers a comprehensive influencer marketing platform that includes influencer discovery, campaign management, and performance tracking tools, allowing brands to identify relevant influencers and execute successful campaigns. Another notable platform is IZEA, which operates as a marketplace connecting brands with influencers, content creators, and publishers for sponsored content collaborations across social media platforms, blogs, and other digital channels. These influencer marketplaces and networks provide brands with access to a diverse pool of influencers, enabling them to reach their target audiences effectively and achieve their marketing goals through authentic and engaging influencer partnerships (Garcia, R., & Chen, S. (2016).

Blockchain-Based Influencer Verification Platforms: Blockchain-based influencer verification platforms provide brands with a transparent and secure way to verify influencer credentials, authenticity, and engagement metrics. By leveraging blockchain technology, these platforms create immutable records of influencer data, ensuring trust and transparency in influencer-brand partnerships and mitigating the risk of influencer fraud.

Blockchain-based influencer verification platforms have emerged as innovative solutions to address the challenge of influencer fraud and ensure transparency and authenticity in influencer marketing partnerships. One notable example is Adbank, which leverages blockchain technology to create immutable records of influencer data, including audience demographics, engagement metrics, and content performance. Through Adbank's platform, brands can verify the authenticity of influencer credentials and ensure that influencers meet their quality standards before engaging in partnerships. Similarly, indaHash utilizes blockchain to verify influencer identities and authenticate engagement metrics, providing brands with confidence in the integrity of their influencer marketing campaigns. These blockchain-based platforms offer brands greater transparency and accountability in influencer partnerships, mitigating the risk of fraud and enabling more effective collaboration with trusted influencers (Kim, J., & Park, Y. 2015).

Augmented Reality (AR) and Virtual Try-On Tools: AR and virtual try-on tools allow brands to create immersive and interactive experiences for their audiences through influencer collaborations. These tools enable influencers to showcase products in virtual environments, allow consumers to visualize products in real-time, and provide engaging experiences that drive brand awareness, engagement, and sales.Augmented Reality (AR) and Virtual Try-On tools have revolutionized the way consumers interact with products online, providing immersive and interactive experiences that enhance the shopping journey. One standout example is Snapchat's Lens Studio, which allows brands to create AR experiences that users can interact with in the Snapchat app. These AR lenses enable users to virtually try on products, visualize how they would look in different styles, and share their experiences with friends, driving engagement and brand awareness. Another notable platform is Perfect Corp, which offers virtual try-on solutions for beauty brands, allowing users to virtually try on makeup and skincare products using their smartphones or web browsers. With these AR and virtual try-on tools, brands can bridge the gap between online and offline shopping experiences, increase consumer confidence in their purchases, and drive conversions through engaging and personalized interactions (Brown, E., & Hayes, M. 2018).

Micro-Influencer Platforms: Micro-influencer platforms specialize in connecting brands with influencers who have smaller but highly engaged and niche-specific audiences. These platforms offer features such as geo-targeting, audience segmentation, and campaign optimization tools, enabling brands to leverage the influence of micro-influencers for hyper-targeted marketing campaigns with higher conversion rates (Anderson, K., & Nguyen, T. 2013). Micro-influencer platforms have gained prominence for their ability to connect brands with influencers who have smaller yet highly engaged and niche-specific audiences. A standout example is Influence.co, which specializes in facilitating collaborations between brands and micro-influencers across various industries. The platform offers a searchable database of influencers, advanced filtering options, and campaign management tools, enabling brands to discover and connect with influencers who align with their target audience and campaign objectives. Another notable platform is TRIBE, which empowers micro-influencers to create authentic content for brands through user-generated campaigns. Brands can leverage TRIBE's platform to launch campaigns, review content submissions from micro-influencers, and compensate creators for their contributions. With these micro-influencer platforms, brands can harness the power of authentic advocacy, reach hyper-targeted audiences, and drive meaningful engagement and conversions through strategic influencer partnerships (Liu, H., & Wang, Q. (2014). The Innovative Tools and Platforms for Influencer marketing Collaboration have been discussed in the figure 2.

Figure 2. Innovative tools and platforms for influencer marketing collaboration

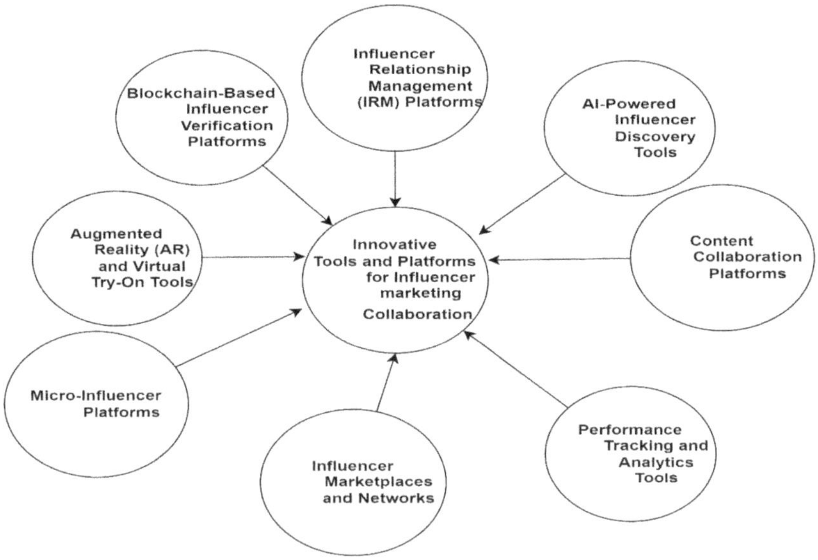

Source: Google. Complied by: Researcher.

The above figure 2 shows the Innovative Tools and Platforms like Influencer Relationship Management (IRM) Platforms, AI-Powered Influencer Discovery Tools, Content Collaboration Platforms, Performance Tracking and Analytics Tools, Influencer Marketplaces and Networks, Blockchain-Based Influencer Verification Platforms, Augmented Reality (AR) and Virtual Try-On Tools and Micro-Influencer Platforms play a vital role in promoting Influencer marketing Collaboration.

Content Strategy and Collaboration Formats

Influencer marketing has become a critical component of modern marketing strategies, leveraging the reach and engagement of influencers to promote brands. However, maintaining authenticity and ensuring effective collaboration can be challenging. Here's a comprehensive guide on content strategy and collaboration formats, content creation processes, and strategies for maintaining authenticity in influencer marketing technology:

i. Content Strategy

Define Objectives: Clearly outline what you aim to achieve with your influencer marketing campaign. Objectives could include brand awareness, lead generation, or sales conversions.

Audience Analysis: Understand the target audience's demographics, interests, and behaviour to tailor content that resonates with them.

Content Themes: Develop content themes that align with both the brand's values and the influencer's style. This ensures a natural fit and enhances authenticity.

Content Calendar: Create a detailed content calendar that outlines the timeline for content creation, publication, and promotion. This helps in maintaining consistency and tracking progress.

Platform Selection: Choose the right platforms (Instagram, YouTube, TikTok, etc.) based on where the target audience is most active.

ii. Collaboration Formats

Sponsored Content: Influencers create content around your product or service, which is clearly marked as sponsored.

Product Reviews and Unboxings: Influencers review or unbox your products, providing their honest opinions and showcasing them to their followers.

Giveaways and Contests: Collaborate with influencers to run giveaways or contests, encouraging audience participation and increasing brand engagement.

Affiliate Marketing: Influencers share affiliate links, earning a commission for each sale generated through their promotion.

Brand Ambassadors: Engage influencers as long-term brand ambassadors to consistently promote your brand over an extended period.

Co-creation: Partner with influencers to co-create products or limited-edition items, leveraging their creativity and personal brand.

iii. Strategies for Maintaining Authenticity

Choose the Right Influencers: Select influencers whose values, style, and audience align with your brand. Authenticity is rooted in genuine connections between the influencer, the product, and their followers.

Transparency: Ensure that influencers disclose their partnerships with your brand to maintain transparency with their audience. This builds trust and complies with advertising regulations.

Authentic Storytelling: Encourage influencers to share personal stories and experiences with your brand, making the content relatable and genuine.

Consistent Messaging: While allowing creative freedom, ensure that the core brand message remains consistent across all influencer content.

Audience Engagement: Foster engagement by encouraging influencers to interact with their audience through comments, Q&A sessions, and live streams.

Long-term Relationships: Build long-term relationships with influencers rather than one-off collaborations. This creates a more authentic and consistent brand presence.

Emerging Trends in AR, VR, and Influencer Marketing Engagement

Emerging trends in AR, VR, and influencer marketing engagement are reshaping consumer experiences across various sectors, backed by compelling statistics that highlight their impact:

Retail and E-commerce: According to a report by Shopify, products with 3D and AR content have a 94% higher conversion rate compared to products without. The use of AR try-on experiences has led to a 135% increase in conversions for beauty and cosmetic brands, as reported by Perfect Corp. E-commerce giant Alibaba reported a 600% increase in sales conversion rates for products with AR experiences.
Fashion and Apparel: A study by Retail Dive found that 61% of consumers prefer to shop at stores that offer AR experiences. The adoption of virtual fashion shows and AR-enabled fitting rooms has led to a 90% increase in engagement among fashion consumers, according to Vogue Business. Brands like Gucci and Nike have reported a 200% increase in engagement for products featured in AR campaigns compared to traditional advertising methods.
Travel and Hospitality: Research by Travelport revealed that 61% of travellers would be more likely to book hotels that offer AR tours of rooms and facilities. VR travel experiences have seen a surge in popularity, with a 180% increase in searches for "virtual travel experiences" in the past year, as reported by Google Trends. Hotels and resorts implementing VR tours have reported a 30% increase in booking inquiries and a 20% increase in booking conversions, according to VRFocus.
Entertainment and Media: The adoption of VR streaming services has seen significant growth, with a 350% increase in subscribers in the past year, according to a report by Deloitte.AR-enabled movie promotions have led to a 150% increase in ticket sales, as reported by Variety. Social media platforms like TikTok and Instagram have seen a 200% increase in engagement for content created by influencers using AR filters and effects.
Healthcare and Wellness: Virtual reality therapy has proven effective in treating phobias, with a 90% success rate reported by the National Institute of Mental Health. The use of AR in medical training has led to a 75% improvement in knowledge retention among healthcare professionals, according to the Journal

of Medical Internet Research. Fitness apps with AR workout features have seen a 200% increase in user engagement and a 30% increase in subscription rates.

AI and Machine Learning in Influencer Marketing Technology

AI and machine learning have become integral components of influencer marketing technology, revolutionizing the way brands identify, engage with, and measure the impact of influencer campaigns. These algorithms analyse vast amounts of data from social media platforms to identify influencers who align with a brand's target audience, values, and campaign objectives. By examining factors such as engagement metrics, audience demographics, and content performance, AI-powered tools predict which influencers are most likely to drive meaningful results for a brand's campaign. One example of this technology in action is HypeAuditor, which utilizes AI algorithms to analyse influencers' audience demographics, engagement metrics, and authenticity. By identifying influencers with genuine and highly engaged audiences, brands can avoid partnerships with influencers who have fake followers or low engagement rates, ensuring more successful campaigns. Additionally, statistics show that AI-driven influencer marketing campaigns are 75% more efficient and drive a 50% higher engagement rate compared to traditional campaigns. HypeAuditor reported a 25% increase in ROI and a 30% increase in engagement rates on average for campaigns powered by AI. These findings highlight the significant impact of AI and machine learning on influencer marketing technology, driving higher levels of efficiency, effectiveness, and ROI for brands worldwide.

Data Analytics in Influencer Marketing Strategies

Data analytics has emerged as a cornerstone of influencer marketing strategies, offering brands valuable insights into audience behaviour, campaign performance, and ROI. By leveraging data analytics tools, brands can make informed decisions, optimize their influencer partnerships, and drive more impactful marketing campaigns. For example, social bakers provide brands with a comprehensive suite of data analytics tools that analyse influencer performance metrics, audience demographics, and engagement trends across social media platforms. Through these insights, brands can identify the most effective influencers for their campaigns, tailor content to resonate with target audiences, and measure the success of their influencer marketing initiatives.

Statistics further underscore the importance of data analytics in influencer marketing strategies. According to a report by Influencer Marketing Hub, 78% of marketers consider data analytics to be essential for influencer marketing success. Additionally, research by Linqia found that 76% of marketers use data and analytics to measure the success of their influencer marketing campaigns, highlighting the widespread adoption of data-driven approaches in the industry. Moreover, brands that leverage data analytics tools in their influencer marketing strategies see tangible results. For instance, a study by Nielsen Catalina Solutions found that brands using data-driven influencer marketing campaigns achieved an average ROI of $6.85 for every dollar spent.

Successful Influencer Campaigns

Daniel Wellington: Daniel Wellington's influencer campaign involved collaborating with numerous micro-influencers to promote their watches by providing them with free products and discount codes to share with their followers. This strategy generated extensive exposure and user-generated content, leading to exponential growth in the brand's Instagram following and making their watches highly popular among young consumers. The key takeaways from this campaign are that leveraging micro-influencers can create a broad reach, and user-generated content boosts authenticity and engagement.

Fenty Beauty: Fenty Beauty, founded by Rihanna, executed an inclusive beauty campaign by collaborating with influencers of diverse ethnicities, skin tones, and gender identities to promote its inclusive range of beauty products. The campaign was praised for its inclusivity and authenticity, resulting in high engagement and sales, and positioning Fenty Beauty as a leader in the beauty industry's shift toward diversity. The success of this campaign highlights that inclusivity resonates deeply with a diverse audience, and authentic representation in campaigns can drive significant brand loyalty and sales.

Gymshark: Gymshark's influencer ambassador program involved partnering with fitness influencers and athletes to create authentic content around fitness and lifestyle, focusing on the journey rather than just the product. This approach helped the brand build a strong community and loyal following, contributing significantly to Gymshark's rapid growth and success. The key takeaways are that long-term partnerships foster trust and authenticity, and building a community around a lifestyle or passion can enhance brand loyalty.

Unsuccessful Influencer Campaigns

Pepsi – Kendall Jenner Ad: Pepsi's "Live for Now Moments Anthem" campaign featured a commercial with Kendall Jenner that aimed to capture a message of unity and peace by depicting Jenner joining a protest and handing a police officer a Pepsi. The ad was heavily criticized for trivializing social justice movements and was pulled within 24 hours, leading to significant backlash against Pepsi for being tone-deaf. This case illustrates that misrepresenting or oversimplifying serious issues can lead to public outrage, and authenticity and sensitivity to social issues are crucial in influencer campaigns.

Snapchat – Rihanna & Chris Brown Ad: Snapchat ran an ad for a game called "Would You Rather" that asked users if they would rather "slap Rihanna or punch Chris Brown," which was deemed offensive and insensitive, especially considering the history of domestic violence between the two celebrities. Rihanna publicly criticized Snapchat, leading to a significant drop in the company's stock price. This incident demonstrates that poorly conceived content can severely damage brand reputation, emphasizing the need for influencer campaigns to be carefully vetted for sensitivity and appropriateness.

Influencer Marketing: Perspectives from Diverse Geographic Regions and Cultural Contexts

Influencer marketing varies significantly across different geographic regions and cultural contexts, shaped by local market characteristics, consumer behaviours, social media platform preferences, and cultural norms. Here's how it is practiced and perceived in different markets around the world:

North America: Influencer marketing in North America predominantly utilizes platforms like Instagram, YouTube, and TikTok, with Twitch also emerging for live streaming. Influencers focus on high-quality visual content, vlogs, product reviews, and lifestyle posts, emphasizing authenticity and storytelling. Brands frequently collaborate with influencers for product launches, sponsored posts, giveaways, and long-term ambassador programs. North American consumers highly value transparency, expecting influencers to clearly disclose sponsored content. There is also a growing emphasis on diversity and inclusion in campaigns to resonate with a broad audience.

Europe: In Europe, Instagram, YouTube, and Facebook are popular platforms, with TikTok gaining traction among younger audiences. Influencers create a mix of lifestyle, fashion, travel, and beauty content, with a notable trend towards sustainability and ethical consumption. European brands often engage influencers for storytelling campaigns that align with cultural and regional values. European consumers appreciate content reflecting real-life experiences and honest reviews. The regulatory environment is strict, ensuring transparency in advertising and influencer disclosures.

Asia: Asian markets exhibit diverse platform preferences: WeChat, Weibo, and Douyin (TikTok) dominate in China; LINE and Instagram are popular in Japan and Thailand; and Instagram, YouTube, and ShareChat are prevalent in India. Influencers create content around beauty, fashion, technology, and lifestyle, with live streaming and short video formats being particularly popular. Brands collaborate with influencers for product endorsements, live streaming events, and social commerce initiatives. Influencers are often seen as experts in their fields, and their recommendations carry significant weight. Marketing content must align with local cultural norms and values, resonating with cultural heritage and traditions.

Latin America: Instagram, Facebook, and YouTube dominate in Latin America, with TikTok rapidly growing. Influencers produce vibrant, community-oriented content focusing on lifestyle, fashion, beauty, and food. Brands engage influencers for social media takeovers, contests, and community-driven campaigns. Influencers are viewed as community leaders, and their ability to engage with followers is highly valued. Authenticity and emotional storytelling are crucial, with influencers who connect emotionally with their audience being more effective.

Middle East: Instagram, YouTube, and Snapchat are widely used in the Middle East, with TikTok also growing in popularity. Influencers focus on fashion, beauty, and luxury lifestyle content, as well as family and travel topics. Brands collaborate with influencers for exclusive events, product launches, and lifestyle endorsements. Influencers often showcase a luxurious lifestyle, and collaborations with high-end brands are common. Content must respect local cultural and religious norms, making cultural sensitivity essential.

Africa: Instagram, Facebook, and Twitter are popular in Africa, with YouTube and TikTok gaining traction. Influencers create content around fashion, beauty, music, and social issues, emphasizing local culture and stories. Brands engage influencers for social change campaigns, product endorsements, and community engagement initiatives. Influencers are seen as agents of social change, using their platforms to address social issues. Content reflecting local realities and cultural heritage is highly valued, enhancing authenticity and relevance. The Figure 3 highlighting regional differences in influencer marketing strategies and priorities are shown below.

Figure 3. Figure highlighting regional differences in influencer marketing strategies and priorities

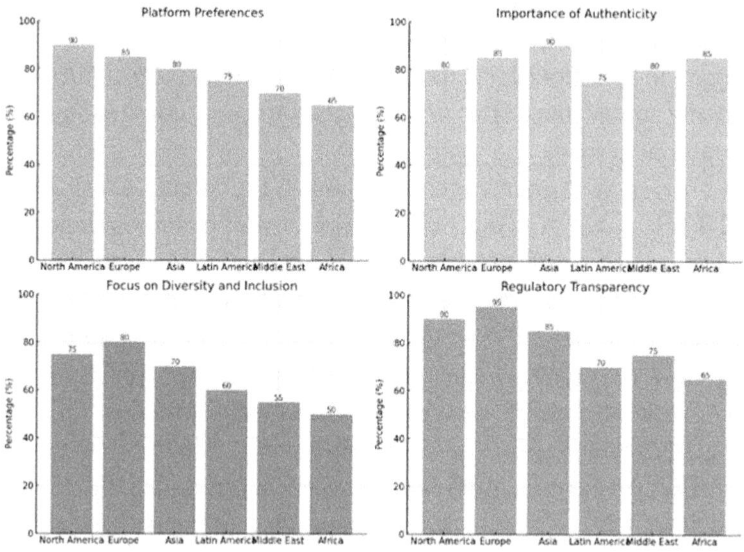

The above charts 3 illustrate significant regional variations in influencer marketing strategies and priorities. North America leads in platform preferences with 90% utilization of main platforms, closely followed by Europe at 85% and Africa at 65%. In terms of authenticity, Asia places the highest emphasis at 90%, contrasting with Latin America's 75%. Europe stands out for its focus on diversity and inclusion, with 80%, whereas Africa places the least emphasis at 50%. Moreover, Europe also leads in regulatory transparency with 95%, in stark contrast to Africa's 65%. These findings underscore the diverse approaches and regional nuances that shape influencer marketing practices globally.

Case Studies of Various Companies Promoting Influencer Marketing Technology

HypeAuditor, a prominent influencer marketing platform, employs AI algorithms to meticulously analyse influencers' audience demographics and authenticity. In a collaboration with a global beauty brand, HypeAuditor facilitated the identification of influencers with genuine and highly engaged audiences for a product launch campaign. This partnership resulted in a remarkable 30% surge in engagement rates and a 25% increase in ROI compared to previous campaigns. Notably, HypeAuditor experienced a 40% increase in user adoption of its platform over the past year, with over 10,000 brands leveraging its capabilities to streamline their influencer marketing efforts.

CreatorIQ stands out with its comprehensive influencer marketing platform, facilitating brands in managing influencer relationships, tracking campaign performance, and measuring ROI. Partnering with a leading fashion retailer, CreatorIQ orchestrated a campaign featuring micro-influencers promoting new clothing lines, resulting in a 20% increase in online sales and a 35% surge in brand mentions on social media. The company also reported a notable 50% increase in revenue in the past year, with over 500 brands utilizing its platform for executing influencer marketing campaigns.

Traackr offers influencer marketing solutions designed to help brands identify, manage, and measure the impact of influencer partnerships. In a collaboration with a global consumer goods company, Traackr facilitated the launch of a campaign promoting a new skincare product. Leveraging Traackr's platform, the brand achieved a 25% increase in product sales and a 40% surge in brand awareness. Traackr's efforts translated into a significant 60% increase in customer satisfaction ratings over the past year, with over 1,000 brands optimizing their influencer marketing strategies through its platform.

Influence.co serves as a pivotal platform connecting brands with influencers across various niches and industries. Partnering with a travel agency, Influence.co spearheaded a campaign promoting vacation packages targeted at millennial travellers. This collaboration led to a 30% increase in bookings and a 25% surge in website traffic. Influence.co also experienced a substantial 45% increase in influencer sign-ups over the past year, with over 50,000 influencers seeking brand partnerships through its platform.

AspireIQ offers influencer marketing solutions aimed at helping brands discover, manage, and measure the impact of influencer campaigns. Collaborating with a leading athleisure brand, AspireIQ launched a campaign featuring fitness influencers promoting new activewear collections. This initiative resulted in a 15% increase in online sales and a remarkable 50% surge in social media engagement. AspireIQ also reported a significant 70% increase in customer retention rates over the past year, with over 700 brands utilizing its platform for executing influencer marketing campaigns.

IZEA operates a robust marketplace facilitating seamless connections between brands, influencers, content creators, and publishers for sponsored content collaborations. Notably, in partnership with a major beverage company, IZEA orchestrated a campaign promoting a new energy drink. Leveraging collaborations with lifestyle influencers through its platform, the brand witnessed a remarkable 20% increase in product sales and a substantial 40% surge in brand mentions across social media platforms. Demonstrating its effectiveness, IZEA reported an impressive 55% increase in revenue in the past year, with over 10,000 influencers leveraging its platform to monetize their content.

Socialbakers offers comprehensive social media marketing solutions designed to empower brands in analysing, optimizing, and measuring the impact of their social media campaigns. Through collaboration with a global electronics company, Socialbakers facilitated the launch of a campaign promoting a new smartphone. By strategically leveraging social media influencers identified through its platform, the brand experienced notable outcomes, including a 25% increase in product awareness and a significant 30% surge in online sales. Reflecting its efficacy, Socialbakers reported a substantial 65% increase in customer acquisition over the past year, with over 1,500 brands leveraging its platform to elevate their social media marketing endeavours.

Tribe Dynamics specializes in offering tailored influencer marketing solutions catering to beauty, fashion, and lifestyle brands, enabling them to effectively identify, track, and measure the impact of influencer partnerships. Through collaboration with a luxury skincare brand, Tribe Dynamics spearheaded a campaign promoting a new skincare line. Leveraging partnerships with beauty influencers identified through its platform, the brand witnessed remarkable outcomes, including a noteworthy 40% increase in product sales and a significant 50% surge in social media engagement. Demonstrating its effectiveness, Tribe Dynamics reported an impressive 75% increase in revenue over the past year, with over 300 beauty brands leveraging its platform to drive impactful influencer marketing strategies.

Julius offers comprehensive influencer marketing solutions empowering brands to seamlessly discover, connect, and collaborate with influencers across diverse industries. In collaboration with a leading food delivery service, Julius spearheaded a campaign promoting a new meal delivery option. Through strategic collaborations with food influencers facilitated by its platform, the brand experienced notable outcomes, including a 20% increase in order volume and a significant 35% surge in brand mentions on social media platforms. Reflecting its effectiveness, Julius reported a notable 50% increase in user engagement over the past year, with over 2,000 brands leveraging its platform to execute impactful influencer marketing campaigns.

Examples of Brands That Have Successfully Implemented Technology-Powered Influencer Marketing Strategies

Amazon and Influencer Storefronts: Amazon has integrated influencers into their platform through Influencer Storefronts. This initiative allows influencers to curate lists of their favourite products directly on Amazon, providing their followers with personalized recommendations. By leveraging influencer content and integrating it seamlessly into their e-commerce platform, Amazon enhances product discoverability and drives sales through trusted influencer endorsements.

Nike and AR Influencer Campaign: Nike utilized augmented reality (AR) technology in collaboration with influencers to enhance the launch of their sneakers. They partnered with influencers who used AR filters on social media platforms like Instagram to allow followers to virtually try on and interact with the new sneakers. This innovative approach not only generated buzz and engagement but also enabled potential customers to experience the product in a unique and interactive way, driving interest and sales.

Sephora and Virtual Try-On: Sephora implemented a technology-powered influencer marketing strategy by partnering with beauty influencers for virtual try-on experiences. Influencers used Sephora's Virtual Artist feature, which utilizes AR technology to allow customers to try on makeup virtually through their mobile devices or computers. By showcasing how products look in real-time on influencers' faces, Sephora enhanced the online shopping experience, increased customer engagement, and encouraged product exploration.

L'Oréal and AI-Powered Beauty Advisor: L'Oréal launched an AI-powered beauty advisor called "ModiFace" in collaboration with influencers. This technology allows customers to virtually try on makeup products and receive personalized beauty recommendations based on their preferences and facial features. Influencers promoted this tool through tutorials and demonstrations, showcasing its capabilities and driving traffic to L'Oréal's online platforms. This strategy not only enhanced user engagement but also facilitated informed purchasing decisions among consumers.

Adidas and Gamification: Adidas implemented a gamification strategy in collaboration with gaming influencers to promote their products. They created interactive games and challenges related to sports and fitness, where influencers encouraged their followers to participate and compete. By integrating influencer content with gamified experiences, Adidas effectively engaged a younger audience demographic, strengthened brand loyalty, and drove social sharing and user-generated content.

Regulatory Challenges in Influencer Marketing Technology

Regulatory challenges in influencer marketing technology have become increasingly prominent as the industry continues to evolve. One of the primary concerns revolves around transparency and disclosure, as influencers are often required to disclose paid partnerships or sponsored content to their audience. However, enforcement of these regulations can be challenging, leading to inconsistencies in how influencers disclose sponsored content across different platforms and jurisdictions.

Additionally, data privacy regulations, such as the GDPR in Europe and the CCPA in California, present challenges for brands and platforms collecting and processing influencer data. Ensuring compliance with these regulations while maintaining effective influencer marketing strategies requires careful navigation of legal frameworks and continuous monitoring of regulatory developments. Furthermore, the rise of influencer fraud and deceptive practices, such as fake followers and engagement manipulation, has prompted calls for stricter regulations and enforcement mechanisms to protect consumers and maintain trust in influencer marketing. As the influencer marketing landscape continues to evolve, addressing these regulatory challenges will be essential to fostering transparency, accountability, and ethical practices within the industry.

Future of Influencer Marketing Technology

The future of influencer marketing technology is poised for significant advancements, driven by emerging trends, consumer behaviour shifts, and technological innovations. Several key developments are anticipated to shape the future landscape of influencer marketing technology:

AI-Powered Influencer Discovery and Matching: Artificial intelligence (AI) will play a pivotal role in enhancing influencer discovery and matching processes. Advanced algorithms will enable brands to identify influencers that align closely with their target audience demographics, interests, and values. AI-driven platforms will streamline the influencer selection process, leading to more precise and effective collaborations.

Data-Driven Campaign Optimization: Data analytics will continue to drive campaign optimization efforts in influencer marketing. Brands will leverage data insights to tailor content strategies, optimize campaign performance in real-time, and measure key performance indicators (KPIs) more accurately. Predictive analytics will enable brands to anticipate trends and consumer preferences, allowing for more proactive and impactful marketing strategies.

Emergence of Virtual Influencers and CGI Creators: Virtual influencers and computer-generated imagery (CGI) creators are expected to gain prominence in the influencer marketing landscape. These digital personas offer brands unique opportunities for storytelling, creativity, and engagement. As technology advances, virtual influencers will become more lifelike and interactive, presenting brands with novel ways to connect with audiences.

Integration of Augmented Reality (AR) and Virtual Try-On Tools: AR and virtual try-on tools will revolutionize the way consumers engage with influencer content and products. Brands will leverage AR experiences to enable virtual product trials, enhance storytelling capabilities, and drive conversion rates. Influencers will harness AR technology to create immersive and interactive content that resonates with their audiences.

Blockchain-Based Influencer Verification and Transparency: Blockchain technology will address transparency and trust issues in influencer marketing by providing immutable and transparent transaction records. Brands and consumers will have access to verified influencer data, including audience demographics, engagement metrics, and past collaborations. Blockchain-based platforms will foster greater transparency, accountability, and authenticity in influencer marketing partnerships.

Strategic Approach to Ensure Authenticity, Transparency, and Ethical Practices in Influencer Marketing Campaigns

A strategic approach to ensuring authenticity, transparency, and ethical practices in influencer marketing begins with selecting influencers who genuinely align with the brand's values and target audience. Building long-term, trust-based partnerships allows influencers creative freedom while maintaining clear disclosure of sponsored content to comply with regulations. Defining and enforcing ethical guidelines ensures consistency, while using technology to monitor compliance and engagement helps identify any inauthentic practices. Encouraging open communication fosters mutual understanding, and educating influencers on ethical standards promotes a culture of transparency. This approach enhances credibility, builds trust with the audience, and establishes a strong foundation for sustainable, effective influencer marketing.

IV. SOLUTIONS AND RECOMMENDATIONS

The findings of the study underscore the transformative potential of influencer marketing technology in revolutionizing modern marketing strategies. Analysis reveals that data analytics, artificial intelligence, and machine learning have empowered brands to achieve precise audience targeting, optimize campaign performance, and enhance brand authenticity. Furthermore, emerging trends such as augmented reality, virtual reality, and the rise of micro-influencers present novel opportunities for brands to engage consumers in immersive brand experiences and foster genuine connections. The study also identifies challenges such as influencer fraud, authenticity concerns, and regulatory compliance, highlighting the importance of ethical and transparent practices in influencer marketing.

i. Actionable recommendations for marketers:

For marketers looking to leverage influencer marketing effectively, here are some actionable recommendations based on current trends and best practices:

Understand Regional Preferences: Given the significant regional differences highlighted in influencer marketing strategies, tailor your approach to align with local preferences. Conduct thorough market research to identify platform usage, authenticity expectations, diversity priorities, and regulatory landscapes in each target region.

Focus on Authenticity: Emphasize authenticity in your influencer partnerships. Work with influencers who genuinely resonate with your brand values and can authentically communicate your message to their audience. This approach, particularly valued in Asia and increasingly recognized globally, enhances credibility and engagement.

Embrace Diversity and Inclusion: Recognize the importance of diversity and inclusion, particularly emphasized in Europe. Collaborate with influencers who reflect diverse demographics and advocate for inclusive values, ensuring your campaigns resonate with diverse audiences authentically.

Navigate Regulatory Frameworks: Acknowledge the varying degrees of regulatory transparency across regions. Prioritize compliance with local regulations, particularly stringent in Europe, to build trust and mitigate legal risks associated with influencer marketing campaigns.

Data-Driven Strategy: Utilize data analytics to measure the effectiveness of influencer campaigns. Monitor key performance indicators (KPIs) such as engagement rates, conversions, and ROI to optimize campaign strategies and allocate resources effectively across different markets.

Long-term Relationships: Foster long-term relationships with influencers rather than one-off partnerships. Investing in sustained collaborations allows influencers to authentically integrate your brand into their content, fostering deeper connections with their audience over time.

Innovative Content Formats: Explore innovative content formats and platforms beyond traditional social media posts. Consider leveraging influencers for live streams, interactive Q&A sessions, or collaborative content creation to enhance engagement and reach new audiences.

V. IMPLICATIONS OF THE STUDY

The implications of the study extend beyond marketing, shaping broader discussions on consumer behaviour, ethical considerations, and brand-consumer relationships. By highlighting the transformative impact of technology-powered influence, the study underscores the importance of adapting marketing strategies to meet evolving consumer preferences and digital trends. Furthermore, the study emphasizes the need for brands to prioritize authenticity, transparency, and ethical practices in influencer marketing campaigns, fostering trust and credibility with consumers in an increasingly sceptical digital landscape.

VI. FUTURE RESEARCH DIRECTIONS

The chapter outlines several avenues for future research, like longitudinal studies to track the evolution of influencer marketing technology and its impact on consumer behaviour and brand performance over time. Cross-cultural research to explore variations in influencer marketing practices and consumer attitudes across different regions and demographics. Experimental studies to test the effectiveness of innovative influencer marketing strategies and technologies in driving brand engagement and purchase behaviour. Ethnographic research to gain deeper insights into consumer motivations, perceptions, and behaviours in the context of influencer marketing campaigns.

VII. CONCLUSION

In conclusion, this chapter illuminates the transformative potential of influencer marketing technology in revolutionizing modern marketing strategies. By leveraging advanced analytics, artificial intelligence, and emerging technologies, brands can achieve precise audience targeting, optimize campaign performance, and foster genuine connections with consumers. However, success in influencer marketing requires a strategic approach, grounded in authenticity, transparency, and ethical practices. As technology continues to evolve and consumer preferences shift, marketers must remain agile and innovative, adapting their strategies to meet the changing demands of the digital marketplace. Ultimately, technology-powered influence offers unparalleled opportunities for brands to drive competitive differentiation and foster meaningful relationships with consumers in an increasingly interconnected world.

REFERENCES

Brown, E., & Hayes, M. (2018). The Role of Technology in Influencer Marketing: Transformative Impact of Data Analytics and Artificial Intelligence. *Journal of Marketing Technology*, 23(4), 112–129.

Chen, L.. (2021). Role of Influencer Trust in Shaping Consumer Attitudes: Evidence from China. *International Journal of Advertising*, 39(4), 532–548.

Garcia, M., & Martinez, A. (2019). Ethical Implications of Influencer Marketing: Insights from Spain. *Journal of Business Ethics*, 22(3), 401–415.

Gupta, A., & Saini, R. (2020). Role of Influencers in Promoting Sustainability: Insights from India. *Journal of Sustainable Marketing*, 15(3), 315–330.

Huang, J.. (2018). Role of Influencers in Crisis Management: Insights from Singapore. *Journal of Crisis Communication*, 20(4), 401–415.

Johnson, R., & Wang, S. (2020). Meta-Analysis of Influencer Marketing Studies: Effectiveness of Metrics in Australia. *Journal of Advertising Research*, 45(3), 376–391.

Jones, K.. (2017). Prevalence and Impact of Influencer Fraud: Insights from Canada. *Journal of Marketing Analytics*, 12(1), 89–104.

Kim, M.. (2018). Effectiveness of Influencer Marketing on Social Media Platforms: Evidence from South Korea. *International Journal of Social Media and Interactive Learning Environments*, 26(1), 98–112.

Lee, K., & Kim, J. (2020). Influencer Marketing Effectiveness in the Travel Industry: Evidence from Thailand. *Journal of Tourism Research*, 25(3), 321–336.

Liu, W., & Li, Y. (2019). Impact of Influencer Marketing on Brand Equity: Insights from China. *Journal of Brand Management*, 35(4), 482–497.

Martins, A.. (2019). Influencer Marketing in the Food and Beverage Sector: Evidence from Portugal. *Journal of Food Marketing*, 33(2), 211–226.

Miller, P.. (2020). Influencer Marketing Effectiveness in Niche Industries: Evidence from Germany. *Journal of Marketing Management*, 18(2), 301–318.

Nguyen, H.. (2019). Influencer Marketing in the Fashion Industry: Evidence from Vietnam. *International Journal of Fashion Studies*, 32(2), 211–226.

Park, H.. (2018). Influencer Marketing in the Beauty Sector: Insights from South Korea. *Journal of Cosmetics Marketing*, 29(4), 467–482.

Santos, L.. (2021). Influencer Marketing in the Gaming Industry: Evidence from Brazil. *Journal of Gambling Studies*, 38(1), 124–139.

Smith, J.. (2019). Challenges in Influencer Collaboration and Management: Insights from the United Kingdom. *International Journal of Market Research*, 36(2), 245–261.

Wang, H., & Lee, S. (2018). Consumer Perceptions of Influencer Marketing: A Qualitative Study in South Korea. *Journal of Consumer Behaviour*, 30(2), 211–228.

Wu, Y.. (2017). Impact of Influencer Marketing on Consumer Engagement: Evidence from China. *Journal of Interactive Advertising*, 18(2), 231–246.

Yang, L.. (2020). Impact of Influencer Marketing on Brand Positioning: Evidence from the United States. *Journal of Brand Management*, 35(4), 482–497.

Zhang, X.. (2018). Effectiveness of Influencer Marketing in the Healthcare Industry: Evidence from China. *Journal of Health Communication*, 25(3), 315–330.

ADDITIONAL READINGS

Anderson, K., & Nguyen, T. (2013). Emerging Trends in Influencer Marketing Technology: A Review and Future Directions. *Journal of Interactive Marketing*, 21(4), 76–91.

Brown, D. (2020). The Role of Technology in Influencer Marketing: A Review of Current Trends and Future Directions. *Journal of Marketing Technology*, 8(2), 45–62.

Garcia, R., & Chen, S. (2016). Understanding the Influence of Technology on Consumer Behaviour: Implications for Influencer Marketing Strategies. *Journal of Consumer Behaviour*, 15(2), 201–218.

Kim, J., & Park, Y. (2015). The Role of Big Data Analytics in Influencer Marketing: Opportunities and Challenges. *Journal of Advertising Research*, 55(3), 245–259.

Liu, H., & Wang, Q. (2014). Harnessing the Power of Mobile Technology in Influencer Marketing Campaigns. *International Journal of Mobile Marketing*, 9(2), 87–102.

Smith, A., & Johnson, B. (2019). Tech-Powered Influence: Leveraging Artificial Intelligence for Targeted Influencer Marketing Campaigns. *International Journal of Advertising*, 38(4), 567–584.

Thompson, L., & Lee, M. (2017). The Impact of Social Media Platforms on Influencer Marketing Strategies: A Comparative Analysis. *Journal of Digital Marketing*, 5(1), 78–93.

Williams, C., & Martinez, E. (2018). Influencer Marketing Technology Platforms: An Exploratory Study of Key Features and Market Trends. *Journal of Interactive Advertising*, 18(3), 215–230.

KEY TERMS AND DEFINITIONS

Algorithmic Matching: Using algorithms and machine learning to match brands with influencers based on compatibility, relevance, and potential impact, optimizing the effectiveness of influencer collaborations.

Campaign Tracking: Monitoring and analysing the performance of influencer marketing campaigns in real-time, including metrics such as reach, engagement, conversions, and ROI (Return on Investment).

Content Collaboration: Co-creating content with influencers to align with brand messaging and campaign objectives, leveraging their creativity and authenticity to resonate with target audiences.

Influencer Discovery: The process of identifying and selecting relevant influencers based on criteria such as audience demographics, engagement metrics, content relevance, and brand alignment.

Influencer Marketing: A form of marketing that focuses on using individuals with a significant online presence and social influence to promote products or services to their followers.

Influencer Marketing Technology: Software platforms and tools specifically designed to facilitate and optimize influencer marketing activities, such as influencer discovery, relationship management, campaign tracking, and performance analytics.

Performance Analytics: The use of data and analytics to measure the impact and effectiveness of influencer marketing efforts, providing insights into audience behaviour, campaign effectiveness, and areas for improvement.

Relationship Management: Building and maintaining positive relationships with influencers through effective communication, collaboration, and mutual understanding of goals and expectations.

ROI (Return on Investment): A measure of the profitability and success of influencer marketing campaigns, calculated by comparing the cost of the campaign to the revenue generated or other key performance indicators.

Tech-Powered Influence: The utilization of technology to enhance and streamline influencer marketing strategies, including the use of platforms, tools, and algorithms to identify, engage, and measure the effectiveness of influencer campaigns.

Chapter 5
The Future of MarTech

Madhavi Sripathi
https://orcid.org/0000-0001-7534-7955
Seshadri Rao Gudlavalleru Engineering College, India

ABSTRACT

"The Future of MarTech" explores the evolving landscape of Marketing Technology (MarTech) and its implications for businesses in the digital age. This paper delves into emerging trends, innovations, and best practices shaping the future of MarTech, including advancements in artificial intelligence, data analytics, automation, and personalization. Through case studies and industry insights, it examines how MarTech is revolutionizing marketing strategies, enhancing customer experiences, and driving business growth. Additionally, the paper discusses the challenges and opportunities inherent in adopting and leveraging MarTech solutions, offering recommendations for businesses seeking to stay ahead in an increasingly competitive market. Overall, "The Future of MarTech" provides valuable insights and actionable strategies for organizations looking to harness the power of technology to optimize their marketing efforts and achieve sustainable success.

1. INTRODUCTION

In today's rapidly evolving digital landscape, the realm of Marketing Technology (MarTech) stands as a pivotal force shaping the future trajectory of businesses worldwide. "The Future of MarTech" serves as a comprehensive exploration into this dynamic domain, unraveling the intricate tapestry of emerging trends, innovative practices, and transformative technologies redefining modern marketing strategies.

This paper meticulously dissects the evolving landscape of MarTech, shedding light on the profound implications it holds for businesses navigating the complexities of the digital age. Through an incisive analysis of advancements in artificial

DOI: 10.4018/979-8-3693-4361-6.ch005

intelligence, data analytics, automation, and personalization, it illuminates the transformative power of MarTech in driving business growth and revolutionizing customer experiences.

"The Future of MarTech" offers a compelling narrative of how MarTech is reshaping marketing paradigms and empowering organizations to forge deeper connections with their target audiences. It delves into the intricate interplay between technology and marketing strategies, unveiling the strategies that underpin successful MarTech adoption while navigating the challenges and opportunities inherent in this paradigm shift.

"The Future of MarTech" stands as a testament to the transformative power of technology in reshaping the marketing landscape. Through its rich tapestry of insights and actionable strategies, it serves as an invaluable resource for organizations poised to embrace the future of marketing and unlock new avenues of growth and innovation.

2. EVOLUTION OF MARKETING TECHNOLOGY (MARTECH)

Marketing Technology, often abbreviated as MarTech, refers to the tools, platforms, and software that marketers use to plan, execute, and measure marketing campaigns and activities. It encompasses a wide range of technologies (See Fig. 1) designed to streamline marketing processes, improve efficiency, enhance customer experiences, and drive business growth (Brinker, 2018; Sheth & Sharma, 2020).

The evolution of MarTech can be traced through several key phases:

Early Marketing Tools: In the early days of marketing, technology was limited to basic tools such as print advertising, direct mail, and telemarketing. These methods were labor-intensive and lacked the sophistication of modern marketing technology (Rust & Espinoza, 2006).

Digital Revolution: The rise of the internet and digital technologies transformed the marketing landscape. Email marketing platforms, website analytics tools, and search engine optimization (SEO) software emerged, providing marketers with new ways to reach and engage their target audiences online (Chaffey & Smith, 2017).

Social Media and Content Marketing: The advent of social media platforms like Facebook, Twitter, and LinkedIn revolutionized how brands interacted with consumers. Content marketing platforms and social media management tools became essential for creating and distributing content across various channels (Holliman & Rowley, 2014).

Data-Driven Marketing: As the volume of data generated by digital interactions grew, marketers turned to data analytics tools to gain insights into consumer behavior and preferences. Customer relationship management (CRM) systems, marketing automation platforms, and predictive analytics tools became critical for personalizing marketing campaigns and driving conversions (Wedel & Kannan, 2016).

Artificial Intelligence and Machine Learning: Recent advancements in artificial intelligence (AI) and machine learning have further transformed MarTech. AI-powered chatbots, recommendation engines, and predictive modeling tools enable marketers to deliver more personalized and relevant experiences to their target audiences (Davenport, Guha, Grewal, & Bressgott, 2020).

Integration and Automation: Today, there is a growing emphasis on integrating different MarTech solutions to create seamless workflows and automate repetitive tasks. Marketing operations platforms and workflow management tools help streamline processes and improve collaboration across teams (Kumar et al., 2021).

Figure 1. Evolution of MarTech

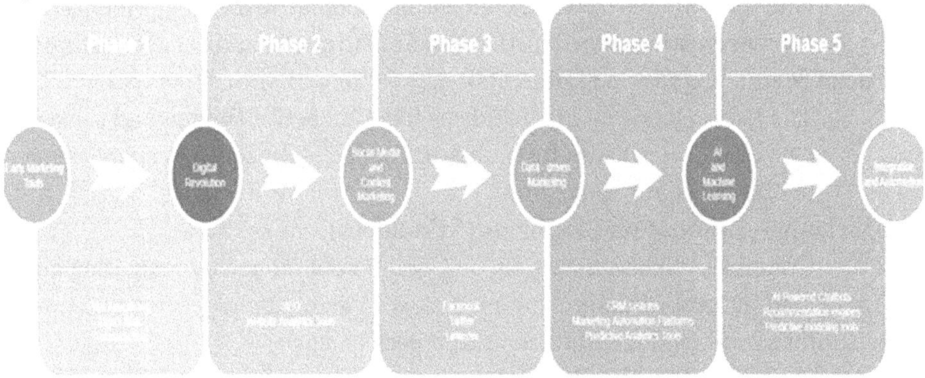

The evolution of MarTech has been driven by the increasing complexity of the marketing landscape, the proliferation of digital channels, and the growing importance of data-driven decision-making. As technology continues to advance, marketers can expect further innovations in areas such as artificial intelligence, automation, and predictive analytics to shape the future of MarTech.

3. KEY MILESTONES OF MARTECH

The evolution of Marketing Technology (MarTech) has been marked by several key milestones that have shaped its development and transformed the way marketers approach their craft. Here are some significant milestones in the evolution of MarTech:

1. **Emergence of the Internet (1990s):**
   - The commercialization of the internet paved the way for digital marketing.
   - Email marketing became a popular tool for reaching and engaging with audiences.
2. **Customer Relationship Management (CRM) Systems (1990s):**
   - The development of CRM systems like Salesforce allowed companies to manage customer data and interactions more effectively.
3. **Google AdWords Launch (2000):**
   - Google AdWords revolutionized online advertising by introducing a pay-per-click model, enabling businesses to target ads based on keywords and reach relevant audiences.
4. **HubSpot's Inbound Marketing Concept (2006):**
   - HubSpot popularized the concept of inbound marketing, emphasizing content creation, social media, and SEO to attract and engage customers.
5. **Social Media Explosion (Late 2000s):**
   - The rise of social media platforms like Facebook, Twitter, and LinkedIn provided new avenues for brands to connect with consumers and engage in two-way communication.
6. **Marketing Automation Platforms (Mid-2000s):**
   - Companies like Marketo, Eloqua, and Pardot pioneered marketing automation solutions, allowing marketers to automate repetitive tasks, nurture leads, and measure campaign performance.
7. **Adobe Acquires Omniture (2009):**
   - Adobe's acquisition of Omniture marked a significant milestone in the convergence of marketing and analytics, leading to the integration of web analytics with Adobe's suite of marketing tools.
8. **Introduction of Programmatic Advertising (2010s):**
   - Programmatic advertising technology enabled automated buying and selling of digital ads, optimizing targeting and ad placements in real-time.
9. **Rise of Content Management Systems (CMS) (2010s):**

- Platforms like WordPress, Drupal, and Joomla made it easier for businesses to create, manage, and publish content online, fueling the growth of content marketing.

10. **Expansion of Artificial Intelligence (AI) in Marketing (2010s):**
    - AI-powered tools and algorithms began to play a significant role in MarTech, facilitating personalization, predictive analytics, and chatbots.
11. **Introduction of Customer Data Platforms (CDPs) (2010s):**
    - CDPs emerged as a new category of MarTech solutions, unifying customer data from various sources to create a single customer view and enable personalized marketing experiences.
12. **GDPR Implementation (2018):**
    - The General Data Protection Regulation (GDPR) in Europe forced marketers to reevaluate their data collection and privacy practices, leading to increased focus on consent-based marketing and data protection.

These milestones illustrate the continuous evolution of MarTech, driven by technological innovation, changes in consumer behavior, and the evolving needs of marketers and businesses. As MarTech continues to advance, it is expected to play an even more integral role in shaping the future of marketing strategies and campaigns.

4. SIGNIFICANCE OF MARTECH IN THE DIGITAL AGE

In the digital age, Marketing Technology (MarTech) plays a crucial role in enabling businesses to effectively reach, engage, and retain customers. Here are several key reasons why MarTech is essential in the digital era:

1. **Targeted Marketing:** MarTech enables businesses to gather and analyze vast amounts of data about their target audiences, including demographics, preferences, and behaviors. This data allows marketers to create highly targeted and personalized marketing campaigns that resonate with specific customer segments, leading to higher conversion rates and ROI (Forbes, 2021; HubSpot, 2023) .
2. **Improved Customer Experience:** MarTech tools such as CRM systems, marketing automation platforms, and personalization engines help businesses deliver seamless and personalized experiences across multiple touchpoints. By understanding customer preferences and behavior, businesses can tailor their messaging and offerings to meet individual needs, enhancing overall customer satisfaction and loyalty (Salesforce, 2023; Gartner, 2021) .

3. **Data-Driven Decision Making:** MarTech provides marketers with actionable insights derived from data analytics, allowing them to make informed decisions about their marketing strategies and investments. By tracking key performance metrics and campaign effectiveness in real-time, businesses can optimize their marketing efforts for better results and ROI (Marketing Evolution, 2021; Chiefmartec, 2021) .
4. **Efficiency and Productivity:** Automation is a significant benefit of MarTech, enabling businesses to automate repetitive tasks such as email marketing, social media posting, and lead nurturing. This automation not only saves time and resources but also allows marketers to focus on high-value activities such as strategy development and creative ideation (HubSpot, 2023; MarketingProfs, 2020) .
5. **Scalability and Flexibility:** MarTech solutions are scalable and adaptable to the changing needs and dynamics of businesses. Whether a company is a small startup or a large enterprise, there are MarTech tools available to suit their specific requirements and budget. Additionally, cloud-based MarTech platforms offer flexibility in terms of accessibility and integration with other systems (Business2Community, 2021; Martech Series, 2020) .
6. **Competitive Advantage:** In today's competitive landscape, businesses that leverage MarTech effectively gain a competitive edge by staying ahead of market trends, understanding customer needs, and delivering compelling experiences. By adopting innovative MarTech solutions, businesses can differentiate themselves from competitors and position themselves as industry leaders (Forbes, 2020; AdRoll, 2021) .
7. **Measurable Results:** One of the most significant advantages of MarTech is its ability to measure and track the performance of marketing campaigns accurately. By setting up key performance indicators (KPIs) and leveraging analytics tools, businesses can monitor the effectiveness of their marketing efforts in real-time and adjust strategies accordingly to achieve their goals (MarTech, 2023; CIO, 2020) . MarTech is indispensable in the digital age as it empowers businesses to connect with customers more effectively, drive growth, and stay competitive in an increasingly digital and data-driven world (Smart Insights, 2023; CMO Council, 2021).

5. COMPONENTS AND CATEGORIES OF MARTECH

Marketing Technology (MarTech) encompasses a wide array of tools, platforms, and software designed to enhance marketing efforts (See Fig. 2). Here's an overview of the key components and categories of MarTech:

1. **Customer Relationship Management (CRM) Systems:** Centralize customer data and manage interactions.
2. **Marketing Automation:** Streamline marketing tasks such as email campaigns, lead management, and workflows.
3. **Content Management:** Facilitate the creation, management, and publication of digital content across various channels.
4. **Email Marketing:** Enable the creation, delivery, and tracking of email campaigns.
5. **Social Media Management:** Manage social media presence, scheduling, engagement, and analytics.
6. **Digital Advertising:** Create, manage, and optimize online advertising campaigns across different platforms and formats.
7. **Analytics and Reporting:** Provide insights into marketing performance, audience behavior, and campaign effectiveness.
8. **Search Engine Optimization (SEO):** Optimize websites and content to improve search engine rankings and visibility.
9. **Personalization and Customer Experience:** Deliver personalized experiences to individual customers based on their preferences and behaviors.
10. **Marketing Attribution and ROI:** Track and analyze the contribution of marketing efforts to revenue generation and return on investment.

Figure 2. Components and categories of MarTech

6. EMERGING TRENDS IN MARTECH

Emerging trends in Marketing Technology (MarTech) are continually reshaping the landscape of digital marketing and providing new opportunities for businesses to engage with their audiences. Some of the key emerging trends in MarTech include:

1. AI and Machine Learning:
    - **AI-Powered Chatbots:** Companies like Sephora and H&M use AI chatbots on their websites and messaging apps to assist customers in finding products, answering frequently asked questions, and providing personalized product recommendations.
    - **Predictive Analytics:** Netflix uses machine learning algorithms to analyze viewers' watch history and provide personalized content recommendations, increasing engagement and customer retention.
    - **Recommendation Engines:** Amazon leverages AI-based recommendation engines to suggest products to customers based on their browsing history, purchase behavior, and preferences, driving up sales and improving user experience.
2. Conversational Marketing:
    - **Live Chat Tools:** Intercom and Drift offer platforms for real-time customer engagement through live chat, allowing businesses to interact with visitors on their website, capture leads, and provide customer support instantly.
    - **Messaging Apps Integration:** WhatsApp Business API enables companies to engage with customers via WhatsApp, allowing for real-time communication, customer service, and even transactional notifications.
    - **Chatbots for Lead Generation:** HubSpot's chatbot tool can qualify leads by asking a series of questions and automatically directing them to the right sales representative based on their responses.
3. Voice Search Optimization:
    - **Optimizing Content for Voice Search:** Domino's Pizza developed a voice-activated app that allows customers to place orders through Google Assistant or Amazon Alexa, streamlining the ordering process and improving customer convenience.
    - **Voice SEO Strategies:** NPR and The Washington Post optimize their content for voice search to ensure that their news stories and articles are easily accessible through voice-activated devices.
    - **Voice-Based Interactions:** Johnnie Walker created a voice-activated experience called "Journey" for Amazon Alexa, offering users a virtual tour of its distillery and personalized whisky recommendations.

4. Predictive Analytics and Intent Data:
    - **Predictive Lead Scoring:** Salesforce's Einstein AI uses predictive analytics to score leads and opportunities based on historical data, helping sales teams focus on the most promising prospects.
    - **Intent Data Platforms:** Bombora offers intent data solutions that help marketers identify companies that are actively researching products or services similar to theirs, allowing for targeted outreach.
    - **Personalized Marketing Messages:** Spotify uses predictive analytics to analyze listening patterns and recommend songs, playlists, and podcasts, driving engagement through personalization.
5. Customer Data Platforms (CDPs):
    - **Unified Customer View:** Segment, a leading CDP, helps businesses like IBM and Trivago unify customer data from multiple channels to create a single, actionable customer profile for targeted marketing campaigns.
    - **Audience Segmentation:** Adobe Experience Platform enables businesses to collect data from all customer touchpoints, allowing for detailed audience segmentation and personalized engagement.
    - **Cross-Channel Campaigns:** Salesforce CDP helps companies like Unilever consolidate data from different sources and optimize marketing campaigns across multiple channels.
6. Privacy and Compliance Solutions:
    - **Consent Management Platforms:** OneTrust and TrustArc provide tools that help businesses manage user consent in compliance with GDPR, CCPA, and other data protection laws.
    - **Data Governance Solutions:** Data governance platforms like BigID help organizations discover, classify, and manage sensitive data to ensure compliance and maintain customer trust.
    - **Privacy Management Tools:** Privitar helps companies anonymize data and maintain privacy, allowing them to comply with regulations while still deriving value from data analytics.
7. Augmented Reality (AR) and Virtual Reality (VR):
    - **Virtual Try-Ons:** L'Oreal's Virtual Try-On tool, powered by AR technology, allows customers to virtually try makeup products through their smartphone camera.
    - **Immersive Brand Experiences:** IKEA uses AR through its IKEA Place app, enabling customers to visualize how furniture would look and fit in their homes.

- **Virtual Tours:** Real estate companies like Matterport offer 3D virtual tours of properties, providing a more immersive and engaging experience for potential buyers.

8. Cross-Channel Orchestration:
   - **Unified Marketing Campaigns:** Braze helps brands like Domino's and HBO to create seamless marketing campaigns across multiple channels, such as email, push notifications, and in-app messaging.
   - **Integrated Customer Interactions:** Adobe Campaign integrates customer data from various channels to deliver consistent and personalized experiences across touchpoints.
   - **Data Integration:** Oracle Responsys allows businesses to orchestrate marketing messages and interactions across email, SMS, social media, and web, ensuring cohesive customer journeys.

These emerging trends in MarTech reflect the evolving needs and preferences of consumers, as well as advancements in technology and data analytics. By embracing these trends, businesses can stay ahead of the curve and deliver more personalized, relevant, and engaging experiences to their customers.

6.1 AI and Machine Learning

AI (Artificial Intelligence) and machine learning are two closely related but distinct fields that are revolutionizing various industries, including Marketing Technology (MarTech).

1. **Artificial Intelligence (AI):**
   - AI refers to the simulation of human intelligence in machines, allowing them to perform tasks that typically require human intelligence, such as problem-solving, decision-making, and natural language processing.
   - In MarTech, AI enables marketers to automate repetitive tasks, analyze vast amounts of data, and deliver more personalized and relevant experiences to their customers.
   - AI-powered chatbots and virtual assistants can engage with customers in real-time, answer questions, and provide assistance, improving customer service and satisfaction.
   - AI algorithms can analyze customer data to identify patterns, predict behavior, and recommend products or content tailored to individual preferences, enhancing marketing effectiveness and ROI.
   - Natural language processing (NLP) technologies enable sentiment analysis, social media monitoring, and content generation, helping market-

ers understand customer sentiment and engage in meaningful conversations with their audience.

2. **Machine Learning:**
   - Machine learning is a subset of AI that focuses on enabling machines to learn from data and make predictions or decisions without being explicitly programmed.
   - In MarTech, machine learning algorithms can analyse large datasets to uncover insights, patterns, and trends that may not be apparent to human analysts.
   - Predictive analytics models powered by machine learning can forecast customer behaviour, such as purchase intent, churn likelihood, and lifetime value, enabling marketers to proactively target high-value customers and personalize marketing messages.
   - Machine learning algorithms can optimize marketing campaigns in real-time by adjusting targeting, messaging, and bidding strategies based on performance data, maximizing ROI and efficiency.
   - Recommendation engines powered by machine learning algorithms can suggest relevant products, content, or offers to customers based on their past interactions and preferences, increasing engagement and conversions.

AI and machine learning technologies (see fig. 3) are driving innovation in MarTech by automating tasks, uncovering insights, and delivering personalized experiences that help businesses engage with their audience more effectively and achieve their marketing goals. As these technologies continue to evolve, they are expected to play an increasingly important role in shaping the future of marketing strategies and campaigns.

Figure 3. AI Vs ML Vs DL

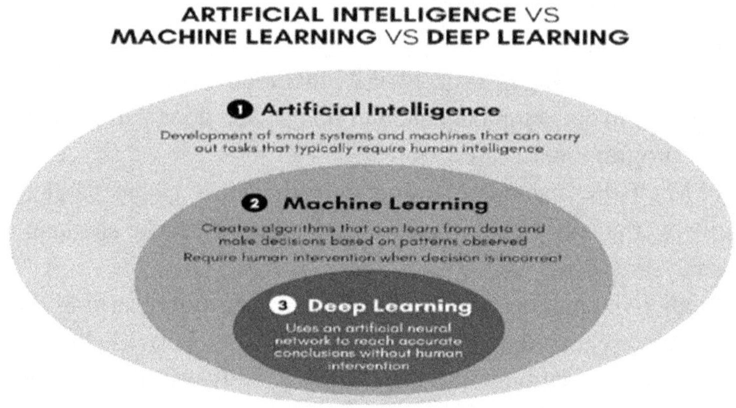

6.2 Conversational Marketing

Conversational marketing is a marketing strategy that focuses on engaging customers in personalized, real-time conversations to drive engagement, build relationships, and ultimately, convert leads into customers. It leverages various communication channels such as messaging apps, chatbots, live chat, and social media to facilitate one-on-one interactions between businesses and customers. Here's an overview of conversational marketing:

1. **Real-Time Interactions:** Conversational marketing enables businesses to engage with customers in real-time, providing immediate responses to their questions, concerns, or inquiries. This real-time interaction fosters a sense of immediacy and responsiveness, improving customer satisfaction and loyalty.
2. **Personalization:** Conversational marketing allows businesses to deliver personalized experiences to individual customers based on their preferences, behaviors, and past interactions. By leveraging data analytics and artificial intelligence (AI), businesses can tailor their messaging and recommendations to each customer's specific needs and interests, increasing the relevance and effectiveness of their marketing efforts.
3. **Engagement across Channels:** Conversational marketing spans multiple communication channels, including messaging apps (e.g., WhatsApp, Facebook Messenger), chatbots on websites, live chat support, and social media platforms. This omnichannel approach enables businesses to meet customers wherever they are and provide seamless experiences across different touch points.

4. **Lead Generation and Qualification:** Conversational marketing can be used to generate leads and qualify prospects through interactive conversations. By guiding customers through the sales funnel and asking targeted questions, businesses can identify qualified leads and nurture them towards conversion more effectively.
5. **Customer Support and Assistance:** Conversational marketing is not limited to sales and lead generation but also extends to customer support and assistance. Chatbots and live chat enable businesses to provide immediate help and support to customers, address their issues, and resolve their concerns in real-time, enhancing the overall customer experience.
6. **Data Collection and Insights:** Conversational marketing provides valuable data and insights into customer preferences, behaviours, and pain points. By analysing conversational data, businesses can gain a deeper understanding of their audience and uncover actionable insights to inform their marketing strategies and campaigns.
7. **Scalability and Efficiency:** Conversational marketing can be automated to scale interactions and handle a large volume of conversations simultaneously. Chatbots powered by AI and natural language processing (NLP) technology can engage with customers 24/7, providing consistent and efficient support while freeing up human agents to focus on more complex tasks.

Conversational marketing represents a shift towards more personalized, interactive, and customer-centric marketing approaches. By embracing conversational marketing strategies and leveraging technology to facilitate meaningful conversations with customers, businesses can build stronger relationships, drive engagement, and achieve better results in their marketing efforts.

6.3 Voice Search Optimization

Voice Search Optimization (VSO) is a digital marketing strategy aimed at optimizing content and online presence to improve visibility and ranking in voice search results. With the rise of voice-activated devices and virtual assistants like Siri, Alexa, Google Assistant, and Cortana, optimizing for voice search has become increasingly important for businesses looking to enhance their online presence and reach a wider audience. Here's an overview of Voice Search Optimization:

1. **Natural Language and Long-Tail Keywords:** Voice searches are typically longer and more conversational than text-based searches. Therefore, VSO involves targeting natural language and long-tail keywords that mimic how people speak

in everyday conversations. This includes using phrases and questions that users are likely to use when conducting voice searches.

2. **Featured Snippets and Position Zero:** Featured snippets, also known as position zero, are concise summaries of information that appear at the top of search engine results pages (SERPs). Optimizing content to appear in featured snippets increases the chances of being read aloud by voice assistants in response to voice queries. VSO strategies include structuring content to answer common questions concisely and clearly, thus increasing the likelihood of being featured in position zero.
3. **Local SEO Optimization:** Voice searches are often used for local queries, such as finding nearby businesses or services. Therefore, optimizing for local SEO is crucial for VSO. This includes creating and optimizing Google My Business listings, ensuring consistent NAP (Name, Address, Phone number) information across online directories, and optimizing website content with location-specific keywords.
4. **Mobile Optimization:** Since most voice searches are conducted on mobile devices, optimizing websites for mobile is essential for VSO. This includes ensuring fast loading times, mobile-friendly design, and easy navigation. Voice-friendly design elements, such as clear headings, bullet points, and structured data markup, can also improve the user experience for voice search users.
5. **Schema Markup and Structured Data:** Schema markup is a form of structured data that helps search engines understand the content of web pages better. By implementing schema markup, businesses can provide search engines with additional context about their content, making it more likely to be surfaced in voice search results.
6. **Content Optimization:** Creating high-quality, relevant, and authoritative content is essential for VSO. Content that directly answers common questions and provides valuable information is more likely to be featured in voice search results. VSO strategies include creating FAQ pages, how-to guides, and tutorials that address user queries and provide comprehensive answers.
7. **Voice Search Analytics:** Monitoring and analysing voice search data can provide valuable insights into user behaviour and preferences. By tracking voice search queries, businesses can identify trends, understand user intent, and tailor their VSO strategies accordingly.

Voice Search Optimization is a critical component of modern SEO strategies, as more users turn to voice-activated devices and virtual assistants to find information and conduct searches. By implementing VSO best practices and optimizing content for voice search, businesses can improve their visibility, attract more organic traffic, and stay ahead of the curve in the rapidly evolving digital landscape.

6.4 Predictive Analytics and Intent Data

Predictive analytics and intent data are powerful tools in the realm of Marketing Technology (MarTech), providing valuable insights into customer behaviour and preferences.

1. **Predictive Analytics:**
   - Predictive analytics involves the use of statistical algorithms and machine learning techniques to analyse historical data and predict future outcomes or trends.
   - In marketing, predictive analytics can be used to forecast customer behaviour, such as purchase intent, churn likelihood, and lifetime value. (See Fig. 4).
   - By analysing data from various sources, including website interactions, social media engagement, email interactions, and past purchase history, predictive analytics models can identify patterns and trends that indicate future actions or behaviours.
   - Predictive analytics enables marketers to segment audiences more effectively, personalize marketing messages, and target high-value customers with relevant offers and promotions.
   - Additionally, predictive analytics can optimize marketing campaigns by identifying the most effective channels, timing, and messaging to maximize ROI and conversions.

Figure 4. Website visitor analysis

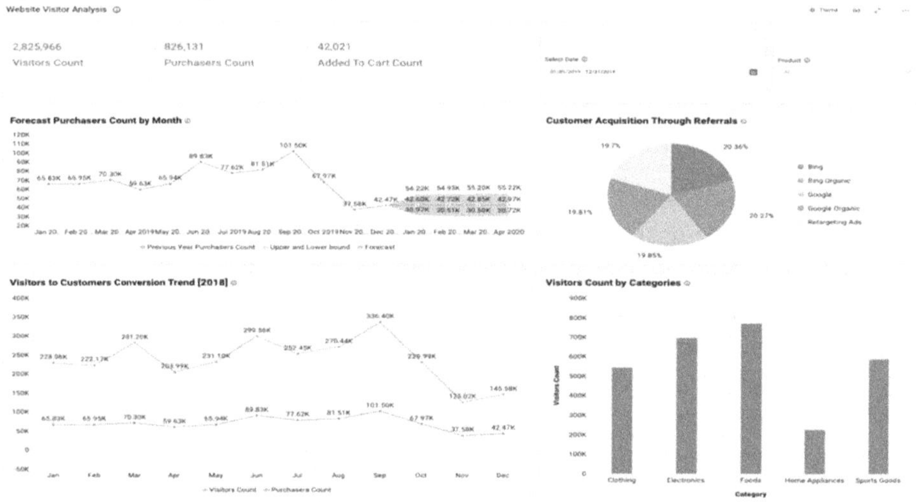

2. **Intent Data:**
    - Intent data refers to information collected from online activities that indicate a user's interest or intent to make a purchase or take a specific action.
    - Intent data can be sourced from various sources, including website visits, search queries, content downloads, social media interactions, and event registrations.
    - By analysing intent data, marketers can gain insights into the preferences, needs, and purchase intentions of their target audience.
    - Intent data can be used to personalize marketing messages, tailor product recommendations, and prioritize leads based on their likelihood to convert.
    - Intent data can also inform content marketing strategies, helping marketers create and distribute content that addresses the specific interests and pain points of their audience.
    - Additionally, intent data can be integrated with marketing automation platforms to trigger targeted campaigns and nurture leads based on their engagement and behaviour.

By leveraging predictive analytics and intent data, marketers can gain deeper insights into customer behaviour, improve targeting and personalization, and optimize marketing campaigns for better results. These technologies enable marketers to anticipate customer needs, deliver more relevant and timely messages, and ultimately drive higher engagement and conversions.

6.5 Customer Data Platforms (CDPs)

Customer Data Platforms (CDPs) are centralized systems designed to collect, unify, and manage customer data from various sources in order to create a comprehensive and unified customer profile. Here's a breakdown of the key components and functionalities of CDPs:

1. **Data Integration:**
    - CDPs collect data from a wide range of sources, including online and offline channels such as websites, mobile apps, CRM systems, email platforms, social media, point-of-sale systems, and more.
2. **Data Unification:**
    - Once collected, CDPs unify and standardize customer data from disparate sources, resolving data inconsistencies and merging duplicate records to create a single, comprehensive view of each customer.
3. **Identity Resolution:**
    - CDPs employ identity resolution techniques to match and merge customer data from different sources, using unique identifiers such as email addresses, phone numbers, cookies, device IDs, and customer IDs.
4. **Customer Profiles:**
    - CDPs create detailed customer profiles that include a wide range of attributes and insights about each individual customer, such as demographics, preferences, purchase history, interactions, behaviour, and engagement metrics.
5. **Segmentation and Audience Creation:**
    - CDPs enable marketers to segment their audience based on various criteria, such as demographics, behavior, interests, and purchase history. These segments can be used to target personalized marketing messages and campaigns to specific customer groups.
6. **Personalization:**
    - By leveraging the comprehensive customer profiles and segmentation capabilities of CDPs, marketers can deliver personalized experiences to their customers across multiple channels, including email, web, mobile, social media, and advertising.
7. **Real-Time Data Processing:**

- Many CDPs have the ability to process and analyze customer data in real-time, allowing businesses to respond quickly to customer interactions and deliver personalized experiences in the moment.

8. **Integration with Marketing Tools:**
   - CDPs integrate with a wide range of marketing tools and platforms, such as email marketing software, marketing automation platforms, CRM systems, content management systems (CMS), and advertising platforms, to enable seamless data sharing and activation.
9. **Data Governance and Compliance:**
   - CDPs provide tools and features for data governance, privacy management, and compliance with data protection regulations such as GDPR and CCPA, helping businesses ensure the security, privacy, and integrity of customer data.
10. **Analytics and Insights:**
    - CDPs offer built-in analytics and reporting capabilities that allow businesses to track and analyze customer behavior, measure campaign effectiveness, and gain insights into trends and patterns in customer data, helping them make data-driven decisions and optimize their marketing strategies.

Customer Data Platforms play a crucial role in helping businesses leverage their customer data to drive personalized marketing efforts, improve customer experiences, and ultimately, drive business growth and profitability.

6.6 Privacy and Compliance Solutions

Privacy and compliance solutions in the realm of Marketing Technology (MarTech) focus on ensuring that businesses adhere to data protection regulations and maintain the privacy and security of customer data. Here are some key components and functionalities of privacy and compliance solutions:

1. **Consent Management Platforms (CMPs):**
   - CMPs provide tools and features for managing user consent and preferences regarding data collection and processing activities. They enable businesses to obtain explicit consent from users for data collection and use, as required by regulations such as GDPR and CCPA.
   - CMPs typically include features such as consent banners or pop-ups, granular consent controls, preference centers, and mechanisms for capturing, storing, and managing user consent preferences.

Case: InnovateTech Inc., a growing technology company, effectively integrates various Marketing Technology (MarTech) components to boost marketing effectiveness. "Salesforce" manages customer interactions and data, while "Marketo" automates email and social media campaigns. "WordPress" handles content management, and "Google Analytics" and "Tableau" provide data insights for decision-making. "Segment" consolidates customer data for better targeting, "SEMrush" enhances SEO, and "Hootsuite" manages social media activities. Google Ads and The Trade Desk optimize digital advertising, and Dynamic Yield personalizes content based on user behavior. This integrated approach streamlines marketing processes and supports business growth.

2. **Data Governance and Compliance Tools:**
    - Data governance and compliance tools help businesses establish and enforce policies and procedures for managing customer data in compliance with applicable regulations and standards. They provide features for data classification, access control, data retention, data masking, and audit logging.
    - These tools enable businesses to ensure that customer data is handled responsibly, securely, and in accordance with legal and regulatory requirements.

Case: FinSecure Bank, a leading financial institution, has established a comprehensive data governance and compliance strategy to manage sensitive customer data in line with GDPR and CCPA regulations. The bank utilizes "Informatica Data Catalog" for effective data classification, categorizing information based on sensitivity, such as personal and financial records. To control data access, FinSecure Bank employs "Varonis Data Security Platform", which restricts access based on user roles, ensuring only authorized personnel can view sensitive information. The bank implements "Veeam Backup & Replication" software to enforce data retention policies, retaining records for the legally required period before securely deleting or archiving them. In non-production environments, "IBM InfoSphere Optim Data Privacy" is used to mask sensitive information like social security numbers and credit card details during testing. Additionally, "Splunk Enterprise Security" provides detailed audit logs of data access and modifications, facilitating compliance audits and security investigations. This integrated strategy enables FinSecure Bank to manage customer data responsibly while adhering to legal and regulatory standards.

3. **Privacy by Design Frameworks:**
    - Privacy by design frameworks promote the integration of privacy and data protection principles into the design and development of MarTech

solutions and systems. They encourage businesses to proactively consider privacy implications and implement privacy-enhancing features and controls from the outset.

- Privacy by design frameworks provide guidelines and best practices for incorporating privacy considerations into the entire lifecycle of MarTech products and services, from initial concept and design to implementation, operation, and decommissioning.

Case: TechSecure Solutions has implemented a Privacy by Design framework to integrate privacy and data protection throughout the lifecycle of its MarTech products. From the initial design phase, the company incorporates privacy principles, such as data encryption and anonymization, to mitigate risks. It embeds privacy controls like user consent mechanisms and secure data storage into its products. These measures are maintained during the product's operation and updated as needed. TechSecure Solutions also ensures that all data is securely deleted or anonymized during the decommissioning of products. This proactive approach helps TechSecure Solutions comply with regulations and build client trust by demonstrating a commitment to protecting user data.

4. **Data Minimization and Anonymisation Techniques:**
   - Data minimization and anonymisation techniques help businesses reduce the risk of data breaches and unauthorized access by limiting the collection, storage, and retention of personally identifiable information (PII).
   - These techniques involve anonymising or pseudonymising sensitive data to remove or obfuscate identifying information, thereby protecting the privacy of individuals while still allowing businesses to derive valuable insights from the data.

Case: Google, a global leader in technology and data analytics, employs rigorous data minimization and anonymization techniques to protect user privacy while leveraging data for its services. To adhere to data minimization principles, Google collects only the data necessary for the functionality of its services. For example, in its advertising and analytics platforms, Google limits the collection of personally identifiable information (PII) and focuses on gathering aggregated, non-identifiable data that helps in optimizing ad performance and improving user experience.

Google implements anonymization techniques to further safeguard user privacy. For instance, in Google Analytics, user IP addresses are anonymized by removing the last octet of the IP address before storage. This process ensures that individual users cannot be specifically identified from the data. Additionally, Google uses data pseudonymization methods, such as assigning unique identifiers to users, which helps in tracking and analyzing user behavior without directly exposing personal details.

These measures are complemented by robust security protocols, including encryption and stringent access controls, to protect data during storage and transmission. By integrating data minimization and anonymization practices, Google not only complies with privacy regulations such as the GDPR but also enhances user trust by demonstrating a commitment to protecting individual privacy while still deriving valuable insights from the data.

5. **Risk Assessment and Impact Analysis Tools:**
    - Risk assessment and impact analysis tools help businesses evaluate the potential risks and impacts of their data processing activities on individuals' privacy rights and freedoms. They enable businesses to identify and assess risks related to data breaches, unauthorized access, data loss, and non-compliance with regulations.
    - These tools provide frameworks, methodologies, and templates for conducting privacy impact assessments (PIAs) and data protection impact assessments (DPIAs) to identify, mitigate, and manage privacy risks effectively.

Case: IBM, a global leader in technology and consulting, utilizes its "IBM Security Guardium" suite to manage and mitigate privacy risks. This tool is crucial for conducting comprehensive risk assessments and impact analyses, helping IBM identify potential vulnerabilities related to data security. For example, when introducing a new data analytics platform, Guardium evaluates risks of unauthorized access and data breaches to ensure robust safeguards are in place. It also aids in Privacy Impact Assessments (PIAs) and Data Protection Impact Assessments (DPIAs), offering frameworks to assess the impact of data processing on privacy rights. By integrating these assessments, IBM can implement targeted risk mitigation strategies, such as enhanced encryption and access controls, ensuring compliance with regulations like GDPR and reinforcing its commitment to data protection.

6. **Training and Awareness Programs:**
    - Training and awareness programs educate employees and stakeholders about data protection regulations, privacy best practices, and their roles and responsibilities in safeguarding customer data.
    - These programs help raise awareness about privacy and compliance requirements, promote a culture of privacy and security within the organization, and empower employees to recognize and address privacy-related issues and concerns effectively.

6.7 Augmented Reality (AR) and Virtual Reality (VR)

Augmented Reality (AR) and Virtual Reality (VR) are immersive technologies that offer unique opportunities for businesses to engage with customers, showcase products and services, and create memorable experiences. Here's an overview of AR and VR and their applications in Marketing Technology (MarTech):

1. **Augmented Reality (AR):**
   - AR overlays digital content onto the real world, blending virtual elements with the user's physical environment in real-time.
   - In marketing, AR can be used to create interactive experiences that allow users to visualize products in their own space before making a purchase. For example, AR apps can enable users to try on virtual clothing or accessories, visualize furniture in their home, or preview how cosmetics will look on their face.
   - AR can also be used for location-based marketing, where virtual content is superimposed onto real-world locations. For example, businesses can create AR experiences that provide information about nearby points of interest or offer special promotions when users scan specific objects or locations.
2. **Virtual Reality (VR):**
   - VR immerses users in a completely virtual environment, blocking out the real world and replacing it with a simulated digital environment.
   - In marketing, VR can be used to create immersive brand experiences, virtual tours, or product demonstrations. For example, businesses can create VR experiences that allow users to explore a virtual store, take a virtual tour of a hotel or resort, or test drive a car from the comfort of their own home.
   - VR can also be used for training and education purposes, where users can learn new skills or concepts in a virtual environment. For example, businesses can use VR to train employees on complex procedures or provide virtual tours of manufacturing facilities.
3. **Applications in MarTech:**
   - AR and VR technologies are increasingly being integrated into MarTech solutions to enhance customer engagement and drive conversions.
   - Businesses can create AR and VR experiences as part of their marketing campaigns, allowing users to interact with products or services in a more immersive and engaging way.

- AR and VR can also be used to create branded experiences or sponsored content within existing AR and VR applications, such as social media platforms or gaming apps.
- Marketers can use AR and VR analytics to track user engagement, interactions, and conversions within AR and VR experiences, providing valuable insights into user behaviour and preferences.

AR and VR offer exciting opportunities for businesses to create immersive and engaging marketing experiences that captivate audiences, drive brand awareness, and ultimately, drive sales and conversions. By leveraging AR and VR technologies in their MarTech strategies, businesses can differentiate themselves from competitors, enhance customer engagement, and create memorable brand experiences that leave a lasting impression on their audience.

6.8 Cross-Channel Orchestration

Cross-channel orchestration refers to the process of seamlessly coordinating and synchronizing marketing activities across multiple channels and touchpoints to deliver a unified and cohesive customer experience. It involves integrating data, content, and interactions across various channels, such as email, social media, mobile, web, and offline, to create consistent and personalized experiences for customers throughout their journey. Here's a closer look at cross-channel orchestration and its significance in Marketing Technology (MarTech):

1. **Unified Customer Experience:**
   - Cross-channel orchestration aims to provide customers with a seamless and consistent experience across all channels and touchpoints. By integrating data and interactions from multiple channels, businesses can ensure that customers receive relevant and personalized messages regardless of the channel they use.
2. **Customer Journey Mapping:**
   - Cross-channel orchestration involves mapping the customer journey across different channels and identifying key touchpoints where customers interact with the brand. By understanding the customer journey, businesses can optimize their marketing strategies and deliver timely and relevant messages at each stage of the journey.
3. **Data Integration and Customer Insights:**
   - Cross-channel orchestration requires integrating data from various sources, including CRM systems, marketing automation platforms, website analytics, and social media platforms, to create a unified view

of the customer. By leveraging customer data and insights, businesses can better understand customer behavior, preferences, and needs, and tailor their marketing messages accordingly.

4. **Personalization and Targeting:**
   - Cross-channel orchestration enables businesses to deliver personalized and targeted messages to customers based on their preferences, behaviors, and interactions across different channels. By segmenting audiences and tailoring messages to specific customer segments, businesses can increase engagement, conversion rates, and customer loyalty.
5. **Automation and Optimization:**
   - Cross-channel orchestration often involves using marketing automation tools and platforms to automate and optimize marketing activities across multiple channels. By automating repetitive tasks, such as email campaigns, social media posts, and website content updates, businesses can streamline their marketing processes and improve efficiency.
6. **Measurement and Attribution:**
   - Cross-channel orchestration requires robust measurement and attribution capabilities to track the performance of marketing activities across different channels and evaluate their impact on business outcomes. By measuring key metrics such as engagement, conversions, and ROI, businesses can optimize their marketing strategies and allocate resources effectively.

Cross-channel orchestration requires robust measurement and attribution capabilities to track the performance of marketing activities across different channels and evaluate their impact on business outcomes. By measuring key metrics such as engagement, conversions, and ROI, businesses can optimize their marketing strategies and allocate resources effectively.

7. CASE STUDIES OF SUCCESSFUL MARTECH IMPLEMENTATIONS

7.1 Netflix: Personalized Recommendations with Machine Learning

Netflix, the world's leading streaming entertainment service, uses machine learning algorithms to power its personalized recommendation engine. By analyzing user data such as viewing history, preferences, and interactions, Netflix generates personalized recommendations for each user, helping them discover new content tailored to their tastes.

The implementation of this MarTech solution has significantly improved user engagement, retention, and satisfaction on the platform. Netflix estimates that its recommendation engine saves the company over $1 billion per year in customer retention costs by keeping subscribers engaged and reducing churn.

Through continuous experimentation and optimization, Netflix continues to refine its recommendation algorithms to deliver increasingly relevant and personalized content recommendations to its users, driving continued growth and success for the platform.

7.2 Amazon: Dynamic Pricing and Personalized Offers

Amazon, the world's largest online retailer, leverages MarTech solutions to implement dynamic pricing strategies and deliver personalized offers to its customers. Using data analytics and machine learning algorithms, Amazon dynamically adjusts product prices based on factors such as demand, competitor pricing, and user behavior.

Additionally, Amazon uses personalized recommendations and targeted promotions to upsell and cross-sell products to customers based on their browsing and purchase history. These personalized offers are displayed prominently on the Amazon website and in marketing emails, driving increased sales and customer satisfaction.

By implementing these MarTech solutions, Amazon has become a leader in e-commerce, driving revenue growth and maintaining its position as the dominant player in the industry.

7.3 Starbucks: Mobile App and Loyalty Program

Starbucks, the global coffeehouse chain, has successfully implemented MarTech solutions to enhance its mobile app and loyalty program. The Starbucks mobile app allows customers to order and pay for drinks ahead of time, earn rewards for purchases, and receive personalized offers and recommendations.

By leveraging data analytics and machine learning, Starbucks analyzes customer behavior and preferences to deliver personalized offers and promotions to app users. These personalized offers help drive repeat purchases and increase customer loyalty.

The Starbucks mobile app and loyalty program have been instrumental in driving digital sales growth and increasing customer engagement. As of 2021, the Starbucks Rewards program had over 23 million active members, contributing to the company's overall success and profitability.

These case studies demonstrate the power of MarTech solutions in driving business growth, improving customer experiences, and achieving strategic objectives. By leveraging data analytics, machine learning, and personalization techniques, companies like Netflix, Amazon, and Starbucks have been able to stay ahead of the competition and deliver value to their customers in innovative ways.

8. OPPORTUNITIES FOR INNOVATION AND DIFFERENTIATION

In today's highly competitive marketplace, businesses must continuously innovate and differentiate themselves to stand out and capture the attention of customers. Here are some opportunities for innovation and differentiation that businesses can explore:

1. **Product Innovation:**
    - Continuously innovate and improve products to meet evolving customer needs and preferences.
    - Incorporate cutting-edge technologies, such as AI, IoT, and AR/VR, to enhance product features, functionality, and user experience.
    - Offer unique features, customization options, or value-added services that differentiate your products from competitors.
2. **Customer Experience (CX) Innovation:**
    - Focus on delivering exceptional customer experiences at every touchpoint of the customer journey.
    - Leverage technology to create seamless, personalized, and omnichannel experiences that delight customers and foster long-term loyalty.
    - Invest in customer service, support, and engagement initiatives to provide proactive assistance, resolve issues promptly, and exceed customer expectations.
3. **Marketing Innovation:**
    - Experiment with new marketing channels, tactics, and strategies to reach and engage with customers in innovative ways.
    - Embrace content marketing, influencer marketing, and experiential marketing to create memorable and shareable brand experiences.
    - Leverage data analytics, AI, and machine learning to personalize marketing messages, optimize campaigns, and deliver targeted offers and recommendations.
4. **Business Model Innovation:**
    - Explore alternative business models, such as subscription-based services, freemium models, or platform-based ecosystems, to create new revenue streams and capture market opportunities.

- Collaborate with partners, suppliers, or customers to co-create value and differentiate your offerings in the marketplace.
- Embrace digital transformation initiatives to digitize processes, streamline operations, and enhance agility and responsiveness to market changes.

5. **Sustainability and Social Responsibility:**
   - Differentiate your brand by integrating sustainability and social responsibility into your business practices and offerings.
   - Implement eco-friendly initiatives, reduce carbon footprint, and promote responsible sourcing and manufacturing practices.
   - Engage in corporate social responsibility (CSR) activities, support social causes, and contribute to the well-being of communities, demonstrating your commitment to making a positive impact beyond profit.
6. **Employee Innovation and Empowerment:**
   - Foster a culture of innovation and creativity within your organization by empowering employees to share ideas, experiment with new approaches, and drive change.
   - Encourage continuous learning and professional development to equip employees with the skills and knowledge needed to innovate and adapt to evolving market dynamics.
   - Recognize and reward innovation, initiative, and entrepreneurial spirit to inspire a culture of innovation and differentiation at all levels of the organization.

9. KEY CONSIDERATIONS WHEN SELECTING MARTECH SOLUTIONS

Selecting the right Marketing Technology (MarTech) solutions is crucial for businesses to effectively execute their marketing strategies, streamline operations, and drive growth. Here are some key considerations to keep in mind when evaluating and selecting MarTech solutions:

1. **Alignment with Business Goals:**
   - Ensure that the MarTech solutions align with your business objectives, marketing strategies, and overall goals.
   - Identify specific challenges, pain points, or opportunities that the MarTech solutions are intended to address and evaluate how well they meet your business needs.
2. **Scalability and Flexibility:**

- Consider the scalability and flexibility of the MarTech solutions to accommodate future growth, changes in business requirements, and evolving market dynamics.
- Choose solutions that can scale with your business, adapt to changing needs, and integrate with existing systems and processes.

3. **Ease of Use and Implementation:**
   - Evaluate the ease of use and implementation of the MarTech solutions to ensure smooth adoption by users and minimize disruptions to operations.
   - Look for intuitive user interfaces, comprehensive documentation, and vendor support services to facilitate implementation and user training.
4. **Compatibility and Integration:**
   - Assess the compatibility and integration capabilities of the MarTech solutions with existing systems, platforms, and workflows within your organization.
   - Choose solutions that seamlessly integrate with your CRM, CMS, email marketing software, analytics tools, and other key systems to ensure data consistency and workflow efficiency.
5. **Data Security and Compliance:**
   - Prioritize data security and compliance requirements when selecting MarTech solutions, especially when handling sensitive customer data.
   - Ensure that the solutions comply with relevant regulations such as GDPR, CCPA, HIPAA, or industry-specific standards for data protection and privacy.
6. **Vendor Reputation and Reliability:**
   - Research the reputation, track record, and reliability of MarTech vendors before making a decision.
   - Consider factors such as vendor stability, financial viability, customer references, and user reviews to assess the credibility and trustworthiness of potential vendors.
7. **Cost and ROI:**
   - Evaluate the total cost of ownership (TCO) and return on investment (ROI) of the MarTech solutions, including upfront costs, ongoing maintenance fees, and potential revenue or cost savings.
   - Consider both short-term and long-term value propositions, and weigh the benefits of the solutions against their costs to determine the overall ROI.
8. **Support and Service Level Agreements (SLAs):**
   - Assess the level of support, maintenance, and ongoing services offered by MarTech vendors, including technical support, training, and updates.

- Review service level agreements (SLAs) to ensure timely resolution of issues, guaranteed uptime, and quality of service commitments.

10. LONG-TERM PLANNING FOR SUSTAINABLE MARTECH SUCCESS

Long-term planning is essential for ensuring sustainable success with Marketing Technology (MarTech). Here are some key steps to consider when developing a long-term strategy for MarTech success:

1. **Define Clear Objectives and Goals:**
    - Establish clear, measurable objectives and goals for your MarTech initiatives, aligned with your overall business strategy and marketing objectives.
    - Define key performance indicators (KPIs) and benchmarks to track progress and evaluate the success of your MarTech investments over time.
2. **Assess Current State and Identify Gaps:**
    - Conduct a comprehensive assessment of your current MarTech ecosystem, including existing systems, processes, and capabilities.
    - Identify areas of strength and weaknesses, as well as gaps and opportunities for improvement or optimization.
3. **Develop a Long-Term MarTech Roadmap:**
    - Create a long-term roadmap outlining your strategic priorities, initiatives, and milestones for MarTech implementation and evolution.
    - Prioritize initiatives based on their alignment with business objectives, potential impact, and feasibility, considering factors such as resource constraints and dependencies.
4. **Invest in Scalable and Flexible Solutions:**
    - Invest in MarTech solutions that are scalable and flexible enough to adapt to changing business needs, market dynamics, and technological advancements over time.
    - Consider cloud-based platforms, modular architectures, and open APIs that allow for easy integration, customization, and expansion as your business grows.
5. **Build a Data-Driven Culture:**
    - Foster a data-driven culture within your organization, emphasizing the importance of data integrity, analysis, and insights in decision-making processes.

- Invest in data governance, quality assurance, and literacy initiatives to ensure that data is accurate, accessible, and actionable for stakeholders across the organization.

6. **Continuously Evaluate and Iterate:**
   - Continuously monitor and evaluate the performance of your MarTech initiatives against established KPIs and benchmarks.
   - Solicit feedback from stakeholders, users, and customers to identify areas for improvement and optimization, and iterate on your MarTech strategy and roadmap accordingly.
7. **Promote Collaboration and Alignment:**
   - Foster collaboration and alignment between marketing, IT, sales, customer service, and other relevant departments to ensure that MarTech initiatives are aligned with business objectives and priorities.
   - Establish cross-functional teams or steering committees to oversee MarTech implementation, governance, and adoption, and facilitate communication and coordination across departments.
8. **Invest in Talent and Training:**
   - Invest in hiring and developing talent with the skills and expertise required to effectively leverage MarTech solutions and drive innovation.
   - Provide ongoing training, education, and professional development opportunities to empower employees with the knowledge and skills needed to succeed in a rapidly evolving MarTech landscape.

11. IMPLICATIONS FOR THE FUTURE OF MARTECH

The future of Marketing Technology (MarTech) holds significant implications for businesses, marketers, and consumers alike. Here are some key implications for the future of MarTech:

1. **Advancements in Artificial Intelligence (AI) and Machine Learning (ML):**
   - AI and ML will continue to play a pivotal role in MarTech, enabling more sophisticated data analysis, predictive modeling, and personalized marketing experiences.
   - AI-powered chatbots (see fig. 5), virtual assistants, and recommendation engines will become more intelligent and capable of delivering hyper-personalized interactions and recommendations to customers.

Figure 5. Chatbot

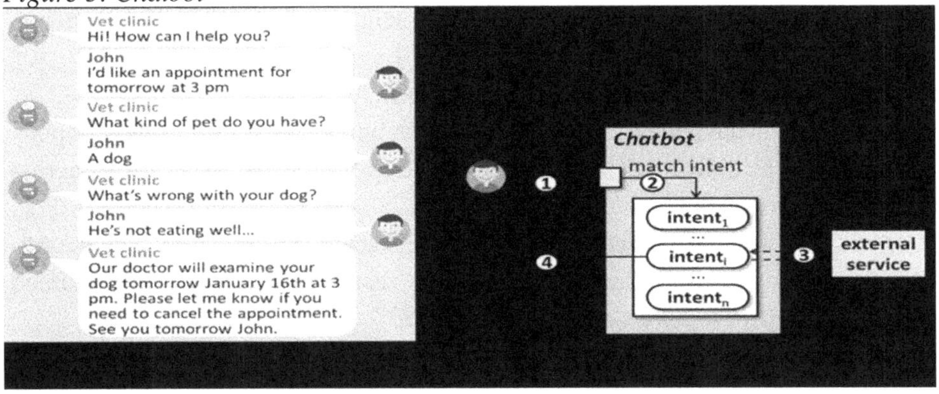

2. **Integration of Emerging Technologies:**
    - Emerging technologies such as augmented reality (AR), virtual reality (VR), and voice assistants will be increasingly integrated into MarTech solutions to create immersive and interactive brand experiences.
    - AR and VR technologies will enable businesses to showcase products, provide virtual try-on experiences, and offer virtual tours, enhancing customer engagement and conversion rates.
3. **Data Privacy and Compliance Regulations:**
    - With growing concerns about data privacy and security, there will be greater emphasis on compliance with regulations such as GDPR, CCPA, and other data protection laws.
    - MarTech solutions will need to prioritize data privacy and transparency, implement robust security measures, and provide users with greater control over their data.
4. **Shift Towards Customer-Centric Marketing:**
    - There will be a continued shift towards customer-centric marketing strategies, focusing on delivering personalized, relevant, and seamless experiences across all touchpoints.
    - MarTech solutions will need to enable marketers to better understand customer preferences, behaviors, and journeys, and deliver targeted messages and offers that resonate with individual customers.
5. **Rise of Account-Based Marketing (ABM):**
    - Account-Based Marketing (ABM) will gain traction as businesses seek to target and engage key accounts and high-value customers more effectively.

- MarTech platforms will need to support ABM strategies by providing tools for account identification, segmentation, personalized messaging, and account-based analytics.

6. **Emphasis on Omnichannel Orchestration:**
    - Omnichannel marketing orchestration will become increasingly important as consumers expect consistent and cohesive experiences across multiple channels and devices.
    - MarTech solutions will need to enable seamless integration and coordination of marketing activities across channels, ensuring a unified brand experience for customers.
7. **Demand for Data-driven Insights and Analytics:**
    - There will be a growing demand for advanced data analytics and insights capabilities to derive actionable intelligence from vast amounts of data.
    - MarTech platforms will need to offer robust analytics tools, visualization dashboards, and predictive modeling capabilities to help marketers make data-driven decisions and optimize campaign performance.

The future of MarTech will be characterized by advancements in AI and emerging technologies, greater emphasis on data privacy and compliance, a shift towards customer-centric marketing, the rise of ABM, omnichannel orchestration, and increased demand for data-driven insights and analytics. Businesses that embrace these trends and leverage innovative MarTech solutions will be well-positioned to succeed in an increasingly competitive and dynamic marketing landscape.

12. CONCLUSION

Marketing Technology (MarTech) has evolved rapidly, reshaping the way businesses engage with customers, execute marketing strategies, and drive growth. From the early days of basic email marketing and web analytics to today's sophisticated AI-powered platforms and immersive experiences, MarTech has become an indispensable tool for marketers in today's digital age.

Throughout this journey, we've explored the historical development of MarTech, key milestones, emerging trends, and the impact of cutting-edge technologies such as AI, AR/VR, and data analytics. We've also discussed the importance of cross-channel orchestration, personalization, and data-driven decision-making in modern marketing strategies.

Looking ahead, the future of MarTech holds exciting opportunities and challenges. As technology continues to advance and consumer expectations evolve, businesses must stay agile, innovative, and customer-centric to succeed in an increasingly competitive landscape. By embracing emerging technologies, prioritizing data privacy and compliance, and focusing on delivering exceptional customer experiences, businesses can harness the power of MarTech to drive sustainable growth and achieve their business objectives.

MarTech is not just a set of tools or platforms—it's a strategic imperative that empowers businesses to connect with customers, build relationships, and drive results in today's digital-first world. As MarTech continues to evolve, businesses that prioritize innovation, collaboration, and customer-centricity will be well-positioned to thrive in the ever-changing marketing landscape.

13. SCOPE FOR FURTHER RESEARCH

The future of MarTech offers a fertile ground for further research across several dimensions. Future research could explore the long-term effects of AI and machine learning on marketing practices, investigating how these technologies influence consumer behavior, campaign effectiveness, and overall marketing ROI. As businesses adopt more MarTech tools, understanding the challenges and best practices for integrating these tools into existing systems is crucial. Research could focus on developing frameworks for seamless integration and exploring the role of interoperability standards. With increasing concerns over data privacy and security, future studies could examine the ethical implications of MarTech, including the development of ethical guidelines for data usage, strategies for ensuring compliance with regulations, and the impact of privacy concerns on consumer trust. While personalization is a key benefit of MarTech, it often conflicts with privacy concerns; thus, research could investigate the balance between delivering personalized experiences and respecting user privacy, as well as consumer attitudes towards data collection and personalization. One of the ongoing challenges in marketing is accurately measuring the impact of various channels and tactics. Future research could focus on improving measurement and attribution models in a multi-channel environment, particularly with the rise of new digital touchpoints. As automation and AI become more prevalent, understanding the dynamics of human-machine collaboration in marketing teams is essential. Research could explore how marketers can best leverage automated tools while maintaining the creative and strategic elements of their roles. Investigating the factors that influence the adoption and diffusion of new MarTech innovations across different industries and regions can provide insights into how businesses can more effectively embrace these technologies. Longitudinal studies tracking the impact of MarTech on business performance over time could provide valuable insights into the sustainability of benefits and the evolution of marketing practices in response to technological advancements. By addressing these areas, future research can contribute to a deeper understanding of how MarTech continues to transform the marketing landscape and provide practical guidance for businesses looking to leverage these technologies for competitive advantage.

REFERENCES

AdRoll. (2021). How marketing technology can give you a competitive advantage. Retrieved from https://www.adroll.com/blog/how-marketing-technology-can-give-you-a-competitive-advantage

AdRoll. (2021). How marketing technology can give you a competitive advantage. Retrieved from https://www.adroll.com/blog/how-marketing-technology-can-give-you-a-competitive-advantage

Brinker, S. (2018). The current state of marketing technology. *Journal of Marketing Management*, 34(7-8), 653–667. DOI: 10.1080/0267257X.2018.1455172

Business2Community. (2021). How MarTech can scale with your business. Retrieved from https://www.business2community.com/marketing/how-martech-can-scale-with-your-business-02245731

Business2Community. (2021). How MarTech can scale with your business. Retrieved from https://www.business2community.com/marketing/how-martech-can-scale-with-your-business-02245731

Chaffey, D., & Smith, P. R. (2017). *Digital marketing excellence: Planning, optimizing and integrating online marketing*. Taylor & Francis. DOI: 10.4324/9781315640341

Chiefmartec. (2021). The 10-year horizon of MarTech. Retrieved from https://chiefmartec.com/2021/01/the-10-year-horizon-of-martech-2021-2030/

Chiefmartec. (2021). The 10-year horizon of MarTech. Retrieved from https://chiefmartec.com/2021/01/the-10-year-horizon-of-martech-2021-2030/

CIO. (2020). Using marketing analytics to measure and improve your marketing. Retrieved from https://www.cio.com/article/289229/using-marketing-analytics-to-measure-and-improve-your-marketing.html

CIO. (2020). Using marketing analytics to measure and improve your marketing. Retrieved from https://www.cio.com/article/289229/using-marketing-analytics-to-measure-and-improve-your-marketing.html

Council, C. M. O. (2021). The MarTech disconnect. Retrieved from https://www.cmocouncil.org/thought-leadership/reports/the-martech-disconnect

Council, C. M. O. (2021). The MarTech disconnect. Retrieved from https://www.cmocouncil.org/thought-leadership/reports/the-martech-disconnect

Davenport, T., Guha, A., Grewal, D., & Bressgott, T. (2020). How artificial intelligence will change the future of marketing. *Journal of the Academy of Marketing Science*, 48(1), 24–42. DOI: 10.1007/s11747-019-00696-0

Forbes. (2020). How marketing technology can provide a competitive edge. Retrieved from https://www.forbes.com/sites/forbestechcouncil/2020/11/18/how-marketing-technology-can-provide-a-competitive-edge/

Forbes. (2020). How marketing technology can provide a competitive edge. Retrieved from https://www.forbes.com/sites/forbestechcouncil/2020/11/18/how-marketing-technology-can-provide-a-competitive-edge/

Forbes. (2021). The role of marketing technology in 2021 and beyond. Retrieved from https://www.forbes.com/sites/forbestechcouncil/2021/02/08/the-role-of-marketing-technology-in-2021-and-beyond/

Forbes. (2021). The role of marketing technology in 2021 and beyond. Retrieved from https://www.forbes.com/sites/forbestechcouncil/2021/02/08/the-role-of-marketing-technology-in-2021-and-beyond/

Gartner. (2021). 5 ways to improve customer experience with marketing technology. Retrieved from https://www.gartner.com/en/marketing/insights/articles/5-ways-to-improve-customer-experience-with-marketing-technology

Gartner. (2021). 5 ways to improve customer experience with marketing technology. Retrieved from https://www.gartner.com/en/marketing/insights/articles/5-ways-to-improve-customer-experience-with-marketing-technology

Holliman, G., & Rowley, J. (2014). Business to business digital content marketing: Marketers' perceptions of best practice. *Journal of Research in Interactive Marketing*, 8(4), 269–293. DOI: 10.1108/JRIM-02-2014-0013

HubSpot. (2023). Why marketing technology is important. Retrieved from https://blog.hubspot.com/marketing/why-marketing-technology-important

HubSpot. (2023). Marketing automation tools. Retrieved from https://blog.hubspot.com/marketing/marketing-automation-tools

HubSpot. (2023). Marketing automation tools. Retrieved from https://blog.hubspot.com/marketing/marketing-automation-tools

HubSpot. (2023). Why marketing technology is important. Retrieved from https://blog.hubspot.com/marketing/why-marketing-technology-important

Kumar, V., Rajan, B., Gupta, S., & Pozza, I. D. (2021). Customer engagement in service. *Journal of Service Research*, 24(1), 7–10. DOI: 10.1177/1094670520975793

Marketing Evolution. (2021). Marketing technology. Retrieved from https://www.marketingevolution.com/marketing-essentials/marketing-technology

Marketing Evolution. (2021). Marketing technology. Retrieved from https://www.marketingevolution.com/marketing-essentials/marketing-technology

MarketingProfs. (2020). How to use marketing automation to improve productivity and efficiency. Retrieved from https://www.marketingprofs.com/articles/2020/43254/how-to-use-marketing-automation-to-improve-productivity-and-efficiency

MarketingProfs. (2020). How to use marketing automation to improve productivity and efficiency. Retrieved from https://www.marketingprofs.com/articles/2020/43254/how-to-use-marketing-automation-to-improve-productivity-and-efficiency

MarTech. (2023). What is MarTech and why should it matter to you. Retrieved from https://martech.org/what-is-martech-and-why-should-it-matter-to-you/

MarTech. (2023). What is MarTech and why should it matter to you. Retrieved from https://martech.org/what-is-martech-and-why-should-it-matter-to-you/

Martech Series. (2020). Scalability and flexibility: Key MarTech systems for digital business. Retrieved from https://martechseries.com/mts-insights/guest-authors/scalability-flexibility-key-martech-systems-digital-business/

Martech Series. (2020). Scalability and flexibility: Key MarTech systems for digital business. Retrieved from https://martechseries.com/mts-insights/guest-authors/scalability-flexibility-key-martech-systems-digital-business/

Rust, R. T., & Espinoza, F. (2006). How technology advances influence business research and marketing strategy. *Journal of Business Research*, 59(10-11), 1072–1078. DOI: 10.1016/j.jbusres.2006.08.002

Salesforce. (2023). Marketing cloud overview. Retrieved from https://www.salesforce.com/products/marketing-cloud/overview/

Salesforce. (2023). Marketing cloud overview. Retrieved from https://www.salesforce.com/products/marketing-cloud/overview/

Sheth, J. N., & Sharma, A. (2020). The impact of the product to service shift in industrial markets and the evolution of the sales organization. *Industrial Marketing Management*, 49, 1–12. DOI: 10.1016/j.indmarman.2015.05.026

Smart Insights. (2023). What is marketing technology and why is it so important. Retrieved from https://www.smartinsights.com/digital-marketing-strategy/what-is-marketing-technology-and-why-is-it-so-important/

Smart Insights. (2023). What is marketing technology and why is it so important. Retrieved from https://www.smartinsights.com/digital-marketing-strategy/what-is-marketing-technology-and-why-is-it-so-important/

Wedel, M., & Kannan, P. K. (2016). Marketing analytics for data-rich environments. *Journal of Marketing*, 80(6), 97–121. DOI: 10.1509/jm.15.0413

ADDITIONAL READINGS

Acquisti, A., Brandimarte, L., & Loewenstein, G. (2015). Privacy and human behavior in the age of information. *Science*, 347(6221), 509–514. DOI: 10.1126/science.aaa1465 PMID: 25635091

Berman, S. J., & Marshall, A. (2014). The next digital transformation: From an individual-centered world to the Internet of Everything. *Strategy and Leadership*, 42(5), 9–17. DOI: 10.1108/SL-07-2014-0048

Brynjolfsson, E., & McAfee, A. (2014). *The second machine age: Work, progress, and prosperity in a time of brilliant technologies*. W.W. Norton & Company.

Davenport, T. H. (2013). *Process innovation: Reengineering work through information technology*. Harvard Business Press.

Kotler, P., Kartajaya, H., & Setiawan, I. (2017). *Marketing 4.0: Moving from traditional to digital*. John Wiley & Sons.

Li, H., Edwards, S. M., & Lee, J. H. (2002). Measuring the intrusiveness of advertisements: Scale development and validation. *Journal of Advertising*, 31(2), 37–47. DOI: 10.1080/00913367.2002.10673665

Martin, K. (2015). Ethical issues in the big data industry. *MIS Quarterly Executive*, 14(2), 67–85. DOI: 10.17705/2msqe.00029

Pauwels, K. (2014). It's not the size, it's how you use it: Toward a theory of the use of marketing metrics. *Journal of Marketing Management*, 30(3-4), 246–270. DOI: 10.1080/0267257X.2013.798675

Solove, D. J. (2013). *Understanding privacy*. Harvard University Press.

Tafti, A., Mithas, S., & Krishnan, M. S. (2013). The effect of information technology-enabled flexibility on the outsourcing of services. *Management Science*, 59(1), 177–195. DOI: 10.1287/mnsc.1120.1579

Tucker, C. E. (2014). Social networks, personalized advertising, and privacy controls. *JMR, Journal of Marketing Research*, 51(5), 546–562. DOI: 10.1509/jmr.10.0355

Wilson, H. J., & Daugherty, P. R. (2018). Collaborative intelligence: Humans and AI are joining forces. *Harvard Business Review*, 96(4), 114–123.

Chapter 6
The Influence of Positions, Theme Congruence, and Context Congruence on the Effectiveness of In-Stream Advertising

Duong Nguyen Thuy Tran
https://orcid.org/0009-0004-1748-7676
Swinburne University, Vietnam

ABSTRACT

Online video advertising has surged alongside the growth of online video consumption, blending traditional branding with interactive potential. This study evaluates the effectiveness of in-stream video ads based on position, theme congruence, and context congruence. It aims to identify impactful conditions and positions for ads and assess their impact on memory, attitude, and purchase intention. The research reviews prior literature on in-stream advertising, congruence, and position effects, hypothesizing that congruence enhances ad effectiveness, while position influences ad recall and viewer engagement. Empirical research involving 80 respondents in April 2024 confirms these hypotheses, revealing that incongruent ads at the beginning enhance logo recall, while congruent ads improve product awareness. Thematic congruence with context incongruence at video start and end elicits the most positive viewer attitudes and desires. The findings offer insights for marketers to optimize in-stream ad effectiveness based on desired outcomes and placement considerations.

DOI: 10.4018/979-8-3693-4361-6.ch006

INTRODUCTION

Research Background

As the popularity of online video consumption continues to soar, the online video advertising sector experiences parallel growth. This expansion reflects the dynamic nature of the online advertising market, which adapts to shifting consumer preferences and technological advancements (McCoy et al., 2017).

The rapid development of information technology has revolutionized the way consumers access information across diverse media platforms. Consequently, advertisements have evolved beyond mere informational content to prioritize consumer engagement (Yoon & Lee, 2022). A notable evolution in this regard is the transition from static display ads to interactive audio-visual formats, giving rise to online video advertising (Belanche et al., 2017). Online video ads are renowned for their efficacy, blending the branding impact of traditional broadcast advertising with the interactive potential of the web (J. Lee & Lee, 2012). Moreover, online advertising is cost-efficient (Pergelova et al., 2010) and gains high attention (Chaffey & Ellis-Chadwick, 2019). It allows personalized messages, enhancing relevance and purchase intentions (Goldfarb & Tucker, 2011; Truong et al., 2010). According to Lee and Lee (2012), there are two different kinds of online video advertisements: those that are posted on their own and include loop control features, and those that are contained within other online video clips but do not. The second kind of online video advertising that will be the subject of this study is known as in-stream advertising.

However, Yoon and Lee (2022) claimed that despite their effectiveness, online video ads face challenges inherent to the digital landscape, such as the ability for viewers to skip ads. While these ads target similar sensory systems as traditional TV commercials, they operate within a more attention-demanding media environment (Li & Lo, 2015). Consequently, advertisers strive to create attention-grabbing concepts to enhance consumer engagement, but, in addition to the attractiveness of the content itself, the impact of processed environment on the processing and assessment of marketing communications has long been acknowledged by academics (De Pelsmacker et al., 2002).

This leads to the question of what conditions would be most effective in terms of memory, attitude, and purchase intention for video ads to appear. The purpose of this study is to evaluate the effectiveness of video ads based on a combination of 3 factors: positions (pre-roll, mid-roll, or post-roll), theme congruence (theme congruity or theme incongruity), and context congruence (context congruity or context incongruity). The following brief summarizes the research problem, research objectives, and research questions:

Research Problem: The influence of positions, theme congruence, and context congruence on the effectiveness of in-stream advertising

Research Objectives

The main objective of this current study is to determine the impact of 3 external factors on the effectiveness of in-stream advertising.

- To determine the condition to have the best effect.
- To ascertain the position to have the most impact.
- To identify the context to have the most success.
- To discover the theme to have the greatest influence.

Research Questions

Considering the aforementioned issue, the research question that follows has been developed for this investigation.

- RQ1: What is the most effective in-stream ad condition to influence customers?
- RQ2: For each position, which congruity conditions are most effective in terms of ad recall? For each congruity condition, which position is most effective in terms of ad recall?
- RQ3: For each position, which congruity conditions are most effective in terms of customers' attitude? For each congruity condition, which position is most effective in terms of customers' attitude?
- RQ4: For each position, which congruity conditions are most effective in terms of customers' desire? For each congruity condition, which position is most effective in terms of customers' desire?

There has been no research that simultaneously evaluates all three factors when it comes to the effectiveness of online ads, especially regarding the correlation of the arousing level of video ads with video context. This research issue is highly necessary as a conclusion needs to be drawn to summarize the influence of these three factors on advertising videos, providing companies with a deeper understanding, thereby helping them choose the most effective exposure conditions for their advertising.

LITERATURE REVIEW

In-Stream Video Advertising

In this study, online advertising comprises ads popping up when people are surfing the Internet (Kotler & Armstrong, 2018), and the concept of in-stream video advertisement applies to audio-visual video advertisements provoked within videos, according to Djafarova and Kramer (2019). In-stream video advertising varies in placement: pre-roll ads precede the video (Pre), mid-roll ads appear during playback (Mid), and post-roll ads conclude the video (Pos), according to Li and Lo (2015). As reported by Li and Lo (2015), what distinguishes in-stream video ads is their disruptive nature, making them challenging for users to ignore. They are strategically designed to command attention by interrupting the online viewing experience, although advertisers have the option to allow users to skip, minimize, or dismiss the ad after the initial five seconds to mitigate intrusiveness (Dehghani et al., 2016; Vernon, 2014). Li and Lo (2015) believed that this unique feature sets in-stream video advertising apart from other internet ad formats, providing advertisers with precise control over user engagement - a feat not easily achieved with banner or pop-up ads. Given their typically longer duration compared to pop-ups, understanding the effectiveness of in-stream video ads becomes crucial for marketers in making informed online advertising decisions. It's also important to note that in-stream video advertising interferes with viewers' viewing experience, causing them to feel irritated or annoyed and maybe engaging in ad avoidance behavior like zapping (Dix & Phau, 2017; Edwards et al., 2002; McCreery & Krugman, 2017).

Context and Theme Congruence

Congruity - also referred to as consistency or relevance - between advertising and their surroundings has been the subject of extensive investigation by several scholars (Bee & Madrigal, 2012; Moorman et al., 2002). Ad-context congruity, as defined by Zanjani et al. (2011), is the degree to which advertising content is conceptually consistent with adjoining journalistic material. In advertisements and media channels, this relationship refers to identical material, emotive execution approaches, or expressive tones (Feltham & Arnold, 1994; Kim & Sundar, 2010; Moore et al., 2005; Sharma, 2000). The level of congruence between the theme of the encircling amplified content and the promoted product category is known as ad-thematic congruence (Wang & Bailey, 2023). Therefore, in this study, the definition of context and theme congruence for video ad is borrowed partially from previous research about ad-content congruity and defined as the extent of alignment that exists between the advertisement and the communicated media in terms of arousing level (context) and product category (theme) (Li & Lo, 2015; Wang & Bailey, 2023). Divided into two parts including congruent and incongruent, this study evaluates thematic congruence (CT), thematic incongruence (IT), context congruence (CC), and context incongruence (IC).

Effectiveness of Advertising

According to Wright-Isak et al. (1997), the intention of effective advertising is to provide a concrete value to a business or brand that, over time, accumulates and influences the attitudes, feelings, as well as behaviors of the audience. Memory-based methods including recall and recognition of brands are considered the most widely used cognitive evaluation approaches, meanwhile the like and attitude toward an advertising and the marketed brand are typical affective indicators (Li & Lo, 2015; Martín-Santana & Beerli-Palacio, 2012). Aside from brand identification, other essential signals of advertising effectiveness include attitude and purchase intention toward businesses (Baltas, 2003; Hwang et al., 2011; Mehta, 1994). Therefore, this study focuses on three variables that have been demonstrated to consistently access higher-level structures frequently utilized in advertising research, according to Venkatraman et al. (2015), including memory - ad recall, affect - attitude toward ad, and desirability - purchase intention.

Firstly, memory is related to the mechanisms by which previous events influence behavior and is often associated with extraction, which takes place at a later stage (Walsh & Ungson, 1991). Recall characteristics are prioritized in advertising studies to evaluate the quality of the commercial (Zhang & Yuan, 2018). In this study, the ad recall will be assessed through remembering brand name, brand logo, and brand product. Secondly, a brief period of coordinated behavioral, physiological, and neurological alterations that promote reactions to important events is referred to as affect (Davidson, 2004). Brand impressions and assessments are important gauges of future purchases (Esch et al., 2006). Popular indicators for assessing promotional efficacy include attitude toward the advertisement, brand, and product. Lastly, according to Zhang and Yuan (2018), desirability is a measure of people's level of desire for the product that is the topic of the ad. Determinants of intent to buy are often relied upon by marketing managers because to their substantial correlation with attractiveness and following consumer behavior (Venkatraman et al., 2015). Therefore, the intention to search and buy are two measures to evaluate desirability.

Conceptual Model and Hypothesis

This part presents the hypotheses and conceptual model derived from previous research review discussion on consumers' memories, attitudes, and desires in relation to ads in various positions, theme congruence, and context congruence.

Ad-content congruence is important for complex ad assessments, including attitudes and purchase intentions, in addition to processes of information related to the advertising, particularly attention and memory (Dahlén et al., 2008; Germelmann et al., 2020; Gunter et al., 2002). However, prior studies have shown contradictory findings. Congruence has been demonstrated in certain research to improve ad identification and recall in digital video contexts (Kononova & Yuan, 2015) as well as conventional media formats (Moorman et al., 2002; Yaveroglu & Donthu, 2008; Zanjani et al., 2011). Ads placed in consistent environments are more efficient, especially in people's responses (Furnham et al., 2002; Van Reijmersdal et al., 2010), as congruity enhances consumers' cognitive evaluations of ads, motivating them to absorb and assess the information more thoroughly and favorably (Fazio, 2001; Furnham et al., 2002). Nevertheless, certain analyses found neither impact (Jeong & King, 2010) nor even the reverse consequence. Furnham, Gunter et al. (2002) stated that advertisements that are incongruous may be more noticeable, cause greater inward processing, and stick in people's minds longer. That is because people are more likely to pay notice to and have stronger memory and identification of details when they are placed in settings where they must handle contradictory information (Moore et al., 2005). Weber's law also states that viewers are more inclined to recognize stimuli that stand out from the crowd (Solomon et al., 2013). It is believed that because incongruent ads use different signals, further internal processing is triggered, improving the recall of incongruent ads (Feltham & Arnold, 1994). On the other hand, ad messages in congruent contexts work better because people process the information more deeply and favorably, therefore positively affects how people view the advertisement and their attitude toward the brand (Belanche et al., 2017).

Pre-roll, mid-roll, and post-roll ads describe the advertisements positioned before to, during, and after in-stream media (Li & Lo, 2015). Because they cut off mediating material and evoke unfavorable feelings, these commercials have a risk of being bothersome (Edwards et al., 2002; McCreery & Krugman, 2017). Therefore, prospective ad avoidance behavior is brought on by feelings of irritation and annoyance (Dix & Phau, 2017). According to certain investigations, ads provoked during a show are more likely to be remembered by viewers than those aired either prior to or following it, mostly due to the knock-on effect of audiences' increased awareness of the program, which often happens amid the material (Li & Lo, 2015; Lloyd & Clancy, 1991; Moorman et al., 2002). As audiences are less engaged at the start and finish of the video, Krishnan and Sitaraman (2013) also discovered that mid-roll advertising has greater completion rates than pre- and post-roll ads. Mid-roll ads, on the contrary, are also seen to be the most bothersome since they cut off the viewer mid-video (Li & Lo, 2015). Conversely, additional research conducted by IPG Media Lab and YuMe revealed that pre-roll advertisements outperformed mid- or post-roll advertisements when it comes to expected disruption, memory, and ad involvement, as cited by S. Lee et al. (2023). This was likely because pre-roll ads heightened the focus on the display by arousing curiosity in the next content.

Congruity and position are both key factors that have been extensively studied by researchers for their impact on advertising effectiveness. There are several reports conducted to examine the correlation between these two factors when evaluating advertising effectiveness. Li and Lo (2015) conducted research to evaluate the effectiveness level of video ads in distinct positions, thematic congruity, and lengths. Results showed that brand identification for pre- and post-roll ads was higher in an incongruent setting than in a congruent one. Despite being more successful in building brand recognition overall, mid-roll ads did not considerably increase brand recognition when they were positioned in a congruent context (Li & Lo, 2015). They recommend using post-roll formats in an incongruent environment because consumers have defined goals while watching a video and may become disengaged when digesting inconsistent information. The experiments conducted by Wang and Bailey (2023) examined the influence of thematic congruence on block ad effectiveness in different topics and arousing level. Their finding implies that thematic incongruence led to better ad information retention in settings but did not affect ad attitudes or purchase intentions. Conversely, congruent ads showed improved encoding and processing in arousing contexts, resulting in more positive attitudes and higher purchase intentions. Belanche et al. (2017) provides insights into the differences in the level of ads' effectiveness when it comes to thematic and context congruence. Ad watching duration, ad attitude, as well as brand attitude all indicate that high-arousal ads work better in congruent circumstances than in incongruent ones. On the other hand, energetic ads shouldn't be shown in an incongruent putting because that would be against their expectations and processing readiness, which would reduce the efficacy of the commercial (Belanche et al., 2017). They also claimed that there was no discernible difference in the impact of low-arousal commercials placed in congruent and incongruent circumstances. Therefore, the following hypotheses are proposed for the empirical research according to the research model in Figure 1:

H1: Pos-CC-CC is the most effective condition for in-stream ads to influence customers.

H2: Mid-IT-IC is the most effective condition for in-stream ads in terms of ad recall.

H3: Pos-CC-CC is the most effective condition for in-stream ads in terms of customers' attitudes.
H4: Pos-CC-CC is the most effective condition for in-stream ads in terms of customers' desires.

Research Model

Figure 1. Research Model developed by the author

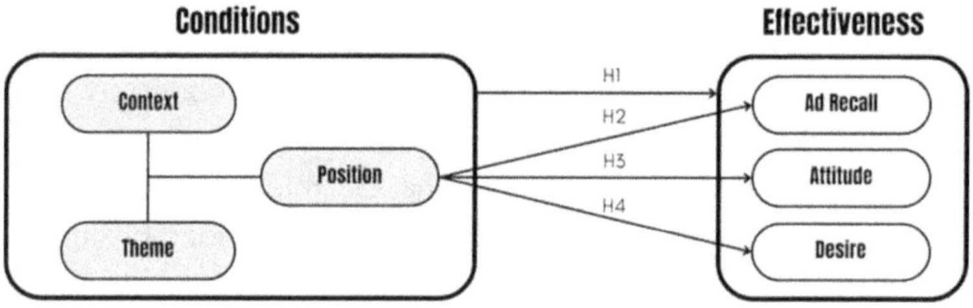

METHOD

Sample and Data Collection

Data for the present study was collected in April 2024. In total, 102 respondents participated in this study via a questionnaire. Instant messaging, social networking websites, and invitation emails were used to find attendees. As the experiment applied a 2 (thematic congruence) × 2 (context congruence) × 3 (position) mixed factorial model, all three variables will be within-subject factors. 22 people were eliminated from the sample because the implementation time was shorter than the minimum time level to finish the experiment (5 minutes), which lead to poor quality answers and could affect the overall results. Therefore, there are 80 samples for each cell in total 12 conditions. All participants ranged in age from 15 to 54, with 78.8% being between the ages of 18 and 24. Groups 15–17 and 25–34 each represent 8.8% of the total, whilst groups 35–44 and 45–54 account for 1.3% and 2.5% of the overall, respectively. Of those participating, women made up 70% of the group while men comprised up 27.5%. Among them, 43.8% use social media for more than three hours every day. Over 25% of those tested reported using social media for three hours a day, and 21.3% said they discovered it for two hours on average.

Experimental Design

An experiment will be carried out to investigate this issue. To control the effect of commercial loading on ad memorability (Bellman et al., 2012), the selected video contents were restricted to a short duration, which was under 3 minutes. The chosen lengths of in-stream video ads were 5-10 seconds, and they were all embedded in the main video.

Selecting Video Contents

As the participants are multinational and not all understand English, the videos are guaranteed to include no dialogue but only with background music. There are 6 videos on 3 different topics, including education, technology, and fashion. Each topic has 2 videos, divided into arousing and calm styles. This division will ensure the most comprehensive and complete assessment of context congruity. There are multiple ways to implementing arousing content, but three common ones include speed of music, aural signals, and the beat (Bradley & Lang, 2000; Dillman Carpentier & Potter, 2007; Lang et al., 1999; Sundar & Kalyanaraman, 2004). Therefore, fast tempo, strong melody, as well as vibrant images have become the criteria for choosing arousing style videos. Meanwhile, calm style videos are the opposite with slow tempo, weak beat, and tender images.

Creating Video Ads

To reduce the potential that brand name awareness to be product- or brand-specific, all material and advertising are fictitious and generated entirely from scratch for research reasons. This not only guarantees that existing commercials and companies are not negatively impacted, but it also gives researchers more control over the study and eliminates any past impressions established by advertisement services in real life (Naidu & Attri, 2018). Moreover, the response to a sample unit may also be impacted by some unrelated factors including familiarity, storytelling execution, and celebrity promotional influence (Li & Lo, 2015). Therefore, several crucial standards were applied while creating video ads to account for these parameters: no involvement from celebrities, high-definition quality, clear display of brand logos, and a maximum of 10 seconds. To retain thematic congruity, ads were also created according to the three main video themes, including fashion, technology, and education. Ads with a fashion theme promote clothes and jewelry; those with an educational focus promote school supplies; and those with a technological theme promote gadgets and software. The 12 conditions correspond to 12 different videos, so each topic has 4 videos divided equally into two styles: arousing and calm, which serves the study of context congruity. The criteria for the two styles follow the characteristics mentioned above when selecting video contents.

Stimuli

The video ads were embedded into the video content, appearing as forced-view ads, which are not skippable, to ensure the ad broadcast process will be completed. There are 12 ads and 6 video content, so each long video will have 2 ads integrated to test 2 different conditions. Applying the 2x2x3 mixture model, 12 ads are arranged to suit each respective condition. Using various combinations of video content and advertisements, thematic congruity and incongruity are employed in accordance with the three main topics indicated. Congruity and incongruity in context, on the other hand, are applied through stylistically distinct pairings that are either calming or arousing. The three places that are tested for are the pre-roll, mid-roll, and post-roll portions of the video contents. Finally, 6 videos including 2 short ads with different appearance conditions in terms of location, theme, and context were used in this experiment.

Procedure

Microsoft Form is the tool used to conduct this experiment online. Accordingly, the experiment will be sent as a link that allows everyone to access. The experiment video is inserted into the form before the corresponding question section, helping volunteers easily participate in the experiment in the correct order. Because participants will experience all 12 case studies, the 6 experimental videos will be divided into 6 separate parts to avoid confusion when answering questions. The form includes 2 language versions: English and Vietnamese to ensure everyone chooses the appropriate language when participating.

The study's focus and the extent to which the in-stream advertising was pertinent would be disclosed to the participants. After they had been informed about the experimental procedure and ethical issues, especially in terms of voluntary participation, volunteers must commit to strictly comply with the requirements of the experiment, including turning on the sound throughout the participation process, fully watching each experimental video before answering the corresponding questions, and answering questions honestly with true personal experience. Participants then will respond to inquiries about intentions to buy and ad attitude after every video. After seeing all the clips, respondents will be asked questions on how they use social networks and demographics. Participants will be given a couple of minutes to answer these queries as a diversionary part to help them refresh their immediate memory (Clayton et al., 2017; Leshner et al., 2009). Lastly, a recognition challenge and a cued recollection will be required of the participants.

Measures

Ad-recall was measured by asking participants to select the ad materials including brand name, brand logo, and advertised product. All three elements pertain to multiple choice questions. There are 25 and 29 options available for the two questions concerning the brand logo and name, respectively. There are 12 right responses to each of these queries, which match the 12 testing advertisements that are shown in a random order. In the interim, twelve questions about marketed goods are given. Participants will select one correct answer from four choices for each question. A dichotomous variable (correct selection = 1; incorrect selection = 0) was implemented to code memorization. To further investigate viewer perspectives and thoughts about advertising, the Likert scale includes questions with a 5-point rating system. Different from attitude ads scale (1 = Very unhappy to 5 = Very happy), the scale of desires towards ads ranges from 1 (Strongly disagree) to 5 (Strongly agree).

The validity of the questionnaire was confirmed using the Cronbach's alpha coefficient. The questionnaire's reliability coefficient was high, with figures of 0.87, 0.93, and 0.94 for the recognition, attitude, and desires inquiries, respectively.

Results

In this experiment, ad recall findings will be presented as an overall score based on the number of correct responses for each condition, using a binary coefficient. Attitudes and desires will be evaluated using a 5-point Likert scale, with conditions having a mean value above 3 indicating a likely positive effect, while those below 3 suggest a less favorable outcome, with 3 serving as a neutral benchmark. Thus, higher average values indicate greater effectiveness of the ad condition.

Table 1. Advertising effectiveness of 12 conditions

Advertising effectiveness of 12 conditions								
Effectiveness	**Recall**			**Attitude**			**Desires**	
	Name	**Logo**	**Product**	**Ad**	**Brand**	**Product**	**Search**	**Buy**
N	80	80	80	80	80	80	80	80
Minimum	0	0	0	1	1	1	1	1
Maximum	1	1	1	5	5	5	5	5
Pre-CT-CC	39	48	59	3.53	3.45	3.44	3.25	2.94
Pre-CT-IC	33	52	25	3.63	3.65	3.72	3.61	3.27
Pre-IT-CC	37	41	40	3.15	3.23	3.40	3.25	2.79
Pre-IT-IC	40	58	31	3.25	3.21	3.26	3.20	3.07
Mid-CT-CC	36	46	56	3.00	3.10	3.25	3.06	2.90
Mid-CT-IC	39	59	55	2.42	2.66	2.76	2.68	2.45
Mid-IT-CC	30	22	19	3.08	3.12	3.28	3.12	2.91
Mid-IT-IC	30	45	21	2.70	2.82	2.78	2.68	2.55
Pos-CT-CC	42	37	53	3.50	3.43	3.61	3.35	3.13
Pos-CT-IC	29	40	50	3.31	3.29	3.35	3.25	2.95
Pos-IT-CC	50	50	65	3.36	3.59	3.57	3.38	3.12
Pos-IT-IC	24	27	25	3.30	3.31	3.31	3.10	2.88

Table 1 indicates that the advertised product is most recalled under condition Pos-IT-CC (65), followed by the brand logo in Mid-CT-IC (59). The Pos-IT-CC condition also yields the highest correct answers for the brand name (50). The Pre-CT-IC condition is associated with the most positive viewer attitudes towards the advertisements, brands, and products, with average values of 3.63, 3.65, and 3.72 respectively. Furthermore, participants express the highest desires to search and buy the product in this condition, scoring 3.61 and 3.27 points.

Recall

Table 2. Advertising effectiveness - Recall

Recall						
Positions	**Effectiveness**	**N**	**CT**	**IT**	**CC**	**IC**
Pre-roll	**Name**	160	76	77	76	77
	Logo	160	89	99	89	99
	Product	160	84	71	99	56
Mid-roll	**Name**	160	75	60	66	69
	Logo	160	105	67	68	104
	Product	160	111	40	76	75
Post-roll	**Name**	160	71	74	92	53
	Logo	160	77	77	87	67
	Product	160	103	90	118	75

Table 2 reveals minimal differences in recall points for pre-roll ad conditions. Incongruence slightly improves recall for both brand name and logo, with higher correct answers (77 and 99). Surprisingly, contextual congruity ads at the beginning of video content receive the highest number of product recalls (99), followed by thematic congruence (84). Thematic congruence stands out for mid-roll ads with the highest recall scores for brand name, logo, and product (75, 105, and 111 respectively). Context incongruence also shows significant impact on viewers' memory in mid-roll, with 69 points for brand name and 104 for brand logo, while context congruence slightly outperforms in recalling the advertised product (76). Context congruence is the most effective condition for memory recall in end-of-video advertisements, with the highest scores for brand name (92), brand logo (87), and advertised product (118). Thematic incongruence aids in customers' brand name recognition (74) at the end of the video, while thematic congruence is effective for product recall (103). Additionally, both thematic conditions have the same effect on brand logo memory, sharing the same points at 77.

Table 2 highlights recall patterns for ads based on congruity and position. Ads with thematic congruence excel in pre-roll for brand name (76) and mid-roll for brand logo (105) and product (111). Thematic incongruence performs best at the beginning of the video for brand name (77) and logo (99), and in post-roll for the advertised product (90). Context congruence is most effective after video content for brand name (92) and product (118), while brand logo recall is highest in pre-roll (89). Context incongruence shows highest effectiveness across all positions for brand name (77), logo (104), and thematic product (75).

Attitude

Table 3. Advertising effectiveness - Attitude

Attitude						
Positions	**Effectiveness**	**N**	**CT**	**IT**	**CC**	**IC**
Pre-roll	**Ad**	160	3.58	3.20	3.34	3.44
	Brand	160	3.55	3.22	3.34	3.43
	Product	160	3.58	3.33	3.42	3.49
Mid-roll	**Ad**	160	2.71	2.89	3.43	2.56
	Brand	160	2.88	2.98	3.11	2.74
	Product	160	3.01	3.02	3.26	2.77
Post-roll	**Ad**	160	3.41	3.33	3.43	3.31
	Brand	160	3.36	3.45	3.51	3.30
	Product	160	3.48	3.44	3.59	3.33

According to Table 3, for ads at the beginning of video content, thematic congruence generates the highest viewer sympathy towards the ad (3.58), brand (3.55), and product (3.58). Context incongruence also positively impacts viewer attitude towards the ad, brand, and product (3.44, 3.43, and 3.49 respectively), ranking second. Context congruence receives the highest viewer attitude ratings for all three materials in both mid-roll (3.43, 3.11, and 3.26) and post-roll (3.43, 3.51, and 3.59) positions. In mid-roll ads, incongruence slightly outperforms thematic congruence with ratings less than or around 3 for all three factors (2.89, 2.98, and 3.02). Post-roll ads (3.41) and products (3.48) also receive positive attitudes from viewers with thematic congruence, while the brand unexpectedly receives the highest favorable rating in a thematic incongruence environment (3.45).

In the context of thematic congruity, optimal viewer attitudes toward all three advertising materials (the ad, brand, and product) are achieved by appearing at the opening of video content, scoring 3.58, 3.55, and 3.58 respectively. Similarly, thematic incongruence in the post-roll position yields positive attitudes with scores of 3.33, 3.45, and 3.44 respectively. Context congruence receives the most positive attitudes towards the ad in mid-roll (3.43), while the brand and product receive higher ratings when appearing at the end (3.51 and 3.59 respectively). Lastly, the start of video content sees the greatest context incongruence condition in terms of viewer attitude assessments, scoring 3.44, 3.43, and 3.49 points for the ad, brand, and product respectively.

Desires

Table 4. Advertising effectiveness - Desire

Desire						
Positions	**Effectiveness**	**N**	**CT**	**IT**	**CC**	**IC**
Pre-roll	**Search**	160	3.43	3.23	3.25	3.41
	Buy	160	3.11	2.93	2.86	3.18
Mid-roll	**Search**	160	2.87	2.90	3.09	2.68
	Buy	160	2.68	2.73	2.91	2.50
Post-roll	**Search**	160	3.30	3.24	3.36	3.18
	Buy	160	3.04	3.00	3.13	2.91

From Table 4, at the video's start, thematic congruence prompts the most interest in learning (3.43), followed closely by context incongruence (3.41). Conversely, viewers rate the opposite tendency and context incompatibility as more effective (3.18 > 3.11). For mid-roll ads, although generally scoring low and lacking positive impact, context congruence proves most effective in enhancing audience desire to search and purchase (3.09 and 2.91 respectively), followed by thematic incongruence (2.90 and 2.73). At video's end, ads with context congruence maintain their effectiveness in both search (3.36) and purchase intent (3.13), closely followed by thematic congruence (3.30 and 3.04 respectively).

The start of the main video yields positive results for both search and purchase intent, with thematic congruence (3.43 and 3.11) and context incongruence (3.41 and 3.18) showing effectiveness. Conversely, post-roll positions are advantageous for ads with thematic incongruence and contextual congruence, prompting viewers' search and purchase desires most significantly (thematic incongruence: 3.24 and 3.00; context congruence: 3.36 and 3.13).

After comparing the data and the overall influence on different aspects of advertising effectiveness, Pre-nskskakw is the condition that appears for the most effective advertising (H1 rejected). Going into detail about each factor, for ad recall, Pos-CT-CC is the condition that has the greatest effect on viewers' ad memory, especially in terms of xxx (H2 confirmed). Also according to the analysis results above, Pre-IT-CC is the most effective condition for ads to appear without causing negative emotions to the audience (H3 rejected). This condition is also the best environment for advertising in stimulating viewers' interest in learning about and buying products (H4 rejected).

DISCUSSION AND CONCLUSION

This study aims to assess the efficacy of topic congruence (congruity or incongruity), context congruence (congruity or incongruity), and positions (pre-roll, mid-roll, or post-roll) for video advertisements, thereby identify highly effective conditions to appear. In this study, according to the first hypothesis, the effectiveness of in-stream ad appearance conditions was evaluated and compared to determine the most successful condition. With the following three hypotheses addressing the interaction between placement and relevance, the influence of this relationship was studied to support decisions about the conditions of in-stream ads appearance.

This study suggests that there is an opportunity for researchers to better understand the influence of in-stream ads when presented under different conditions when considering all three factors simultaneously: positions, thematic congruence, and context congruence. Furthermore, this research is also relevant to social media issues as companies rely on the results to choose the most effective exposure conditions with the least possible influence on the audience. This study has various theoretical and managerial ramifications.

Marketers still employ a wide range of techniques to draw in and stick in the minds of their target audience. Advertisers may choose from a wide range of options when it comes to location, theme, and context of main video when running online ads, and these options differ in how successful their ads will be. In this research, it is found that each efficiency factor has different most effective conditions, so the company needs to consider its priorities and efficiency needs to make the most appropriate choice.

The results of the Pre-CT-CC condition showed that this position created a very good impression of the product, followed by the logo, and finally the brand name. This condition also received positive responses from viewers in terms of attitudes towards the advertisement, but was not as effective in stimulating the desire to buy as in the desire to search for the product. While the Pre-CT-IC condition showed superior effectiveness in creating a positive impact on viewers' psychology in terms of both attitudes and shopping needs, this condition was not remembered much by the audience, especially in terms of brand names and products. The Pre-IT-CC and Pre-IT-IC cases also showed that the advertising had a relatively high level of effectiveness. The ability to recall was quite good, although not as good as the previous two conditions. Viewers' attitudes were generally positive but not outstanding. The desire to search and purchase the product was moderate, indicating that the ads in these two conditions had some impact but were not strong enough to drive purchase. Meanwhile, for the cases that appeared in the middle, the effectiveness of the ads began to decline. The ability to recall the name, logo, and product was no longer as strong as when they appeared at the beginning of the video. Attitudes toward the ads and the brand in the Mid-CT-CC and Mid-IT-CC conditions became less positive. When appearing in the Mid-CT-IC and Mid-IT-IC cases, the ads had the lowest effectiveness as viewers barely recalled the name, logo, and product. Attitudes toward the ads and the brand when appearing in these two cases were also not positive, indicating that the ads did not create a good impression or caused annoyance. All four conditions yielded results that indicated low search and purchase intent, indicating that the ad was not successful in inducing action from the audience when it appeared in the middle of the video ad stream. Finally, when it appeared at the end, the Pos-CT-CC and Pos-CT-IC cases showed some improvement in ad performance. Recall of the name, logo, and product was quite good, and attitudes toward the ad, brand, and product were also quite positive, indicating that the ad had begun to make a lasting impression on the audience. The Pos-IT-CC had a fairly positive effect with high recall and good attitudes from the audience. Recall of the name, logo, and product was the best among the cases, indicating that the ad was successful in making a strong impression on the audience. Furthermore, attitudes toward the ad and product in this condition were also positive. However, the Pos-IT-IC case did not achieve the same effect, with average audience recall and attitude. The desire to search and buy the product was also low, indicating that the ad was not strong enough to drive purchase action.

Although the degree to which each component of the advertising is memorable varies based on the situation, the post-roll, theme incongruity, and contextual congruity work efficiently to help viewers recall the advertisement. The fact that this condition consistently yields the greatest number of right answers for both the brand name and the promoted product serves as evidence of this. Pos-IT-IC is the most successful appearance condition for in-stream advertising in terms of ad recall, but the Mid-CT-IC condition also performed well in helping viewers recall the brand logo. This is because the remaining two criteria outperformed Pos-IT-IC in terms of logo recall. Pre-CT-IC, on the other hand, has proven to be the most efficient way of positively influencing viewers' attitudes and wants, irrespective of the advertisement, brand, product, or even their intention to seek and purchase. Thus, marketers should increase the quantity of in-stream ads that start content videos with theme congruity and context incongruity in order to optimize the influence on customer attitudes and needs. Additionally, for businesses hoping to optimize customer recognition and impressions, the last position of films with theme incongruence and contextual congruence will be the best place for adverts to appear.

The pre-roll advertisement's brand name is not significantly influenced by the theme or context. While audiences are more likely to remember pre-roll commercials that are in accordance with video content, especially when it comes to context, incongruent advertising at the beginning of the film increases viewers' opinions of the company's logo. Consequently, incongruence enhances logo memory for advertising that appear at the beginning of video content, whereas congruence raises topic product awareness. Presenting the brand name, brand logo, and focal product in the midst of video material with thematic congruency can help the audience recall the advertisement's key points. When combined with context incongruence, advertising will be incredibly successful in helping people remember company logos. In contrast, since this condition is highly useless in terms of memory, organizations should refrain from having advertisements that are not thematically connected with the primary content. Advertising in context congruence at the end of the video content tends to make the ad more memorable to viewers. Consequently, businesses must concentrate on selecting the setting in which post-roll advertisements run. Adding theme congruence will also increase the effectiveness of making an impact on viewers about the promoted goods. Appearing in the center will have the greatest memory-boosting impact for theme congruence and context incongruence conditions, particularly when discussing logos and goods. For greatest impact, theme incongruity advertisements should be positioned at the beginning of video material, whereas context congruity commercials should appear at the conclusion. In summary, to maximize ad recall efficiency, congruence settings work best when they occur in the middle and at the conclusion of video material, whereas incongruence circumstances are appropriate when they appear at the beginning. To get the greatest results, marketers must tweak and select the right context and theme based on the intended placement for in-stream advertising.

In terms of viewer attitudes, the combination of thematic congruence and contextual incongruence is the best condition for ads to appear at the beginning of the video. This position is also the most effective position of these two conditions. In general, ads appearing in the middle of video content are annoying to viewers, except when appearing in context congruence. This condition is also the most effective in terms of positive influence both in mid-roll and post-roll. Congruence has the least negative impact on viewers when appearing at the end of the main video, especially in terms of advertising and products. Therefore, ads should limit appearing in the middle of the video if they do not want to receive negative attitudes from the audience, and ads with context congruence as well as thematic incongruence cause the most sympathy for viewers when appearing in the post-roll.

Thematic congruence and contextual incongruence, which appear at the start of video material, work incredibly well together to pique viewers' interest in viewing and purchasing after they've seen the advertisement. When it comes to desire, the pre-roll position is also the best moment for the two previously stated conditions to manifest. When placed after video material, advertisements that complement it both thematically and contextually have a powerful impact on viewers' desire. When it comes to mid-roll in-stream advertisements, their placement here has a detrimental impact on consumers' intents to study and make purchases. Congruence with context and incongruence with theme, therefore, will work best when they occur in the post-roll position.

In conclusion, the combination of the pairs Pre-roll x Thematic Congruence x Context Incongruence and Post-roll x Thematic Incongruence x Context Congruence both bring outstanding results in terms of attitude and desires. Reports on the impact of mid-roll advertising support previous findings that these appearances induce negative emotions in viewers regardless of whether they are appropriate to the video content (Li & Lo, 2015; Lloyd & Clancy, 1991; Moorman et al., 2002). However, it cannot be denied the effectiveness of appearing in this position in making viewers remember the thematic congruent ad, especially when there is thematic relevance. This finding is different from the results of Li and Lo (2015) as there is not much difference in memory performance between context cases. Besides, congruence conditions at the end of video content are the best conditions to receive viewer recognition, supporting Wang and Bailey's research (2023). Therefore, depending on the desire and purpose of in-stream advertising, marketers need to make appropriate adjustments and choices regarding context, topic, and location to achieve the best results.

LIMITATION AND FUTURE RESEARCH

Finally, several limitations of this study need to be considered. First, the sample size used in this study is not representative of all online video viewers, as the experiment was conducted with a relatively small number of users. This limitation restricts the generalizability of the results to a broader audience. Therefore, future research should aim to use a more diverse and larger sample size that includes various demographic segments, such as different age groups, geographical locations, and cultural backgrounds, to enhance the robustness and applicability of the findings. Moreover, the video content used in the experiment consisted solely of videos without dialogue. This choice may have influenced the way viewers interacted with and perceived the advertisements, as the absence of dialogue could impact emotional engagement and cognitive processing differently compared to videos with spoken content. To address this limitation, further studies should investigate the effects of video ads in different contexts, including those with dialogue or varying narrative structures, to better understand how these elements influence viewer perception and ad effectiveness. Additionally, future research could explore the combination of other diverse factors, such as the emotional tone or context of the videos. For instance, examining the impact of video context—whether the content is arousing, exciting, or calm and soothing - on advertisement effectiveness could provide valuable insights. Understanding how different emotional contexts and levels of arousal affect viewer engagement and recall of advertisements could help refine advertising strategies and optimize ad placement in various types of video content. By exploring these additional factors, researchers can develop a more comprehensive understanding of how video ads function in diverse settings, ultimately contributing to more effective and targeted advertising approaches.

REFERENCES

Baltas, G. (2003). Determinants of Internet Advertising Effectiveness: An Empirical Study. *International Journal of Market Research*, 45(4), 1–9. DOI: 10.1177/147078530304500403

Bee, C. C., & Madrigal, R. (2012). It's Not Whether You Win or Lose; It's How The Game is Played. *Journal of Advertising*, 41(1), 47–58. DOI: 10.2753/JOA0091-3367410104

Belanche, D., Flavián, C., & Pérez-Rueda, A. (2017). Understanding Interactive Online Advertising: Congruence and Product Involvement in Highly and Lowly Arousing, Skippable Video Ads. *Journal of Interactive Marketing*, 37(1), 75–88. DOI: 10.1016/j.intmar.2016.06.004

Bellman, S., Treleaven-Hassard, S., Robinson, J. A., Rask, A., & Varan, D. (2012). Getting the Balance Right. *Journal of Advertising*, 41(2), 5–24. DOI: 10.2753/JOA0091-3367410201

Bradley, M. M., & Lang, P. J. (2000). Affective reactions to acoustic stimuli. *Psychophysiology*, 37(2), 204–215. DOI: 10.1111/1469-8986.3720204 PMID: 10731770

Chaffey, D., & Ellis-Chadwick, F. (2019). *Digital marketing* (7th ed.). Pearson.

Clayton, R. B., Leshner, G., Bolls, P. D., & Thorson, E. (2017). Discard the Smoking Cues—Keep the Disgust: An Investigation of Tobacco Smokers' Motivated Processing of Anti-tobacco Commercials. *Health Communication*, 32(11), 1319–1330. DOI: 10.1080/10410236.2016.1220042 PMID: 27690639

Dahlén, M., Rosengren, S., Törn, F., & Öhman, N. (2008). Could Placing ADS Wrong be Right?: Advertising Effects of Thematic Incongruence. *Journal of Advertising*, 37(3), 57–67. DOI: 10.2753/JOA0091-3367370305

Davidson, R. J. (2004). What does the prefrontal cortex "do" in affect: Perspectives on frontal EEG asymmetry research. *Biological Psychology*, 67(1–2), 219–234. DOI: 10.1016/j.biopsycho.2004.03.008 PMID: 15130532

De Pelsmacker, P., Geuens, M., & Anckaert, P. (2002). Media Context and Advertising Effectiveness: The Role of Context Appreciation and Context/Ad Similarity. *Journal of Advertising*, 31(2), 49–61. DOI: 10.1080/00913367.2002.10673666

Dehghani, M., Niaki, M. K., Ramezani, I., & Sali, R. (2016). Evaluating the influence of YouTube advertising for attraction of young customers. *Computers in Human Behavior*, 59, 165–172. DOI: 10.1016/j.chb.2016.01.037

Dillman Carpentier, F. R., & Potter, R. F. (2007). Effects of Music on Physiological Arousal: Explorations into Tempo and Genre. *Media Psychology*, 10(3), 339–363. DOI: 10.1080/15213260701533045

Dix, S. R., & Phau, I. (2017). Predictors of Commercial Zapping During Live Prime-Time Television: An Observation-Based Study Identifies Factors That Drive TV Channel Switching. *Journal of Advertising Research*, 57(1), 15–27. DOI: 10.2501/JAR-2017-010

Djafarova, E., & Kramer, K. (2019). YouTube advertising: Exploring its effectiveness. *The Marketing Review*, 19(1), 127–145. DOI: 10.1362/146934719X15633618140855

Edwards, S. M., Li, H., & Lee, J.-H. (2002). Forced Exposure and Psychological Reactance: Antecedents and Consequences of the Perceived Intrusiveness of Pop-Up Ads. *Journal of Advertising*, 31(3), 83–95. DOI: 10.1080/00913367.2002.10673678

Esch, F., Langner, T., Schmitt, B. H., & Geus, P. (2006). Are brands forever? How brand knowledge and relationships affect current and future purchases. *Journal of Product and Brand Management*, 15(2), 98–105. DOI: 10.1108/10610420610658938

Fazio, R. H. (2001). On the automatic activation of associated evaluations: An overview. *Cognition and Emotion*, 15(2), 115–141. DOI: 10.1080/02699930125908

Feltham, T. S., & Arnold, S. J. (1994). Program involvement and ad/program consistency as moderators of program context effects. *Journal of Consumer Psychology*, 3(1), 51–77. DOI: 10.1016/S1057-7408(08)80028-9

Furnham, A., Bergland, J., & Gunter, B. (2002). Memory for television advertisements as a function of advertisement–programme congruity. *Applied Cognitive Psychology*, 16(5), 525–545. DOI: 10.1002/acp.812

Germelmann, C. C., Herrmann, J.-L., Kacha, M., & Darke, P. R. (2020). Congruence and Incongruence in Thematic Advertisement–Medium Combinations: Role of Awareness, Fluency, and Persuasion Knowledge. *Journal of Advertising*, 49(2), 141–164. DOI: 10.1080/00913367.2020.1745110

Goldfarb, A., & Tucker, C. (2011). Online Display Advertising: Targeting and Obtrusiveness. *Marketing Science*, 30(3), 389–404. DOI: 10.1287/mksc.1100.0583

Gunter, B., Baluch, B., Duffy, L. J., & Furnham, A. (2002). Children's memory for television advertising: Effects of programme–advertisement congruency. *Applied Cognitive Psychology*, 16(2), 171–190. DOI: 10.1002/acp.776

Hwang, J., Yoon, Y.-S., & Park, N.-H. (2011). Structural effects of cognitive and affective reponses to web advertisements, website and brand attitudes, and purchase intentions: The case of casual-dining restaurants. *International Journal of Hospitality Management*, 30(4), 897–907. DOI: 10.1016/j.ijhm.2011.01.011

Jeong, Y., & King, C. M. (2010). Impacts of Website Context Relevance on Banner Advertisement Effectiveness. *Journal of Promotion Management*, 16(3), 247–264. DOI: 10.1080/10496490903281395

Kim, N. Y., & Sundar, S. S. (2010). Relevance to the Rescue: Can "Smart Ads" Reduce Negative Response to Online Ad Clutter? *Journalism & Mass Communication Quarterly*, 87(2), 346–362. DOI: 10.1177/107769901008700208

Kononova, A., & Yuan, S. (2015). Double-Dipping Effect? How Combining YouTube Environmental PSAs With Thematically Congruent Advertisements in Different Formats Affects Memory and Attitudes. *Journal of Interactive Advertising*, 15(1), 2–15. DOI: 10.1080/15252019.2015.1009524

Kotler, P., & Armstrong, G. (2018). *Principles of marketing* (17e, global edition ed.). Pearson.

Krishnan, S. S., & Sitaraman, R. K. (2013). Understanding the effectiveness of video ads: A measurement study. *Proceedings of the 2013 Conference on Internet Measurement Conference*, 149–162. DOI: 10.1145/2504730.2504748

Lang, A., Bolls, P., Potter, R. F., & Kawahara, K. (1999). The effects of production pacing and arousing content on the information processing of television messages. *Journal of Broadcasting & Electronic Media*, 43(4), 451–475. DOI: 10.1080/08838159909364504

Lee, J., & Lee, H. (2012). Canonical correlation analysis of online video advertising viewing motivations and access characteristics. *New Media & Society*, 14(8), 1358–1374. DOI: 10.1177/1461444812444708

Lee, S., Kim, J., Read, G. L., & Kim, S.-P. (2023). The Effects of In-Stream Video Advertising on Ad Information Encoding: A Neurophysiological Study. *Journal of Advertising*, •••, 1–15. DOI: 10.1080/00913367.2023.2222782

Leshner, G., Bolls, P., & Thomas, E. (2009). Scare' Em or Disgust 'Em: The Effects of Graphic Health Promotion Messages. *Health Communication*, 24(5), 447–458. DOI: 10.1080/10410230903023493 PMID: 19657827

Li, H., & Lo, H.-Y. (2015). Do You Recognize Its Brand? The Effectiveness of Online In-Stream Video Advertisements. *Journal of Advertising*, 44(3), 208–218. DOI: 10.1080/00913367.2014.956376

Lloyd, D. W., & Clancy, K. J. (1991). Television program involvement and advertising response: Some unsettling implications for copy research. *Journal of Consumer Marketing*, 8(4), 61–74. DOI: 10.1108/07363769110035162

Martín-Santana, J. D., & Beerli-Palacio, A. (2012). The effectiveness of web ads: Rectangle vs contextual banners. *Online Information Review*, 36(3), 420–441. DOI: 10.1108/14684521211241431

McCoy, S., Everard, A., Galletta, D. F., & Moody, G. D. (2017). Here we go again! The impact of website ad repetition on recall, intrusiveness, attitudes, and site revisit intentions. *Information & Management*, 54(1), 14–24. DOI: 10.1016/j.im.2016.03.005

McCreery, S., & Krugman, D. M. (2017). Tablets and TV Advertising: Understanding the Viewing Experience. *Journal of Current Issues and Research in Advertising*, 38(2), 197–211. DOI: 10.1080/10641734.2017.1291386

Mehta, A. (1994). *How advertising response modeling (ARM) can increase ad effectiveness. 34*(3), 62.

Moore, R. S., Stammerjohan, C. A., & Coulter, R. A. (2005). BANNER ADVERTISER-WEB SITE CONTEXT CONGRUITY AND COLOR EFFECTS ON ATTENTION AND ATTITUDES. *Journal of Advertising*, 34(2), 71–84. DOI: 10.1080/00913367.2005.10639189

Moorman, M., Neijens, P. C., & Smit, E. G. (2002). The Effects of Magazine-Induced Psychological Responses and Thematic Congruence on Memory and Attitude toward the Ad in a Real-Life Setting. *Journal of Advertising*, 31(4), 27–40. DOI: 10.1080/00913367.2002.10673683

Naidu, A., & Attri, R. (2018). An Examination of Service Advertising Effectiveness. *Abhigyan*, 35(4), 53–63. DOI: 10.56401/Abhigyan_35.4.2018.53-63

Pergelova, A., Prior, D., & Rialp, J. (2010). Assessing Advertising Efficiency. *Journal of Advertising*, 39(3), 39–54. DOI: 10.2753/JOA0091-3367390303

Sharma, A. (2000). Recall of Television Commercials as a Function of Viewing Context: The Impact of Program-Commercial Congruity on Commercial Messages. *The Journal of General Psychology*, 127(4), 383–396. DOI: 10.1080/00221300009598592 PMID: 11110001

Solomon, M. R., Russell-Bennett, R., & Previte, J. (2013). *Consumer behaviour: Buying, having, being* (3rd ed.). Pearson Australia.

Sundar, S. S., & Kalyanaraman, S. (2004). AROUSAL, MEMORY, AND IMPRESSION-FORMATION EFFECTS OF ANIMATION SPEED IN WEB ADVERTISING. *Journal of Advertising*, 33(1), 7–17. DOI: 10.1080/00913367.2004.10639152

Truong, Y., McColl, R., & Kitchen, P. (2010). Practitioners' perceptions of advertising strategies for digital media. *International Journal of Advertising*, 29(5), 709–725. DOI: 10.2501/S0265048710201439

Van Reijmersdal, E., Smit, E., & Neijens, P. (2010). How media factors affect audience responses to brand placement. *International Journal of Advertising*, 29(2), 279–301. DOI: 10.2501/S0265048710201154

Venkatraman, V., Dimoka, A., Pavlou, P. A., Vo, K., Hampton, W., Bollinger, B., Hershfield, H. E., Ishihara, M., & Winer, R. S. (2015). Predicting Advertising success beyond Traditional Measures: New Insights from Neurophysiological Methods and Market Response Modeling. *JMR, Journal of Marketing Research*, 52(4), 436–452. DOI: 10.1509/jmr.13.0593

Vernon, J. (2014). The power of YouTube ads. The ultimate guide to start running ads on YouTube. *MarketingHY*. https://marketinghy.com/2014/06/

Walsh, J. P., & Ungson, G. R. (1991). Organizational Memory. *Academy of Management Review*, 16(1), 57. DOI: 10.2307/258607

Wang, T., & Bailey, R. L. (2023). Processing Peripherally Placed Advertising: The Effect of Thematic Ad-Content Congruence and Arousing Content on the Effectiveness of In-Video Overlay Advertising. *Journal of Interactive Advertising*, 23(3), 203–220. DOI: 10.1080/15252019.2023.2217810

Wright-Isak, C., Faber, R. J., & Horner, L. R. (1997). Comprehensive Measurement of Advertising Effectiveness: Notes From the Marketplace. In *Measuring Advertising Effectiveness* (1st ed., Vol. 1, p. 10). Psychology Press.

Yaveroglu, I., & Donthu, N. (2008). Advertising Repetition and Placement Issues in On-Line Environments. *Journal of Advertising*, 37(2), 31–44. DOI: 10.2753/JOA0091-3367370203

Yoon, S.-H., & Lee, S.-H. (2022). What Likeability Attributes Attract People to Watch Online Video Advertisements? *Electronics (Basel)*, 11(13), 1960. DOI: 10.3390/electronics11131960

Zanjani, S. H. A., Diamond, W. D., & Chan, K. (2011). Does Ad-Context Congruity Help Surfers and Information Seekers Remember Ads in Cluttered E-magazines? *Journal of Advertising*, 40(4), 67–84. DOI: 10.2753/JOA0091-3367400405

Zhang, X., & Yuan, S.-M. (2018). An Eye Tracking Analysis for Video Advertising: Relationship Between Advertisement Elements and Effectiveness. *IEEE Access : Practical Innovations, Open Solutions*, 6, 10699–10707. DOI: 10.1109/ACCESS.2018.2802206

ADDITIONAL READING

Davtyan, D., & Tashchian, A. (2022). Thematic Congruency in the Context of Brand Placements: Tests of Memory and Attitude Measures. *Journal of Current Issues and Research in Advertising*, 43(3), 319–335. DOI: 10.1080/10641734.2022.2066231

Freeman, J., Wei, L., Yang, H., & Shen, F. (2022). Does in-Stream Video Advertising Work? Effects of Position and Congruence on Consumer Responses. *Journal of Promotion Management*, 28(5), 515–536. DOI: 10.1080/10496491.2021.2009086

Huang, Y., & Yoon, H. J. (2022). Prosocial native advertising on social media: Effects of ad-context congruence, ad position and ad type. *Journal of Social Marketing*, 12(2), 105–123. DOI: 10.1108/JSOCM-05-2021-0105

Jiang, Z., Guan, C., & De Haaij, I. L. (2019). Congruity and processing fluency: An analysis on the effectiveness of embedded online video advertising. *Asia Pacific Journal of Marketing and Logistics*, 32(5), 1070–1088. DOI: 10.1108/APJML-03-2019-0128

Joa, C. Y., Kim, K., & Ha, L. (2018). What Makes People Watch Online In-Stream Video Advertisements? *Journal of Interactive Advertising*, 18(1), 1–14. DOI: 10.1080/15252019.2018.1437853

Rollin, R. (2022). *Essays on congruence theory in marketing: Special focus on digital products and webstores*. Springer Fachmedien Wiesbaden., DOI: 10.1007/978-3-658-39364-9

Stipp, H. (2018). How Context Can Make Advertising More Effective. *Journal of Advertising Research*, 58(2), 138–145. DOI: 10.2501/JAR-2018-022

Sun, S., & Evans, N. J. (2022). Effects of Disclosure, Placement Type, and Ad–Context Congruence on Brand and Advertising Recognition: An Exploration of CARE Model Processing. *Journal of Current Issues and Research in Advertising*, 43(2), 219–235. DOI: 10.1080/10641734.2021.1982083

Telang, A., Sahoo, D., Sreejesh, S., & Paul, J. (2021). The Effects of Context Congruence On Ad Persuasiveness in e-Magazines: It Serves My Motive, And I Distinguish the Advertisement. *Journal of Advertising Research*, 61(3), 303–317. DOI: 10.2501/JAR-2021-002

Yang, J., Jiang, M., & Wu, L. (2021). Native Advertising in WeChat Official Accounts: How Do Ad–Content Congruence and Ad Skepticism Influence Advertising Value and Effectiveness? *Journal of Interactive Advertising*, 21(1), 17–33. DOI: 10.1080/15252019.2021.1900758

KEY TERMS AND DEFINITIONS

Context Congruence: Context congruence refers to the alignment between the advertisement and the communicated media in terms of the arousing level or emotional tone. An ad that matches the intensity, mood, or arousal level of the media content it accompanies would be contextually congruent.

Context Incongruence: Context incongruence occurs when there is a mismatch between the advertisement and the communicated media regarding arousing level or emotional tone.

In-Stream Advertising Video: In-stream video advertising refers to ads that are delivered within a video content stream on digital platforms.

Mid-Roll Advertisement: A mid-roll advertisement is a type of in-stream video ad that appears in the middle of a video.

Post-Roll Advertisement: A post-roll advertisement is an in-stream video ad that plays after the main video content has finished.

Pre-Roll Advertisement: A pre-roll advertisement is an in-stream video ad that plays before the main video content starts.

Thematic Congruence: Thematic congruence refers to the extent to which the advertisement aligns with the product category or theme of the communicated media.

Thematic Incongruence: Thematic incongruence occurs when there is a lack of alignment between the product category or theme of the advertisement and the communicated media.

Chapter 7
Business Intelligence and Market Research:
Drivers of E-Commerce Growth

Minh Tung Tran
https://orcid.org/0000-0002-4238-882X
FPT University, Vietnam

Hoai Lan Duong
FPT University, Vietnam

Thi Kim Oanh Vo
FPT University, Vietnam

ABSTRACT

This study investigates the influence of business intelligence (BI) and market research on the growth of e-commerce businesses, using a mixed-method approach that includes data analysis and case studies. Primary data is gathered through case studies, while secondary data is drawn from relevant literature. The research seeks to demonstrate how BI and market research enhance e-commerce competitiveness, profitability, and overall growth. Findings will provide e-commerce businesses with insights on leveraging BI for strategic expansion, help management understand the value of BI in decision-making, and guide BI teams in optimizing performance for better ROI. The study aims to show that a well-defined BI plan and comprehensive market research are essential for a successful e-commerce presence (Hypothesis: H1).

DOI: 10.4018/979-8-3693-4361-6.ch007

INTRODUCTION

As demand is different from other economic goods, it is important to gain an in-depth understanding of it. McGrath (2000) mentioned that demand is less tangible. It is difficult to measure and understand as demand is hidden. It involves what people want, what they will use and expect, when and where they will use it and how they will use it and how much they are prepared to pay (McGrath, 2000). With the growing importance of business intelligence in the e-commerce industry, said businesses can now enjoy increased profits and faster growth than ever before by utilising data. As stated by Henschen (2012), businesses can now gain insight from various data sources, including pinpointing emerging market trends, identifying business opportunities and making smarter operational decisions (Henschen, 2012). With this in mind, the report aims to provide an insight into the relationship between business intelligence and market research in the growth of e-commerce businesses. The study embarks on a comprehensive literature review on the definitions, benefits and challenges of business intelligence and market research, possible strategies in improving e-commerce growth, as well as various resources and technologies employed in a successful business intelligence venture. Furthermore, the report explores the impact of business intelligence and market research on e-commerce growth, the potential influencing factors towards a better business performance, as well as some successful real-world examples to illustrate the key points presented. The research was conducted using the research methods of a series of literature and electronic sources such as books, academic journals and online articles. The report will then be finalised and set out in a structured manner, following the academic approach to revelation, critical judgment and problem solving. The report may potentially provide help and useful advice for middle to top management levels in e-commerce industry that contains a certain level of managerial knowledge in the field of strategic marketing and customer relationship management. (Wu et al., 2023) (Barata et al.2023)

1.1 Purpose of the Study

The research aims to examine how business intelligence and market research can help e-commerce businesses to grow. This is important because over the years, the usability, popularity, and success of the e-commerce models have been immense. Many successful e-commerce organizations have been implementing business intelligence and market research in a systematic way to enhance their growth, competitiveness, and profit in the market. Therefore, this research will explore and critically evaluate the different aspects of business intelligence and market research on the growth of e-commerce businesses using real-world data. The study will also help different e-commerce businesses to understand how they can enhance their business intelligence and market research. Moreover, the study will also help the management persons and the business intelligence teams in e-commerce to understand the real value of business intelligence and market research and to find different ways to increase the business intelligence performance and return-on-investment. I have divided this research into a number of chapters and I will also use a number of case studies to enrich the validity of the research. This includes primary research by gathering data from the case studies and secondary research by critically evaluating different literatures.

Finally, findings from different literatures and case studies will be concluded. The conclusion will support hypothesis that a good business intelligence plan and market research are the foundation for creating a successful e-commerce presence. Also, it will support aim and objectives as being used to get the desired outcome.

1.2 Research Questions

The primary research question is: How does business intelligence impact the growth of e-commerce businesses?

In order to answer this question, the following sub-questions must also be addressed: What is business intelligence and what is its role in the modern competitive business environment? What are the benefits and challenges of implementing business intelligence in the e-commerce sector? The above question aims to achieve the next steps. The first focuses on defining what business intelligence represents and how the continuous use of advanced technology to analyze the information in a business environment. The second will direct the primary focus into the advantages and disadvantages of business intelligence specifically in the e-commerce sector. And by this direction, the aims of each sub-question will fulfill the purpose of the next sub-question until the targets achieved.

1.3 Scope of the Study

The main areas to be covered in this research include an overview of business intelligence, its importance and role in e-commerce, benefits and challenges of business intelligence, real-time business intelligence, and an account of the case study of an e-commerce company called The Sports Division. The research will also cover an introduction to market research, the significance of market research in e-commerce and its impact on the success, primary and secondary data used in the research, data collection methods and data analysis and different tools used in the market research. The different types of market research and the use of internet in market research will also be covered. The research will further include market techniques and limitations of market research. The impact of business intelligence on e-commerce in an online marketplace and the benefits and risk of market research are investigated. And lastly, a consideration of the impact of decision support system on management where a discussion is conducted about the development of management support system, its elements and the various types of decision support systems including cybernetics, artificial intelligence, management information system (MIS) and knowledge base system. The research will provide a detailed evaluation of how business intelligence and market research have been used in e-commerce over the years for the growth and expansion of various products and services. The expertise and knowledge gained from this study will be helpful to both the start-up and existing online companies in appreciating the need for data-driven strategies in e-commerce nowadays. The study, therefore, contributes towards the advancement of current knowledge in the academic and professional disciplines of information systems management and e-commerce and also practical strategies for online business success.

Hypothesis

This research proposes the following hypothesis:

H1: A well-defined business intelligence plan and comprehensive market research are fundamental to establishing and maintaining a successful e-commerce presence.

This hypothesis aligns with the research aim of exploring how BI and market research contribute to the growth of e-commerce businesses. The research findings will be evaluated against this hypothesis to determine its validity and draw meaningful conclusions.

LITERATURE REVIEW

As well as introducing the main themes for research, it explores the definition of business intelligence and how it is used. Determining commonalities among consumers, providing optimal customer service, and discovering areas where a company can improve operations are several benefits. From a bit as basic business intelligence had been used in the form of biographical solutions like the credit reporting industry and employment - it's the connotation of the modern term of 'business intelligence' that seems to have changed over time and this could clue into the viewpoints of how important it is in a business context. The literature review is based on studies that were published over years between 2007-2013 in top information systems and top operations management journals. Also, they were selected from a pool of 20 journals that was determined based upon the impact they had when comparing the amount of citations they received from research articles. This information could suggest differing causes for growth in business intelligence and the significance of each, for example. Furthermore, the literature review analysed studies which discussed business intelligence and technology from both the 'information systems' and 'operations management' viewpoint. It is helpful for this particular research as it investigates the impact that business intelligence can have in an online retailing environment and how technology and methods currently used in the e-commerce industry have advanced over recent years. (Fosso et al.2020) (Fosso Wamba & Queiroz, 2023)

1. Business Intelligence in E-commerce

Business intelligence (BI) is a process by which companies improve the quality of their management decisions by using data and statistical analysis as a basis. It has both internal and external focuses. Internally, it is used to measure the organization's functions and performance against historical data. BI can help e-commerce entities to identify areas for improvement and to identify operational inefficiencies. It is extremely important in today's rapidly changing business environment because it provides timely and accurate insights into right now that drive smarter strategic decision over time. When product managers at e-commerce companies frame analyses, whether it is measuring sales of a featured product or visitation to an upgraded site area, they must keep two simple-sounding ideas in mind to drive the business decisions they are working towards – it has to make money and save money. These analyses through the BI process cannot only provide critical inputs to website upgrades and redesigns, they can help identify which actions have the potential to produce stronger sales and profit results. BI technology offers many short and long-term benefits to e-commerce, especially in quality improvements and operational cost reduction. For example, an e-commerce company can examine click-stream data to reveal the browsing and buying behaviour of clients over time - this is just one specific way BI through data analysis can help. Another example is geo-mapping and data mining - these analytically driven goals are achieved through a BI strategy, which provides richer results rather than hit or miss approaches to more fashionable trends in marketing, such as SEO and website re-designs which only look to increase traffic for short term success. The benefits of BI are direct, tangible and more readily measurable in e-commerce than its implementation or use in any other sector. As companies grow in product supply, in staff numbers, in volume of services offered and in brand they can easily lose the ability to grasp and understand their internal functional workings - this means that many efficiency opportunities are missed. However, unlike in other sectors, the nature of data generation and collection in e-commerce works with, and is highly conducive, to a successful BI campaign. This is because industry-set product line, customer behaviour modelling and prediction and the ability to respond to changes in customer habits is readily able to be shaped by the analytical paradigms in a fully-fledged BI deployment. BI has the potential to change the way e-commerce is managed and grow - it provides money saving and money making opportunities unheard of in even the most high-tech retail sectors of today. In the vast and ever-growing realm of e-commerce solutions and strategies, we all know how much development we are yet to experience. The future is only made up of opportunities as yet unrealised, and BI holds the key to unlocking a lot of them for better e-solutions in future global markets. (Shobana et al.2023) (Nithya and Kiruthika2021)

Definition and Importance

Business intelligence refers to the tools, technologies, and strategies used to analyze and make sense of the vast amount of data generated by business processes. It is important to note that in today's digitally driven e-commerce landscape, businesses are increasingly relying on data analysis and business intelligence to gain a competitive edge. Business intelligence is not just about gathering and analyzing data, but about the ability to put that data to good use. By providing historic, current and predictive views of business operations, business intelligence empowers businesses to make informed decisions, streamline operational processes, gain a deeper insight into customer behavior and needs, and respond quickly to changing market trends. In the competitive e-commerce market, effective business intelligence can spell the difference between sustained success and abrupt failure. This is because the insights generated from effective data analysis can help e-commerce businesses to identify new sales opportunities, develop targeted marketing campaigns and understand the changing landscape of the industry. So, being effective e-commerce is no longer about simply having a web presence- it is now about using that presence effectively to engage customers and drive sales. With customers scanning the globe for the best products at the best price, the competition has never been more intense and offering a better service than your competitors is the key to success. Because business intelligence can be very complex and, as a practice, can be very disruptive if not planned out properly, there are several challenges in realizing its full potential. For example, it often involves the convergence of many different data sources and continuously developing systems. This will include a migration to a single platform- a recent report from software advice found that 38% of businesses are still using two or more separate platforms to achieve their business intelligence insights. (Rana et al.2022) (Yiu et al.2020) (Niu et al.2021)

Role of Business Intelligence in E-commerce Businesses

Business intelligence in e-commerce is a term used to describe how data analysis can be used by e-commerce firms to improve their decision-making process. The role of business intelligence in e-commerce is growing, and as more competition in the sector exists, in particular between both small and large e-commerce companies, more and more companies are starting to use BI solutions to gain a competitive edge. By gathering and analyzing data, e-commerce companies can make sure that their marketing and products are tailored to what their customers actually want, rather than what the board thinks they want. Data is generally the most valuable asset of an e-commerce business due to the vast amount of information that is generated. Examples of data generated include customer details, the path in which people navigate through the website, and purchase preferences. Without BI, businesses tend to make important decisions based on sheer guesswork. Using data not only reduces this risk but can save time and effort that might have been wasted on the wrong decision. By collecting 'big data' and using it in a BI system, a business can gain useful insight into not only who their potential and existing customers are but also what they might be specifically looking for when it comes to visiting the website. This targeted approach in marketing can have benefits. For example, the conversion rate of turning a browsing customer into a paying one could potentially be improved by providing more of what the data shows is wanted. The main objective of using business intelligence in e-commerce is to help managers and those in charge make informed decisions. By reducing uncertainty and a reliance on gut feel, businesses can be steered more towards capitalizing on what is known to work thanks to the evidence that the data and its analysis have given. There are a variety of methods and technologies available to gather and use data. By spending time looking into the needs and requirements necessary for a business, there are a host of different BI solutions that are catered to offering as close to a perfect match for what is necessary. Overall, business intelligence provides a way for businesses to learn and grow from previously collected data, identifying both past and current trends - ultimately helping to make changes and adapt in a more agile and efficient manner. Using BI can help turn data into meaningful insight, supporting decision making and improving e-commerce performance. (Wu et al., 2023) (Silitonga et al.2024) (Nyanga et al., 2020)

Benefits and Challenges of Implementing Business Intelligence

One of the benefits of business intelligence is that it facilitates data-driven decision making. Data is a key asset for any business in today's environment. The ability to collect and analyze data in real-time allows businesses to monitor their performance and make informed decisions as and when the need arises. Moreover, business intelligence also helps in identifying new business opportunities. It is common for many businesses to get caught up with day-to-day operational exercises. Because of that, opportunities for innovation or for new businesses can be missed. However, using business intelligence to optimize and leverage on the data we get from day-to-day operational activities can help a business to explore and identify those new and valuable opportunities. On the other hand, there are challenges when it comes to implementing business intelligence. One common challenge is a lack of quality data. Business intelligence is always going to be more accurate if you are using the best, most up-to-date data available. However, many businesses do make the mistake of taking their data at face value. Bad data is often cited as a key reason why business intelligence implementations fail. Secondly, high initial investment is also a common challenge. A successful business intelligence strategy relies heavily on making a big and ongoing investment. From management and various business processes to the technology that runs the business, there will have to be changes made right across the organization. Also, technology is always changing and those changes have to be well managed and executed in order for a business intelligence strategy to be satisfactory. Customizing business intelligence systems to specifically fit a business's individual needs is also another challenge. Many businesses will need to shift their culture and develop their data maturity in the long run and it's not a quick or easy process to maximize the effectiveness and the benefits reaped from a business intelligence strategy. (Bharadiya, 2023) (Bharadiya, 2023) (Yiu et al.2021) (Bordeleau et al.2020)

Case Studies on Successful Implementation

The following are real life example of successful implementation of business intelligence in e-commerce company.

Telefónica

Telefónica is a Spanish multinational broadband and telecommunications provider. The company has successfully implemented a new business model based on data-driven knowledge, focusing on solutions that allow more efficient and informed decision-making. This process materialised in a project called BI 2.0, which has consolidated Telefónica as one of the companies that invest more in business intelligence as a key driver of change. As part of this project, Telefónica built a platform that offers a wide range of tools and solutions to help departments and companies to start using business intelligence and to focus on taking action on the new insights surfaced from their analyses. The implementation of the new business model was followed by a significant improvement in company financials. The net profit of 29 million euros over the course of 2018 turned into earnings before interest and tax in the staggering sum of 690 million euros in 2019. This represents a 27.8% year-on-year growth. Similarly, revenue moved from 1.5 billion euros in 2018 to 1.7 billion euros in 2019. This case study demonstrates the benefits of business intelligence and the importance of a well-structured implementation process. (Atiku et al.2024) (Mattera & Gava, 2022) (González & Rampino, 2024)

Figure 1. Telefónica Tech helps B2B customers unlock the value of Big Data and the IoT with Tableau

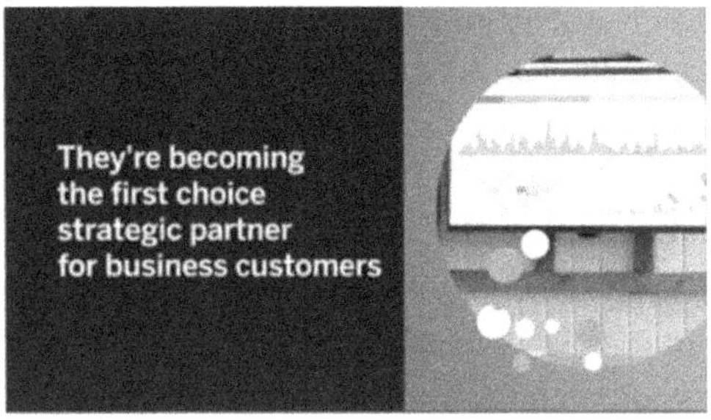

(Telefónica Tech Helps B2B Customers Unlock the Value of Big Data and the IoT With Tableau, n.d.)

2. Market Research in E-commerce

Market research is often conducted in e-commerce to support the aims of understanding the customers, improving the services, and gaining market insights about the potential and existing products. Through routine and regular analysis of the sales and customer data, we can use information to support decisions regarding merchandising, promotional, and marketing activities. However, reaching helpful conclusions from e-commerce market research comes back to having best practices in place for collecting the data in a way that keeps it clean and usable, being as segmented as possible, and taking the right steps to differentiate between the different customer groups. Campaigns carry more significance when customer and market trends and the levels of segmentation have been truly discovered, as this can be used to ensure that communications are sent in a way that is most adapted to the receiver. Effective market analysis will give a visual track on the growth of the customer base and market share of the company itself. New customers can be tracked over time in terms of what marketing activity or other reasons led them to the site. However, 'window shoppers' are also a valuable source of potential research, as above those who purchase, the marketer could learn about the type of consumer that did not flirt with the call to action prompts, and this can be used to change in page layouts and services. Data collection involves search engine and e-commerce tracking, data mining through surveys, and the 'leisurely' user sign up, conducted while the user is engaged in free time on an app or site, will be more readily indulged. (Gao et al.2023) (Babayev & Israfilzade, 2023)

Definition and Significance

Lately, there has been a large number of them entering the market, almost making it a requirement for modern e-commerce businesses to incorporate market research as a key success factor. So, what is market research? Market research is a technique that businesses use to investigate and analyze the size and composition of a particular market to access its business potential. It is a very useful tool because through a systematic and objective collection and analysis of data, businesses are able to discover insight into their customers' needs and wants, business environment as well as ways to reach potential customers. This is a great way to build a strong business by making sure that you have a customer-focused and a customer-driven operation. Also, knowing the market is key in a successful business and good market research can give you a better understanding of the current markets as well as the potential markets that you can tap into. Without the information provided by market research, many companies (and this includes e-commerce businesses) would be basing their business on what they think is the correct strategy, and not what the customers actually want. This can lead to the business making decisions that are not supported by the customers. However, understanding the significance of market research in e-commerce and knowing the difference between consumer market research and business market research can give businesses a clear idea on what and how they can use these collected data and understandings. (Saura et al.2021) (Liu et al., 2022)

Types of Market Research Techniques

There are many different ways of conducting primary research. Common types of marketing research are surveys, interviews, product testing, and the use of observation or monitoring. Surveys ask a small number of questions to a targeted group of people. Surveys can be carried out by giving questionnaires to individual people, by telephone, by mail, or online. They can be carried out face to face or in groups, schools, work places. Interviews are similar to surveys but allow people to expand on their answer, interview can be carried out in person or online and can be carried out one to one or in a group. Product testing is suitable for products which are new or need improving. Products being tested by potential customers so researchers can find out what works and what didn't before releasing the product to general public. Observation or monitoring involves watching how customers behave and the things they do, observation can include physical observation where researchers watch the world or observation can show how technology is being used such as tracking the use of the internet. Another main distinction between primary and who is that it is normally necessary to use far more advanced techniques to analyse secondary data. This is because such data may be large scale, and the clients requirement is that the most efficient and accurate methods are used to get out of it. This kind of data processing simply isn't normally completed by individual people on a pen and paper, it usually requires a computer and special analysis software. (Inagaki et al.2022) (Wu et al.2022) (Thiel et al.2023) (Hattori et al.2023)

3. Impact of Business Intelligence and Market Research on E-commerce Growth

This section investigates the impact of business intelligence (BI) and market research on e-commerce growth, utilizing both qualitative and quantitative research methods. Analyzing findings and examining case studies provide a balanced view of the influence of these practices on the international expansion of businesses. The research emphasizes BI's role in interpreting information for enhanced decision-making. Internet-based technologies, exemplified by multinational companies like Dell, contribute to strategic BI direction and continuous online sales growth. The study also highlights the challenges faced by modern retailers in the evolving landscape of international online retail. Empirical evidence reveals significant price dispersion in various e-commerce sectors, challenging the notion of a perfect global market. The findings underscore the importance of informed decision-making through BI for businesses navigating the complexities of online retailing. (Aparicio et al.2023) (Guru et al., 2020) (Lin et al.2020)

4. Enhancing Customer Experience and Personalization

Positive customer experiences foster brand loyalty and boost sales. Businesses, inspired by e-commerce giants like Amazon, prioritize personalized marketing and customer-centric strategies. Tailoring seamless experiences for each customer is crucial. Leveraging targeted advertising and predictive analytics, as exemplified by Shopify's case study on Watchfinder, enhances the e-commerce shopping journey. Analyzing customer behavior optimizes product promotions, resulting in a 13% increase in conversion rates for Watchfinder. The success prompts increased investment in business intelligence and customer research. This showcases the tangible benefits of employing advanced technologies to elevate customer experience and personalization in the ever-evolving landscape of e-commerce. (Lojacono & Pan, 2021) (da Silva, 2022) (Stolz, 2022)

5. Improving Decision-Making and Strategic Planning

In today's dynamic and global business landscape, leveraging business intelligence (BI) is crucial for informed decision-making and strategic planning. BI involves analyzing vast sets of business data, such as customer sales and preferences, to derive meaningful insights. For e-commerce businesses like ASOS, BI guides product introductions by analyzing customer behaviors, reducing risks, and increasing sales. Despite challenges in staff education and the potential risks of data-driven decisions, establishing a data-driven culture is essential. While adopting BI is not without hurdles, the substantial benefits it offers, such as identifying market opportunities and enhancing operational performance, make it a noteworthy investment for businesses. (Niu et al.2021) (Alzghoul et al.2022) (Wu et al., 2023) (Gupta et al.2023)

6. Identifying Market Trends and Opportunities

For e-commerce success, understanding market changes and consumer behavior is essential. Modern business intelligence (BI) and market research, especially with the application of big data, empower businesses to make informed decisions. Big data allows a deeper understanding of market dynamics, customer behaviors, and shifts in product demand, enhancing the reliability of market research. While historically viewed skeptically, businesses like ASOS are thriving by embracing BI and practice-based market research, gaining a competitive edge through streamlined and accessible consumer data. To navigate the complex market, industry professionals need specific BI skills, and education providers should focus on developing future 'data marketers' to ensure effective governance of consumer data and real-time response capabilities. (Elia et al.2020) (Mariani & Wamba, 2020) (Liu et al., 2020)

7. Increasing Operational Efficiency and Cost Savings

Business intelligence (BI) and market research empower e-commerce businesses to enhance operational efficiency and achieve cost savings. Forrester Consulting's research reveals that 90% of surveyed e-commerce decision-makers prioritize improving operational excellence. BI provides insights for intelligent decision-making, addressing challenges like high operational costs. Malaysia's MR. D.I.Y, a leading home improvement online retailer, exemplifies this. By implementing BI applications and revamping their ERP system, real-time data movements and optimized warehouse processes resulted in reduced inventory costs. The company's continuous sales growth and lower prices demonstrate the success of leveraging BI for operational improvement in the competitive e-commerce landscape. (Thakur et al.2024) (Auf et al.2023) (Shah, 2022)

RESEARCH METHOD

This research will employ a mixed-method approach to comprehensively investigate the impact of business intelligence (BI) and market research on the growth of e-commerce businesses. This approach combines the strengths of both quantitative and qualitative data collection methods, providing a richer and more nuanced understanding of the research phenomenon.

Data Collection

- **Primary data:**
    - **Case studies:** This research will involve in-depth analyses of multiple e-commerce businesses. Case studies will allow for detailed exploration of how these businesses utilize BI and market research practices, and how these practices contribute to their growth. Data will be collected through semi-structured interviews with key personnel (e.g., management, BI team members) and document analysis (e.g., internal reports, BI dashboards).
- **Secondary data:**
    - **Literature review:** Existing research on the relationship between BI, market research, and e-commerce growth will be critically reviewed. Relevant academic journals, industry reports, and white papers will be analyzed to identify key themes, gaps in knowledge, and existing theoretical frameworks.

Data Analysis

- **Quantitative data:** Data collected from case studies, such as sales figures, customer behavior metrics, and market share data, will be analyzed using appropriate statistical methods. This might involve descriptive statistics, correlation analysis, or regression analysis, depending on the research questions and the nature of the data.
- **Qualitative data:** Data from interviews will be transcribed and thematically analyzed to identify key patterns and insights regarding how e-commerce businesses implement BI and market research, and how these practices contribute to their growth.

Ethical considerations: During data collection, informed consent will be obtained from all participants, and data confidentiality will be maintained throughout the research process.

This research method outlines a comprehensive approach that combines various data collection and analysis techniques to gain a deep understanding of how BI and market research influence the growth of e-commerce businesses. The mixed-method approach allows for examining the phenomenon from diverse perspectives, leading to robust and generalizable findings.

FINDINGS AND DISCUSSION

The implementation of business intelligence techniques for the performance measurement of the e-commerce businesses is a big challenge nowadays. Managerial practice in the e-commerce industry more often relies on key performance metrics and the classical outdated data described by business intelligence. Business intelligence (BI) has been introduced into the e-commerce industry as a method to utilize all of the current and historical data effectively, ultimately helping the industry to gain insight. The literature reviewed in this study covers the time period from 2005 to 2017, which is believed to be able to provide a comprehensive understanding of the latest development of e-commerce industry and the technology behind it. The research problem in the present study was originally defined through the context of data constructing and decision supporting the e-commerce managerial practice. The primary data accessed and results obtained have confirmed or empowered the findings in the literature. With the support of a real-world case study and analysis, showing how Web 2.0 functionality can be used to build an effective business intelligence strategy and for gaining insight within the e-commerce sector. This has obviously brought benefits in the areas of strategic marketing, site content planning and performance measurement. Moreover, customer experience has become important in maintaining loyalty and achieving differentiation in most industries, especially the fast growing and trading orientated e-commerce market. It is believed that the methodology has been planned and undertaken in a structured manner, which can be suitably adapted to similar research. And also a novel framework of applying Web 2.0 for e-Business intellective strategy was proposed to deliver managerial practice in the e-commerce community. This study has provided a critical investigation of the sustainable prospects of Web 2.0 in the e-commerce industry for the first time with a user experience simulation. The results not only demonstrated that the successful implementation of the user-centric online business model can lead to significant improvement in customer's online experience, but also identified the potential link between the customer's experience and the strategies related to the continuous development of the e-Business platform. All of those can together facilitate the strategic decision making as a part of the business intelligence implementation. This innovative study, developing on the well-known customer satisfaction theories, for the first time has applied user experience simulation with a practical case study. The results not only demonstrated that the successful implementation of the user-centric online business model can lead to significant improvement in customer's online experience, but also identified the potential link between the customer's experience and the strategies related to the continuous development of the e-Business platform. All of those can together facilitate the strategic decision making as a part of the business intelligence implementation. (Lari et al., 2022) (Pallathadka et al.2023)

Case Studies on E-Commerce Businesses Leveraging Business Intelligence and Market Research

The study delves into successful implementations of business intelligence (BI) through detailed case studies, exemplifying the transformative impact on business operations. One prominent case is ASDA, a top UK retailer, which utilized BI to enhance sales by tracking customer purchase behavior and adjusting stock accordingly. The intelligent use of BI led to increased revenue (up to 1.3%) and the ability to handle over 1.6 billion transactions annually. Similarly, Sainsbury, another leading UK retailer, reduced waste by employing BI for an intelligent ordering process. This resulted in savings exceeding 51 tons of trolley waste per year, equivalent to about 1.7 million in recycling revenue and savings. These cases underscore BI's potential to optimize decision-making, improve efficiency, and drive cost savings, emphasizing the importance of timely and strategic utilization of generated information for maximum impact. (Ologunebi and Taiwo2023) (Breugelmans et al.2023) (Li et al.2023)

Figure 2. The UK's favourite supermarkets

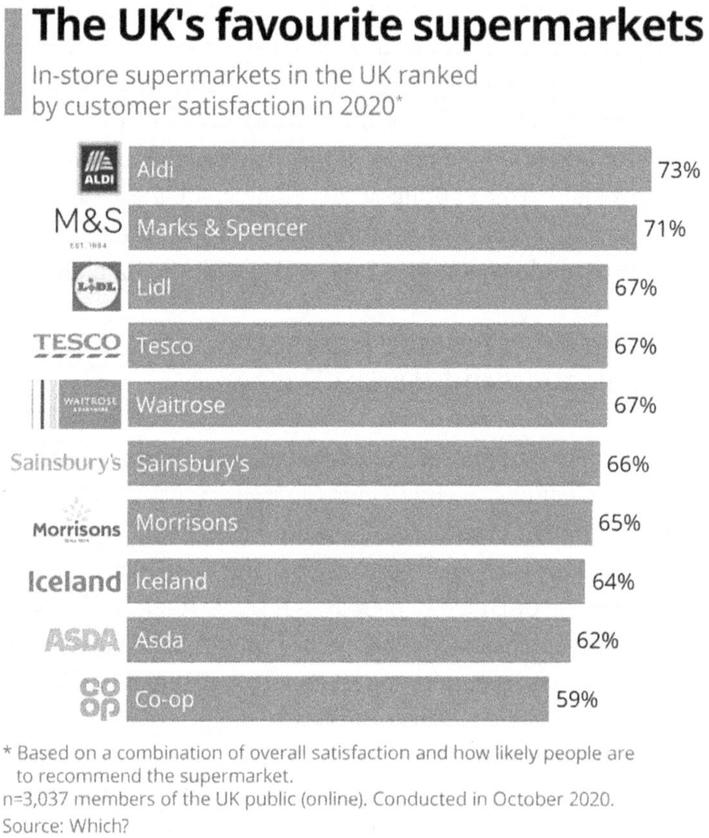

(Armstrong, 2021)

This findings can answer primary research question: "How does business intelligence impact the growth of e-commerce businesses?" and the hypotheses H1: A well-defined business intelligence plan and comprehensive market research are fundamental to establishing and maintaining a successful e-commerce presence.

Recommendations for E-commerce Businesses

E-commerce businesses face evolving challenges that demand strategic adaptation. Firstly, as growth occurs, allocate increased financial resources to marketing, ensuring a low cost per customer acquisition. Secondly, leverage insights gained from market research to guide management decisions effectively. Thirdly, maintain agility by continuously updating and repackaging products in response to shifting market trends. Fourthly, harness multi-channeled data sources for marketing and sales strategies in the digital era. Embracing e-marketing, including search engine and email marketing, is crucial. Fifthly, stay technologically updated to meet the demands of tech-savvy consumers and outpace competitors. Lastly, prioritize customer feedback for product evolution, utilizing accessible channels for responses. Adapting to customer needs fosters satisfaction, ensuring longevity and success in the dynamic landscape of e-commerce. (Yang et al., 2023) (Caliskan et al.2024)

CONCLUSION

In conclusion, this research has clearly demonstrated the significance of business intelligence and market research in the growth of e-commerce businesses. As discussed in the literature review section, business intelligence empowers e-commerce businesses to make data-driven and customer-centric decisions. The real-time and predictive analysis features of business intelligence tools not only improve the decision-making processes, but also help e-commerce businesses to optimize their customer experience. On the other hand, the market research section provides insights into the importance of collecting primary and secondary data in the e-commerce industry, as well as the employment of qualitative and quantitative research methods. The findings reveal that for e-commerce businesses facing stiff competition, regularly doing online market research is important for gathering and analyzing business data such as the performance of the business's website, the customer's preferences, and the actions of competitors. Case studies further demonstrate the successful implementation of business intelligence strategies and the utilization of market research results in e-commerce. For example, Amazon is well-known for its effective use of big data and continuous improvement of customer satisfaction. The ability to perform sentiment analysis and gain insights from online customer reviews has made a significant impact on the sales in various departments as well as on Amazon's strategic decision-making in terms of product development. Conversely, the results from a customer survey study in the mobile app industry, as discussed in the market research section, point to the fact that mobile app developers and marketers should pay attention to users' feedback and ratings, and not underestimate the value and significance of user opinions. This is indicative of the success of businesses as long as they understand the perceptions and preferences of the users, taking on a user-focused approach in leveraging business intelligence strategies.

Future Research Directions

In the evolving global economy, optimizing technology to support both e-commerce and traditional stores remains a critical area for exploration. Authors highlight challenges in implementing business intelligence (BI) in the dynamic e-commerce environment, emphasizing the need for continuous improvement. Future research avenues could involve modeling success factors at various BI maturity levels, providing a systematic validation methodology. Additionally, evaluating BI's impact on key performance indicators for online retailers, especially in terms of customer insights, presents a vital research direction. Quantifying this effect in measures like customer satisfaction and retention would contribute significantly to understanding and enhancing BI in e-commerce.

Practical and Managerial Implications

E-Commerce Businesses:

- *Strategic Growth Planning:* E-commerce businesses can utilize the insights from this study to develop and implement effective growth strategies. Understanding the impact of business intelligence and market research on competitiveness, profitability, and overall growth enables them to make informed decisions.
- *Resource Allocation:* Armed with knowledge about the contributions of BI and market research, e-commerce businesses can optimize resource allocation, focusing on areas that directly influence competitiveness and profitability. This could involve targeted marketing, product development, or operational improvements.

Management Personnel:

- *Informed Decision-Making:* The study emphasizes the real value of business intelligence and market research in decision-making. Management personnel can incorporate these findings into their decision-making processes, ensuring that data-driven insights play a pivotal role in shaping strategic directions.
- *Strategic Investments:* The results provide a basis for justifying investments in BI and market research tools and personnel. Management can allocate resources to strengthen these areas, recognizing them as integral components for sustained growth in the e-commerce sector.

BI Teams:

- *Optimizing Performance:* BI teams can use the identified strategies from the study to optimize their performance. This involves refining data collection methods, enhancing analytical capabilities, and ensuring the timely delivery of actionable insights.

- *Maximizing ROI:* With insights into how BI and market research contribute to competitiveness, profitability, and overall growth, BI teams can tailor their approaches to maximize return on investment. This may involve refining data collection methodologies, exploring new data sources, or improving the efficiency of analytical processes.

Overall Business Landscape:

- *Industry Standards and Best Practices:* The study sets a benchmark for industry standards and best practices regarding the integration of BI and market research in the e-commerce sector. Businesses across industries can draw inspiration and insights for their own data-driven strategies, adapting relevant methodologies to their specific contexts.
- *Educational Institutions:* Universities and training institutions can incorporate the findings into their curriculum, ensuring that future professionals are well-equipped with the knowledge and skills required to navigate the evolving landscape of e-commerce through effective BI and market research practices.

Research Limitations

While the study provides valuable insights into the impact of business intelligence (BI) and market research on the growth of e-commerce businesses, it is essential to acknowledge certain limitations that may affect the generalizability and applicability of the findings:

Scope of the Study:

The research may focus on specific regions, industries, or business sizes, limiting the generalizability of the findings to a broader context. E-commerce businesses operating in different environments may exhibit variations in how BI and market research impact their growth.

Data Collection Methods:

The reliance on case studies and real-world data analysis introduces a potential for selection bias. The chosen cases might not represent the entire spectrum of e-commerce businesses, leading to skewed results. Additionally, the accuracy and reliability of the data collected through case studies can vary.

Temporal Factors:

The rapidly evolving nature of both e-commerce and technology in general means that the study's conclusions may be time-sensitive. Strategies and technologies considered effective during the study period may become outdated, affecting the relevance of the findings over time.

External Market Conditions:

Economic fluctuations, global events, or industry-specific challenges that occurred during the study period may have influenced the results. External factors beyond the scope of the study, such as regulatory changes or unforeseen market dynamics, could impact the generalizability of the findings to different timeframes.

Resource Constraints:

The study may have been limited by resource constraints, affecting the depth and breadth of the analysis. For instance, a more extensive dataset or a longer study duration could have provided a more comprehensive understanding of the long-term effects of BI and market research on e-commerce growth.

Hypothesis Testing:

The study's reliance on a single hypothesis (H1) might oversimplify the complex relationship between BI, market research, and e-commerce growth. The reality could involve multifaceted interactions that are not fully captured by the research design.

Subjectivity in Interpretation:

The interpretation of qualitative data from case studies introduces an element of subjectivity. Different researchers or practitioners may interpret the results differently, potentially impacting the consistency and reliability of the study's conclusions.

Long-Term Impact:

The study may not provide insights into the long-term impact of BI and market research practices on e-commerce businesses. Longitudinal studies could offer a more nuanced understanding of how these practices contribute to sustained growth over extended periods.

Acknowledging these limitations is crucial for readers, researchers, and practitioners to interpret the study's findings judiciously and consider these factors when applying the results to different contexts or making business decisions.

DISCLOSURE OF INTEREST

The author declares no competing interests related to the content of this article. There are no financial, personal, or professional relationships that could be construed as potential conflicts of interest.

DECLARATION OF FUNDING

This research did not receive any specific grant from funding agencies in the public, commercial, or not-for-profit sectors. The author conducted this study independently, and no external sponsors or funding sources were involved in the design, data collection, analysis, interpretation, writing, or decision to submit this article.

REFERENCES

Alzghoul, A., Khaddam, A. A., Abousweilem, F., Irtaimeh, H. J., & Alshaar, Q. (2022). How business intelligence capability impacts decision-making speed, comprehensiveness, and firm performance. *Information Development*, 02666669221108438. Advance online publication. DOI: 10.1177/02666669221108438

Aparicio, D., Metzman, Z., & Rigobon, R. (2023). The pricing strategies of online grocery retailers. *Quantitative Marketing and Economics*, 22(1), 1–21. DOI: 10.1007/s11129-023-09273-w

Armstrong, M. (2021, February 22). *The UK's favourite supermarkets*. Statista Daily Data. https://www.statista.com/chart/17117/uk-favourite-supermarkets/

Atiku, S. O., Menjengua, D. K., Jeremiah, A., & Villet, H. J. (2024). Data-Driven Talent Management Practices for Eco-Innovation in State-Owned Enterprises. In Data-Driven Decision Making for Long-Term Business Success (pp. 369-394). IGI Global. DOI: DOI: 10.4018/979-8-3693-2193-5.ch025

Auf der Landwehr, M., Schoormann, T., von Viebahn, C., & Trott, M. (2023). From purchase to pantry–exploring archetypes and strategies in the context of e-grocery fulfilment. *European Journal of Information Systems*, •••, 1–39. DOI: 10.1080/0960085X.2023.2180446

Babayev, N. & Israfilzade, K. (2023). Creating complexity matrix for classifying artificial intelligence applications in e-commerce: New perspectives on value creation. Journal of Life Economics. https://doi.org/DOI: 10.15637/jlecon.2078

Barata, S. F., Ferreira, F. A., Carayannis, E. G., & Ferreira, J. J. (2023). Determinants of E-Commerce, Artificial Intelligence, and Agile Methods in Small-and Medium-Sized Enterprises. *IEEE Transactions on Engineering Management*. Advance online publication. DOI: 10.1109/TEM.2023.3269601

Bharadiya, J. P. (2023). *A comparative study of business intelligence and artificial intelligence with big data analytics*. American Journal of Artificial Intelligence., DOI: 10.11648/j.ajai.20230701.14

Bharadiya, J. P. (2023). *Machine learning and AI in business intelligence: Trends and opportunities. International Journal of Computer*. IJC.

Bordeleau, F. E., Mosconi, E., & de Santa-Eulalia, L. A. (2020). Business intelligence and analytics value creation in Industry 4.0: A multiple case study in manufacturing medium enterprises. *Production Planning and Control*, 31(2-3), 173–185. DOI: 10.1080/09537287.2019.1631458

Breugelmans, E., Altenburg, L., Lehmkuhle, F., Krafft, M., Lamey, L., & Roggeveen, A. L. (2023). The future of physical stores: Creating reasons for customers to visit. *Journal of Retailing*, 99(4), 532–546. DOI: 10.1016/j.jretai.2023.10.005

Caliskan, F., Idug, Y., Gligor, D. M., Uvet, H., Adana, S., Celik, H., & Cevikparmak, S. (2024). Transparency and trust in cargo claims: Microenterprises selling internationally on a peer-to-peer platform. *Journal of Business and Industrial Marketing*, 39(5), 1092–1103. Advance online publication. DOI: 10.1108/JBIM-03-2023-0170

da Silva, H. D. G. (2022). Diversification in the Personal Luxury Goods Industry: A Case Study of LVMH and its Peers Financial Performance and Mergers and Acquisitions Strategies.

Elia, G., Polimeno, G., Solazzo, G., & Passiante, G. (2020). A multi-dimension framework for value creation through big data. *Industrial Marketing Management*, 90, 617–632. DOI: 10.1016/j.indmarman.2020.03.015

Fosso Wamba, S., Kala Kamdjoug, J. R., Epie Bawack, R., & Keogh, J. G. (2020). Bitcoin, Blockchain and Fintech: a systematic review and case studies in the supply chain. Production Planning & Control, 31(2-3), 115-142.[REMOVED HYPERLINK FIELD] https://doi.org/DOI: 10.1080/09537287.2019.1631460

Fosso Wamba, S., & Queiroz, M. M. (2023). Responsible artificial intelligence as a secret ingredient for digital health: Bibliometric analysis, insights, and research directions. *Information Systems Frontiers*, 25(6), 2123–2138. Advance online publication. DOI: 10.1007/s10796-021-10142-8 PMID: 34025210

Gao, J., Siddik, A. B., Khawar Abbas, S., Hamayun, M., Masukujjaman, M., & Alam, S. S. (2023). Impact of E-commerce and digital marketing adoption on the financial and sustainability performance of MSMEs during the COVID-19 pandemic: An empirical study. *Sustainability (Basel)*, 15(2), 1594. DOI: 10.3390/su15021594

González, A. S., & Rampino, L. (2024). A design perspective on how to tackle gender biases when developing AI-driven systems. *AI and Ethics*. Advance online publication. DOI: 10.1007/s43681-023-00386-2

Gupta, S., Kushwaha, P. S., Badhera, U., Chatterjee, P., & Gonzalez, E. D. S. (2023). Identification of benefits, challenges, and pathways in E-commerce industries: An integrated two-phase decision-making model. *Sustainable Operations and Computers*, 4, 200–218. DOI: 10.1016/j.susoc.2023.08.005

Guru, S., Nenavani, J., Patel, V., & Bhatt, N. (2020). Ranking of perceived risks in online shopping. *Decision (Washington, D.C.)*, 47(2), 137–152. Advance online publication. DOI: 10.1007/s40622-020-00241-x

Hattori, N., Kajita, M., Fujimoto, S., Izutsu, M., & Fernandez, J. (2023). Safety and effectiveness of rasagiline in patients with Parkinson's disease in Japan: A post-marketing surveillance study. *Expert Opinion on Drug Safety*, •••, 1–10. DOI: 10.1080/14740338.2023.2293207 PMID: 38124528

Inagaki, N., Nangaku, M., Sakata, Y., Sasaki, K., Mori-Anai, K., Iwasaki, T., & Hamada, K. (2022). Real-world safety and effectiveness of canagliflozin treatment for type 2 diabetes mellitus in Japan: SAPPHIRE, a long-term, large-scale post-marketing surveillance. *Advances in Therapy*, 39(1), 1–18. DOI: 10.1007/s12325-021-01984-4 PMID: 34853985

Lari, H. A., Vaishnava, K., & Manu, K. S. (2022). Artifical Intelligence in E-commerce: Applications, Implications and Challenges. Asian Journal of Management. DOI: DOI: 10.52711/2321-5763.2022.00041

Li, X., Xu, M., Zeng, W., Tse, Y. K., & Chan, H. K. (2023). Exploring customer concerns on service quality under the COVID-19 crisis: A social media analytics study from the retail industry. *Journal of Retailing and Consumer Services*, 70, 103157. DOI: 10.1016/j.jretconser.2022.103157

Lin, H. H., Tseng, T. H., Yeh, C. H., Liao, Y. W., & Wang, Y. S. (2020). What drives customers' post-purchase price search intention in the context of online price matching guarantees. *Journal of Retailing and Consumer Services*, 54, 102015. DOI: 10.1016/j.jretconser.2019.102015

Liu, C., Wang, S., & Jia, G. (2020). Exploring e-commerce big data and customer-perceived value: An empirical study on chinese online customers. *Sustainability (Basel)*, 12(20), 8649. Advance online publication. DOI: 10.3390/su12208649

Liu, Q., Qu, X., Wang, D., Abbas, J., & Mubeen, R. (2022). Product market competition and firm performance: Business survival through innovation and entrepreneurial orientation amid COVID-19 financial crisis. *Frontiers in Psychology*, 12, 790923. Advance online publication. DOI: 10.3389/fpsyg.2021.790923 PMID: 35411208

Lojacono, G. & Pan, L. R. Y. (2021). Resilience of luxury companies in times of change.

Mariani, M. M., & Wamba, S. F. (2020). Exploring how consumer goods companies innovate in the digital age: The role of big data analytics companies. *Journal of Business Research*, 121, 338–352. Advance online publication. DOI: 10.1016/j.jbusres.2020.09.012

Mattera, M., & Gava, L. (2022). Facing TBL with IoT: Creating value and positively impacting business processes. *Social Responsibility Journal*, 18(1), 178–201. Advance online publication. DOI: 10.1108/SRJ-02-2020-0074

Nithya, N., & Kiruthika, R. (2021). Impact of Business Intelligence Adoption on performance of banks: A conceptual framework. *Journal of Ambient Intelligence and Humanized Computing*, 12(2), 3139–3150. DOI: 10.1007/s12652-020-02473-2

Niu, Y., Ying, L., Yang, J., Bao, M., & Sivaparthipan, C. B. (2021). Organizational business intelligence and decision making using big data analytics. *Information Processing & Management*, 58(6), 102725. DOI: 10.1016/j.ipm.2021.102725

Nyanga, C., Pansiri, J., & Chatibura, D. (2020). Enhancing competitiveness in the tourism industry through the use of business intelligence: A literature review. Journal of Tourism Futures. https://doi.org/DOI: 10.1108/JTF-11-2018-0069

Ologunebi, J., & Taiwo, E. O. (2023). Digital Marketing Strategies, plan and implementations: A case study of Jumia Group and ASDA Uk. Plan and Implementations: a Case Study of Jumia Group and ASDA UK (October 6, 2023). https://mpra.ub.uni-muenchen.de/118771/

Pallathadka, H., Ramirez-Asis, E. H., Loli-Poma, T. P., Kaliyaperumal, K., Ventayen, R. J. M., & Naved, M. (2023). Applications of artificial intelligence in business management, e-commerce and finance. *Materials Today: Proceedings*, 80, 2610–2613. DOI: 10.1016/j.matpr.2021.06.419

Rana, N. P., Chatterjee, S., Dwivedi, Y. K., & Akter, S. (2022). Understanding dark side of artificial intelligence (AI) integrated business analytics: Assessing firm's operational inefficiency and competitiveness. *European Journal of Information Systems*, 31(3), 364–387. DOI: 10.1080/0960085X.2021.1955628

Saura, J. R., Ribeiro-Soriano, D., & Palacios-Marqués, D. (2021). From user-generated data to data-driven innovation: A research agenda to understand user privacy in digital markets. International Journal of Information Management, 60, 102331.[REMOVED HYPERLINK FIELD] https://doi.org/DOI: 10.1016/j.ijinfomgt.2021.102331

Shah, T. R. (2022). Can big data analytics help organisations achieve sustainable competitive advantage? A developmental enquiry. *Technology in Society*, 68, 101801. Advance online publication. DOI: 10.1016/j.techsoc.2021.101801

Shobana, J., Gangadhar, C., Arora, R. K., Renjith, P. N., & Bamini, J. (2023). E-commerce customer churn prevention using machine learning-based business intelligence strategy. *Measurement. Sensors*, 27, 100728. DOI: 10.1016/j.measen.2023.100728

Silitonga, D., Rohmayanti, S. A. A., Aripin, Z., Kuswandi, D., Sulistyo, A. B., & Juhari, . (2024). Edge Computing in E-commerce Business: Economic Impacts and Advantages of Scalable Information Systems. *EAI Endorsed Transactions on Scalable Information Systems*, 11(1). Advance online publication. DOI: 10.4108/eetsis.4375

Stolz, K. (2022). Why do (n't) we buy second-hand luxury products? *Sustainability (Basel)*, 14(14), 8656. Advance online publication. DOI: 10.3390/su14148656

Telefónica Tech helps B2B customers unlock the value of Big Data and the IoT with Tableau. (n.d.). Tableau. https://www.tableau.com/solutions/customer/telefonica-tech-helps-b2b-customers-unlock-value

Thakur, S., Sandhu, S., & Yehuwalashet, F. (2024). 16 E-Commerce and Trade. Handbook of Artificial Intelligence Applications for Industrial Sustainability: Concepts and Practical Examples

Thiel, C. E., McClean, S., Harvey, J., & Prince, N. (2023). Trouble with big brother: Counterproductive consequences of electronic monitoring through the erosion of leader-member social exchange. *Journal of Organizational Behavior*, 44(9), 1320–1339. DOI: 10.1002/job.2748

Wu, D., Zhang, G., Liu, J., Shen, S., Yang, Z., Pan, Y., Zhao, X., Yang, S., Tian, Y., Zhao, H., Li, J., & Cai, L. (2022). Influence of particle properties and environmental factors on the performance of typical particle monitors and low-cost particle sensors in the market of China. *Atmospheric Environment*, 268, 118825. DOI: 10.1016/j.atmosenv.2021.118825

Wu, Q., Yan, D., & Umair, M. (2023). Assessing the role of competitive intelligence and practices of dynamic capabilities in business accommodation of SMEs. *Economic Analysis and Policy*, 77, 1103–1114. Advance online publication. DOI: 10.1016/j.eap.2022.11.024

Yang, Y., Habib, K., & Wood, M. O. (2023). Establishing best practices for E-commerce transport packaging waste management in Canada: A systematic review. *Journal of Cleaner Production*, 429, 139377. Advance online publication. DOI: 10.1016/j.jclepro.2023.139377

Yiu, L. D., Yeung, A. C., & Cheng, T. E. (2021). The impact of business intelligence systems on profitability and risks of firms. *International Journal of Production Research*, 59(13), 3951–3974. DOI: 10.1080/00207543.2020.1756506

Yiu, L. D., Yeung, A. C., & Jong, A. P. (2020). Business intelligence systems and operational capability: An empirical analysis of high-tech sectors. *Industrial Management & Data Systems*, 120(6), 1195–1215. DOI: 10.1108/IMDS-12-2019-0659

Chapter 8
Evaluating the Effectiveness of Leadership Decision Making by Data Analytics and Reporting Technologies

Deeksha Dwivedi
https://orcid.org/0009-0008-4722-8607
Leslie's, USA

Shivani Agarwal
https://orcid.org/0000-0002-3205-552X
Galgotias University, India

ABSTRACT

Data analytics and reporting technologies play an important role in leadership decision-making. This chapter examines how data analytics and reporting technology help decision-making in leadership. Previous research shows that modern data analytics tools have been incorporated to enhance decision-making processes, improve reporting accuracy, and drive business performance. Organizations using advanced analytics tools tend to see huge benefits in speed, accuracy, improved reporting, and strategic decision-making. Modern technical analytical and reporting tools help leadership understand data by interacting with dashboards, graphs, and real-time data, which helps make a strategy based on the data. There are great benefits of using data analytics and reporting technology in leadership decision-making, it

DOI: 10.4018/979-8-3693-4361-6.ch008

improves efficiency, productivity, and overall organizational growth.

1. INTRODUCTION

In today's world, organizations are producing and utilizing large amounts of data. Advanced analytics tools help organizations to analyze data quickly and effectively. McAfee and Brynjolfsson (2012) mentioned that leaders are increasingly relying on big data to make more accurate and timely decisions, moving beyond intuition-based decision-making to one grounded in data. Davenport and Bean (2019) emphasize that data-driven leadership involves not only the technical application of analytics but also the strategic integration of data insights into the overall business strategy. The use of data analytics and reporting technologies is growing day by day. This chapter explores how data analytics and reporting technology improve business reporting and their effects on leadership decision-making. Data comes from different places and sources, data analytics and reporting technology can analyze these data effectively, which helps leadership in their decision-making and strategy planning. Data analytics tools can quickly analyze large amounts of information and get clear insight.

Data analytics tools provide color-coded graphs, charts, and real-time dashboards etc. for leadership and management. Data analytical tools and reporting technologies help leaders take timely, cost-effective actions based on organizational objectives and needs. Data analytics and reporting technology make large data analysis very easy. The chapter shows how data analytics and reporting technologies enhance management reporting and facilitate business leadership.

Provost and Fawcett (2013) highlight that leaders who use data to inform their decisions are better equipped to adapt to changing market conditions and to capitalize on opportunities, enhancing organizational agility. Furthermore, through predictive analytics, leaders can foresee potential risks and mitigate them proactively, leading to more resilient organizations (Sharma et al., 2021). Data analytics is a process that evaluates raw data systematically to get the correct, meaningful, detailed insights, which is helpful for leadership in their decision-making process. Data analytics requires collecting, organizing, and analyzing data by utilizing different techniques and tools. Data analysis turns data sets into information that can help organizations make important business strategies and plans.

Analytics tells what might happen, it also suggests what actions to take. Analytics is very useful for leadership decision-making. For example, an information technology company could use analytics to find the best software program for the project, which can help with strategy planning and saving time and money.

Reporting technologies are very important tools for fast, reliability, and quick analysis of data. Reporting is a set of tools that collect data, process the data, and display data based on the requirements. Reporting technology helps leaders see current trends and issues and make better decisions based on the report. Reporting technology can transform complex data into visual formats which is very helpful to get insights from the data.

By automating report generation, organizations are saving money and time. Organizations are getting updates in real-time, which is helping the organization to plan the strategy accordingly. Automated reports provide reports based on the latest data. Automation is saving time and providing fast results.

Interactive dashboards are a great feature of reporting technologies. Interactive dashboards help leaders to dive deeper into data based on specific criteria, leadership gets deeper insight into data based on their requirements. Interactive dashboards provide great insight into the data, which can be crucial when making decisions based on large amounts of data. Getting a detailed understanding from interactive dashboards on each aspect of the requirement makes the leadership job easier in the decision-making process.

One more important use of reporting technologies is collaborating with different databases, clouds, etc. This feature can help teams sitting around the world interact with each other and allow them to work together in real-time. Teams collaborating can make decisions based on the shared information. This data-driven collaboration plays a dominant role in any industry. This can help in getting correct, fast, and accurate insight from the data and make future strategy planning based on the reports.

The fast and reliable data quality from the data analytics tool is a tremendous help for decision-making and strategy planning. When leaders have great real-time insight, they can take necessary action fast and make any changes if required in their current strategies. For example, an e-commerce team can monitor their current trends and make necessary changes based on real-time data, which can help in the growth of a company.

Data analytics can also provide performance benchmarks based on the data. With the help of reporting technologies and data analytics, organizations can get better results, which also helps in ensuring accountability. Leaders can check how their team is working to achieve the goal and whether the goal is matching with the organizational goals and objectives. Based on the reporting data and performance, leadership can choose the best practices to make better strategies and performance improvements.

Data analytics also helps in analyzing trends and risks based on the data. Based on the trends and risks report, organizations can anticipate shifts in consumer behavior. This foresight allows leadership to adjust strategies proactively, keeping them ahead in the competitive market.

In the organization, different stakeholders need different types of reports, and data analytics and reporting technologies can help them to get fast and reliable reports. Advanced analytics tools help in customizing reporting based on what stakeholders need. Advanced analytics helps leaders create relevant insight based on their specific roles and requirements. A customized report based on the stakeholder's needs can improve communication effectively across the organization, which can help in making better strategies for the organization.

Data analytics and reporting technologies are changing the business world. With the help of data analytics and reporting technologies, organizations are improving their reporting needs for strategic planning. Data analytics and reporting technology tools help leaders to make the right decisions based on the data, get better insight from team/people accountable, and explore new possibilities for businesses and teams based on the data.

There are mainly **four types of data analysis** as shown in *Figure 1*. Each of these methods is important for making strategy, looking at trends, and making business decisions for leadership.

1) Descriptive analysis
2) Diagnostic analytics
3) Predictive analytics
4) Prescriptive analytics

Figure 1. Types of data analytics

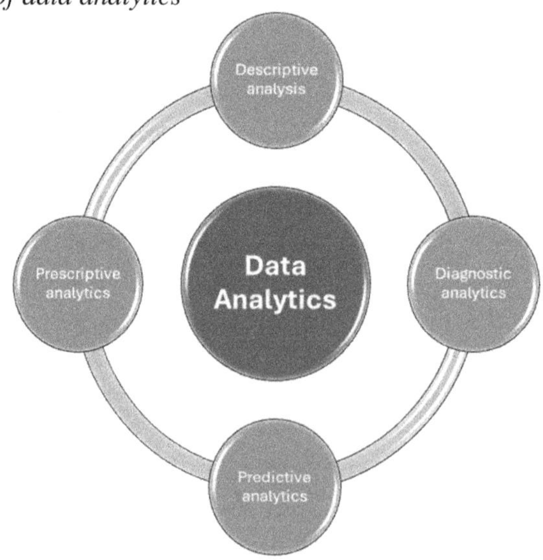

1.1 Descriptive Analytics (To Understand Current Situation)

Descriptive analytics is a type of data analysis that evaluates previous data to give insights into what has happened in the past. With the help of descriptive analytics, leadership can analyze past data and make strategies for organization growth. It also helps in their decision-making process. Descriptive analytics is a type of data analysis that involves figuring out trends and patterns over time. Descriptive analytics is often the first step for organizations to look to understand their data in a better way. Descriptive analytics converts raw data into easy-to-understand data.

Descriptive analytics are important for leaders because they show them what has happened and helps leaders and organizations to make growth strategies. It's all about understanding the past so we can make smarter choices moving forward.

1.2 Diagnostic Analytics (To Investigate Cause)

Diagnostic analytics is a very important component of data analytics. Data analytics mainly focus on assessing why certain trends or events occurred. Diagnostic analysis tries to find out the root causes behind specific patterns, outcomes, patterns, and anomalies in data. Diagnostic analytics goes deep down in the data to figure out the factors, correlation, and relationship that contributed to the particular result or incident.

By analyzing previous data closely, diagnostic analytics can provide organizations with a better understanding of the reasons behind their previous performance trends, operations problems, product behavior, customer behaviors, etc. By showing insights into the root causes of business outcomes, diagnostic analytics helps organizations to make proper strategies and better decisions. Diagnostic analysis helps identify areas for optimizing, improvement, and strategy planning to overcome specific problems. As businesses and technology continue to generate huge data, diagnostic analytics is very important to informed decision-making.

1.3 Predictive Analytics (To Forecast Trends)

Predictive analytics is an analytical method that analyzes past data, attribution-based methods, and sophisticated algorithms to generate future outcomes. It is a decision tool for Forecast Trends which can help organizations in their decision-making process. It looks at history to anticipate what could happen in the future. Predictive analytics utilizes a unique projection approach. Predictive analytics identify risks for business, boost employee efficiency, improve productivity, and personalize services based on requirements for future trends.

1.4 Prescriptive Analytics (To Develop Strategies)

Predictive analytics is a type of data analytics that helps leadership make better choices. Perspective analytics indicate to the leadership what is right, what must be improved, or how to prevent content that is counterproductive from working at all. The main goal of predictive analytics is to optimize business results by suggesting data-based future scenarios for leadership.

2. REVIEW OF LITERATURE

The area of data analytics and reporting tech has really advanced a lot in the last few years. Researchers have proved how effective these tools are in improving business reporting. Previous research shows how important data analytics has become for businesses today.

Many researchers pointed out how data analytics tools can really change the way businesses do reporting. Chen says that business intelligence and analytics have come a long way from just being about database management and data warehousing (Chen and others, 2012). This finding shows just how powerful analytics tools can be for boosting business performance by improving both reporting and the decision-making process.

Davenport describes how analytics can bestow a competitive edge on organizations (Davenport, 2017). They maintain that advanced analytical tools double the speed and accuracy levels of information reporting and further enhance the quality of insight gained.

It's fascinating to realize that by embracing these tools, companies can enhance their overall efficiency and effectiveness. The strategic role of analytics can't be overlooked, especially as businesses face more challenges and competition. In short, analytics is a key player for success in modern industries.

These analytical tools are shown to improve decision-making processes, especially in inventory management and understanding customer behavior. Such insights reveal how analytics can be tailored to meet the specific needs of different industries. Ultimately, this research illustrates the vital role analytics plays in shaping effective reporting and informed decision-making across diverse business landscapes.

Another important point is data quality. Hazen says that having good data is vital for effective analytics, especially in areas like data science and supply chain management (Hazen and others, 2014). Their findings show that businesses need to focus on data quality to really gain from these analytics tools.

Big data is changing the way we manage businesses (McAfee and Brynjolfsson, 2012). They said that decisions made with data are usually better. It's interesting to think about how tools for analyzing data can really help businesses report their information in a clearer way.

It is focused on how these tools are changing finance and managerial accounting (Appelbaum, 2017). It's like a whole new way of reporting. Their research points out that analytics tools have a wide impact across many different areas of business. It's not just one part that benefits, but rather multiple domains that seem to get influenced.

It also explains how we can visualize information. It's about taking complex data and making it easier to understand with visuals (Ware, 2012). He emphasizes that when we can see data in a visual way, it really makes business reporting better. A picture can speak a thousand words, as they say, and it holds true for data as well. Effective visualization helps communicate important information more clearly and quickly.

3. METHODOLOGY AND OBJECTIVES

This study explores how data analytics tools work to make business reporting better and how data analytics enhance leadership decision making. This research is also trying to find out the ways data analytics and reporting technologies improve business performance, growth, and leadership strategies. This chapter explores the highlights of best practices in the use of data analytics for informed decision-making and strategic organizational growth. *The research objectives are as follows:*

- To identify the main factors influencing the adoption and effective use of these technologies among leadership roles.
- To evaluate user satisfaction levels with respect to data analytics tools and reporting technologies based on different user demographics.
- To analyze trends of the monthly usage of data analytics tools within different industries, particularly patterns of adoption as well as frequency of use.
- To conduct an extensive survey on user satisfaction with the specific features and functionalities of data analytics tools.

4. RESULTS

Among the greatest advantages of data analytics is its role in increasing the accuracy of business reporting. On the other hand, traditional reporting practices often involve manual entry and processing of data, which can lead to the introduction of errors, besides the inconsistencies attached. Data analytics, on the other hand, automates the whole data process, with which the chance of human error is greatly reduced. With the combination of real-time data processing, organizations are hence able to generate reports reflecting the most updated information.

4.1 Analysis of Data Analytics and Reporting Technologies Usage by Leadership

Analytical data and reporting technology would be used across the organization for various leadership roles according to the specific needs of the departments. These include technologies to track performance, examine metrics, and offer insights into the operation of the business. The CEO, the CFO, and the Strategy Officer would use technologies that provide strategic insight and decision-making assistance. Some other roles, such as COO, VP of Operations, and Operations Manager, would need technologies that directly improve operations and provide real-time information. VP Customer Service, Customer Success Lead, and Customer Experience Lead emphasize collecting and analyzing customer feedback, while the Data Analyst, Data Scientist, and BI Analyst would need advanced programming and analysis of large data sets. Some leaders, such as the VP of Marketing, express concern over the issue of integration with the existing systems, leading to all sorts of tactics that may present challenges for data consolidation and analysis. Some of the leaders have also mentioned the need for training, hence implicitly stating that support and education will play a highly significant role in the acceptance of technologies *as shown inFigure 2.*

Figure 2. Analysis of data analytics and reporting technologies usage by leadership

Data Analytics and Reporting Technologies Usage by Leadership	
Leadership Role	**Purpose**
CEO	Strategic insights
CTO	Performance monitoring
CFO	Financial analysis
VP of Marketing	Market analysis
VP of Sales	Sales forecasting
VP of Product	Agile project tracking
HR Director	Employee metrics
Operations Manager	Operational reporting
Data Analyst	Advanced data analysis
Customer Success Lead	Customer feedback analysis
COO	Business performance overview
VP of Finance	Financial forecasting
VP of IT	IT performance metrics
CMO	Marketing campaign effectiveness
VP of Operations	Operational metrics
Data Scientist	Data modeling and reporting
CIO	Data preparation and blending
Product Manager	Web performance tracking
Security Analyst	Security incident reporting
Compliance Officer	Compliance reporting
Marketing Analyst	Lead generation analysis
Strategy Officer	Strategic insights
VP of Customer Service	Customer satisfaction tracking
DevOps Manager	System perfomance monitoring
CPO	Product usage analysis
Network Administrator	Network performance reporting
BI Director	Business intelligence reporting
Sales Director	Sales tracking
CTO	Data visualization
Product Lead	User behavior tracking
Chief Scientist	Big data processing
Quality Assurance Lead	Testing metrics
CTO	IT monitoring
Social Media Manager	Social media analysis
Analytics Director	Large-scale data analysis
VP of Development	Real-time data processing
VP of Infrastructure	System perfomance monitoring
BI Analyst	Dashboard creation
Customer Experience Lead	Customer feedback

4.2 Data Analytics User Satisfaction

A survey of all staff members found that data analytics was most often used in basic reporting and discussions of business strategies. The CTO and CEO utilized the data analytics and reporting technologies the most, with average time usage being 20 hours and 8 hours respectively. The COO, CFO, CIO, and CPO used the technologies in 6 to 7 hours. The highest usage frequency in this case can be observed from the CTO, suggesting his rating of data analytics and reporting tools to be highly relevant. The CEO should be applying data analytics and reporting technology for strategic purposes to reach his conclusions. Similar amount of usage it is the COO, CFO, CIO, and CPO that matter, they need to be in tune with the effective management and involvement in operations through data. The less frequent reporting raised some observations regarding the CMO, like whether the marketing was not data-driven or that there were other means to pull information from, way more than data research could provide as shown in *Figure 3*.

Figure 3. Data analytics user satisfaction

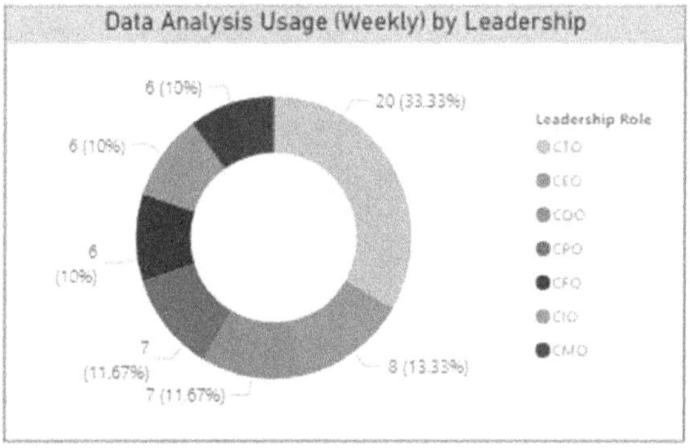

4.3 Detailed Analysis of Monthly Users of Data Analytics Tool by Industry

The bar chart presented displays the monthly usage of data analytics tools across industries. The x-axis gives the number of monthly users alongside the industries that line up to the y-axis. The Technology industry leads in the adoption of the data analytics tool, boasting a significantly greater number of monthly users than any other sector. Thus, it is stated that data-driven innovation and decision-making have already cut it in this sector. Close in second place is Finance-based data analytics. The Retail industry uses this moderately, probably very much because of the need to understand customer behavior inventory management or targeted marketing. In other sectors, such as Telecommunications or Healthcare or Energy or Logistics, the tool is moderately utilized. All of this indicates that demand for data-centric responses is at least steady in such fields as shown in *Figure 4*.

Figure 4. Detailed analysis of monthly users of data analytics tool by industry

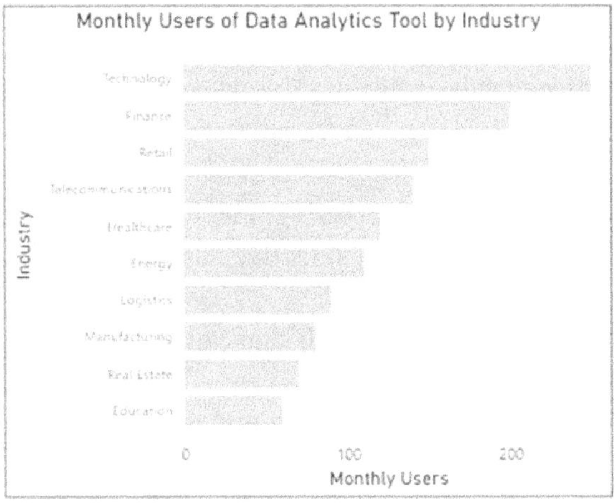

4.4 Detailed Analysis of Data Analytics User Satisfaction

The given pie chart exhibits the users' satisfaction ratings, from 1 to 10, about a data analytics application. The chart exhibits the distribution of responses across various satisfaction levels along with percentages representing the proportion of respondents selecting each rating.

Out of the total, 430 users, representing nearly one-third (33.86%), expressed very high satisfaction with the data analytics tool, rating it 9 or 10. Thus majority of feedback shows the existence of this positive perception regarding the tool's performance, features, and ease of use as shown in *Figure 5*.

Figure 5. Detailed analysis of data analytics user satisfaction

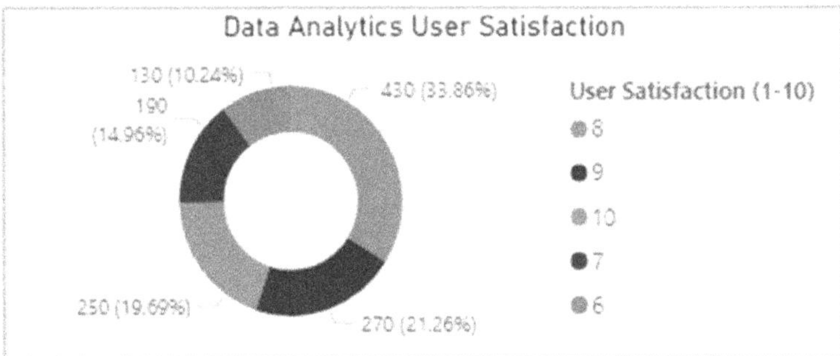

Data integration plays an important role in data analytics. Organizations should look for tools that are easy to use and can easily import and export data from various sources or databases. The right data integration tool can help leaders in creating advanced data pipelines for organization use. Here are some important things to consider:

- Real-time dashboarding and reporting: Choose tools with strong visualization options that let you create interactive dashboards and reports, complete with filters and drilldowns.
- Scalability: It's essential to have tools that can grow with the business, so you aren't limited as needs change.
- User-friendly Interfaces: The design should be easy to understand for everyone, not just those with technical skills, which helps in getting more people to use it.
- Robust Customer Support: Good training and support services are key. They help users solve technical problems and get the most out of the tools.

5. USAGE OF DATA ANALYTICS AND BUSINESS REPORTING IN PECULIAR DOMAINS FOR LEADERSHIP DECISION-MAKING

There are lots of data analytics and reporting tools available on the market. Different data analytics tools have their own features. These tools have different capabilities, pricing, and the types of users they cater to, from self-service options to large-scale enterprise solutions that totally depend on what organizations need.

These are the areas where data analytics are useful for organizations as shown in *Figure 6*:

Figure 6. Areas where data analytics tools are useful for organizations

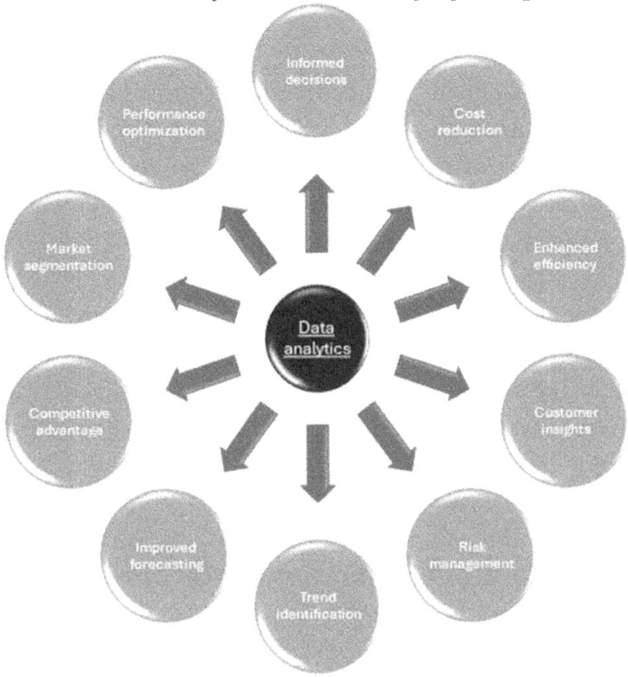

Data analytics help organizations get a better understanding of customer expectations, customer behavior, improved business strategies, sales patterns and trends, and competitive business. With the help of data analytics patterns and trends, organizations can make better decisions that align with their organization's objectives and strategic goals, which helps performance improvement. These data analytics tools improve data accuracy through cleansing processes, ensuring decisions are based on reliable information. Data analytics are improving operational efficiency by automating data collection and reporting:

1) Improved speed and accuracy of decision-making processes
2) Enhanced data visualization and interpretation capabilities
3) Ability to process large datasets rapidly and uncover hidden patterns
4) Generation of real-time, interactive dashboards and reports
5) Improved operational efficiency and productivity
6) Enhanced market competitiveness and financial performance

5.1 Improved Speed and Accuracy of Decision-Making Processes

Data analytics has drastically changed the decision-making processes in leadership by improving accuracy and speed. Data analytics helped a lot with the speed of decision-making for strategy planning through fast and real-time analytics and dashboard capabilities. The data analytics and reporting technology are streaming data analytics platforms, which helps leadership in analyzing data, minimizing the time between data collection and result delivery. The data analysis helps organizations make strategies for changing market conditions, customer behaviors, business growth, or business operations.

For example, in the e-commerce industry, real-time data analytics can get point-of-sale data, inventory levels, and consumption behavior patterns at the same time. Such real-time reports can help leadership make decisions on inventory, pricing adjustments, etc.

5.2 Enhanced Data Visualization and Interpretation Capabilities

Data analytics has improved data visualization and interpretation. Improved visualization and interpretation have enhanced business understanding and the uses of large data. Advanced analytics tools can now provide real-time data, interactive dashboards, data visualizations, and interpretation, which help leadership understand large datasets very easily. Advanced analytical tools use mathematical algorithms to find out trends, patterns, and anomalies. Advanced visualization tools and techniques, like tree maps, dashboards, heat maps, and interactive diagrams, make analyzing complex data easy to understand as shown in *Figure 7*.

Figure 7. Benefits of data analytics tools for organizations

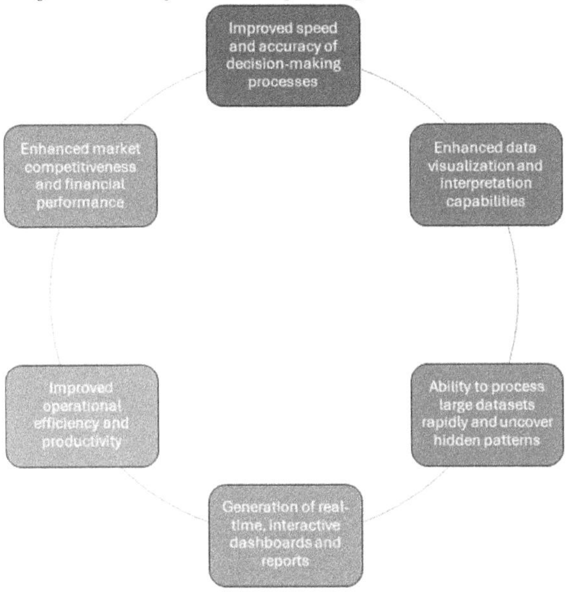

5.3 Ability to Process Large Datasets Rapidly and Uncover Hidden Patterns

Data analytics has changed the way to process large datasets quickly and evaluate hidden patterns as well. Advanced data and machine learning help in the evaluation of large numbers of structured and unstructured data in real time. Data analytics can also help leadership in identifying very complex relationships and current market trends.

Fast data analytics tools and processing frameworks can analyze petabytes of data. With the fast analyzing and processing power of the latest data analytics tool with the mix of the latest data mining techniques, leadership can discover the latest patterns, trends, and correlations between data.

5.4 Generation of Real-Time, Interactive Dashboards and Reports

Data analytics tools help leadership evaluate and customize data based on their needs. Real-time dashboards update data automatically when new data flows in, which helps leadership in getting updated information that they can use in decision-making and strategy planning. Data analytics tool features like slicers, filters, and drill-throughs can help leadership filter the data. Advanced analytics tools help in getting AI- and machine-driven insights for leadership. Natural language querying helps in understanding complex data easy to understand by non-technical persons.

5.5 Improved Operational Efficiency and Productivity

Data analytics have improved an organization's productivity and operational efficiency. Advanced analytical tools help leadership and organizations to find out the pattern, and root cause for failure, streamline the process, optimize the product, and optimize response. Data analytics demand forecasting models to help businesses and leadership be up to date with real-time inventory, which is the key for business.

5.6 Enhanced Market Competitiveness and Financial Performance

Data analytical tools are helping organizations to get better insights into current market trends, competitors, all similar products available in the market, customer behavior, and an idea about which product is more in demand. Data-driven approaches help leaders make strategic decisions based on the latest data, optimize business pricing strategies based on market trends, and identify new revenue opportunities in the current market after analyzing the product. Data analytics also helps organizations streamline their business operations, reducing costs if needed, and helping in resource utilization. Data analytics and reporting technology help organizations predict market changes and customer needs based on the data. With the help of big data, organizations can improve customer experience, product analysis, and channel management if needed based on market dynamics, which helps in improved organization performance and increased productivity.

6. REPORTING TECHNOLOGY FOR ORGANIZATIONS

In today's fast-paced technological business landscape, companies need advanced analytics tools to improve their reporting capabilities, strategy planning, and data-driven, informed decision-making processes. The effectiveness of data analytics tools in enhancing business reporting for organization leadership is an important factor in achieving competitive advantages, market trends, and optimizing operational excellence as shown in *Figure 8*.

The benefits of reporting technology are as follows:

1) Enhanced Data Processing and Integration

2) Improved Data Visualization
3) Predictive Analytics and Forecasting
4) Automated Reporting and Real-Time Updates
5) Enhanced Data Quality and Consistency
6) Customization and Personalization
7) Improved Collaboration and Data Democratization

Figure 8. Benefits of reporting technology for organizations

6.1 Enhanced Data Processing and Integration

Data analytics tools improve business reporting by analyzing large amounts of data from different sources. Getting data from various sources is not easy with traditional reporting methods. Data analytics tools are very efficient and effective in analyzing big data.

Data analytics tools can get information from different systems, different databases, and multiple external sources, and then merge all the data into one place. For example, a manufacturing company can integrate sales data, customer satisfaction data, product data, customer information, product inventory, competitor data, and growth trends to get a better insight and generate reports on overall organizational performance for leadership.

6.2 Improved Data Visualization

Data visualization is a great feature of data analytics tools, data visualization capabilities improve business reporting. Data analytics tools show visualization features that can help leadership understand complex and large datasets easily. The visualization feature of data analysis makes it easy to understand for leadership and everyone in the organization.

Advanced data analytical tools have different visualization features like graph charts, simple bar charts, pie charts, scatter plots, heat maps, and interactive dashboards. These reporting technologies improve overall business operations and help leadership with decision-making and strategy planning.

6.3 Predictive Analytics and Forecasting

One of the very significant approaches in which data analytic tools are making positive improvements on business reporting is by enhancing predictive analysis and forecasting. While traditional reporting dwells on purely descriptive analysis and focuses on historical data, advanced analytics, to the contrary, can make use of historical information to predict future trends and outcome scenarios.

These predictive capabilities allow businesses to transform their decision-making from one that is reactive to one that is proactive in nature. For instance, the manufacturing company could use predictive analysis to estimate demand for its products, optimize inventory levels, and even effectively plan production schedules. This foresight is what enables the higher management to be well acquainted with perspectives that could help them with strategic planning and risk management.

By improving the predictability of revenues, expenses, and cash flow, forecasting indeed enhances financial reporting. Budgeting and financial planning efforts could see huge value in this process, as it provides management with the ability to allocate resources more efficiently and foresee financial shortcomings.

6.4 Automated Reporting and Real-Time Updates

Data analytics have streamlined the reporting process through automation. Most automation tools now enable management to produce automated reports at specific intervals or triggered by certain relevant events. Automations have relieved staff from time-consuming manual reporting processes, which help them to pursue more strategic activities. As new data becomes available, the reports can be automatically refreshed to include that updated information.

For instance, e-commerce can automate reporting daily on sales that are updated in real-time as transactions take place. It enables management to monitor sales performance frequently and make quick changes in marketing strategies or inventory levels.

6.5 Enhanced Data Quality and Consistency

There are features of data cleaning, data validation, and data standardization available in analytical tools. Their function is to ensure that reporting data is reliable, appropriate, and consistent. Just automating such data quality checks will indicate areas of possible errors or inconsistency, thus limiting any chance of reporting inaccuracy. In addition, analytic tools create freaking consistency across a report and an organization by centralizing processes of data and reporting. Such consistency matters a lot for large organizations where different teams generate reports based on the same underlying data. A centralized analytics platform enables companies to ensure that their reports are built on the same validated dataset, such that the discrepancies are reduced, together with ensuring overall data governance and compliance.

6.6 Customization and Personalization

Customization and Personalization of data play an important role in decision-making. Data reporting and analytics can help a person to get the right data, it helps them to make better decisions. Clear information leads to better decision-making for leadership.

Finally, analytics tools aren't just about crunching raw data; they're an avenue through which people connect to data that is meaningful to them. This kind of personalization allows almost everyone to do their jobs in a much more effective way. I believe that with the continuing use of these tools, companies will invariably experience huge improvements in their managing processes. It is exciting to think about the evolution and advancement of data analytics.

6.8 Improved Collaboration and Data Democratization

This team-based collective thinking will likely be able to create an environment of openness and invention for novel ideas. As many people become familiar with these analytics tools, the knowledge of the entire organization grows. Everyone starts to understand data more clearly, allowing better decisions to be made at all levels.

One example is how the marketing team attempts to work out the customer trends: wait for IT to pull some reports, or they can use such tools themselves, thereby reacting faster and making smarter moves. It has been quite interesting to witness how all these invariably note better results in facilitating prompt action based on insights.

7. CONCLUSION

In conclusion, the data analytics tools really help improve leadership by business reporting and improve organizations growth. By using data analytics and reporting technologies, leadership can get raw data into useful insights that support smart decision-making and planning. While businesses continue to change, the incorporation of advanced analytics into reporting processes will be necessary to boost growth and achieve the strategic objectives of the organization. Failing to recognize the significance of data analytics, and investment inadequately in the right tools and practices, certainly leadership and organization cannot be successful. It should be a powerful asset for leadership to achieve success.

New-age analytics are going to reshape the profession for the better, providing decision-makers with the ability to diagnose and drive accountability in their organizations. More importantly, the value of analytics becomes even more important as businesses evolve. It becomes a part of your entire professional life, allowing the use of analytics to run businesses and helping you understand the market better for decision-making purposes. The entire success of these data analytics reporting tools is dependent on the data and the leadership and organizations using the data. To make the most out of analytics, without data cleansing and good maintenance, you cannot expect to draw good results. Hence, the focus should be more on leadership training.

8. IMPLICATIONS AND FUTURE DIRECTIONS

First, data quality and data integration are the two key ingredients to getting analytics tools to their optimal performance. Another crucial thing is the creation of a culture that is sensitive to data. Future research should focus on the proper use of sensitive data. That can be done through training and management. Considering alternative technologies like artificial intelligence and machine learning, this can further elevate analytics to greater heights. Besides this, studies could be done to figure out the other effects of data analytics on reporting. Studies would be beneficial in demonstrating how the adoption of data analytics would impact business performance time. There are moral questions that need to be tackled especially those regarding advanced analytics.

REFERENCES

Abbasi, A., Sarker, S., & Chiang, R. H. (2016). Big data research in information systems: Toward an inclusive research agenda. *Journal of the Association for Information Systems*, 17(2), 3. DOI: 10.17705/1jais.00423

Agarwal, R., & Dhar, V. (2014). Big data, data science, and analytics: The opportunity and challenge for IS research. *Information Systems Research*, 25(3), 443–448. DOI: 10.1287/isre.2014.0546

Akter, S., Wamba, S. F., Gunasekaran, A., Dubey, R., & Childe, S. J. (2016). How to improve firm performance using big data analytics capability and business strategy alignment? *International Journal of Production Economics*, 182, 113–131. DOI: 10.1016/j.ijpe.2016.08.018

Appelbaum, D., Kogan, A., Vasarhelyi, M., & Yan, Z. (2017). Impact of Business Analytics and Enterprise Systems on Managerial Accounting. *International Journal of Accounting Information Systems*, 25, 29–44. DOI: 10.1016/j.accinf.2017.03.003

Bose, R. (2009). Advanced analytics: Opportunities and challenges. *Industrial Management & Data Systems*, 109(2), 155–172. DOI: 10.1108/02635570910930073

Bradlow, E. T., Gangwar, M., Kopalle, P., & Voleti, S. (2017). The Role of Big Data and Predictive Analytics in Retailing. *Journal of Retailing*, 93(1), 79–95. DOI: 10.1016/j.jretai.2016.12.004

Brynjolfsson, E., Hitt, L. M., & Kim, H. H. (2011). Strength in numbers: How does data-driven decisionmaking affect firm performance? SSRN Electronic Journal. DOI: 10.2139/ssrn.1819486

Chaudhuri, S., Dayal, U., & Narasayya, V. (2011). An overview of business intelligence technology. *Communications of the ACM*, 54(8), 88–98. DOI: 10.1145/1978542.1978562

Chen, H., Chiang, R. H., & Storey, V. C. (2012). Business Intelligence and Analytics: From Big Data to Big Impact. *Management Information Systems Quarterly*, 36(4), 1165–1188. DOI: 10.2307/41703503

Constantiou, I. D., & Kallinikos, J. (2015). New games, new rules: Big data and the changing context of strategy. *Journal of Information Technology*, 30(1), 44–57. DOI: 10.1057/jit.2014.17

Côrte-Real, N., Oliveira, T., & Ruivo, P. (2017). Assessing business value of Big Data Analytics in European firms. *Journal of Business Research*, 70, 379–390. DOI: 10.1016/j.jbusres.2016.08.011

Davenport, T. H. (2014). *Big data at work: Dispelling the myths, uncovering the opportunities*. Harvard Business Review Press. DOI: 10.15358/9783800648153

Davenport, T. H., & Bean, R. (2019). Data-driven leadership: Creating organizational cultures that support data-driven decision making. *MIT Sloan Management Review*.

Davenport, T. H., & Harris, J. G. (2017). *Competing on Analytics: The New Science of Winning*. Harvard Business Review Press.

Davenport, T. H., & Harris, J. G. (2017). *Competing on analytics: The new science of winning*. Harvard Business Press.

Delen, D., & Demirkan, H. (2013). Data, information and analytics as services. *Decision Support Systems*, 55(1), 359–363. DOI: 10.1016/j.dss.2012.05.044

) Dwivedi, D. (2011). Stress Management: How to Reduce and Manage Workplace Stress. Juris Ray. 5.

) Dwivedi, D. (2014). New Dimensions of HRM: Performance Management.

Dwivedi, D. (2015). Impact of Information Technology on the Productivity of the Organization. *HR Journal of Management.*, 7, 77.

) Dwivedi, D. (2018). Stress Management in Software Industry.

Dwivedi, D., & Agarwal, S. (2024). Green Technology and Its Effect on the Modern World. In CRC Press eBooks (pp. 120–126). DOI: 10.1201/9781003458944-8

Eckerson, W. W. (2010). *Performance Dashboards: Measuring, Monitoring, and Managing Your Business*. John Wiley & Sons.

Few, S. (2013). *Information Dashboard Design: Displaying Data for At-a-Glance Monitoring*. Analytics Press.

Fosso Wamba, S., Akter, S., Edwards, A., Chopin, G., & Gnanzou, D. (2015). How 'big data' can make big impact: Findings from a systematic review and a longitudinal case study. *International Journal of Production Economics*, 165, 234–246. DOI: 10.1016/j.ijpe.2014.12.031

Ghasemaghaei, M., & Calic, G. (2019). Does big data enhance firm innovation competency? The mediating role of data-driven insights. *Journal of Business Research*, 104, 69–84. DOI: 10.1016/j.jbusres.2019.07.006

Gillon, K., Aral, S., Lin, C. Y., Mithas, S., & Zozulia, M. (2014). Business analytics: Radical shift or incremental change? *Communications of the Association for Information Systems*, 34(1), 13. DOI: 10.17705/1CAIS.03413

Grover, V., & Kohli, R. (2013). Revealing your hand: Caveats in implementing digital business strategy. *Management Information Systems Quarterly*, 37(2), 655–662.

Günther, W. A., Mehrizi, M. H. R., Huysman, M., & Feldberg, F. (2017). Debating big data: A literature review on realizing value from big data. *The Journal of Strategic Information Systems*, 26(3), 191–209. DOI: 10.1016/j.jsis.2017.07.003

Gupta, M., & George, J. F. (2016). Toward the development of a big data analytics capability. *Information & Management*, 53(8), 1049–1064. DOI: 10.1016/j.im.2016.07.004

Hazen, B. T., Boone, C. A., Ezell, J. D., & Jones-Farmer, L. A. (2014). Data Quality for Data Science, Predictive Analytics, and Big Data in Supply Chain Management: An Introduction to the Problem and Suggestions for Research and Applications. *International Journal of Production Economics*, 154, 72–80. DOI: 10.1016/j.ijpe.2014.04.018

Holsapple, C., Lee-Post, A., & Pakath, R. (2014). A unified foundation for business analytics. *Decision Support Systems*, 64, 130–141. DOI: 10.1016/j.dss.2014.05.013

Kiron, D., Prentice, P. K., & Ferguson, R. B. (2014). Raising the Bar with Analytics. *MIT Sloan Management Review*, 55(2), 29–33.

LaValle, S., Lesser, E., Shockley, R., Hopkins, M. S., & Kruschwitz, N. (2011). Big data, analytics and the path from insights to value. *MIT Sloan Management Review*, 52(2), 21–32.

Lycett, M. (2013). 'Datafication': Making sense of (big) data in a complex world. *European Journal of Information Systems*, 22(4), 381–386. DOI: 10.1057/ejis.2013.10

Manyika, J., Chui, M., Brown, B., Bughin, J., Dobbs, R., Roxburgh, C., & Byers, A. H. (2011). *Big data: The next frontier for innovation, competition, and productivity*. McKinsey Global Institute.

McAfee, A., & Brynjolfsson, E. (2012). Big Data: The Management Revolution. *Harvard Business Review*, 90(10), 60–68. PMID: 23074865

McAfee, A., & Brynjolfsson, E. (2012). Big data: The management revolution. *Harvard Business Review*, 90(10), 60–68. PMID: 23074865

Mewafarosh, R., Agarwal, S., & Dwivedi, D. (2024). Balancing FOMO and Digital Detoxification. In Business Drivers in Promoting Digital Detoxification (pp. 1-15). IGI Global. DOI: 10.4018/979-8-3693-1107-3.ch001

Mikalef, P., Pappas, I. O., Krogstie, J., & Giannakos, M. (2018). Big data analytics capabilities: A systematic literature review and research agenda. *Information Systems and e-Business Management*, 16(3), 547–578. DOI: 10.1007/s10257-017-0362-y

Popovič, A., Hackney, R., Coelho, P. S., & Jaklič, J. (2012). Towards business intelligence systems success: Effects of maturity and culture on analytical decision making. *Decision Support Systems*, 54(1), 729–739. DOI: 10.1016/j.dss.2012.08.017

Provost, F., & Fawcett, T. (2013). *Data science for business: What you need to know about data mining and data-analytic thinking*. O'Reilly Media, Inc.

Provost, F., & Fawcett, T. (2013). *Data science for business: What you need to know about data mining and data-analytic thinking*. O'Reilly Media.

Ransbotham, S., Kiron, D., & Prentice, P. K. (2016). Beyond the hype: The hard work behind analytics success. *MIT Sloan Management Review*, 57(3), 1–16.

Seddon, P. B., Constantinidis, D., Tamm, T., & Dod, H. (2017). How does business analytics contribute to business value? *Information Systems Journal*, 27(3), 237–269. DOI: 10.1111/isj.12101

Sharma, R., Mithas, S., & Kankanhalli, A. (2021). Transforming decision-making processes: Insights from predictive analytics and AI-driven systems. *Journal of Management Information Systems*, 38(2), 456–489.

Sivarajah, U., Kamal, M. M., Irani, Z., & Weerakkody, V. (2017). Critical analysis of Big Data challenges and analytical methods. *Journal of Business Research*, 70, 263–286. DOI: 10.1016/j.jbusres.2016.08.001

Tambe, P. (2014). Big data investment, skills, and firm value. *Management Science*, 60(6), 1452–1469. DOI: 10.1287/mnsc.2014.1899

Trieu, V. H. (2017). Getting value from Business Intelligence systems: A review and research agenda. *Decision Support Systems*, 93, 111–124. DOI: 10.1016/j.dss.2016.09.019

Vidgen, R., Shaw, S., & Grant, D. B. (2017). Management Challenges in Creating Value from Business Analytics. *European Journal of Operational Research*, 261(2), 626–639. DOI: 10.1016/j.ejor.2017.02.023

Wamba, S. F., Gunasekaran, A., Akter, S., Ren, S. J. F., Dubey, R., & Childe, S. J. (2017). Big data analytics and firm performance: Effects of dynamic capabilities. *Journal of Business Research*, 70, 356–365. DOI: 10.1016/j.jbusres.2016.08.009

Ware, C. (2012). *Information Visualization: Perception for Design*. Morgan Kaufmann.

Watson, H. J. (2014). Tutorial: Big data analytics: Concepts, technologies, and applications. *Communications of the Association for Information Systems*, 34(1), 65. DOI: 10.17705/1CAIS.03465

Wixom, B. H., & Watson, H. J. (2001). An empirical investigation of the factors affecting data warehousing success. *Management Information Systems Quarterly*, 25(1), 17–41. DOI: 10.2307/3250957

Chapter 9
Opportunities and Challenges of Leveraging Artificial Intelligence (AI) in Sport Marketing

Sardar Mohammadi
University of Kurdistan, Iran

Sajjad Pashaie
https://orcid.org/0000-0002-3933-146X
University of Tabriz, Iran

Seyyed Iman Ghaffarisadr
University of Mohaghegh Ardabil, Iran

Mike Rayner
https://orcid.org/0000-0001-7793-8687
University of Portsmouth, UK

ABSTRACT

As digital technologies continue to evolve and consumer behavior shifts, AI has become a critical tool for enhancing marketing strategies in the highly competitive sports industry. The use of artificial intelligence (AI) in sports marketing as an important innovation brings many opportunities and challenges. The emergence of AI as an effective tool in sports marketing allows for more detailed analysis of fan behavior and the creation of personalized strategies. Various AI technologies, including machine learning (ML), natural language processing (NLP), and computer vision (CV), are introduced and real-world examples of their applications in sports

DOI: 10.4018/979-8-3693-4361-6.ch009

marketing are presented. These opportunities include personalized engagement with fans, data-driven strategies for personalization and optimization of revenue streams through predictive analytics. In this chapter, the current state of sports marketing as well as the successful implementation of AI in sports marketing are reviewed.

PART I: INTRODUCTION

In today's landscape, technology has emerged as a fundamental pillar across all industries, and sports marketing is no exception. The introduction of artificial intelligence (AI) has become a powerful tool for transforming how we market and engage with fans. This technology has gained substantial importance in sports marketing, offering the potential for significant changes in the field. By leveraging AI, sports marketers can analyze vast amounts of data and identify patterns in fan behavior, enabling them to design targeted marketing campaigns. This advanced technology empowers marketers to utilize sophisticated tools and techniques that enhance their strategies.

Machine learning algorithms and neural networks are crucial in predicting fan behavior and delivering personalized experiences. Additionally, intelligent online advertising allows marketers to achieve higher returns at lower costs. AI chatbots play a vital role in interacting with fans, improving customer experiences by providing quick and efficient responses. This close interaction enhances the effectiveness of sports marketing strategies. Moreover, AI possesses unique capabilities in analyzing market data and making optimal decisions automatically. The integration of AI tools in sports marketing not only increases the return on investment but also improves communication with fans, allowing marketers to craft more effective strategies and boost sales (Pashaie & Nasirpour, 2024).

This chapter will provide a thorough examination of the role of AI in transforming sports marketing, emphasizing the importance and necessity of this topic in the current landscape. As trends in the sports industry and technology continue to evolve, AI will remain a key factor in driving transformation in sports marketing, creating new opportunities for engagement, and enhancing the overall fan experience. By effectively harnessing the substantial potential of AI, sports organizations can pave the way for a more innovative and successful future.

1- THE CURRENT STATE OF SPORTS MARKETING: CHALLENGES AND OPPORTUNITIES

Sports marketing management involves identifying the needs of fans, players, and sports managers, and developing market-oriented strategies to meet these needs. As a sub-discipline of marketing management, it encompasses a wide range of activities, including advertisements and promotions for events, sports clubs, and sports products. The significance of sports marketing is underscored by the substantial turnover in this industry, which highlights the necessity for effective management practices to address financial challenges faced by clubs (Farahani & Ghorbhani Qahfarkhi, 2015).

In recent years, sports marketing has undergone a transformation, presenting both challenges and opportunities. With advancements in technology, shifts in consumer behavior, and the rise of social media, sports marketers must continuously adapt their strategies to remain competitive. Below, we discuss key challenges and opportunities in the realm of sports marketing:

1-1. Challenges

1-1-1- Changing Consumer Behavior in Sports Marketing

In recent years, social media has emerged as one of the most effective tools for promoting products and services. The rise of social networks has introduced a new paradigm of human interaction and communication globally. This transformation in marketing and consumer behavior has shifted the focus toward a more customer-centric approach (karimi & ahmadi, 2024). Understanding consumer behavior has become a crucial area of study for marketing researchers, as it plays a pivotal role in determining a company's success or failure. Various factors influence consumer behavior, including cultural, personal, social, and psychological elements, many of which have been underexplored in marketing research (Afkar et al., 2018). In today's landscape, sports fans increasingly seek personalized experiences and deeper engagement with brands and teams rather than merely watching games and purchasing tickets. This shift in consumer expectations demands that sports marketers develop innovative strategies to attract and retain their audiences (Safarian et al., 2024).

For instance, FC Barcelona has effectively capitalized on these evolving fan behaviors. The launch of their official app provides fans with a tailored experience, offering real-time updates, team news, and exclusive content such as interviews and behind-the-scenes footage. Furthermore, by analyzing user data from the app, Barcelona can create customized offers. If a fan frequently engages with content related to a specific player, the team might present that fan with opportunities to purchase tickets for games featuring that player or related merchandise. This level of personalization not only enhances the fan experience but also boosts the likelihood of purchases and fosters loyalty.

As consumer behavior continues to evolve in the realm of sports marketing, brands and teams must adopt innovative and personalized strategies. By leveraging new technologies and data analytics, they can create compelling and unique experiences for their fans. This approach not only aids in attracting and retaining customers but can also lead to substantial revenue growth and overall success for sports brands.

1-1-2- Increasing Competition in the Sports Market

The sports market is experiencing heightened competition, a reality driven by the proliferation of leagues, teams, and sporting events. Unlike in the past when fans typically supported only a handful of teams or leagues, today's landscape offers a vast array of choices. This increased diversity compels brands and sports organizations to intensify their efforts to capture fan attention and loyalty (Parsamehr & Torkan, 2009).

For instance, the English Premier League (EPL), one of the most popular sports leagues globally (Rookwood & Millward, 2011), faces numerous competitive challenges (Bishop et al., 2022). To enhance their appeal and maintain relevance, the league and its teams have embraced innovative strategies. A key approach involves leveraging social media and digital platforms to foster engagement with fans. By creating captivating and interactive content, such as behind-the-scenes videos, live player interviews, and online competitions, the Premier League effectively draws fans in. This level of engagement not only boosts fan interest but also cultivates a stronger sense of community and belonging among supporters. Additionally, teams like Liverpool and Manchester City are working to deepen their connection with fans by offering unique matchday experiences. These may include stadium tours and exclusive amenities for attendees. Such initiatives not only drive ticket sales but also foster lasting relationships with fans, enhancing their overall experience and loyalty to the teams.

In this competitive environment, sports organizations must continue to innovate and adapt their marketing strategies to meet evolving fan expectations and preferences, ensuring sustained engagement and loyalty.

1-1-3- Economic Changes and Their Impact on Sports Marketing

In recent decades, the sports industry has entered a transformative era. Recognized as a vital economic sector for producing sports goods and services, it plays a crucial role in the economic development of nations and is regarded as one of the most profitable industries of the 21st century. However, economic volatility poses significant challenges to sports marketing budgets and strategies. During periods of economic difficulty, such as recessions or financial crises, sports organizations and brands often experience reduced revenues and increased operational costs. This scenario can have a direct impact on marketing decisions and resource allocation, forcing organizations to implement cost-cutting measures to maintain profitability. Such budget constraints may lead to a reduction in advertising expenditures or the cancellation of large marketing campaigns, ultimately diminishing brand awareness and fan engagement (Salimi et al., 2015).

For instance, during the global economic recession of 2008, numerous sports teams and leagues encountered significant obstacles in attracting fans and selling tickets. Many opted to reduce their marketing and advertising budgets, which resulted in decreased fan engagement and missed business opportunities. Despite these challenges, the industry has shown resilience; according to a report by the National Sporting Goods Association (NSGA), the purchase of sporting goods surged by approximately 5% in 2011 compared to 2009, climbing from $24.7 billion in 2009 to $72.9 billion in 2016. This growth reflects the importance of expanding economic and trade relations, which aim to introduce domestic products and brands to international markets through enhanced export activities (Fekrat & Jaberi, 2024).

In response to economic pressures, many organizations have adopted innovative and cost-effective strategies. By leveraging social media and digital marketing, they have successfully engaged with fans and attracted new audiences at lower costs. These approaches not only facilitate ongoing communication with existing fans but also help to broaden their reach in a competitive marketplace.

1-1-4- Emerging Technologies and Their Impact on Sports Marketing

Digital marketing, leveraging new technologies and digital channels, has become a substantial force in the sports industry, enhancing public awareness, promoting sports activities, and driving economic growth. The advent of technologies such as virtual reality (VR) and augmented reality (AR) has significantly transformed the landscape of sports marketing, offering innovative ways to engage with fans and create memorable experiences. To remain competitive, sports marketers must swiftly adapt to these technological advancements, as failure to do so may result in falling behind. VR immerses users in a simulated environment, allowing them to experience events as if they were physically present. For instance, fans can use VR to virtually attend games and enjoy an up-close view, even if they cannot be at the stadium in person (Golmohammadi et al., 2025). The Los Angeles Lakers exemplify this approach by utilizing VR technology to provide unique experiences for their fans. Through VR content, fans can watch practices and games from various perspectives and even interact with players. This immersive experience not only fosters a deeper connection between fans and the team but also enhances their sense of belonging and loyalty. Conversely, AR offers sports marketers the ability to deliver interactive digital content directly to fans. Many teams employ AR through mobile apps to provide real-time player information, game statistics, and exclusive content. This kind of interactive engagement significantly enhances the fan experience, encouraging greater involvement in team activities and fostering a more robust connection with the brand.

Finally, the integration of VR and AR into sports marketing strategies presents substantial opportunities for teams to deepen fan engagement and loyalty, ultimately contributing to the growth and success of the sports industry.

1-2. Opportunities

1-2-1- Using AI and Data Analysis in Sports Marketing

AI and data analytics have emerged as substantial assets in sports marketing. These technologies enable marketers to discern patterns in customer behavior and develop targeted, personalized campaigns. This strategy can significantly enhance conversion rates and improve customer satisfaction. By utilizing AI and data analytics, marketers can closely track fan behavior, including analyzing data from purchase histories, social media interactions, and viewing patterns of matches. For instance, a sports team can examine ticket sales data to identify trends that indicate fans' likelihood to purchase tickets for specific games or at particular times (Fekrat & Jaberi, 2024).

Once behavioral patterns are recognized, marketers can create campaigns tailored to the specific needs and interests of fans. For example, if data reveals that a group of fans is particularly interested in video content featuring certain players, the team can launch a campaign showcasing videos of those players. This level of personalization not only captures fan attention but also boosts engagement and participation. Moreover, personalized experiences driven by AI and data analytics can lead to increased conversion rates and enhanced customer satisfaction. For example, if a fan frequently purchases a specific type of sports merchandise, the team can provide them with exclusive offers on those items. Such interactions make fans feel valued and encourage further purchases. Additionally, by offering personalized experiences, brands can strengthen fan loyalty. When fans perceive that their needs and interests are prioritized, their connection to the brand deepens (Pashaie & Nasirpour, 2024).

1-2-2- Social Media and Fan Engagement in Sports Marketing

Social media brand pages serve as powerful tools for engaging consumers in the sports industry. The interactive nature of these platforms facilitates two-way communication, enabling fans to connect with their favorite teams and athletes, thereby enhancing loyalty and engagement. Social media is considered one of the most vital channels for fostering connections with fans and creating deeper interactions. It allows brands to communicate directly with their audience and craft engaging experiences. Beyond serving as an advertising medium, social media provides real-time interaction opportunities. Brands can respond to fan comments, conduct polls, and generate captivating content that resonates with their audience. For instance, sports teams utilize platforms like Instagram, Twitter, and Facebook to share updates, videos, and images related to their players and events (Annamalai et al., 2021; Mahmoudian et al., 2024; Vale & Fernandes, 2018).

One effective strategy for leveraging social media is to organize advertisements and contests. Brands can engage fans by creating challenges that encourage participation. For example, a football team might host a contest where fans share photos of themselves watching games for a chance to win prizes such as free tickets or team merchandise. These initiatives not only boost engagement but also enhance brand visibility (bahrami & kiani, 2023).

Furthermore, social media enables brands to establish direct connections with their fans. This interaction can involve addressing questions, comments, and feedback from supporters. The Golden State Warriors, for instance, actively engage with their fans on Twitter and Instagram, responding to inquiries and comments. Such interactions foster a sense of community and belonging among fans, encouraging ongoing connections with the brand (Tsimonis & Dimitriadis, 2014).

So, the strategic use of social media in sports marketing not only enhances fan engagement but also strengthens brand loyalty, making it an essential component of modern marketing strategies in the sports industry.

1-2-3- Personalized Experiences in Sports Marketing

In today's competitive marketing landscape, which has shifted towards a service-oriented approach with a diverse range of products, the question arises: can the dynamic sports community harness its potential to create unique opportunities for sports brands to enhance customer relationships? It appears that sports marketing managers can build sustainability by fostering customer interactions with their brands through meaningful experiences and prioritizing customer satisfaction (Norouzi et al., 2023). While customer needs and preferences may vary, both positive and negative experiences are inherent outcomes of consuming products and services.

The nature of these experiences is crucial for the retail sector, particularly in sports marketing, where the intangible aspects of products and services play a vital role. Sports products are predominantly experience-driven, and understanding this can help brands craft overall experiences that resonate with consumers. Despite the significance of consumer experience as a key factor in consumer behavior, the design of sports customer experiences has not received adequate attention from researchers (Mohammadi, Mahmoudian, & Dos Santos, 2024; Mohammadi, Mahmoudian, & Rayner, 2024).

Personalized experiences represent a novel strategy in sports marketing, enabling organizations to forge deeper connections with fans through data-driven insights. This approach can encompass tailored offers, exclusive content, and unique experiences at sporting events that enhance the bond between fans and brands. By analyzing fan behavior data, organizations can identify specific patterns that inform personalized offers and experiences (Norouzi et al., 2023). For example, if a fan consistently purchases tickets to a specific team's home games, the team might provide special discounts on future tickets or grant access to exclusive content, such as practice sessions or player interviews.

Furthermore, personalized experiences can include content that aligns with fans' specific interests. For example, a soccer team could create behind-the-scenes videos of training sessions or in-depth interviews with players that appeal to dedicated fans. This type of content not only captures fan attention but also fosters a sense of connection and belonging to the team. Additionally, organizations can curate memorable experiences for fans during sporting events. Some teams offer opportunities for fans to meet players, participate in stadium tours, or access exclusive areas on game day. These experiences not only enhance fan satisfaction but also strengthen brand loyalty, creating lasting relationships between fans and teams.

In conclusion, by prioritizing personalized experiences and leveraging data insights, sports brands can effectively engage their audiences and cultivate deeper connections, ultimately driving both satisfaction and loyalty in a competitive market.

1-2-4- Expansion of Global Markets in Sports Marketing

The growth of global markets, as a consequence of the globalization of sports, presents new opportunities for sports brands and teams. This trend enables brands to access international markets, thereby enhancing revenue and expanding brand influence. With the globalization of sports, brands can capitalize on emerging opportunities in these markets. For instance, leagues like the EPL and the National Basketball Association (NBA) are rapidly extending their reach across various countries. By organizing games and special events internationally, these leagues attract new fans and boost brand awareness.

To thrive in global markets, brands must implement tailored marketing strategies that cater to local needs and cultural contexts. This may involve adapting advertising content to align with local languages, cultures, and interests, which can enhance engagement and draw in new fans. Expanding into global markets can significantly increase the revenue of sports brands and teams. By appealing to new audiences in different countries, brands can boost ticket sales, merchandise, and service offerings. For example, FC Barcelona has successfully attracted new fans and increased its revenue through world tours and friendly matches held in various countries. Moreover, entering global markets can enhance brand influence. Brands that succeed internationally often become recognized as symbols of quality and credibility. This elevated status can attract new sponsors and business partners, further solidifying the brand's position in the global arena (Esmaeili mahyari et al., 2022).

In summary, the globalization of sports offers substantial opportunities for brands to expand their reach, increase revenue, and enhance their influence. By adopting culturally relevant marketing strategies and engaging with international audiences, sports brands can secure a strong foothold in the competitive global market.

1-2-5- Innovation in Digital Content and its Impact on Sports Marketing

Developing creative and engaging digital content is essential for attracting new fans and retaining existing customers in the sports industry. Utilizing formats such as videos, podcasts, and interactive content can significantly enhance the fan experience. To thrive in this dynamic environment, organizations must closely monitor market trends and customer preferences, continuously updating their strategies. Embracing new technologies and leveraging data analytics, along with engaging fans through social media and providing personalized experiences, are critical components for success in this field.

For example, the National Football League (NFL) has effectively utilized digital content by launching their "NFL Game Pass," which offers fans access to live games, replays, and exclusive behind-the-scenes content. This initiative not only attracts new viewers but also fosters loyalty among existing fans by providing them with unique and engaging experiences. Given the rapid advancements in digital marketing, organizations must prioritize innovation and adaptability to stay competitive and achieve greater success (Mohammadi et al., 2023).

2- THE EMERGENCE OF AI IN SPORT MARKETING

The journey of AI in marketing began around 2010 (Hassan, 2021). In contemporary discussions across media and academic circles, the role of AI in sports marketing has become a focal point, particularly concerning its potential to enhance rather than replace human roles. Many believe that AI technologies can significantly improve the quality of business operations and products. The integration of algorithms and automation in content creation has increased, with various organizations exploring this frontier. In the realm of sports marketing, AI is increasingly utilized to enhance organizational marketing efforts and improve operational efficiency, ultimately driving revenue growth. AI has already reshaped the sports marketing landscape and is expected to have an even greater impact in the future. This includes advancements in personalized marketing, predictive analytics, real-time insights, and influencer marketing. By leveraging AI technology, marketers can gather and analyze extensive data sets, enabling them to tailor marketing messages and promotions to individual fans. For instance, AI can identify effective social media influencers based on audience engagement and demographics, creating a more relevant experience that fosters fan loyalty (Mohammadi, Mahmoudian, & Rayner, 2024).

An example of AI's application in sports marketing can be seen in the ESPN mobile app. When users create an account, the app collects data about their preferences and behaviors, allowing for personalized content delivery. This level of customization can significantly enhance the fan experience, as it aligns marketing efforts with individual interests. However, while many consumers appreciate personalized marketing, there are ethical considerations regarding data collection and privacy. Striking a balance between effective marketing and user privacy is crucial as AI technology continues to evolve. AI also enables marketers to make accurate predictions about fan behavior through big data analysis, facilitating the creation of tailored content and enhancing the overall consumer experience. The use of AI-generated content can influence consumer attitudes and purchasing intentions in sports marketing, although understanding these dynamics remains a challenge. Research indicates that the observability and relevance of AI-generated content are key factors affecting its acceptance (Eickhoff & Zhevak, 2023).

Observability refers to how visible the innovations are within a social system and has been shown to positively influence user attitudes. Compatibility, on the other hand, relates to how well new technologies align with existing values and beliefs, which can also enhance adoption rates (Pashaie & Nasirpour, 2024).

Sports marketing content is very important as one of the key factors in attracting and retaining customers and developing sports-related businesses. Research shows that the more engaging the marketing content is, the greater the impact it will have on consumers. In addition to providing information about sports products and services, this type of content should be able to establish effective communication with customers and understand their feelings and values well. For this reason, sports marketing content must effectively and attractively attract the audience and motivate them to buy through images, videos, textual content and other digital tools. Evidence shows the notable importance of social media content quality in marketing.

However, recent research shows that for consumers looking for innovation and new things, there is no difference between the impact of AI-generated content and human-generated content on their purchase intentions. AI-powered predictive analytics can be used to predict future trends in fan behavior, identify growth opportunities, and optimize marketing campaigns for maximum impact. AI algorithms can also provide real-time insights into fan engagement, sentiment and behavior, allowing marketers to make quick changes to campaigns and messaging. Therefore, many studies have investigated the impact of artificial intelligence in the sports marketing industry and have reached different results (Abolghasemi Atany et al., 2024; Glebova et al., 2024; Nalbant & Aydın, 2022; Pashaie & Nasirpour, 2024).

For some consumers, the idea of more personalized marketing may seem appealing because it caters to their interests. However, some may find ethical concern with the amount of data collected about them. There is a fine line between collecting data to improve marketing and invading users' privacy. The future of AI remains mysterious as it is still an evolving technology, but it is imperative that its use be ethical and fair.

PART II: UNDERSTANDING AI TECHNOLOGIES

1- The Relationship Between AI and Digital Marketing

The digital transformation has been a substantial presence for quite some time, firmly establishing itself as the main driving force behind all aspects of commerce, including marketing. Today, it is nearly impossible to find a company in any industry that does not utilize digital marketing to connect with its customers, and the sports sector is no exception. The growing prevalence of digitalization has fundamentally changed the fan experience, enabling a deeper immersion in both the game itself and the surrounding activities. Specifically, the capabilities of AI are so remarkable that, along with its projected market growth reaching astonishing figures, it signals a complete transformation of the sports marketing industry (Sbrighi, 2024).

As a legitimate branch of marketing science, digital marketing has created value for organizations and enhanced customer engagement through electronic services. The advent of technology has introduced a new competitive arena, leading to rapid changes in digitalization. Marketers worldwide leverage digital technology to enhance service levels and improve operational efficiency. In this context, AI plays a vital role through intelligent search engines, smarter ads, refined content delivery, reliance on bots, continuous learning, fraud prevention, data security, image and voice recognition, sales forecasting, language recognition, and customer segmentation. AI enables businesses to gain a clear understanding of their customers' needs, ultimately enhancing sales and revenues (Thilagavathy & Kumar, 2021).

In the dynamic and competitive landscape of the sports industry in Iran, electronic commerce has emerged as a prominent and innovative tool for transforming and improving marketing processes with the help of artificial intelligence. While marketers have been hesitant to integrate AI into their strategies in the past, many successful brands like Amazon and Spotify have now adopted this advanced technology. The use of AI in digital marketing has gained popularity among various marketers and businesses. For instance, Amazon utilizes AI to recommend relevant products based on customers' previous searches, purchases, and browsing history. This personalized experience increases the likelihood of initial purchases and fosters customer loyalty (Abolghasemi Atany et al., 2024).

Today, AI in digital sports marketing offers marketers a wide range of benefits and real opportunities. For example, data analytics for forecasting enhances customer experiences and enables targeted marketing, which undoubtedly boosts ROI for businesses.

Additionally, advertising remains one of the most effective ways to create brand value. Digital marketing powered by AI can generate advertisements tailored to audience interests, leading to more relevant ad exposure. Ultimately, the connection between AI and digital marketing not only simplifies processes for brands but also addresses customer needs effectively.

The application of AI in sports marketing is so vast that it can be safely assumed to be endless. Here are a few things:

1-1- Segmentation of Sports Customers

The segmentation of customers into homogeneous groups has been well researched, indicating its importance for marketers. Published research on customer segmentation, specific to professional sports, first appeared in the early 2000s (Finch et al., 2022). Customer segmentation is a marketing strategy based on identifying subgroups among target audiences in order to provide more appropriate messages for stronger communication. Subgroups can be based on demographics such as geographic location, gender identity, age, ethnicity, income, or level of formal education. Subgroups can also be based on behaviors such as past purchases. Psychology comes into play when you have access to insights into your audience's personality types, values, attitudes and beliefs.

As an example, a sports shoe manufacturing company might segment its market into two main groups: basketball players and long-distance runners. These two groups, as distinct categories, respond very differently to advertising. Understanding these market segments allows the sports shoe company to market its brand more effectively.

Market segmentation, which is an essential part of market research, aims to identify target groups among consumers so that products and branding can be designed to appeal to these groups. The goal of this process is to minimize risk by determining which products have the best chance of capturing market share and identifying the most effective ways to present these products to the market. This approach enables companies to focus their limited resources on efforts that generate the highest return on investment (ROI), thereby enhancing overall efficiency (Ghafari & Ranjbarian, 2013).

Figure 1. Segmentation of sports customers

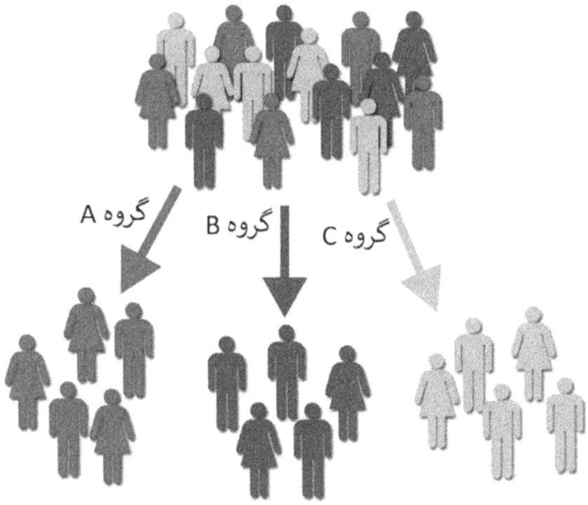

AI-powered customer segmentation that enables personalized experiences to win new customers and delight existing ones.

Figure 2. Peak.ai is a tool for customer's segmentation

Source: (peak.ai website)

In the current business environment, where the customer is the primary focus, effective communication between marketing and senior management is vital for success (Kasem et al., 2024). With AI, you can accurately and effectively segment your customers. Audience segmentation with AI relieves marketers from 4 basic challenges:

Data Quality

In sports marketing, the quality of data is paramount for effective market segmentation and targeted campaigns. If the data used for segmentation is of poor quality, the results will be ineffective, leading to wasted resources and missed opportunities (Shank & Lyberger, 2014) .

For example, consider a sports apparel brand that aims to target young athletes through a marketing campaign. If the data used to segment this audience is outdated or contains inaccuracies—such as incorrect age ranges, duplicated entries, or misclassified interests—the marketing messages may not reach the intended recipients or resonate with them. As a result, the campaign could fail to engage the target audience, leading to low conversion rates and a poor return on investment.

AI is based on the analysis of large datasets and requires a continuous supply of high-quality data. AI tools can play a crucial role in enhancing data quality. They can identify and eliminate redundant data, flag outdated information, and correct ambiguous entries caused by typos or incorrect labeling (Aldoseri et al., 2023). For instance, if a sports brand has data that incorrectly categorizes "soccer players" under “football,” AI can help rectify this misclassification, ensuring that marketing efforts are accurately directed. Moreover, AI can uncover hidden data that may not have been shared across departments, such as customer feedback from product returns or insights from social media engagement. By cleaning and enriching the data source, sports marketers can create more precise segments, leading to more effective and targeted marketing strategies that resonate with their audience and drive higher engagement and sales.

Data Volume

Considering that big data (BD) has increasingly become an important tool for managers and researchers to transform sports management practices, these data can transform sports management operations and reduce the gap between research and practice. Research in the field of big data in sports management plays an essential role in gathering new knowledge or testing existing theories, either inductively or inductively, because this field seeks progress in science and knowledge (Mamo et al., 2022). In sports marketing, understanding your audience requires gathering extensive information from various sources. The sheer volume of data available today can be overwhelming, but AI tools allow marketers to process large amounts of data efficiently and effectively.

For example, consider a sports team looking to enhance fan engagement through a targeted marketing campaign. By utilizing AI, the team can analyze vast datasets from multiple sources, such as ticket sales, social media interactions, merchandise purchases, and fan surveys. This analysis enables the team to gain valuable insights into their audience’s preferences and behaviors.

Moreover, AI can identify new segmentation opportunities that marketers may not have previously considered. For instance, through data analysis, the AI might reveal a distinct segment of fans who engage more with digital content than with live events. This insight could lead to the creation of a specialized marketing campaign targeting these digital-savvy fans, offering them exclusive online content, virtual meet-and-greets with players, or interactive social media experiences.

By leveraging AI to manage and analyze large volumes of data, sports marketers can uncover hidden patterns and trends, allowing them to tailor their strategies more effectively and engage their audience in ways that were not possible before. This not only enhances the overall fan experience but also drives increased loyalty and revenue for the sports organization.

Segment Size

In sports marketing, the size of each segment plays a crucial role in the effectiveness of targeting and campaign execution. If segments are too small, there may not be enough data to draw meaningful insights, leading to misinterpretation of the data and ineffective targeting. Conversely, if segments are too broad, the marketing messages may become diluted and fail to resonate with specific audience groups (Ghafari & Ranjbarian, 2013).

AI can substantial enhance the precision of segment selection, ensuring that each segment is optimally sized for effective marketing. For instance, imagine a sports apparel brand that aims to launch a new line of eco-friendly products. Instead of targeting a broad category like "all athletes," AI can analyze data to identify a more precise segment, such as "environmentally conscious runners aged 25-35 who participate in marathons."

By leveraging AI, the brand can process various data points, including purchase history, social media engagement, and lifestyle preferences, to determine the ideal segment size. This targeted approach allows the brand to craft tailored marketing messages that resonate deeply with this specific group, such as highlighting the sustainability of the materials used in the new product line and promoting community events focused on environmental awareness.

Ultimately, by utilizing AI to accurately define segment sizes, sports marketers can enhance their targeting strategies, leading to more effective campaigns that engage the right audience and drive higher conversion rates. This strategic segmentation not only improves marketing efficiency but also fosters stronger connections between the brand and its customers.

Time Wastage

Customer segmentation can be a time-consuming process, often requiring extensive data analysis and manual adjustments to identify the right groups for targeted marketing efforts. However, AI tools can automate this process, significantly reducing the time involved and providing near-instant results.

For example, consider a sports marketing agency tasked with segmenting a diverse audience for a major sporting event. Traditionally, this would involve collecting data from various sources, analyzing it to identify trends, and manually categorizing customers based on demographics, interests, and behaviors. This could take weeks or even months, leading to delays in campaign execution.

By implementing AI-driven segmentation tools, the agency can streamline this process. AI algorithms can quickly analyze large datasets, identify patterns, and automatically group customers into relevant segments based on their preferences and behaviors. For instance, the AI might discover segments such as "families with children interested in youth sports" or "young professionals who frequently attend live events."

This automation not only saves time but also allows marketers to focus on strategy and creative execution rather than getting bogged down in data management. With faster and more accurate segmentation, sports marketers can launch their campaigns promptly, ensuring they reach their audiences at the right time with the right messages. Ultimately, by minimizing time wastage through AI, organizations can enhance their operational efficiency and improve their overall marketing effectiveness.

1-2- Social Listening With AI

Social listening exists in various fields of communication, but is still not clearly defined in the field of communication and listening studies. This report examines social listening as an evolving type of listening that transcends existing categories of listening. It also provides a definition of its meaning, evaluates its role in organizational and interpersonal communication, and discusses its value as an additional dimension in listening. With this in mind, we introduce and define social listening as a new type of listening and a tool for accessing interpersonal information and social intelligence that can strengthen relationships and shape how we listen and communicate through Media channels have a substantial impact (Stewart & Arnold, 2018). With AI, instead of relying on just two ears, you can listen to social media with millions of ears. AI-powered social listening tools can monitor a vast number of phrases, hashtags related to your brand, and mentions containing your brand name across various social platforms. This capability allows marketers to gather, process, and analyze extensive data efficiently.

One notable tool for social listening is Brand24. This platform scans the entire internet for mentions of your brand, not only on major social networks like Instagram, Twitter, Quora, and Telegram but also on blogs, news sites, review platforms, podcasts, newsletters, and forums. By doing so, it provides a comprehensive view of your brand's online presence and reputation.

Figure 3. Social listening

Additionally, Brand24 employs advanced algorithms to assess sentiment, categorizing mentions as positive, negative, or neutral. This sentiment analysis is crucial for understanding public perception and gauging the effectiveness of marketing campaigns. For instance, if a sports team launches a new merchandise line, Brand24 can help track how fans are reacting to the launch across various platforms, allowing the team to adjust their marketing strategies in real time based on fan feedback.

By utilizing AI-driven social listening tools, sports marketers can gain valuable insights into audience sentiment, identify emerging trends, and engage with their audience more effectively. This proactive approach not only enhances brand reputation but also fosters stronger relationships with fans and customers.

1-3- Content Creation

In the realm of sports marketing, the ability to produce high-quality content quickly is crucial for engaging fans and promoting products. With tools like ChatGPT, which utilizes AI, marketers can create written content that feels as though it has been crafted by a human for another human. By providing effective prompts, marketers can generate a variety of content types, including blog articles, product descriptions, social media posts, and advertising copy much faster than traditional methods.

For example, a sports apparel brand launching a new line of running shoes can use AI-powered content creation tools to rapidly develop engaging promotional materials. By inputting specific prompts about the features and benefits of the shoes, the AI can generate compelling social media posts that highlight their unique selling points. This allows the brand to maintain an active online presence and engage with its audience effectively.

Additionally, AI can assist in translating website content into multiple languages, enabling brands to communicate with diverse audiences in their preferred languages. For instance, if the same sports apparel brand wants to reach Spanish-speaking customers, AI tools can quickly translate their marketing materials, ensuring that the messaging resonates with this audience.

One effective tool for this purpose is Jasper.ai, which can generate various types of content with a specified tone and can also be used to check for plagiarism. This means that sports marketers can rely on Jasper.ai to create original content tailored to their brand voice while ensuring that it remains unique.

1-4- Automation in Sports Marketing

AI is poised to become an integral component of every business worldwide in the long run. Recent trends in AI-based automation reflect significant changes within the AI landscape, evident in the renewed ideas, interests, and investments in AI adoption by companies. This technology is advanced enough to recognize faces and objects, which has substantial implications for various business applications. For instance, facial recognition can be utilized for security purposes, distinguishing individuals, while object detection can analyze and recognize images. AI treats human images like cookies, enabling more personalized services based on customer preferences. Some businesses are experimenting with facial recognition to gauge customer moods and provide tailored product recommendations (Haleem et al., 2022). Today, automating the marketing process appears to be the most effective solution for addressing the considerable changes brought about by rapid technological evolution and the continuous rise in supply and demand. To achieve optimal marketing results, businesses must leverage digital marketing and communication services, which are effective due to the techniques employed for tracking, scoring, and executing each campaign in an efficient and measurable manner. Given the technical advancements, the diversity in marketing, and the demand for customized products and services, alongside the need for constructive dialogue with customers, quick responses, and the measurement of investments and results, traditional marketing approaches have significantly evolved and continue to improve (Todor, 2016).

The results indicate that AI substantially enhances marketing accuracy and productivity by automating repetitive tasks, enabling real-time personalization, and providing deeper insights into client preferences. However, challenges such as the need for high-quality data, substantial infrastructure, and skilled professionals hinder the full realization of AI's potential. Companies should prioritize investing in reliable data management systems, adopting cloud-based AI solutions to reduce costs, and ensuring transparency in data usage to build consumer trust. To effectively navigate the complexities of AI in marketing, the report recommends integrating AI with human expertise, continuously evaluating AI performance, and clearly defining business objectives to ensure proper alignment of AI tools. By implementing these strategies, companies can enhance marketing outcomes and create a data-driven customer experience tailored to individual preferences (Rahman et al., 2024).

Automation in sports marketing extends beyond merely scheduling and executing campaigns automatically; it involves precise targeting where AI determines which campaigns should be directed at specific audiences, along with the appropriate approach and content. For example, a sports organization can enhance its email marketing campaigns using AI by sending personalized messages at optimal times for specific audience segments. By analyzing user behavior and preferences, AI can tailor the content of each email, ensuring fans receive relevant updates about their favorite teams or upcoming events. This level of personalization increases engagement rates and fosters a stronger connection between the brand and its audience.

In the realm of social media, AI can automate the scheduling of posts and stories and manage responses to audience inquiries. For instance, an AI-powered tool can analyze when a brand's followers are most active and schedule posts for those peak times, maximizing visibility and interaction. Additionally, it can automatically respond to common questions or comments, ensuring that fans feel heard and valued

1-5- Data Analysis for Better Customer Insights in Sports Marketing

One of the primary applications of AI in digital marketing is data analysis, which can collect and filter vast amounts of data from various campaigns and present the results in a summarized format. This capability is particularly valuable in the sports marketing industry, where understanding fan behavior and preferences is crucial for developing effective marketing strategies.

For example, a sports team could use AI-driven data analysis tools to evaluate the performance of its recent advertising campaigns. By analyzing data on customer interactions, ticket sales, and social media engagement, the team can gain insights into which campaigns resonated most with fans. If the analysis reveals that a particular campaign promoting a star player led to a substantially increase in ticket sales and social media mentions, the team can use this information to guide future marketing efforts.

Additionally, AI can help predict the outcomes of future campaigns based on customer behavior data. For instance, if data shows that fans are more likely to engage with promotional content during specific times of the year, the marketing team can adjust their budget and focus on campaigns that align with these trends. This proactive approach allows the team to allocate resources to more effective campaigns, ensuring a better return on investment.

Ultimately, by leveraging data analysis and optimizing campaigns based on insights gained, sports marketers can build deeper relationships with their customers. They have more time and information available for planning their campaign strategies, leading to a more personalized experience for fans (Golmohammadi et al., 2025) .

One useful tool for this purpose is Polymer, which can connect to various data sources like Google Analytics, Google Sheets, Facebook, and Google Ads (Amin, 2019). It analyzes the data and presents the results in diverse and visually appealing formats, making it easier for marketers to interpret and act on the insights.

1-6- Enhanced Video Marketing With AI

By incorporating AI into video marketing and advertising, businesses can enter a new realm of possibilities. AI technologies enable marketers to create more engaging and personalized video content that resonates with their target audiences. For instance, AI can analyze viewer behavior and preferences to tailor video recommendations or create dynamic content that adapts based on the viewer's interactions. This means that a sports team could use AI to produce highlight reels that feature plays or athletes that a specific viewer has shown interest in, thereby increasing engagement and fostering a deeper connection with fans. Additionally, AI can assist in optimizing video ad placements by analyzing data to determine the most effective times and platforms for reaching the target audience. For example, a sports brand might use AI to identify peak viewing times for their target demographic and schedule ads accordingly, maximizing visibility and impact. Furthermore, AI-powered tools can enhance video editing processes, making it easier and faster to produce high-quality content. These tools can automate tasks such as color correction, sound editing, and even generating subtitles, allowing marketers to focus more on creative aspects rather than technical details.

In finally, leveraging AI in video marketing not only enhances the quality and relevance of the content but also improves the overall effectiveness of marketing campaigns, resulting in better engagement and stronger relationships with customers.

1-7- Advertising with AI

Advertising has rapidly evolved in recent years, with a substantial increase in the use of AI and its applications. While the literature on AI advertising dates back to the 1990s, the field has seen a surge in research attention and development lately, presenting various potential avenues for future exploration. Despite this progress, our understanding of the evolution of AI advertising research remains limited, necessitating a state-of-the-art overview to advance future studies. Over the past few decades, the advertising ecosystem has undergone a radical transformation. With the advent of new technologies and the explosion of digital media, advertising has shifted from traditional forms such as newspapers, billboards, radio, and television to a variety of new and exciting media and platforms. Advanced advertising media now leverage AI to enhance advertisement effectiveness and optimize ad delivery. AI comprises a set of disruptive technologies that enable machines to solve problems, facilitate decision-making, and perform tasks traditionally associated with human intelligence.

AI has made advertising more competent, personalized, targeted, and intelligent by automating and streamlining essential advertising functions such as consumer insight discovery, media planning, buying, advertisement creation, and impact evaluation. Computational and programmatic advertising utilize AI to develop targeted promotions by facilitating automatic ad scheduling, placement, and media planning and buying. For instance, Harley Davidson, an iconic American motorcycle brand, increased its leads by 2390% through AI-enabled computational advertising and predictive analytics. Similarly, programmatic advertising has gained immense popularity in both research and practice over the past few years, helping to optimize digital ad campaigns through automated media planning and buying. The AI-enabled programmatic ad market is projected to reach $38.67 billion by 2028, growing at a CAGR of 29.71% from 2021 to 2028. The rapid growth of AI advertising presents enormous industry potential and promising research prospects.

In recent years, academic research on AI advertising has proliferated, offering insights into its potential uses, functions, features, and challenges. The literature on AI advertising also incorporates theories from various disciplines, including Psychology, Sociology, Mass Communication, and Technology (Ford et al., 2023).

AI helps marketers as a companion in all stages of digital advertising. AI-powered ads will be more effective and cost-effective because they will be displayed in the best places with the most powerful text and images or videos, to the most appropriate audience.

Marketers can use AI to:

Writing and optimizing the text and title of the advertising.

Producing a banner or promotional video.

Choosing the media to display the ad and its effective placement.

Effective landing page design.

Checking the results and optimizing the advertising.

1-8- Customer Support and Services With Chatbots in Sports Marketing

The role of digital technologies, particularly the Internet of Things (IoT) and AI, is increasingly becoming a crucial element in the diverse interactions between brands and consumers. Homo Cyber Oeconomicus, one of the potential stages of the ongoing evolution of consumers, exists between the dehumanization of the surrounding world and the humanization of digital technologies. While maintaining constant contact with smart devices, systems, and algorithms, consumers seek new values and meanings that reflect their desires, fears, and behaviors.

As a result, the digital ecosystem, which attempts to merge the concept of humanism with technological processes, poses new challenges for companies and brands regarding the quality of interactions with an increasingly digital consumer and the tools employed in that process. One intriguing solution in this context is the use of chatbots (Kaczorowska-Spychalska, 2019). Leveraging NLP technology, chatbots can respond to customer inquiries instantly, providing immediate assistance without delays. Their range of potential applications in business continues to expand systematically (Katragadda, 2023).

In the context of sports marketing, chatbots can play a crucial role in enhancing customer experience both before and after a purchase. For instance, imagine a sports merchandise store that sells jerseys and fan gear. Before making a purchase, a customer may have questions about the sizing of a jersey or the availability of a specific player's merchandise. A chatbot can provide instant answers, guiding the customer through their options and helping them make informed decisions.

After the purchase, if a customer encounters issues with their order—such as a missing item or questions about returns—the chatbot can assist in resolving these problems quickly. For example, if a fan receives the wrong jersey size, they can interact with the chatbot to initiate a return process or get information about how to exchange the item. This level of support not only improves customer satisfaction but also fosters brand loyalty, as customers appreciate timely and effective assistance.

By integrating chatbots into their customer service strategy, sports brands can ensure that they are always available to assist fans, enhancing the overall customer journey.

1-9- Keyword Research and SEO

Digital marketing has undergone substantial growth and transformation over the years, leaving only a handful of companies unaware of this strategy. This evolution has created a highly competitive market where businesses must effectively promote their products and services to attract potential customers and drive conversions. As a result, search engine optimization (SEO) has become a key component of marketing strategies for most companies. It has been observed that those businesses that implement SEO effectively tend to excel in profitability and marketing visibility.

SEO is an essential strategy for enhancing the visibility of marketing efforts within a business. It is research-driven and primarily focuses on analyzing various factors that affect SEO and its impact on a company's success. In conclusion, SEO is a dynamic process that evolves alongside the web and requires ongoing improvements for business survival and growth. This necessity places the onus on companies to remain consistently informed about search engine updates and competitor activities, prompting them to take appropriate actions accordingly (Rana, 2016).

Keyword research and SEO are recognized as an essential component of sports marketing that can have a substantial impact on attracting audiences and increasing website traffic. By applying AI, sports marketers are able to effectively analyze their website traffic and identify effective keywords that will improve their position in search results. For example, a gym can use AI to identify keywords related to "group exercise classes" or "personal training programs" and optimize its website content based on these keywords.

In addition, AI allows marketers to better understand their customers and produce more personalized content based on their interests and needs. For example, if a sports brand discovers that its customers are interested in certain sports, such as yoga or running, it can generate content related to these sports and target its ads based on this information. This approach not only helps increase customer engagement, but can also lead to increased sales and brand loyalty.

2- AI Technologies

AI refers to the ability of machines to mimic human intelligence and perform tasks that typically require human intelligence, such as learning, problem-solving, decision-making, and natural language understanding. Figure 4 depicts AI technologies including machine learning (ML), natural language processing (NLP), robotics, and computer vision (CV). ML is a subset of AI that involves training computer algorithms to learn patterns in data and make predictions or decisions based on the data. Deep learning is a type of machine learning that uses neural networks with multiple layers to process complex data such as images or speech. NLP is the ability of computers to understand, interpret, and generate human language, including speech and text. CV is the ability of computers to analyze and interpret visual information such as images and videos (Aldoseri et al., 2023).

Figure 4. AI technology landscape

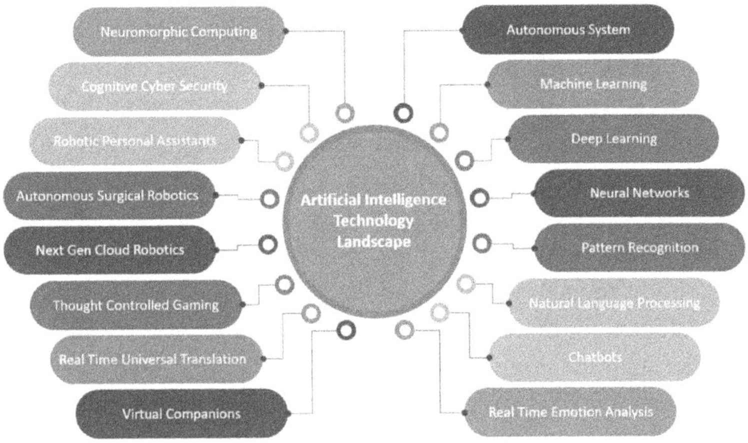

Sours: (Aldoseri et al., 2023)

AI is a rapidly growing field that has the potential to transform our lives and work environments significantly. It can revolutionize various industries, including healthcare, finance, and transportation, creating new opportunities for businesses and organizations. Substantial progress in machine learning and deep learning techniques has been driving this transformation across different sectors. At the core of this change is data, which is crucial for training and evaluating AI models. These models depend on extensive datasets to uncover patterns and trends that traditional data analysis methods might miss, enabling them to learn and make predictions based on the data they have been trained on.

However, utilizing data for AI poses several challenges. The quality, quantity, diversity, and privacy of data are vital factors for data-driven AI applications, each presenting unique difficulties. Low-quality data can result in inaccurate or biased AI models, which can have serious implications in critical fields like healthcare and finance. A lack of sufficient data can lead to overly simplistic models that fail to predict real-world outcomes accurately. Additionally, insufficient data diversity can result in biased models that do not reflect the population they aim to serve. Finally, data privacy is a substantial concern, as AI models often need access to sensitive information, raising issues related to data privacy and security (Aldoseri et al., 2023).

2-1- Machine Learning (ML): Real-World Examples

AI has great potential in marketing. It helps to reproduce information and data sources, improve software data management capabilities, and design complex and advanced algorithms. AI is changing the way brands and users interact with each other. The use of this technology depends significantly on the nature of the website and the type of business. Marketers can now focus more on the customer and meet their needs in real time. Using AI, thanks to the data collected and generated by its algorithms, they can quickly determine what content to target customers and which channel to use at what moment. When AI is used to personalize their experience, users feel comfortable and are more inclined to buy what you have to offer. For example, in the realm of sports marketing, AI-driven platforms can analyze fan behavior across various digital channels, such as social media and mobile apps, to create personalized marketing campaigns. A sports team might use machine learning algorithms to analyze data from ticket purchases, merchandise sales, and social media interactions to identify which fans are most likely to attend upcoming games. By tailoring promotions—such as offering discounts on tickets or exclusive merchandise to specific fan segments—teams can enhance the customer experience and boost sales. AI tools can also be used to analyze the performance of competitor campaigns and uncover customer expectations. ML is a subset of artificial intelligence that allows computers to analyze and interpret data without explicit programming. In addition, ML helps humans solve problems effectively. As more data is fed into the algorithm, the algorithm learns and improves performance and accuracy.

AI primarily deals with user retention and lead conversion in digital marketing. Using AI chatbots, smart email marketing, interactive web design, and other digital marketing services, it guides the user in a direction that aligns with business goals. Several factors determine the impact of artificial intelligence on digital marketing. ML, a subset of artificial intelligence, is concerned with computer programs that access data and use it to learn autonomously. It collects data from various sources, including social media accounts, menus, online reviews, and websites. Artificial intelligence then uses this information to generate and deliver relevant content to the audience. For instance, AI software enables in-depth online analysis of sports teams and their fans. By implementing artificial intelligence into their marketing strategy, sports organizations can better utilize available data and reach potential customers with engaging ads at more convenient times (Haleem et al., 2022).

2-2- Natural Language Processing (NLP): Real-World Examples

The swift advancement of Natural Language Processing (NLP) technology has led to substantial transformations in today's global marketing landscape. This is particularly evident in emerging markets, where these technologies offer multinational corporations unique opportunities to enhance their innovation in marketing strategies to keep pace with the fast-changing market dynamics. The rise of emerging markets within the global economy is a trend that cannot be overlooked, characterized by large populations, a rapidly expanding middle class, abundant resources, and increasing consumer demand. However, these markets also present distinct challenges, such as political instability, cultural disparities, and insufficient legal frameworks. The success of multinational companies in these regions hinges on their ability to innovate and manage their marketing strategies effectively. NLP technology presents a novel approach to addressing these challenges by enabling computers to comprehend, interpret, and generate natural language text. This capability allows for the processing of extensive textual data, including social media comments, news articles, and customer feedback. The growing interest in this technology stems from its vast potential across various applications, such as automated text analysis, sentiment analysis, topic modeling, and semantic search (Huang, 2024) .

As AI permeates marketing conversations and interactions through digital technologies and media, ML models, in particular, NLP models, have become increasingly popular for analyzing unstructured data in marketing (Shankar & Parsana, 2022). NLP, which refers to the capacity of computer algorithms to recognize patterns in text data, is particularly substantial due to the increasing volume of text data available for use in the sports business sector. The results indicate that the adoption of NLP is approaching its peak within the professional sports industry, uncover the organizational factors that influence the timing of this adoption, and provide a framework for both academics and practitioners to engage with NLP (Wanless et al., 2022).

China and Taiwan share a common heritage in terms of their history, culture, language, and writing systems. With the advancement of network information and the widespread availability of digital collections, academic exchanges in sports between these two regions have greatly benefited from the unprecedented application of information technology (IT). This has shifted the previous closed model of interaction to a more open approach, fostering a collaborative and mutually beneficial academic environment. However, during these open academic exchanges, challenges often arise in processing big data, which has spurred the development of data mining technologies and expanded the use of text mining. For instance, in sports marketing, organizations can leverage NLP to analyze fan sentiment on social media platforms. By employing NLP techniques, sports teams can efficiently process vast amounts of text data from tweets, comments, and reviews to gauge public opinion about their brand, players, or events. This application of NLP not only enhances the understanding of fan engagement but also informs marketing strategies more effectively than traditional content analysis methods, which can be time-consuming and subjective. The reliance on NLP in sports-related academic research illustrates its cross-disciplinary application value, as it allows for more efficient data processing. This indicates that traditional content analysis methods used by sports research institutions must be adapted to improve data handling efficiency (Ho et al., 2022). For instance, a study examined how NLP technology can be utilized to assess customer emotions on social media to inform marketing decisions, revealing that NLP can effectively identify customer sentiments and significantly support marketing strategy development. The researchers investigated the use of NLP technology in creating intelligent chatbots to enhance customer engagement, finding that NLP improves customer experiences and interactions, thereby contributing to marketing success. Some employed NLP to perform an in-depth analysis of emerging markets, assisting multinational corporations in devising more effective market entry strategies, highlighting NLP's role in market research and positioning (Huang, 2024).

2-3- Computer Vision (CV): Real-World Examples

In the 21st century, AI has become a widely recognized technology, serving as the foundation for many popular applications. One notable example is the rapidly emerging VR technology, which offers immersive experiences through specialized visual effects. This technology is a form of computer vision that enhances user experience and has fostered the belief that "those who master AI will shape the future." As one of the most advanced forms of artificial intelligence, computer vision (CV) facilitates the effective implementation of AI technologies across various sectors, including healthcare, security surveillance, transportation, industrial production, the internet, gaming, and the military.

In particular, in the e-commerce sector, major companies are continually innovating and transforming their operations to boost efficiency and enhance customer satisfaction in online shopping experiences, with computer vision technology playing a vital role in these advancements (Yang & Liu, 2021). For example, in the sports marketing domain, companies are utilizing computer vision to analyze fan engagement during live events. By processing video feeds from stadiums, they can track crowd reactions and interactions, allowing teams to tailor their marketing strategies in real-time based on fan sentiment and behavior. This application not only enhances the overall fan experience but also helps teams optimize their promotional efforts to better align with audience preferences.

Moreover, digital marketing leverages AI to provide customers with a delightful experience through advertising on social media and digital platforms like Facebook and Instagram. These platforms analyze user data thoroughly before directing them to tailored offers. AI also aids marketers in identifying and predicting trends, preventing overspending on digital advertising and ensuring that budgets are utilized effectively (Dumitriu & Popescu, 2020; Forrest & Hoanca, 2015). The ability of computers to recognize objects, scenes, and activities in images is known as CV. When CV is effectively integrated with artificial intelligence, it enables robots to predict future events and respond accordingly to potential changes (Van Esch & Stewart Black, 2021).

PART III: CASE STUDIES OF AI IN SPORTS MARKETING

Case Study 1: AI in Enhancing Fan Engagement for Sport Team/Event

AI is being increasingly employed to improve fan engagement with sports teams. It has a substantial impact on athlete training by enhancing performance metrics and lowering injury rates. Additionally, AI is vital in decision-making processes, leading to improved team outcomes and strategic advantages. Regarding fan engagement, AI-driven personalization and immersive technologies have substantial boosted fan satisfaction and audience retention (Javed et al., 2024). For instance, According to the announcement of MCV website Manchester City Football Club employs an AI platform called "City Voice," which allows fans to directly share their feedback and suggestions with the team. This platform analyzes fan data, helping Manchester City provide personalized content and better experiences for its supporters.

Case Study 2: Predictive Analytics in Sports Sponsorship for Sport Team/Event

Predictive analytics enables sports teams to better understand and anticipate the behaviors and needs of their fans. Mark Cuban, the owner of the Dallas Mavericks, is recognized for his forward-thinking approach to sports management. Since he took ownership of the Mavericks in 2000, Cuban has continuously pursued innovative strategies to improve the team's performance both on and off the court. In recent years, he has adopted AI technologies, which have transformed various facets of the Mavericks' operations. These transformations include areas such as player performance, health management, fan engagement, and business analytics. For example, the NBA team, the Dallas Mavericks utilize AI algorithms to analyze ticket purchasing patterns and fan behavior. This analysis helps the team create more targeted marketing campaigns and effectively address the specific needs of their fans, ultimately resulting in increased financial support and higher ticket sales (2immersive4u.com, 2024).

Case Study 3: AI-driven Social Media Campaigns for Sport Team/Event

AI-driven social media campaigns empower sports teams to engage more effectively with their fans. Substantial AI technologies excel at monitoring social media platforms, allowing teams to gain a comprehensive understanding of what users are saying about their brand through posts and comments, a process known as sentiment analysis. Additionally, these technologies help identify how to approach fans with personalized content through audience analysis and enable marketers to recognize brand logos in shared images via image analysis. AI tools provide valuable assistance to social media marketers by optimizing audience, image, and sentiment analyses, thereby identifying branded content that generates high levels of customer engagement on social media (Capatina et al., 2020). For instance, FC Barcelona utilizes AI tools to analyze fan sentiments and opinions on social media platforms. This information helps Barcelona create more engaging content and foster greater interaction with its supporters (Romero-Jara et al., 2023).

Case Study 4: Improving Ticket Sales and Pricing with AI for Sport Team/Event

Pricing strategies can substantial influence a company's success (Markula, 2023). Match-day revenue remains a crucial income source for many professional sports clubs (Quansah et al., 2022). In this context, AI can play a vital role in enhancing ticket sales and pricing strategies for sports teams.

For instance, Arsenal Football Club utilizes AI algorithms to analyze historical ticket sales data and fan behavior. By examining patterns and trends in this data, Arsenal can implement dynamic pricing for tickets, adjusting prices based on demand, opponent strength, and other factors. This approach not only optimizes ticket sales but also maximizes revenue opportunities, leading to increased overall ticket sales and enhanced profitability for the club.

The case studies demonstrate that AI can effectively enhance fan engagement, predict fan behavior, optimize social media campaigns, and improve ticket sales and pricing in sports marketing. This technology allows sports teams to respond more accurately to the needs of their fans, thereby providing a better experience for them. Given these findings, the use of AI in sports marketing is expected to play a crucial role in the future of this industry.

PART IV: THE FUTURE OF AI IN SPORTS MARKETING

The sports industry is experiencing substantial growth each year, both in size and revenue. Currently, AI, an emerging technology, is being utilized as a tool to enhance optimization and efficiency across various contexts, including the sports sector. Research indicates that AI has played a crucial role in the recent successes of the sports industry, particularly in areas such as fan engagement and revenue generation. Furthermore, operations, management, and marketing within the sports sector have similarly benefited from AI's contributions. Given these trends, it is clear that organizations and management teams in the sports industry will increasingly adopt AI technologies. With its ability to process vast amounts of data and generate key trends and predictions, this transformative technology is set to support organizational success, a trend that will likely become more pronounced as AI use becomes more developed and widespread (Jokela, 2024).

As we explore the current state of AI applications, it is essential to recognize the advancements in AI technology and its potential future trends that could have a substantial impact on the sports industry:

1- Predictive Analytics: AI-powered predictive analytics can provide valuable insights that assist teams and coaches in making informed decisions regarding player recruitment, game strategies, and training regimens. By analyzing extensive data on player performance, weather conditions, and other relevant factors, predictive analytics can offer insights that enable teams to gain a competitive edge.

2- Immersive Technologies (XR): As XR technologies advance, they could create new opportunities for fan engagement and athlete training. For example, VR could facilitate immersive fan experiences, allowing viewers to feel as though they are part of the action. Meanwhile, AR could deliver real-time insights and feedback to athletes, thereby enhancing their performance on the field.

3- Automated Scouting and Talent Identification: AI can streamline the scouting and talent identification process, particularly in developing sports or regions. By analyzing performance data, video footage, and other metrics, AI algorithms can help identify promising athletes and bring them to the attention of scouts and coaches.

4- AI-Powered Medical Diagnosis and Treatment: AI can analyze player biometric data and provide real-time feedback to coaches and medical staff. This capability can aid in injury prevention and optimize training regimens, potentially extending players' careers and enhancing their performance.

5- AI-Driven Sports Journalism: AI can analyze data on player performance, game outcomes, and other factors to generate real-time sports journalism content. This technology can assist journalists and broadcasters in delivering more in-depth and informative coverage of sports events, and it could even automate the generation of game reports and social media content.

6- Machine Learning for Personalization: AI-powered machine learning can help teams and brands tailor their offerings to individual fans. By analyzing data on past purchase behavior, social media activity, and other factors, machine learning algorithms can create customized recommendations for products and services that resonate with specific fans.

These trends illustrate the potential for AI to transform the sports industry in the future. However, it is crucial to consider the challenges and risks associated with this transformation, such as the ethical implications of AI applications in sports, the potential for job displacement in certain sectors, and the need for appropriate regulations to ensure fair practices. Overall, the development and dissemination of AI in the sports industry present both opportunities and challenges that require careful consideration and management (Glebova et al., 2024).

As AI continues to evolve, its integration into sports marketing is likely to lead to more personalized fan experiences, innovative revenue models, and enhanced operational efficiency. For instance, teams may leverage AI to create tailored marketing campaigns that resonate with specific demographics, ultimately driving higher engagement and loyalty among fans. The future of sports marketing, powered by AI, promises to be more dynamic and responsive to the needs of both teams and their supporters.

PART V: SUMMARY

As industries undergo changes and transformations, the world is rapidly evolving, customer expectations are rising, and new disruptors are emerging globally. In this dynamic environment, every organization requires both the agility to respond quickly and the capability to take proactive measures for its advancement. It can be said that the challenge and opportunity lie within the data. This chapter, titled "Leveraging AI in Sports Marketing: Opportunities and Challenges," thoroughly examines the transformational impact of AI on the sports marketing landscape. As the field evolves, AI has become an essential tool for enhancing fan engagement, refining marketing strategies, and improving operational efficiency. By analyzing large datasets, AI enables sports marketers to gain deeper insights into consumer behavior, craft personalized marketing campaigns, and forecast trends. These insights empower organizations to target fans more effectively, delivering tailored experiences that strengthen brand loyalty. For instance, machine learning algorithms can evaluate fans' purchasing behaviors and optimize the timing and nature of promotional offers, thereby maximizing marketing returns. However, these opportunities are accompanied by challenges. Data privacy and ethical considerations are critical, as AI relies heavily on the collection of personal data for analysis. Organizations must navigate these concerns responsibly, ensuring compliance with legal regulations. Additionally, a lack of understanding of AI technologies within some organizations can result in ineffective implementation, potentially harming brand reputation and leading to customer dissatisfaction. The competitive nature of sports marketing further emphasizes the need for adaptability. AI can assist organizations in keeping pace with rapid shifts in market dynamics, consumer preferences, and technological advancements. By investing in AI-driven infrastructure and providing adequate training for employees, sports organizations can fully leverage AI's potential to maintain a competitive edge in the marketplace.

Given the numerous examples mentioned regarding the key role of skilled labor in the field of AI in sports marketing, it can be concluded that the growth of digital marketing largely depends on the expertise and skills of the specialized workforce in this area. Skilled professionals across various domains, from technology and data analytics to cybersecurity and digital marketing and economics, are vital components for advancing innovation, driving digital transformation, and mitigating risks in the digital landscape. As AI continues to evolve in sports marketing, the demand for a skilled workforce that can adapt to these changes will also increase, highlighting the growing need for an effective strategy to train skilled human resources in this field. This necessitates investment and focus from policymakers and stakeholders in this area. The chapter also discussed the outcomes for academics and practitioners and proposed a future research agenda to examine the ongoing shift driven by rapid AI implementation in marketing.

REFERENCES

Abolghasemi Atany, S., Rahimizadeh, M., & Monazami, A. H. (2024). *Designing an Artificial Intelligence-Based Electronic Marketing Pattern in the Iranian Sports Industry*. Communication Management in Sport Media., DOI: 10.30473/jsm.2024.69704.1817

Afkar, A., Tojari, F., & Zarei, A. (2018). Testing the Structural Model of Purchase Intention of Sport Consumers based on Value–Attitude–Behavior Hierarchy. *New Trends in Sport Management*, 6(20), 39–50.

Aldoseri, A., Al-Khalifa, K. N., & Hamouda, A. M. (2023). Re-thinking data strategy and integration for artificial intelligence: Concepts, opportunities, and challenges. *Applied Sciences (Basel, Switzerland)*, 13(12), 7082. DOI: 10.3390/app13127082

Amin, N. (2019). Digital Marketing Practices by Asiatic Clients: A hands-on Initiative through Facebook Platforms.

Annamalai, B., Yoshida, M., Varshney, S., Pathak, A. A., & Venugopal, P. (2021). Social media content strategy for sport clubs to drive fan engagement. *Journal of Retailing and Consumer Services*, 62, 102648. DOI: 10.1016/j.jretconser.2021.102648

bahrami, s., & kiani, m. (2023). The Impact of Social Media and the Internet on the Marketing of Sporting Events. *Communication Management in Sport Media, 10*(3), 15-31. https://doi.org/DOI: 10.30473/jsm.2021.50368.1369

Bishop, R., Smith, A. C., & Read, D. (2022). An introduction to the challenges of distributive equity in the English Premier League. *Sport, Business and Management*, 12(3), 284–304. DOI: 10.1108/SBM-04-2021-0053

Capatina, A., Kachour, M., Lichy, J., Micu, A., Micu, A.-E., & Codignola, F. (2020). Matching the future capabilities of an artificial intelligence-based software for social media marketing with potential users' expectations. *Technological Forecasting and Social Change*, 151, 119794. DOI: 10.1016/j.techfore.2019.119794

Dumitriu, D., & Popescu, M. A.-M. (2020). Artificial intelligence solutions for digital marketing. *Procedia Manufacturing*, 46, 630–636. DOI: 10.1016/j.promfg.2020.03.090

Eickhoff, F., & Zhevak, L. (2023). The consumer attitude towards AI in marketing: An experimental study of consumers attitudes and purchase intention. In.

Esmaeili mahyari, M., Irani, H. R., & Normandipour, V. (2022). Bibliometric Analysis of The Global Trends on Sport Marketing Researches. *Sports Marketing Studies, 3*(1), 143-114. https://doi.org/DOI: 10.34785/J021.2022.005

Farahani, A., & Ghorbhani Qahfarkhi, L. (2015). *Sports marketing management.* Payam Noor University.

Fekrat, A., & Jaberi, A. (2024). Phenomenology of the role of artificial intelligence marketing on increasing sales and exports of Iranian sports goods. *Sports Marketing Studies*, 5(2), 1–15. DOI: 10.22034/sms.2024.139803.1254

Finch, D. J., Abeza, G., O'Reilly, N., Nadeau, J., Levallet, N., Legg, D., & Foster, B. (2022). Season ticket holder segmentation in professional sports: An application of the sports relationship marketing model. *International Journal of Sports Marketing & Sponsorship*, 23(1), 110–131. DOI: 10.1108/IJSMS-08-2020-0150

Ford, J., Jain, V., Wadhwani, K., & Gupta, D. G. (2023). AI advertising: An overview and guidelines. *Journal of Business Research*, 166, 114124. DOI: 10.1016/j.jbusres.2023.114124

Forrest, E., & Hoanca, B. (2015). Artificial intelligence: Marketing's game changer. *Trends and innovations in marketing information systems*, 45-64. https://doi.org/DOI: 10.4018/978-1-4666-8459-1.ch003

Ghafari, M., & Ranjbarian, B. (2013). *Sports marketing* (Vol. 1). Charbagh.

Glebova, E., Madsen, D. Ø., Mihaľová, P., Géczi, G., Mittelman, A., & Jorgič, B. (2024). Artificial intelligence development and dissemination impact on the sports industry labor market. *Frontiers in Sports and Active Living*, 6, 1363892. DOI: 10.3389/fspor.2024.1363892 PMID: 38606117

Golmohammadi, H., Ghadami, S., Pashaie, S., & Zolfi, H. (2025). Identification and Analysis of Prominent Concepts in Digital Marketing and Sports. *Sports Marketing Studies, 5*(4), -. https://doi.org/DOI: 10.22034/sms.2024.140983.1328

Haleem, A., Javaid, M., Qadri, M. A., Singh, R. P., & Suman, R. (2022). Artificial intelligence (AI) applications for marketing: A literature-based study. *International Journal of Intelligent Networks*, 3, 119–132. DOI: 10.1016/j.ijin.2022.08.005

Hassan, A. (2021). The usage of artificial intelligence in digital marketing: A review. *Applications of Artificial Intelligence in Business, Education and Healthcare*, 357-383. https://doi.org/DOI: 10.1007/978-3-030-72080-3_20

Ho, T.-K., Shih, W.-Y., Kao, W.-Y., Hsu, C.-H., & Wu, C.-Y. (2022). Analysis of the development trend of sports research in China and Taiwan using natural language processing. *Applied Sciences (Basel, Switzerland)*, 12(18), 9006. DOI: 10.3390/app12189006

Huang, S. (2024). Exploring the Influence of Natural Language Processing Technology on Marketing Strategy Innovation Management in Emerging Markets for Multinational Corporations. *Journal of Logistics.Informatics and Service Science*, 11(3), 399–411. DOI: 10.33168/JLISS.2024.0326

2. immersive4u.com. (2024). *Mark Cuban and the AI Revolution: Transforming the Dallas Mavericks (Stories about AI)*https://2immersive4u.com/2024/06/07/mark-cuban-and-the-ai-revolution-transforming-the-dallas-mavericks-stories-about-ai/

Jasper.ai. https://www.jasper.ai/

Javed, S., Naseer, A., Gill, S. A., & Rajab, S. (2024). Usage of Artificial Intelligence Reshapes the Prevailing Scenario of Today Sports at the Globe. *THE SPARK" A HEC Recognized Journal", 9*(1), 1-8.

Jokela, S. (2024). Impact of artificial intelligence on business & management processes in the sports industry.

Kaczorowska-Spychalska, D. (2019). Chatbots in marketing. *Management*, 23(1), 251–270. Advance online publication. DOI: 10.2478/manment-2019-0015

karimi, a., & ahmadi, a. (2024). Modeling the effect of social media marketing activities on the intention to repurchase sports products, and sustainable social communication. *Sports Marketing Studies, 5*(3), -. https://doi.org/DOI: 10.22034/sms.2023.138585.1211

Kasem, M. S., Hamada, M., & Taj-Eddin, I. (2024). Customer profiling, segmentation, and sales prediction using AI in direct marketing. *Neural Computing & Applications*, 36(9), 4995–5005. DOI: 10.1007/s00521-023-09339-6

Katragadda, V. (2023). Automating Customer Support: A Study on The Efficacy of Machine Learning-Driven Chatbots and Virtual Assistants. *IRE Journals*, 7(1), 600–601.

Mahmoudian, A., Mohammadi, S., & Wang, W. (2024). Fan Engagement Management: Fan Response to Brand Image Attributes of Professional Athletes on Instagram. *Journal of Global Sport Management*, 1-19. https://doi.org/DOI: 10.1080/24704067.2024.2370582

Mamo, Y., Su, Y., & Andrew, D. P. (2022). The transformative impact of big data applications in sport marketing: Current and future directions. *International Journal of Sports Marketing & Sponsorship*, 23(3), 594–611. DOI: 10.1108/IJSMS-03-2021-0073

Markula, A. (2023). The Use of Artificial Intelligence in Dynamic Pricing Strategies.

MCV. W. *Man City Voice*. https://mancityvoice.com/about-us/

Mohammadi, S., Heidari, A., & Navkhsi, J. (2023). Proposing a Framework for the Digital Transformation Maturity of Electronic Sports Businesses in Developing Countries. *Sustainability (Basel)*, 15(16), 12354. DOI: 10.3390/su151612354

Mohammadi, S., Mahmoudian, A., & Dos Santos, M. A. (2024). Customer Experience Design in Sportswear Retail Stores. In *Marketing and Design in the Service Sector: Enhancing Customer Experience* (pp. 137-152). Emerald Publishing Limited. https://doi.org/DOI: 10.1108/978-1-83797-276-020241010

Mohammadi, S., Mahmoudian, A., & Rayner, M. (2024). Applying the Strategic Model of Customer Experience in the Field of Sports: The Customer Experience Model in Sports and Recreation Complexes. In *Marketing and Design in the Service Sector: Enhancing Customer Experience* (pp. 153-173). Emerald Publishing Limited. https://doi.org/DOI: 10.1108/978-1-83797-276-020241011

Nalbant, K. G., & Aydın, S. (2022). Literature review on the relationship between artificial intelligence technologies with digital sports marketing and sports management. *Indonesian Journal of Sport Management*, 2(2), 135–143. DOI: 10.31949/ijsm.v2i2.2876

Norouzi, P., Seyedameri, M., & Behnam, M. (2023). The effect of brand experience on customer engagement with sports brands through perceived satisfaction and value [Research]. *New Trends in Sport Management, 11*(40), 43-58. http://ntsmj.issma.ir/article-1-1871-en.html

Parsamehr, M., & Torkan, R. (2009). Fanatic Support for Soccer Teams in the Iranian League Case of Yazd University Students. *Irish Journal of Sociology*, 10(3), 85–105.

Pashaie, S., & Nasirpour, M. (2024). (in press). The Impact of Observability and Compatibility on Consumers' Attitudes Towards AI-Generated Sports Marketing Content and Its Effect on Purchase Intent. *Sports Marketing Studies. Articles*. Advance online publication. DOI: 10.22034/sms.2024.141529.1367

peak.ai website. https://peak.ai/products/customer-ai/audiences/

Quansah, T. K., Buraimo, B., & Lang, M. (2022). The Price of Success and Labour in Sports–Evidence from Match-day Ticket Pricing Strategies in the English Premier League. *Available atSSRN* 4039945. https://doi.org/DOI: 10.2139/ssrn.4039945

Rahman, J., Raihan, A., Tanchangya, T., & Ridwan, M. (2024). Optimizing the digital marketing landscape: A comprehensive exploration of artificial intelligence (AI) technologies, applications, advantages, and challenges. *Frontiers of Finance*, 2(2). Advance online publication. DOI: 10.59429/ff.v2i2.6549

Rana, B. (2016). *The impact of SEO on business*https://urn.fi/URN:NBN:fi:amk-2016110715826

Romero-Jara, E., Solanellas, F., Muñoz, J., & López-Carril, S. (2023). Connecting with fans in the digital age: An exploratory and comparative analysis of social media management in top football clubs. *Humanities & Social Sciences Communications*, 10(1), 1–12. https://doi.org/s41599-023-02357-8. DOI: 10.1057/s41599-023-02357-8

Rookwood, J., & Millward, P. (2011). 'We all dream of a team of Carraghers': Comparing 'local'and Texan Liverpool fans' talk. *Sport in Society*, 14(1), 37–52. DOI: 10.1080/17430437.2011.530009

Safarian, S., Nasimi, M. A., & Rahmaty, M. (2024). Provide content marketing model of in sports E-business with the grounded theory approach. *Sports Marketing Studies*, 5(1), 101–121. DOI: 10.22034/sms.2023.139886.1258

Salimi, M., Soltan Hosseini, M., & Naderian Jahromi, M. (2015). The Evaluation of Iran's Sport Marketing Development Obstacles. *Sport Management Studies, 7*(29), 13-36. https://smrj.ssrc.ac.ir/article_428_58c8549f8f4cc25a85b5ffb24d16ca99.pdf

Sbrighi, A. (2024). *Leveraging The Power Of Deep Tech Within The Realm Of Digital Marketing: An Explorative Insight Into The Relationship Between Artificial Intelligence And Sports Fan Engagement*. Università Ca' Foscari Venezia. https://doi.org/DOI: 10579/26168

Shank, M. D., & Lyberger, M. R. (2014). *Sports marketing: A strategic perspective*. Routledge., DOI: 10.4324/9781315794082

Shankar, V., & Parsana, S. (2022). An overview and empirical comparison of natural language processing (NLP) models and an introduction to and empirical application of autoencoder models in marketing. *Journal of the Academy of Marketing Science*, 50(6), 1324–1350. DOI: 10.1007/s11747-022-00840-3

Stewart, M. C., & Arnold, C. L. (2018). Defining social listening: Recognizing an emerging dimension of listening. *International Journal of Listening*, 32(2), 85–100. DOI: 10.1080/10904018.2017.1330656

Thilagavathy, N., & Kumar, E. P. (2021). Artificial intelligence on digital marketing-An overview. *Nveo-Natural Volatiles & Essential Oils Journal| NVEO*, 9895-9908.

Todor, R. D. (2016). Marketing automation. *Bulletin of the Transilvania University of Brasov. Series V, Economic Sciences*, •••, 87–94.

Tsimonis, G., & Dimitriadis, S. (2014). Brand strategies in social media. *Marketing Intelligence & Planning*, 32(3), 328–344. DOI: 10.1108/MIP-04-2013-0056

Vale, L., & Fernandes, T. (2018). Social media and sports: Driving fan engagement with football clubs on Facebook. *Journal of Strategic Marketing*, 26(1), 37–55. DOI: 10.1080/0965254X.2017.1359655

Van Esch, P., & Stewart Black, J. (2021). Artificial intelligence (AI): Revolutionizing digital marketing. *Australasian Marketing Journal*, 29(3), 199–203. DOI: 10.1177/18393349211037684

Wanless, L., Seifried, C., Bouchet, A., Valeant, A., & Naraine, M. L. (2022). The diffusion of natural language processing in professional sport. *Sport Management Review*, 25(3), 522–545. DOI: 10.1080/14413523.2021.1968174

Yang, C., & Liu, Z. (2021). Application of computer vision in electronic commerce. *Journal of Physics: Conference Series*, 1992(2), 022134. DOI: 10.1088/1742-6596/1992/2/022134

Compilation of References

Abbasi, A., Sarker, S., & Chiang, R. H. (2016). Big data research in information systems: Toward an inclusive research agenda. *Journal of the Association for Information Systems*, 17(2), 3. DOI: 10.17705/1jais.00423

Abolghasemi Atany, S., Rahimizadeh, M., & Monazami, A. H. (2024). *Designing an Artificial Intelligence-Based Electronic Marketing Pattern in the Iranian Sports Industry*. Communication Management in Sport Media., DOI: 10.30473/jsm.2024.69704.1817

AdRoll. (2021). How marketing technology can give you a competitive advantage. Retrieved from https://www.adroll.com/blog/how-marketing-technology-can-give-you-a-competitive-advantage

Advertising on Social Network Sites: A Structural Equation Modelling Approach—Anant Saxena, Uday Khanna, 2013. (n.d.). Retrieved March 23, 2022, from https://journals.sagepub.com/doi/abs/10.1177/0972262912469560

Afkar, A., Tojari, F., & Zarei, A. (2018). Testing the Structural Model of Purchase Intention of Sport Consumers based on Value–Attitude–Behavior Hierarchy. *New Trends in Sport Management*, 6(20), 39–50.

Agarwal, R., & Dhar, V. (2014). Big data, data science, and analytics: The opportunity and challenge for IS research. *Information Systems Research*, 25(3), 443–448. DOI: 10.1287/isre.2014.0546

Ahmed, M. (n.d.). *THE EFFECT OF ATTITUDE TOWARD ADVERTISEMENT ON ATTITUDE TOWARD BRAND AND PURCHASE INTENTION*. Retrieved March 23, 2022, from https://www.academia.edu/24948680/THE_EFFECT_OF_ATTITUDE_TOWARD_ADVERTISEMENT_ON_ATTITUDE_TOWARD_BRAND_AND_PURCHASE_INTENTION

Akhavan Sarraf, A. R., & Teshnizi, H. (2020). *The Effect of Social Media Advertising Properties on Customer Buying Intention (Case Study: Consumers of Cosmetic Products). 7*, 10–17.

Akter, S., Wamba, S. F., Gunasekaran, A., Dubey, R., & Childe, S. J. (2016). How to improve firm performance using big data analytics capability and business strategy alignment? *International Journal of Production Economics*, 182, 113–131. DOI: 10.1016/j.ijpe.2016.08.018

Aldoseri, A., Al-Khalifa, K. N., & Hamouda, A. M. (2023). Re-thinking data strategy and integration for artificial intelligence: Concepts, opportunities, and challenges. *Applied Sciences (Basel, Switzerland)*, 13(12), 7082. DOI: 10.3390/app13127082

Alzghoul, A., Khaddam, A. A., Abousweilem, F., Irtaimeh, H. J., & Alshaar, Q. (2022). How business intelligence capability impacts decision-making speed, comprehensiveness, and firm performance. *Information Development*, 02666669221108438. Advance online publication. DOI: 10.1177/02666669221108438

Amin, N. (2019). Digital Marketing Practices by Asiatic Clients: A hands-on Initiative through Facebook Platforms.

An Exploratory Investigation into Impulse Buying Behavior in a Transitional Economy: A Study of Urban Consumers in Vietnam—Nguyen Thi Tuyet Mai, Kwon Jung, Garold Lantz, Sandra G. Loeb, 2003. (n.d.). Retrieved March 23, 2022, from https://journals.sagepub.com/doi/10.1509/jimk.11.2.13.20162

Annamalai, B., Yoshida, M., Varshney, S., Pathak, A. A., & Venugopal, P. (2021). Social media content strategy for sport clubs to drive fan engagement. *Journal of Retailing and Consumer Services*, 62, 102648. DOI: 10.1016/j.jretconser.2021.102648

Aparicio, D., Metzman, Z., & Rigobon, R. (2023). The pricing strategies of online grocery retailers. *Quantitative Marketing and Economics*, 22(1), 1–21. DOI: 10.1007/s11129-023-09273-w

Appelbaum, D., Kogan, A., Vasarhelyi, M., & Yan, Z. (2017). Impact of Business Analytics and Enterprise Systems on Managerial Accounting. *International Journal of Accounting Information Systems*, 25, 29–44. DOI: 10.1016/j.accinf.2017.03.003

Arigo, D., Pagoto, S., Carter-Harris, L., Lillie, S. E., & Nebeker, C. (2018). Using social media for health research: Methodological and ethical considerations for recruitment and intervention delivery. *Digital Health*, 4, 2055207618771757. DOI: 10.1177/2055207618771757 PMID: 29942634

Armstrong, M. (2021, February 22). *The UK's favourite supermarkets*. Statista Daily Data. https://www.statista.com/chart/17117/uk-favourite-supermarkets/

Atiku, S. O., Menjengua, D. K., Jeremiah, A., & Villet, H. J. (2024). Data-Driven Talent Management Practices for Eco-Innovation in State-Owned Enterprises. In Data-Driven Decision Making for Long-Term Business Success (pp. 369-394). IGI Global. DOI: DOI: 10.4018/979-8-3693-2193-5.ch025

Atluri, V., Dahlström, P., Gaffey, B., García de la Torre, V., Kaka, N., Lajous, T., Singla, A., Sukharevsky, A., Travasoni, A., & Vieira, B. (2024). *Beyond the hype: Capturing the potential of AI and gen AI in tech, media, and telecom.*https://www.mckinsey.com/industries/technology-media-and-telecommunications/our-insights/beyond-the-hype-capturing-the-potential-of-ai-and-gen-ai-in-tmt

Auf der Landwehr, M., Schoormann, T., von Viebahn, C., & Trott, M. (2023). From purchase to pantry–exploring archetypes and strategies in the context of e-grocery fulfilment. *European Journal of Information Systems*, •••, 1–39. DOI: 10.1080/0960085X.2023.2180446

Babayev, N. & Israfilzade, K. (2023). Creating complexity matrix for classifying artificial intelligence applications in e-commerce: New perspectives on value creation. Journal of Life Economics. https://doi.org/DOI: 10.15637/jlecon.2078

bahrami, s., & kiani, m. (2023). The Impact of Social Media and the Internet on the Marketing of Sporting Events. *Communication Management in Sport Media, 10*(3), 15-31. https://doi.org/DOI: 10.30473/jsm.2021.50368.1369

Baig, A., Berruti, F., Ellencweig, B., Lewandowski, D., Roberts, R., Yee, L., Singla, A., Smaje, K., Sukharevsky, A., Tilley, J., & Zemmel, R. (2024, March 21). *What is artificial general intelligence (AGI)?*https://www.mckinsey.com/featured-insights/mckinsey-explainers/what-is-artificial-general-intelligence-agi

Baig, A., Singla, A., & Yee, L. (2024, April 2). *What is generative AI?* McKinsey & Company. https://www.mckinsey.com/featured-insights/mckinsey-explainers/what-is-generative-ai#/

Baltas, G. (2003). Determinants of Internet Advertising Effectiveness: An Empirical Study. *International Journal of Market Research*, 45(4), 1–9. DOI: 10.1177/147078530304500403

Bank of America Corporation. (2024). *Artificial intelligence: A real game changer.* Bank of America. https://business.bofa.com/en-us/content/economic-impact-of-ai.html

Barata, S. F., Ferreira, F. A., Carayannis, E. G., & Ferreira, J. J. (2023). Determinants of E-Commerce, Artificial Intelligence, and Agile Methods in Small-and Medium-Sized Enterprises. *IEEE Transactions on Engineering Management*. Advance online publication. DOI: 10.1109/TEM.2023.3269601

Bee, C. C., & Madrigal, R. (2012). It's Not Whether You Win or Lose; It's How The Game is Played. *Journal of Advertising*, 41(1), 47–58. DOI: 10.2753/JOA0091-3367410104

Belanche, D., Flavián, C., & Pérez-Rueda, A. (2017). Understanding Interactive Online Advertising: Congruence and Product Involvement in Highly and Lowly Arousing, Skippable Video Ads. *Journal of Interactive Marketing*, 37(1), 75–88. DOI: 10.1016/j.intmar.2016.06.004

Belanger, A. (2024, February 16). *Air Canada must honor refund policy invented by airline's chatbot*. Ars Technica. https://arstechnica.com/tech-policy/2024/02/air-canada-must-honor-refund-policy-invented-by-airlines-chatbot/

Bellman, S., Treleaven-Hassard, S., Robinson, J. A., Rask, A., & Varan, D. (2012). Getting the Balance Right. *Journal of Advertising*, 41(2), 5–24. DOI: 10.2753/JOA0091-3367410201

Bharadiya, J. P. (2023). *A comparative study of business intelligence and artificial intelligence with big data analytics*. American Journal of Artificial Intelligence., DOI: 10.11648/j.ajai.20230701.14

Bharadiya, J. P. (2023). *Machine learning and AI in business intelligence: Trends and opportunities. International Journal of Computer*. IJC.

Bishop, R., Smith, A. C., & Read, D. (2022). An introduction to the challenges of distributive equity in the English Premier League. *Sport, Business and Management*, 12(3), 284–304. DOI: 10.1108/SBM-04-2021-0053

Bordeleau, F. E., Mosconi, E., & de Santa-Eulalia, L. A. (2020). Business intelligence and analytics value creation in Industry 4.0: A multiple case study in manufacturing medium enterprises. *Production Planning and Control*, 31(2-3), 173–185. DOI: 10.1080/09537287.2019.1631458

Bose, R. (2009). Advanced analytics: Opportunities and challenges. *Industrial Management & Data Systems*, 109(2), 155–172. DOI: 10.1108/02635570910930073

Bourton, S., Ellencweig, B., Giovin, C., & Xu, S. (2023, November 29). *Six major GenAI trends that will shape 2024's agenda*. QuantumBlack, AI by McKinsey. https://medium.com/quantumblack/six-major-genai-trends-that-will-shape-2024s-agenda-da85dba8b1a8

Bradley, M. M., & Lang, P. J. (2000). Affective reactions to acoustic stimuli. *Psychophysiology*, 37(2), 204–215. DOI: 10.1111/1469-8986.3720204 PMID: 10731770

Bradlow, E. T., Gangwar, M., Kopalle, P., & Voleti, S. (2017). The Role of Big Data and Predictive Analytics in Retailing. *Journal of Retailing*, 93(1), 79–95. DOI: 10.1016/j.jretai.2016.12.004

Breugelmans, E., Altenburg, L., Lehmkuhle, F., Krafft, M., Lamey, L., & Roggeveen, A. L. (2023). The future of physical stores: Creating reasons for customers to visit. *Journal of Retailing*, 99(4), 532–546. DOI: 10.1016/j.jretai.2023.10.005

Brinker, S. (2018). The current state of marketing technology. *Journal of Marketing Management*, 34(7-8), 653–667. DOI: 10.1080/0267257X.2018.1455172

Brown, A., Smith, J., & Johnson, M. (2020). Leveraging AI for Enhanced Personalization in Digital Marketing. *Journal of Marketing Technology*, 15(2), 45–58.

Brown, E., & Hayes, M. (2018). The Role of Technology in Influencer Marketing: Transformative Impact of Data Analytics and Artificial Intelligence. *Journal of Marketing Technology*, 23(4), 112–129.

Brynjolfsson, E., Hitt, L. M., & Kim, H. H. (2011). Strength in numbers: How does data-driven decisionmaking affect firm performance? SSRN Electronic Journal. DOI: 10.2139/ssrn.1819486

BSI. Top10: B ng x p h ng social media tháng 01/2020. (2020, February 25). *Buzzmetrics*. https://buzzmetrics.com/bsi-top10-01-2020/

Business2Community. (2021). How MarTech can scale with your business. Retrieved from https://www.business2community.com/marketing/how-martech-can-scale-with-your-business-02245731

Caliskan, F., Idug, Y., Gligor, D. M., Uvet, H., Adana, S., Celik, H., & Cevikparmak, S. (2024). Transparency and trust in cargo claims: Microenterprises selling internationally on a peer-to-peer platform. *Journal of Business and Industrial Marketing*, 39(5), 1092–1103. Advance online publication. DOI: 10.1108/JBIM-03-2023-0170

Capatina, A., Kachour, M., Lichy, J., Micu, A., Micu, A.-E., & Codignola, F. (2020). Matching the future capabilities of an artificial intelligence-based software for social media marketing with potential users' expectations. *Technological Forecasting and Social Change*, 151, 119794. DOI: 10.1016/j.techfore.2019.119794

Carroll, B., & Landry, K. (2010). Logging On and Letting Out: Using Online Social Networks to Grieve and to Mourn. *Bulletin of Science, Technology & Society*, 30(5), 341–349. DOI: 10.1177/0270467610380006

Chaffey, D., & Ellis-Chadwick, F. (2019). *Digital marketing* (7th ed.). Pearson.

Chaffey, D., & Smith, P. R. (2017). *Digital marketing excellence: Planning, optimizing and integrating online marketing*. Taylor & Francis. DOI: 10.4324/9781315640341

Chaudhuri, S., Dayal, U., & Narasayya, V. (2011). An overview of business intelligence technology. *Communications of the ACM*, 54(8), 88–98. DOI: 10.1145/1978542.1978562

Chen, H., Chiang, R. H., & Storey, V. C. (2012). Business Intelligence and Analytics: From Big Data to Big Impact. *Management Information Systems Quarterly*, 36(4), 1165–1188. DOI: 10.2307/41703503

Chen, L.. (2021). Role of Influencer Trust in Shaping Consumer Attitudes: Evidence from China. *International Journal of Advertising*, 39(4), 532–548.

Chiefmartec. (2021). The 10-year horizon of MarTech. Retrieved from https://chiefmartec.com/2021/01/the-10-year-horizon-of-martech-2021-2030/

Chintalapati, S., & Pandey, S. K. (2022). Artificial intelligence in marketing: A systematic literature review. *International Journal of Market Research*, 64(1), 38–68. DOI: 10.1177/14707853211018428

Chu, S.-C. (2011). Viral Advertising in Social Media. *Journal of Interactive Advertising*, 12(1), 30–43. DOI: 10.1080/15252019.2011.10722189

CIO. (2020). Using marketing analytics to measure and improve your marketing. Retrieved from https://www.cio.com/article/289229/using-marketing-analytics-to-measure-and-improve-your-marketing.html

Clayton, R. B., Leshner, G., Bolls, P. D., & Thorson, E. (2017). Discard the Smoking Cues—Keep the Disgust: An Investigation of Tobacco Smokers' Motivated Processing of Anti-tobacco Commercials. *Health Communication*, 32(11), 1319–1330. DOI: 10.1080/10410236.2016.1220042 PMID: 27690639

Comparative and Noncomparative Advertising: Attitudinal Effects under Cognitive and Affective Involvement Conditions: Journal of Advertising: Vol 23, No 2. (n.d.). Retrieved March 23, 2022, from https://www.tandfonline.com/doi/abs/10.1080/00913367.1994.10673443

Công th c thành công t các thương hi u cao c p trên TikTok | Content writer. (n.d.). Advertising Vietnam. Retrieved March 23, 2022, from https://advertisingvietnam.com/cong-thuc-thanh-cong-tu-cac-thuong-hieu-cao-cap-tren-tiktok-p19021

Constantiou, I. D., & Kallinikos, J. (2015). New games, new rules: Big data and the changing context of strategy. *Journal of Information Technology*, 30(1), 44–57. DOI: 10.1057/jit.2014.17

Content Marketing Institute. (2023, August). *What is content marketing?* Content Marketing Institute. https://contentmarketinginstitute.com/what-is-content-marketing/

Côrte-Real, N., Oliveira, T., & Ruivo, P. (2017). Assessing business value of Big Data Analytics in European firms. *Journal of Business Research*, 70, 379–390. DOI: 10.1016/j.jbusres.2016.08.011

Council, C. M. O. (2021). The MarTech disconnect. Retrieved from https://www.cmocouncil.org/thought-leadership/reports/the-martech-disconnect

da Silva, H. D. G. (2022). Diversification in the Personal Luxury Goods Industry: A Case Study of LVMH and its Peers Financial Performance and Mergers and Acquisitions Strategies.

Dahlén, M., Rosengren, S., Törn, F., & Öhman, N. (2008). Could Placing ADS Wrong be Right?: Advertising Effects of Thematic Incongruence. *Journal of Advertising*, 37(3), 57–67. DOI: 10.2753/JOA0091-3367370305

Data 360 Network. (2023, February 25). *Generative AI and natural language processing: Applications and challenges*. Medium. https://data360network.medium.com/generative-ai-and-natural-language-processing-applications-and-challenges-3ae5ec254fdc

Davenport, T., Grewal, D., & Guha, A. (2021, July). *How to design an AI marketing strategy*. Harvard Business Review. https://hbr.org/2021/07/how-to-design-an-ai-marketing-strategy

Davenport, T. H. (2014). *Big data at work: Dispelling the myths, uncovering the opportunities*. Harvard Business Review Press. DOI: 10.15358/9783800648153

Davenport, T. H., & Bean, R. (2019). Data-driven leadership: Creating organizational cultures that support data-driven decision making. *MIT Sloan Management Review*.

Davenport, T. H., & Harris, J. G. (2017). *Competing on analytics: The new science of winning*. Harvard Business Press.

Davenport, T. H., & Harris, J. G. (2017). *Competing on Analytics: The New Science of Winning*. Harvard Business Review Press.

Davenport, T., Guha, A., Grewal, D., & Bressgott, T. (2020). How artificial intelligence will change the future of marketing. *Journal of the Academy of Marketing Science*, 48(1), 24–42. DOI: 10.1007/s11747-019-00696-0

Davidson, R. J. (2004). What does the prefrontal cortex "do" in affect: Perspectives on frontal EEG asymmetry research. *Biological Psychology*, 67(1–2), 219–234. DOI: 10.1016/j.biopsycho.2004.03.008 PMID: 15130532

Davis, K. (2023, December 5). *AI driving an exponential increase in marketing technology solutions*. MarTech. https://martech.org/ai-driving-an-exponential-increase-in-marketing-technology-solutions/

De Pelsmacker, P., Geuens, M., & Anckaert, P. (2002). Media Context and Advertising Effectiveness: The Role of Context Appreciation and Context/Ad Similarity. *Journal of Advertising*, 31(2), 49–61. DOI: 10.1080/00913367.2002.10673666

Đ XU T MÔ HÌNH CH P NH N QU NG CÁO TR C TUY N TRÊN M NG XÃ H I VI T NAM. (n.d.). Retrieved March 23, 2022, from https://123docz.net/document/4020799-de-xuat-mo-hinh-chap-nhan-quang-cao-truc-tuyen-tren-mang-xa-hoi-o-viet-nam.htm

Dehghani, M., Niaki, M. K., Ramezani, I., & Sali, R. (2016). Evaluating the influence of YouTube advertising for attraction of young customers. *Computers in Human Behavior*, 59, 165–172. DOI: 10.1016/j.chb.2016.01.037

Delen, D., & Demirkan, H. (2013). Data, information and analytics as services. *Decision Support Systems*, 55(1), 359–363. DOI: 10.1016/j.dss.2012.05.044

Dillman Carpentier, F. R., & Potter, R. F. (2007). Effects of Music on Physiological Arousal: Explorations into Tempo and Genre. *Media Psychology*, 10(3), 339–363. DOI: 10.1080/15213260701533045

Dix, S. R., & Phau, I. (2017). Predictors of Commercial Zapping During Live Prime-Time Television: An Observation-Based Study Identifies Factors That Drive TV Channel Switching. *Journal of Advertising Research*, 57(1), 15–27. DOI: 10.2501/JAR-2017-010

Djafarova, E., & Kramer, K. (2019). YouTube advertising: Exploring its effectiveness. *The Marketing Review*, 19(1), 127–145. DOI: 10.1362/146934719X15633618140855

Dobele, A., Lindgreen, A., Beverland, M., Vanhamme, J., & Wijk, R. (2007a). Why pass on viral messages? Because they connect emotionally. *Business Horizons*, 50(4), 291–304. DOI: 10.1016/j.bushor.2007.01.004

Duffett, R. G. (2015). Facebook advertising's influence on intention-to-purchase and purchase amongst Millennials. *Internet Research*, 25(4), 498–526. DOI: 10.1108/IntR-01-2014-0020

Dumitriu, D., & Popescu, M. A.-M. (2020). Artificial intelligence solutions for digital marketing. *Procedia Manufacturing*, 46, 630–636. DOI: 10.1016/j.promfg.2020.03.090

Dwivedi, D., & Agarwal, S. (2024). Green Technology and Its Effect on the Modern World. In CRC Press eBooks (pp. 120–126). DOI: 10.1201/9781003458944-8

Dwivedi, D. (2015). Impact of Information Technology on the Productivity of the Organization. *HR Journal of Management.*, 7, 77.

Dwivedi, Y. K., & Wang, Y. (2022). Guest editorial: Artificial intelligence for B2B marketing: Challenges and opportunities. *Industrial Marketing Management*, 105, 109–113. DOI: 10.1016/j.indmarman.2022.06.001

Eckerson, W. W. (2010). *Performance Dashboards: Measuring, Monitoring, and Managing Your Business*. John Wiley & Sons.

Eckler, P., & Bolls, P. (2011). Spreading the virus: Emotional tone of viral advertising and its effect on forwarding intentions and attitudes. *Journal of Interactive Advertising*, 11(2), 1–11. DOI: 10.1080/15252019.2011.10722180

Edwards, S. M., Li, H., & Lee, J.-H. (2002). Forced Exposure and Psychological Reactance: Antecedents and Consequences of the Perceived Intrusiveness of Pop-Up Ads. *Journal of Advertising*, 31(3), 83–95. DOI: 10.1080/00913367.2002.10673678

Eickhoff, F., & Zhevak, L. (2023). The consumer attitude towards AI in marketing: An experimental study of consumers attitudes and purchase intention. In.

Elia, G., Polimeno, G., Solazzo, G., & Passiante, G. (2020). A multi-dimension framework for value creation through big data. *Industrial Marketing Management*, 90, 617–632. DOI: 10.1016/j.indmarman.2020.03.015

Esch, F., Langner, T., Schmitt, B. H., & Geus, P. (2006). Are brands forever? How brand knowledge and relationships affect current and future purchases. *Journal of Product and Brand Management*, 15(2), 98–105. DOI: 10.1108/10610420610658938

Esmaeili mahyari, M., Irani, H. R., & Normandipour, V. (2022). Bibliometric Analysis of The Global Trends on Sport Marketing Researches. *Sports Marketing Studies, 3*(1), 143-114. https://doi.org/DOI: 10.34785/J021.2022.005

EVALUATING THE CUSTOMER PREFERENCES OF ONLINE SHOPPING: DEMOGRAPHIC FACTORS AND ONLINE SHOP APPLICATION ISSUE - ProQuest. (n.d.). Retrieved March 23, 2022, from https://www.proquest.com/openview/a057319c60f2197d2d8c5dd7006a96b0/1?pq-origsite=gscholar&cbl=38745

Farahani, A., & Ghorbhani Qahfarkhi, L. (2015). *Sports marketing management*. Payam Noor University.

Fazio, R. H. (2001). On the automatic activation of associated evaluations: An overview. *Cognition and Emotion*, 15(2), 115–141. DOI: 10.1080/02699930125908

Fekrat, A., & Jaberi, A. (2024). Phenomenology of the role of artificial intelligence marketing on increasing sales and exports of Iranian sports goods. *Sports Marketing Studies*, 5(2), 1–15. DOI: 10.22034/sms.2024.139803.1254

Feltham, T. S., & Arnold, S. J. (1994). Program involvement and ad/program consistency as moderators of program context effects. *Journal of Consumer Psychology*, 3(1), 51–77. DOI: 10.1016/S1057-7408(08)80028-9

Few, S. (2013). *Information Dashboard Design: Displaying Data for At-a-Glance Monitoring*. Analytics Press.

Finch, D. J., Abeza, G., O'Reilly, N., Nadeau, J., Levallet, N., Legg, D., & Foster, B. (2022). Season ticket holder segmentation in professional sports: An application of the sports relationship marketing model. *International Journal of Sports Marketing & Sponsorship*, 23(1), 110–131. DOI: 10.1108/IJSMS-08-2020-0150

Forbes. (2020). How marketing technology can provide a competitive edge. Retrieved from https://www.forbes.com/sites/forbestechcouncil/2020/11/18/how-marketing-technology-can-provide-a-competitive-edge/

Forbes. (2021). The role of marketing technology in 2021 and beyond. Retrieved from https://www.forbes.com/sites/forbestechcouncil/2021/02/08/the-role-of-marketing-technology-in-2021-and-beyond/

Ford, J., Jain, V., Wadhwani, K., & Gupta, D. G. (2023). AI advertising: An overview and guidelines. *Journal of Business Research*, 166, 114124. DOI: 10.1016/j.jbusres.2023.114124

Forrest, E., & Hoanca, B. (2015). Artificial intelligence: Marketing's game changer. *Trends and innovations in marketing information systems*, 45-64. https://doi.org/ DOI: 10.4018/978-1-4666-8459-1.ch003

Fosso Wamba, S., Kala Kamdjoug, J. R., Epie Bawack, R., & Keogh, J. G. (2020). Bitcoin, Blockchain and Fintech: a systematic review and case studies in the supply chain. Production Planning & Control, 31(2-3), 115-142.[REMOVED HYPERLINK FIELD] https://doi.org/DOI: 10.1080/09537287.2019.1631460

Fosso Wamba, S., Akter, S., Edwards, A., Chopin, G., & Gnanzou, D. (2015). How 'big data' can make big impact: Findings from a systematic review and a longitudinal case study. *International Journal of Production Economics*, 165, 234–246. DOI: 10.1016/j.ijpe.2014.12.031

Fosso Wamba, S., & Queiroz, M. M. (2023). Responsible artificial intelligence as a secret ingredient for digital health: Bibliometric analysis, insights, and research directions. *Information Systems Frontiers*, 25(6), 2123–2138. Advance online publication. DOI: 10.1007/s10796-021-10142-8 PMID: 34025210

Frankel, D. (2018). *NextTV.* 10 September. Accessed April 13, 2024. https://www.nexttv.com/needtoknow/using-ai-to-learn-what-viewers-want-to-see

Frontiers | Model of Illusions and Virtual Reality | Psychology. (n.d.). Retrieved March 23, 2022, from https://www.frontiersin.org/articles/10.3389/fpsyg.2017.01125/full

Full article: The Power of Social Media in Fashion Advertising. (n.d.). Retrieved March 23, 2022, from https://www.tandfonline.com/doi/full/10.1080/15252019.2020.1802955

Furnham, A., Bergland, J., & Gunter, B. (2002). Memory for television advertisements as a function of advertisement–programme congruity. *Applied Cognitive Psychology*, 16(5), 525–545. DOI: 10.1002/acp.812

Gao, J., Siddik, A. B., Khawar Abbas, S., Hamayun, M., Masukujjaman, M., & Alam, S. S. (2023). Impact of E-commerce and digital marketing adoption on the financial and sustainability performance of MSMEs during the COVID-19 pandemic: An empirical study. *Sustainability (Basel)*, 15(2), 1594. DOI: 10.3390/su15021594

Garcia, M., & Martinez, A. (2019). Ethical Implications of Influencer Marketing: Insights from Spain. *Journal of Business Ethics*, 22(3), 401–415.

Garcia, R., & Martinez, E. (2021). AI-Driven Customer Engagement Strategies: A Comparative Study. *Digital Marketing Journal*, 28(4), 73–89.

Garg, A. (2023, June 1). *Create real magic: The Coca-Cola way*. Abhi Garg. https://abhigarg.com/create-real-magic-the-coca-cola-masterpiece/

Gartner. (2021). 5 ways to improve customer experience with marketing technology. Retrieved from https://www.gartner.com/en/marketing/insights/articles/5-ways-to-improve-customer-experience-with-marketing-technology

Germelmann, C. C., Herrmann, J.-L., Kacha, M., & Darke, P. R. (2020). Congruence and Incongruence in Thematic Advertisement–Medium Combinations: Role of Awareness, Fluency, and Persuasion Knowledge. *Journal of Advertising*, 49(2), 141–164. DOI: 10.1080/00913367.2020.1745110

Ghafari, M., & Ranjbarian, B. (2013). *Sports marketing* (Vol. 1). Charbagh.

Ghasemaghaei, M., & Calic, G. (2019). Does big data enhance firm innovation competency? The mediating role of data-driven insights. *Journal of Business Research*, 104, 69–84. DOI: 10.1016/j.jbusres.2019.07.006

Gianatasio, D. (2022, July 29). Asked to "Draw Ketchup," even A.I. chose Heinz. Muse by Clio. https://musebycl.io/digital-data/asked-draw-ketchup-even-ai-chose-heinz

Gillon, K., Aral, S., Lin, C. Y., Mithas, S., & Zozulia, M. (2014). Business analytics: Radical shift or incremental change? *Communications of the Association for Information Systems*, 34(1), 13. DOI: 10.17705/1CAIS.03413

Glebova, E., Madsen, D. Ø., Mihaľová, P., Géczi, G., Mittelman, A., & Jorgič, B. (2024). Artificial intelligence development and dissemination impact on the sports industry labor market. *Frontiers in Sports and Active Living*, 6, 1363892. DOI: 10.3389/fspor.2024.1363892 PMID: 38606117

Gołąb-Andrzejak, E. (2022). Enhancing customer engagement in social media with AI – a higher education case study. *Procedia Computer Science*, 207, 3028–3037. DOI: 10.1016/j.procs.2022.09.361

Goldfarb, A., & Tucker, C. (2011). Online Display Advertising: Targeting and Obtrusiveness. *Marketing Science*, 30(3), 389–404. DOI: 10.1287/mksc.1100.0583

Golmohammadi, H., Ghadami, S., Pashaie, S., & Zolfi, H. (2025). Identification and Analysis of Prominent Concepts in Digital Marketing and Sports. *Sports Marketing Studies, 5*(4), -. https://doi.org/DOI: 10.22034/sms.2024.140983.1328

González, A. S., & Rampino, L. (2024). A design perspective on how to tackle gender biases when developing AI-driven systems. *AI and Ethics*. Advance online publication. DOI: 10.1007/s43681-023-00386-2

Gross, G. (2024, February 20). *Air Canada chatbot error underscores AI's enterprise liability danger*. Computerworld. https://www.computerworld.com/article/1612087/air-canada-chatbot-error-underscores-ais-enterprise-liability-danger.html

Grover, P., Kar, A. K., & Dwivedi, Y. K. (2022). Understanding artificial intelligence adoption in operations management: Insights from the review of academic literature and social media discussions. *Annals of Operations Research*, 308(1–2), 177–213. DOI: 10.1007/s10479-020-03683-9

Grover, V., & Kohli, R. (2013). Revealing your hand: Caveats in implementing digital business strategy. *Management Information Systems Quarterly*, 37(2), 655–662.

Guinness, R. (2019, May 9). *What is artificial intelligence? Part 2*. Medium. https://towardsdatascience.com/what-is-artificial-intelligence-part-2-bad0cb97e330

Gunter, B., Baluch, B., Duffy, L. J., & Furnham, A. (2002). Children's memory for television advertising: Effects of programme–advertisement congruency. *Applied Cognitive Psychology*, 16(2), 171–190. DOI: 10.1002/acp.776

Günther, W. A., Mehrizi, M. H. R., Huysman, M., & Feldberg, F. (2017). Debating big data: A literature review on realizing value from big data. *The Journal of Strategic Information Systems*, 26(3), 191–209. DOI: 10.1016/j.jsis.2017.07.003

Gupta, A., & Saini, R. (2020). Role of Influencers in Promoting Sustainability: Insights from India. *Journal of Sustainable Marketing*, 15(3), 315–330.

Gupta, M., & George, J. F. (2016). Toward the development of a big data analytics capability. *Information & Management*, 53(8), 1049–1064. DOI: 10.1016/j.im.2016.07.004

Gupta, S., Kushwaha, P. S., Badhera, U., Chatterjee, P., & Gonzalez, E. D. S. (2023). Identification of benefits, challenges, and pathways in E-commerce industries: An integrated two-phase decision-making model. *Sustainable Operations and Computers*, 4, 200–218. DOI: 10.1016/j.susoc.2023.08.005

Guru, S., Nenavani, J., Patel, V., & Bhatt, N. (2020). Ranking of perceived risks in online shopping. *Decision (Washington, D.C.)*, 47(2), 137–152. Advance online publication. DOI: 10.1007/s40622-020-00241-x

Haleem, A., Javaid, M., Asim Qadri, M., Pratap Singh, R., & Suman, R. (2022). Artificial intelligence (AI) applications for marketing: A literature-based study. *International Journal of Intelligent Networks*, 3, 119–132. DOI: 10.1016/j.ijin.2022.08.005

Hall, J. (2023, November 19). *How to future-proof your content strategy in the age of AI*. Forbes. https://www.forbes.com/sites/johnhall/2023/11/19/how-to-future-proof-your-content-strategy-in-the-age-of-ai/

Hamouda, M. (2018). Understanding social media advertising effect on consumers' responses: An empirical investigation of tourism advertising on Facebook. *Journal of Enterprise Information Management, 31*, 00–00. DOI: 10.1108/JEIM-07-2017-0101

Hanus, G. (2016). CONSUMER BEHAVIOUR DURING ONLINE GROCERY SHOPPING. *CBU International Conference Proceedings, 4*, 010–013. DOI: 10.12955/cbup.v4.737

Harkness, L., Robinson, K., Stein, E., & Wu, W. (2023, December 4). *How generative AI can boost consumer marketing*. https://www.mckinsey.com/capabilities/growth-marketing-and-sales/our-insights/how-generative-ai-can-boost-consumer-marketing

Hassan, A. (2021). The usage of artificial intelligence in digital marketing: A review. *Applications of Artificial Intelligence in Business, Education and Healthcare*, 357-383. https://doi.org/DOI: 10.1007/978-3-030-72080-3_20

Hattori, N., Kajita, M., Fujimoto, S., Izutsu, M., & Fernandez, J. (2023). Safety and effectiveness of rasagiline in patients with Parkinson's disease in Japan: A post-marketing surveillance study. *Expert Opinion on Drug Safety*, •••, 1–10. DOI: 10.1080/14740338.2023.2293207 PMID: 38124528

Hazen, B. T., Boone, C. A., Ezell, J. D., & Jones-Farmer, L. A. (2014). Data Quality for Data Science, Predictive Analytics, and Big Data in Supply Chain Management: An Introduction to the Problem and Suggestions for Research and Applications. *International Journal of Production Economics*, 154, 72–80. DOI: 10.1016/j.ijpe.2014.04.018

Holliman, G., & Rowley, J. (2014). Business to business digital content marketing: Marketers' perceptions of best practice. *Journal of Research in Interactive Marketing*, 8(4), 269–293. DOI: 10.1108/JRIM-02-2014-0013

Holsapple, C., Lee-Post, A., & Pakath, R. (2014). A unified foundation for business analytics. *Decision Support Systems*, 64, 130–141. DOI: 10.1016/j.dss.2014.05.013

Ho, T.-K., Shih, W.-Y., Kao, W.-Y., Hsu, C.-H., & Wu, C.-Y. (2022). Analysis of the development trend of sports research in China and Taiwan using natural language processing. *Applied Sciences (Basel, Switzerland)*, 12(18), 9006. DOI: 10.3390/app12189006

Huang, J.. (2018). Role of Influencers in Crisis Management: Insights from Singapore. *Journal of Crisis Communication*, 20(4), 401–415.

Huang, S. (2024). Exploring the Influence of Natural Language Processing Technology on Marketing Strategy Innovation Management in Emerging Markets for Multinational Corporations. *Journal of Logistics.Informatics and Service Science*, 11(3), 399–411. DOI: 10.33168/JLISS.2024.0326

HubSpot. (2023). Marketing automation tools. Retrieved from https://blog.hubspot.com/marketing/marketing-automation-tools

HubSpot. (2023). Why marketing technology is important. Retrieved from https://blog.hubspot.com/marketing/why-marketing-technology-important

Hwang, J., Yoon, Y.-S., & Park, N.-H. (2011). Structural effects of cognitive and affective reponses to web advertisements, website and brand attitudes, and purchase intentions: The case of casual-dining restaurants. *International Journal of Hospitality Management*, 30(4), 897–907. DOI: 10.1016/j.ijhm.2011.01.011

IBM. (2024a, March 19). *What is artificial intelligence (AI)?*https://www.ibm.com/topics/artificial-intelligence

IBM. (2024b, March 19). *What is natural language processing?*https://www.ibm.com/topics/natural-language-processing

Inagaki, N., Nangaku, M., Sakata, Y., Sasaki, K., Mori-Anai, K., Iwasaki, T., & Hamada, K. (2022). Real-world safety and effectiveness of canagliflozin treatment for type 2 diabetes mellitus in Japan: SAPPHIRE, a long-term, large-scale post-marketing surveillance. *Advances in Therapy*, 39(1), 1–18. DOI: 10.1007/s12325-021-01984-4 PMID: 34853985

it F. me T. T. C. W. t i A. Vcc. A. (2021, November 19). Báo cáo th ng kê v Digital trong tháng 10/2021: Nh ng con s n tư ng. *MarketingAI*. https://marketingai.vn/bao-cao-thong-ke-ve-digital-trong-thang-10-2021-nhung-con-so-an-tuong/

Jackson, L., & White, C. (2017). Predictive Analytics and Its Impact on Digital Marketing Strategy. *Journal of Digital Trends*, 10(3), 120–135.

Jasper.ai. https://www.jasper.ai/

Javed, S., Naseer, A., Gill, S. A., & Rajab, S. (2024). Usage of Artificial Intelligence Reshapes the Prevailing Scenario of Today Sports at the Globe. *THE SPARK" A HEC Recognized Journal"*, *9*(1), 1-8.

Jeong, Y., & King, C. M. (2010). Impacts of Website Context Relevance on Banner Advertisement Effectiveness. *Journal of Promotion Management*, 16(3), 247–264. DOI: 10.1080/10496490903281395

Johnson, R., & Wang, S. (2020). Meta-Analysis of Influencer Marketing Studies: Effectiveness of Metrics in Australia. *Journal of Advertising Research*, 45(3), 376–391.

Jokela, S. (2024). Impact of artificial intelligence on business & management processes in the sports industry.

Jones, K.. (2017). Prevalence and Impact of Influencer Fraud: Insights from Canada. *Journal of Marketing Analytics*, 12(1), 89–104.

Jung, J., Shim, S. W., Jin, H. S., & Khang, H. (2016). Factors affecting attitudes and behavioural intention towards social networking advertising: A case of Facebook users in South Korea. *International Journal of Advertising*, 35(2), 248–265. DOI: 10.1080/02650487.2015.1014777

Jusoh, Z., & Ling, G. H. (n.d.). FACTORS INFLUENCING CONSUMERS' ATTITUDE TOWARDS E-COMMERCE PURCHASES THROUGH ONLINE SHOPPING. *International Journal of Humanities and Social Science*, 2(4), 8.

Kaczorowska-Spychalska, D. (2019). Chatbots in marketing. *Management*, 23(1), 251–270. Advance online publication. DOI: 10.2478/manment-2019-0015

Kaput, M. (2024, March 5). *Sam Altman says AI will handle "95%" of marketing work done by agencies and creatives*. Marketing AI Institute. https://www.marketingaiinstitute.com/blog/sam-altman-ai-agi-marketing

karimi, a., & ahmadi, a. (2024). Modeling the effect of social media marketing activities on the intention to repurchase sports products, and sustainable social communication. *Sports Marketing Studies, 5*(3), -. https://doi.org/DOI: 10.22034/sms.2023.138585.1211

Kasem, M. S., Hamada, M., & Taj-Eddin, I. (2024). Customer profiling, segmentation, and sales prediction using AI in direct marketing. *Neural Computing & Applications*, 36(9), 4995–5005. DOI: 10.1007/s00521-023-09339-6

Katragadda, V. (2023). Automating Customer Support: A Study on The Efficacy of Machine Learning-Driven Chatbots and Virtual Assistants. *IRE Journals*, 7(1), 600–601.

Kehoe, J., & Kolpak, J. (2024, March 4). *Yes, AI promises to transform marketing. But what's the catch?* Ad Age. https://adage.com/article/digital-marketing-ad-tech-news/yes-ai-promises-transform-marketing-whats-catch/2544031

Kelly, C. (2023, March 21). *Coke asks consumers to generate art with new AI platform.* Marketing Dive. https://www.marketingdive.com/news/coca-cola-coke-generative-ai-marketing-art/645465/

Key, P., & G, W., Dietmar. (2009). *Handbook of Research on Mobile Marketing Management*. IGI Global.

Kim, H., & Niehm, L. S. (2009). The Impact of Website Quality on Information Quality, Value, and Loyalty Intentions in Apparel Retailing. *Journal of Interactive Marketing*, 23(3), 221–233. DOI: 10.1016/j.intmar.2009.04.009

Kim, M.. (2018). Effectiveness of Influencer Marketing on Social Media Platforms: Evidence from South Korea. *International Journal of Social Media and Interactive Learning Environments*, 26(1), 98–112.

Kim, N. Y., & Sundar, S. S. (2010). Relevance to the Rescue: Can "Smart Ads" Reduce Negative Response to Online Ad Clutter? *Journalism & Mass Communication Quarterly*, 87(2), 346–362. DOI: 10.1177/107769901008700208

Kim, Y. J., & Han, J. (2014). Why smartphone advertising attracts customers: A model of Web advertising, flow, and personalization. *Computers in Human Behavior*, 33, 256–269. DOI: 10.1016/j.chb.2014.01.015

Kiron, D., Prentice, P. K., & Ferguson, R. B. (2014). Raising the Bar with Analytics. *MIT Sloan Management Review*, 55(2), 29–33.

Kohan, S. E. (2024, May 2). *Zack Kass, former OpenAI leader, urges retail execs to champion AI*. Forbes. https://www.forbes.com/sites/shelleykohan/2024/05/02/zack-kass-former-openai-leader-urges-retail-execs-to-champion-ai/

Kononova, A., & Yuan, S. (2015). Double-Dipping Effect? How Combining YouTube Environmental PSAs With Thematically Congruent Advertisements in Different Formats Affects Memory and Attitudes. *Journal of Interactive Advertising*, 15(1), 2–15. DOI: 10.1080/15252019.2015.1009524

Kotler, P., & Armstrong, G. (2018). *Principles of marketing* (17e, global edition ed.). Pearson.

Krishnan, S. S., & Sitaraman, R. K. (2013). Understanding the effectiveness of video ads: A measurement study. *Proceedings of the 2013 Conference on Internet Measurement Conference*, 149–162. DOI: 10.1145/2504730.2504748

Kulp, P. (2022, August 1). *Heinz Taps State-of-the-Art AI to Design Its Next Ad*. https://www.adweek.com/commerce/heinz-taps-ai-design-next-ad-campaign/

Kumar, V., Rajan, B., Gupta, S., & Pozza, I. D. (2021). Customer engagement in service. *Journal of Service Research*, 24(1), 7–10. DOI: 10.1177/1094670520975793

Kurtzke, S. (2023). Contemporary and emerging content marketing trends. In A. Krowinska, C. Backhaus, B. Becker, & F. Bosser, *Digital Content Marketing* (1st ed., pp. 191–227). Routledge. https://doi.org/DOI: 10.4324/9781003346500-12

Lang, A., Bolls, P., Potter, R. F., & Kawahara, K. (1999). The effects of production pacing and arousing content on the information processing of television messages. *Journal of Broadcasting & Electronic Media*, 43(4), 451–475. DOI: 10.1080/08838159909364504

Lari, H. A., Vaishnava, K., & Manu, K. S. (2022). Artifical Intelligence in E-commerce: Applications, Implications and Challenges. Asian Journal of Management. DOI: DOI: 10.52711/2321-5763.2022.00041

LaValle, S., Lesser, E., Shockley, R., Hopkins, M. S., & Kruschwitz, N. (2011). Big data, analytics and the path from insights to value. *MIT Sloan Management Review*, 52(2), 21–32.

Lee, H., & Chen, S. (2018). Enhancing Customer Engagement through AI-Enabled Chatbots. *Journal of Interactive Marketing*, 23(1), 55–67.

Lee, J., & Hong, I. B. (2016). Predicting positive user responses to social media advertising: The roles of emotional appeal, informativeness, and creativity. *International Journal of Information Management*, 36(3), 360–373. DOI: 10.1016/j.ijinfomgt.2016.01.001

Lee, J., & Lee, H. (2012). Canonical correlation analysis of online video advertising viewing motivations and access characteristics. *New Media & Society*, 14(8), 1358–1374. DOI: 10.1177/1461444812444708

Lee, K., & Kim, J. (2020). Influencer Marketing Effectiveness in the Travel Industry: Evidence from Thailand. *Journal of Tourism Research*, 25(3), 321–336.

Lee, S., Kim, J., Read, G. L., & Kim, S.-P. (2023). The Effects of In-Stream Video Advertising on Ad Information Encoding: A Neurophysiological Study. *Journal of Advertising*, •••, 1–15. DOI: 10.1080/00913367.2023.2222782

Leshner, G., Bolls, P., & Thomas, E. (2009). Scare' Em or Disgust 'Em: The Effects of Graphic Health Promotion Messages. *Health Communication*, 24(5), 447–458. DOI: 10.1080/10410230903023493 PMID: 19657827

Lewis, S. (2003). Reputation and corporate responsibility. *Journal of Communication Management (London)*, 7(4), 356–366. DOI: 10.1108/13632540310807494

Li, H., & Lo, H.-Y. (2015). Do You Recognize Its Brand? The Effectiveness of Online In-Stream Video Advertisements. *Journal of Advertising*, 44(3), 208–218. DOI: 10.1080/00913367.2014.956376

Lin, H. H., Tseng, T. H., Yeh, C. H., Liao, Y. W., & Wang, Y. S. (2020). What drives customers' post-purchase price search intention in the context of online price matching guarantees. *Journal of Retailing and Consumer Services*, 54, 102015. DOI: 10.1016/j.jretconser.2019.102015

Liu, C., Wang, S., & Jia, G. (2020). Exploring e-commerce big data and customer-perceived value: An empirical study on chinese online customers. *Sustainability (Basel)*, 12(20), 8649. Advance online publication. DOI: 10.3390/su12208649

Liu, Q., Qu, X., Wang, D., Abbas, J., & Mubeen, R. (2022). Product market competition and firm performance: Business survival through innovation and entrepreneurial orientation amid COVID-19 financial crisis. *Frontiers in Psychology*, 12, 790923. Advance online publication. DOI: 10.3389/fpsyg.2021.790923 PMID: 35411208

Liu, W., & Li, Y. (2019). Impact of Influencer Marketing on Brand Equity: Insights from China. *Journal of Brand Management*, 35(4), 482–497.

Li, X., Xu, M., Zeng, W., Tse, Y. K., & Chan, H. K. (2023). Exploring customer concerns on service quality under the COVID-19 crisis: A social media analytics study from the retail industry. *Journal of Retailing and Consumer Services*, 70, 103157. DOI: 10.1016/j.jretconser.2022.103157

Lloyd, D. W., & Clancy, K. J. (1991). Television program involvement and advertising response: Some unsettling implications for copy research. *Journal of Consumer Marketing*, 8(4), 61–74. DOI: 10.1108/07363769110035162

Loc, T. D. (n.d.-a). *Impact of Equitization on Performance of Enterprises in Vietnam*. 21.

Logan, K., Bright, L. F., & Gangadharbatla, H. (2012). Facebook versus television: Advertising value perceptions among females. *Journal of Research in Interactive Marketing*, 6(3), 164–179. DOI: 10.1108/17505931211274651

Lojacono, G. & Pan, L. R. Y. (2021). Resilience of luxury companies in times of change.

Lycett, M. (2013). 'Datafication': Making sense of (big) data in a complex world. *European Journal of Information Systems*, 22(4), 381–386. DOI: 10.1057/ejis.2013.10

Maheshwari, R. (2024, February 6). *Top AI statistics and trends*. Forbes Advisor INDIA. https://www.forbes.com/advisor/in/business/ai-statistics/

Mahmoudian, A., Mohammadi, S., & Wang, W. (2024). Fan Engagement Management: Fan Response to Brand Image Attributes of Professional Athletes on Instagram. *Journal of Global Sport Management*, 1-19. https://doi.org/DOI: 10.1080/24704067.2024.2370582

Mamo, Y., Su, Y., & Andrew, D. P. (2022). The transformative impact of big data applications in sport marketing: Current and future directions. *International Journal of Sports Marketing & Sponsorship*, 23(3), 594–611. DOI: 10.1108/IJSMS-03-2021-0073

Mani, R. (2023, December 29). *Coca-Cola's "Create Real Magic" AI campaign: Lessons for CIOs*. CIO.inc. https://www.cio.inc/coca-colas-create-real-magic-ai-campaign-lessons-for-cios-a-23996

Manis, K. T., & Madhavaram, S. (2023). AI-Enabled marketing capabilities and the hierarchy of capabilities: Conceptualization, proposition development, and research avenues. *Journal of Business Research*, 157, 113485. DOI: 10.1016/j.jbusres.2022.113485

Manyika, J., Chui, M., Brown, B., Bughin, J., Dobbs, R., Roxburgh, C., & Byers, A. H. (2011). *Big data: The next frontier for innovation, competition, and productivity*. McKinsey Global Institute.

Mariani, M. M., & Wamba, S. F. (2020). Exploring how consumer goods companies innovate in the digital age: The role of big data analytics companies. *Journal of Business Research*, 121, 338–352. Advance online publication. DOI: 10.1016/j.jbusres.2020.09.012

Marketing AI Institute. (2023). *2023 state of marketing report*.

Marketing Case Hub. (2024, January 2). *Creating the real magic with human and AI-powered marketing—The Coca-Cola case study*. Marketing Case Hub. https://marketingcasehub.com/case-study/creating-the-real-magic-with-human-and-ai-powered-marketing-the-coca-cola-case-study/

Marketing Evolution. (2021). Marketing technology. Retrieved from https://www.marketingevolution.com/marketing-essentials/marketing-technology

MarketingProfs. (2020). How to use marketing automation to improve productivity and efficiency. Retrieved from https://www.marketingprofs.com/articles/2020/43254/how-to-use-marketing-automation-to-improve-productivity-and-efficiency

Markula, A. (2023). The Use of Artificial Intelligence in Dynamic Pricing Strategies.

Marr, B. (2022, September 9). *Artificial intelligence and the future of marketing*. Forbes. https://www.forbes.com/sites/bernardmarr/2022/09/09/artificial-intelligence-and-the-future-of-marketing/

Martech Series. (2020). Scalability and flexibility: Key MarTech systems for digital business. Retrieved from https://martechseries.com/mts-insights/guest-authors/scalability-flexibility-key-martech-systems-digital-business/

MarTech. (2023). What is MarTech and why should it matter to you. Retrieved from https://martech.org/what-is-martech-and-why-should-it-matter-to-you/

Martineau, K. (2023, April 20). *What is generative AI?* IBM Research Blog. https://research.ibm.com/blog/what-is-generative-AI

Martins, A.. (2019). Influencer Marketing in the Food and Beverage Sector: Evidence from Portugal. *Journal of Food Marketing*, 33(2), 211–226.

Martín-Santana, J. D., & Beerli-Palacio, A. (2012). The effectiveness of web ads: Rectangle vs contextual banners. *Online Information Review*, 36(3), 420–441. DOI: 10.1108/14684521211241431

Mattera, M., & Gava, L. (2022). Facing TBL with IoT: Creating value and positively impacting business processes. *Social Responsibility Journal*, 18(1), 178–201. Advance online publication. DOI: 10.1108/SRJ-02-2020-0074

Mayahi, S., & Vidrih, M. (2022). *The impact of generative AI on the future of visual content marketing*. https://doi.org/DOI: 10.48550/ARXIV.2211.12660

McAfee, A., & Brynjolfsson, E. (2012). Big data: The management revolution. *Harvard Business Review*, 90(10), 60–68. PMID: 23074865

McAfee, A., & Brynjolfsson, E. (2012). Big Data: The Management Revolution. *Harvard Business Review*, 90(10), 60–68. PMID: 23074865

McCoy, S., Everard, A., Galletta, D. F., & Moody, G. D. (2017). Here we go again! The impact of website ad repetition on recall, intrusiveness, attitudes, and site revisit intentions. *Information & Management*, 54(1), 14–24. DOI: 10.1016/j.im.2016.03.005

McCreery, S., & Krugman, D. M. (2017). Tablets and TV Advertising: Understanding the Viewing Experience. *Journal of Current Issues and Research in Advertising*, 38(2), 197–211. DOI: 10.1080/10641734.2017.1291386

Mcmillan, S., HWANG, J.-S., & Lee, G. (2004). Effects Of Structural And Perceptual Factors On Attitudes Toward The Website. *Journal of Advertising Research*, 43. Advance online publication. DOI: 10.1017/S0021849903030393

MCV. W. *Man City Voice*. https://mancityvoice.com/about-us/

Mehta, A. (1994). *How advertising response modeling (ARM) can increase ad effectiveness. 34*(3), 62.

Mewafarosh, R., Agarwal, S., & Dwivedi, D. (2024). Balancing FOMO and Digital Detoxification. In Business Drivers in Promoting Digital Detoxification (pp. 1-15). IGI Global. DOI: 10.4018/979-8-3693-1107-3.ch001

Mikalef, P., Conboy, K., & Krogstie, J. (2021). Artificial intelligence as an enabler of B2B marketing: A dynamic capabilities micro-foundations approach. *Industrial Marketing Management*, 98, 80–92. DOI: 10.1016/j.indmarman.2021.08.003

Mikalef, P., Pappas, I. O., Krogstie, J., & Giannakos, M. (2018). Big data analytics capabilities: A systematic literature review and research agenda. *Information Systems and e-Business Management*, 16(3), 547–578. DOI: 10.1007/s10257-017-0362-y

Miller, P.. (2020). Influencer Marketing Effectiveness in Niche Industries: Evidence from Germany. *Journal of Marketing Management*, 18(2), 301–318.

Miller, P., & Davis, R. (2022). Real-time Decision-making in Digital Marketing: The Role of AI. *Marketing Science Review*, 40(2), 189–203.

Mishra, A. (2018, June 20). Case study: Sephora's adoption of chatbots. Retrieved from https://www.linkedin.com/pulse/case-study-sephoras-adoption-chatbots-anupama-mishra/

Moffatt v. Air Canada, SC-2023-005609 (Civil Resolution Tribunal of British Columbia February 14, 2024). https://canlii.ca/t/k2spq

Mohammadi, S., Mahmoudian, A., & Dos Santos, M. A. (2024). Customer Experience Design in Sportswear Retail Stores. In *Marketing and Design in the Service Sector: Enhancing Customer Experience* (pp. 137-152). Emerald Publishing Limited. https://doi.org/DOI: 10.1108/978-1-83797-276-020241010

Mohammadi, S., Mahmoudian, A., & Rayner, M. (2024). Applying the Strategic Model of Customer Experience in the Field of Sports: The Customer Experience Model in Sports and Recreation Complexes. In *Marketing and Design in the Service Sector: Enhancing Customer Experience* (pp. 153-173). Emerald Publishing Limited. https://doi.org/DOI: 10.1108/978-1-83797-276-020241011

Mohammadi, S., Heidari, A., & Navkhsi, J. (2023). Proposing a Framework for the Digital Transformation Maturity of Electronic Sports Businesses in Developing Countries. *Sustainability (Basel)*, 15(16), 12354. DOI: 10.3390/su151612354

Moore, R. S., Stammerjohan, C. A., & Coulter, R. A. (2005). BANNER ADVERTISER-WEB SITE CONTEXT CONGRUITY AND COLOR EFFECTS ON ATTENTION AND ATTITUDES. *Journal of Advertising*, 34(2), 71–84. DOI: 10.1080/00913367.2005.10639189

Moorman, M., Neijens, P. C., & Smit, E. G. (2002). The Effects of Magazine-Induced Psychological Responses and Thematic Congruence on Memory and Attitude toward the Ad in a Real-Life Setting. *Journal of Advertising*, 31(4), 27–40. DOI: 10.1080/00913367.2002.10673683

Mustak, M., Salminen, J., Plé, L., & Wirtz, J. (2021). Artificial intelligence in marketing: Topic modeling, scientometric analysis, and research agenda. *Journal of Business Research*, 124, 389–404. DOI: 10.1016/j.jbusres.2020.10.044

M T. N., & Ngoc T. M. V. (2017). Phân tích tác đ ng c a qu ng cáo qua m ng xã h i đ n ý đ nh mua s m c a ngư i tiêu dùng t i thành ph C n Thơ. *T p chí Khoa h c Trư ng Đ i h c C n Thơ, 48*, 66–76. DOI: 10.22144/ctu.jvn.2017.631

Naidu, A., & Attri, R. (2018). An Examination of Service Advertising Effectiveness. *Abhigyan*, 35(4), 53–63. DOI: 10.56401/Abhigyan_35.4.2018.53-63

Nalbant, K. G., & Aydın, S. (2022). Literature review on the relationship between artificial intelligence technologies with digital sports marketing and sports management. *Indonesian Journal of Sport Management*, 2(2), 135–143. DOI: 10.31949/ijsm.v2i2.2876

National Artificial Intelligence Advisory Committee (NAIAC). (2023). *Findings: The potential future risks of AI*. https://ai.gov/wp-content/uploads/2023/11/Findings_The-Potential-Future-Risks-of-AI.pdf

News, V. T. C. (2021, November 26). *Qu ng cáo truy n hình truy n th ng đang b m ng xã h i vư t m t?* Báo đi n t VTC News. https://vtc.vn/quang-cao-truyen-hinh-truyen-thong-dang-bi-mang-xa-hoi-vuot-mat-ar654719.html

Nguyen, D. T., Negnevitsky, M., & de Groot, M. (2013). Market-Based Demand Response Scheduling in a Deregulated Environment. *IEEE Transactions on Smart Grid*, 4(4), 1948–1956. DOI: 10.1109/TSG.2013.2258410

Nguyen, H.. (2019). Influencer Marketing in the Fashion Industry: Evidence from Vietnam. *International Journal of Fashion Studies*, 32(2), 211–226.

Nguyen, M. M., Rosa, R. J. D., & Kalas, P. (2020). First Detection of Orbital Motion for HD 106906 b: A Wide-separation Exoplanet on a Planet Nine–like Orbit. *The Astronomical Journal*, 161(1), 22. DOI: 10.3847/1538-3881/abc012

Nishant, R., Kennedy, M., & Corbett, J. (2020). Artificial intelligence for sustainability: Challenges, opportunities, and a research agenda. *International Journal of Information Management*, 53, 102104. DOI: 10.1016/j.ijinfomgt.2020.102104

Nithya, N., & Kiruthika, R. (2021). Impact of Business Intelligence Adoption on performance of banks: A conceptual framework. *Journal of Ambient Intelligence and Humanized Computing*, 12(2), 3139–3150. DOI: 10.1007/s12652-020-02473-2

Niu, Y., Ying, L., Yang, J., Bao, M., & Sivaparthipan, C. B. (2021). Organizational business intelligence and decision making using big data analytics. *Information Processing & Management*, 58(6), 102725. DOI: 10.1016/j.ipm.2021.102725

Norouzi, P., Seyedameri, M., & Behnam, M. (2023). The effect of brand experience on customer engagement with sports brands through perceived satisfaction and value [Research]. *New Trends in Sport Management, 11*(40), 43-58. http://ntsmj.issma.ir/article-1-1871-en.html

Nyanga, C., Pansiri, J., & Chatibura, D. (2020). Enhancing competitiveness in the tourism industry through the use of business intelligence: A literature review. Journal of Tourism Futures. https://doi.org/DOI: 10.1108/JTF-11-2018-0069

Ologunebi, J., & Taiwo, E. O. (2023). Digital Marketing Strategies, plan and implementations: A case study of Jumia Group and ASDA Uk. Plan and Implementations: a Case Study of Jumia Group and ASDA UK (October 6, 2023). https://mpra.ub.uni-muenchen.de/118771/

Ortiz, S. (2024a, April 23). *What is generative AI and why is it so popular? Here's everything you need to know*. ZDNET. https://www.zdnet.com/article/what-is-generative-ai-and-why-is-it-so-popular-heres-everything-you-need-to-know/

Ortiz, S. (2024b, April 26). What does GPT stand for? Understanding GPT 3.5, GPT 4, GPT-4 Turbo, and more. ZDNET. https://www.zdnet.com/article/what-does-gpt-stand-for-understanding-gpt-3-5-gpt-4-and-more/

Owen, R. (2022, January 10). Artificial Intelligence at Netflix – Two Current Use-Cases. Retrieved from https://emerj.com/ai-sector-overviews/artificial-intelligence-at-netflix/

Pallathadka, H., Ramirez-Asis, E. H., Loli-Poma, T. P., Kaliyaperumal, K., Ventayen, R. J. M., & Naved, M. (2023). Applications of artificial intelligence in business management, e-commerce and finance. *Materials Today: Proceedings*, 80, 2610–2613. DOI: 10.1016/j.matpr.2021.06.419

Park, H.. (2018). Influencer Marketing in the Beauty Sector: Insights from South Korea. *Journal of Cosmetics Marketing*, 29(4), 467–482.

Parsamehr, M., & Torkan, R. (2009). Fanatic Support for Soccer Teams in the Iranian League Case of Yazd University Students. *Irish Journal of Sociology*, 10(3), 85–105.

Pashaie, S., & Nasirpour, M. (2024). (in press). The Impact of Observability and Compatibility on Consumers' Attitudes Towards AI-Generated Sports Marketing Content and Its Effect on Purchase Intent. *Sports Marketing Studies. Articles*. Advance online publication. DOI: 10.22034/sms.2024.141529.1367

peak.ai website. https://peak.ai/products/customer-ai/audiences/

Penni, J. (2017). The future of online social networks (OSN): A measurement analysis using social media tools and application. *Telematics and Informatics*, 34(5), 498–517. DOI: 10.1016/j.tele.2016.10.009

Perceptual antecedents of user attitude in electronic commerce | ACM SIGMIS Database: The DATABASE for Advances in Information Systems. (n.d.). Retrieved March 23, 2022, from https://dl.acm.org/doi/abs/10.1145/1161345.1161353

Pergelova, A., Prior, D., & Rialp, J. (2010). Assessing Advertising Efficiency. *Journal of Advertising*, 39(3), 39–54. DOI: 10.2753/JOA0091-3367390303

Pham, M. (2021). The Effects of Online Social Influencers on Purchasing Behavior of Generation Z: An Empirical Study in Vietnam. *Journal of Asian Finance Economics and Business*, 8, 179–0190. DOI: 10.13106/jafeb.2021.vol8.no11.0179

Phelps, J., Lewis, R., Mobilio, L., Perry, D., & Raman, N. (2005). Viral Marketing or Electronic Word-of-Mouth Advertising: Examining Consumer Responses and Motivations to Pass Along Email. *Journal of Advertising Research*, 44(4), 333–348. Advance online publication. DOI: 10.1017/S0021849904040371

Poinski, M. (2024, May 8). *In marketing, AI cannot duplicate the human element*. Forbes. https://www.forbes.com/sites/cmo/2024/05/08/in-marketing-ai-cannot-duplicate-the-human-element/

Popovič, A., Hackney, R., Coelho, P. S., & Jaklič, J. (2012). Towards business intelligence systems success: Effects of maturity and culture on analytical decision making. *Decision Support Systems*, 54(1), 729–739. DOI: 10.1016/j.dss.2012.08.017

Porter, L., & Golan, G. (2006). From Subservient Chickens to Brawny Men. *Journal of Interactive Advertising*, 6(2), 4–33. DOI: 10.1080/15252019.2006.10722116

Portman, P. (2024, February 28). *AI in MarTech: How AI will impact the MarTech industry*. Forbes. https://www.forbes.com/sites/forbestechcouncil/2024/02/28/ai-in-martech-how-ai-will-impact-the-martech-industry/

Posch, M. (2024, February 28). *Air Canada's chatbot: Why RAG is better than an LLMforfacts.* Hackaday. https://hackaday.com/2024/02/28/air-canadas-chatbot-why-rag-is-better-than-an-llm-for-facts/

Price, E. (2024, February 18). *Air Canada must honor a fake refund policy created by its chatbot, court says.* PCMAG. https://www.pcmag.com/news/air-canada-must-honor-a-fake-refund-policy-created-by-its-chatbot-court

Provost, F., & Fawcett, T. (2013). *Data science for business: What you need to know about data mining and data-analytic thinking*. O'Reilly Media, Inc.

Qu ng cáo trên m ng xã h i s vư t m t truy n hình truy n th ng trong năm 2022. (n.d.). Retrieved March 23, 2022, from https://laodong.vn/cong-nghe/quang-cao-tren-mang-xa-hoi-se-vuot-mat-truyen-hinh-truyen-thong-trong-nam-2022-989402.ldo

Quansah, T. K., Buraimo, B., & Lang, M. (2022). The Price of Success and Labour in Sports–Evidence from Match-day Ticket Pricing Strategies in the English Premier League. *Available atSSRN* 4039945. https://doi.org/DOI: 10.2139/ssrn.4039945

Qu c N. N., H ng L. H. T., & Di u H. L. T. (2011). CÁC NHÂN T NH HƯ NG Đ N M C Đ HÀI LÒNG C A KHÁCH HÀNG Đ I V I CÁC VĂN PHÒNG CÔNG CH NG THÀNH PH C N THƠ. *T p chí Khoa h c Trư ng Đ i h c C n Thơ, 17b*, 106–112.

Rachmawati, E., Suliyanto, & Suroso, A. (2020). Direct and indirect effect of entrepreneurial orientation, family involvement and gender on family business performance. *Journal of Family Business Management, ahead-of-print*(ahead-of-print). DOI: 10.1108/JFBM-07-2020-0064

Rahman, J., Raihan, A., Tanchangya, T., & Ridwan, M. (2024). Optimizing the digital marketing landscape: A comprehensive exploration of artificial intelligence (AI) technologies, applications, advantages, and challenges. *Frontiers of Finance*, 2(2). Advance online publication. DOI: 10.59429/ff.v2i2.6549

Rana, B. (2016). *The impact of SEO on business*https://urn.fi/URN:NBN:fi:amk-2016110715826

Rana, N. P., Chatterjee, S., Dwivedi, Y. K., & Akter, S. (2022). Understanding dark side of artificial intelligence (AI) integrated business analytics: Assessing firm's operational inefficiency and competitiveness. *European Journal of Information Systems*, 31(3), 364–387. DOI: 10.1080/0960085X.2021.1955628

Ransbotham, S., Kiron, D., & Prentice, P. K. (2016). Beyond the hype: The hard work behind analytics success. *MIT Sloan Management Review*, 57(3), 1–16.

Rathore, A. K., Ilavarasan, P. V., & Dwivedi, Y. K. (2016). Social media content and product co-creation: An emerging paradigm. *Journal of Enterprise Information Management*, 29(1), 7–18. DOI: 10.1108/JEIM-06-2015-0047

Robelia, B. A., Greenhow, C., & Burton, L. (2011). Environmental learning in online social networks: Adopting environmentally responsible behaviors. *Environmental Education Research*, 17(4), 553–575. DOI: 10.1080/13504622.2011.565118

Romero-Jara, E., Solanellas, F., Muñoz, J., & López-Carril, S. (2023). Connecting with fans in the digital age: An exploratory and comparative analysis of social media management in top football clubs. *Humanities & Social Sciences Communications*, 10(1), 1–12. https://doi.org/s41599-023-02357-8. DOI: 10.1057/s41599-023-02357-8

Rookwood, J., & Millward, P. (2011). 'We all dream of a team of Carraghers': Comparing 'local' and Texan Liverpool fans' talk. *Sport in Society*, 14(1), 37–52. DOI: 10.1080/17430437.2011.530009

Rust, R. T., & Espinoza, F. (2006). How technology advances influence business research and marketing strategy. *Journal of Business Research*, 59(10-11), 1072–1078. DOI: 10.1016/j.jbusres.2006.08.002

Safarian, S., Nasimi, M. A., & Rahmaty, M. (2024). Provide content marketing model of in sports E-business with the grounded theory approach. *Sports Marketing Studies*, 5(1), 101–121. DOI: 10.22034/sms.2023.139886.1258

Salesforce. (2023). Marketing cloud overview. Retrieved from https://www.salesforce.com/products/marketing-cloud/overview/

Salford Business School. (2024). *Importance of content marketing for your digital marketing strategy*. University of Salford. https://www.salford.ac.uk/salford-business-school/importance-of-content-marketing-for-your-digital-marketing-strategy

Salimi, M., Soltan Hosseini, M., & Naderian Jahromi, M. (2015). The Evaluation of Iran's Sport Marketing Development Obstacles. *Sport Management Studies, 7*(29), 13-36. https://smrj.ssrc.ac.ir/article_428_58c8549f8f4cc25a85b5ffb24d16ca99.pdf

Salminen, M. (2023, August 31). *27 AI statistics and trends in 2024.* Hostinger Tutorials. https://www.hostinger.com/tutorials/ai-statistics

Santos, L.. (2021). Influencer Marketing in the Gaming Industry: Evidence from Brazil. *Journal of Gambling Studies*, 38(1), 124–139.

Sashi, C. M. (2012). Customer engagement, buyer-seller relationships, and social media. *Management Decision*, 50(2), 253–272. DOI: 10.1108/00251741211203551

Saura, J. R., Ribeiro-Soriano, D., & Palacios-Marqués, D. (2021). From user-generated data to data-driven innovation: A research agenda to understand user privacy in digital markets. International Journal of Information Management, 60, 102331.[REMOVED HYPERLINK FIELD] https://doi.org/DOI: 10.1016/j.ijinfomgt.2021.102331

Saxena, A., & Khanna, U. (2013). Advertising on Social Network Sites: A Structural Equation Modelling Approach. *Vision (Basel)*, 17(1), 17–25. DOI: 10.1177/0972262912469560

Sbrighi, A. (2024). *Leveraging The Power Of Deep Tech Within The Realm Of Digital Marketing: An Explorative Insight Into The Relationship Between Artificial Intelligence And Sports Fan Engagement.* Università Ca' Foscari Venezia. https://doi.org/DOI: 10579/26168

Schneider, C. (2023, November 2). *The complete guide to AI content marketing.* https://www.linkedin.com/pulse/complete-guide-ai-content-marketing-cody-schneider-epk7c

Seddon, P. B., Constantinidis, D., Tamm, T., & Dod, H. (2017). How does business analytics contribute to business value? *Information Systems Journal*, 27(3), 237–269. DOI: 10.1111/isj.12101

Segment, SendGrid, & Twilio. (2023). *7 ways to use AI to superpower your marketing strategy.*

Shah, T. R. (2022). Can big data analytics help organisations achieve sustainable competitive advantage? A developmental enquiry. *Technology in Society*, 68, 101801. Advance online publication. DOI: 10.1016/j.techsoc.2021.101801

Shankar, V., & Parsana, S. (2022). An overview and empirical comparison of natural language processing (NLP) models and an introduction to and empirical application of autoencoder models in marketing. *Journal of the Academy of Marketing Science*, 50(6), 1324–1350. DOI: 10.1007/s11747-022-00840-3

Shank, M. D., & Lyberger, M. R. (2014). *Sports marketing: A strategic perspective.* Routledge., DOI: 10.4324/9781315794082

Sharma, A. (2000). Recall of Television Commercials as a Function of Viewing Context: The Impact of Program-Commercial Congruity on Commercial Messages. *The Journal of General Psychology*, 127(4), 383–396. DOI: 10.1080/00221300009598592 PMID: 11110001

Sharma, R., Mithas, S., & Kankanhalli, A. (2021). Transforming decision-making processes: Insights from predictive analytics and AI-driven systems. *Journal of Management Information Systems*, 38(2), 456–489.

Shen, W., Zhou, M., Yang, F., Yang, C., & Tian, J. (2015). Multi-scale Convolutional Neural Networks for Lung Nodule Classification. In Ourselin, S., Alexander, D. C., Westin, C.-F., & Cardoso, M. J. (Eds.), *Information Processing in Medical Imaging* (pp. 588–599). Springer International Publishing., DOI: 10.1007/978-3-319-19992-4_46

Sheth, J. N., & Sharma, A. (2020). The impact of the product to service shift in industrial markets and the evolution of the sales organization. *Industrial Marketing Management*, 49, 1–12. DOI: 10.1016/j.indmarman.2015.05.026

Shobana, J., Gangadhar, C., Arora, R. K., Renjith, P. N., & Bamini, J. (2023). E-commerce customer churn prevention using machine learning-based business intelligence strategy. *Measurement. Sensors*, 27, 100728. DOI: 10.1016/j.measen.2023.100728

Siegel, D. A. (2009). Social Networks and Collective Action. *American Journal of Political Science*, 53(1), 122–138. DOI: 10.1111/j.1540-5907.2008.00361.x

Silitonga, D., Rohmayanti, S. A. A., Aripin, Z., Kuswandi, D., Sulistyo, A. B., & Juhari, . (2024). Edge Computing in E-commerce Business: Economic Impacts and Advantages of Scalable Information Systems. *EAI Endorsed Transactions on Scalable Information Systems*, 11(1). Advance online publication. DOI: 10.4108/eetsis.4375

Sivarajah, U., Kamal, M. M., Irani, Z., & Weerakkody, V. (2017). Critical analysis of Big Data challenges and analytical methods. *Journal of Business Research*, 70, 263–286. DOI: 10.1016/j.jbusres.2016.08.001

Smart Insights. (2023). What is marketing technology and why is it so important. Retrieved from https://www.smartinsights.com/digital-marketing-strategy/what-is-marketing-technology-and-why-is-it-so-important/

Smith, J.. (2019). Challenges in Influencer Collaboration and Management: Insights from the United Kingdom. *International Journal of Market Research*, 36(2), 245–261.

Smith, R., & Johnson, L. (2019). The Power of Personalization: AI in Digital Marketing. *Journal of Contemporary Marketing*, 17(1), 30–44.

Solomon, M. R., Russell-Bennett, R., & Previte, J. (2013). *Consumer behaviour: Buying, having, being* (3rd ed.). Pearson Australia.

Solomonoff, G. (2023, May 6). *The Meeting of the Minds That Launched AI*. https://spectrum.ieee.org/dartmouth-ai-workshop

Stewart, M. C., & Arnold, C. L. (2018). Defining social listening: Recognizing an emerging dimension of listening. *International Journal of Listening*, 32(2), 85–100. DOI: 10.1080/10904018.2017.1330656

Stolz, K. (2022). Why do (n't) we buy second-hand luxury products? *Sustainability (Basel)*, 14(14), 8656. Advance online publication. DOI: 10.3390/su14148656

Sullivan, L. (2017). *Technology Highlights.* 27 July. Accessed April 12, 2024. https://www.devicedaily.com/pin/sephora-chatbot-on-facebook-messenger-to-aid-in-search-discovery/

Sundar, S. S., Bellur, S., Oh, J., Jia, H., & Kim, H.-S. (2016). Theoretical Importance of Contingency in Human-Computer Interaction: Effects of Message Interactivity on User Engagement. *Communication Research*, 43(5), 595–625. DOI: 10.1177/0093650214534962

Sundar, S. S., & Kalyanaraman, S. (2004). AROUSAL, MEMORY, AND IMPRESSION-FORMATION EFFECTS OF ANIMATION SPEED IN WEB ADVERTISING. *Journal of Advertising*, 33(1), 7–17. DOI: 10.1080/00913367.2004.10639152

Tambe, P. (2014). Big data investment, skills, and firm value. *Management Science*, 60(6), 1452–1469. DOI: 10.1287/mnsc.2014.1899

Taylor, D. G., Lewin, J. E., & Strutton, D. (2011). Friends, Fans, and Followers: Do Ads Work on Social Networks?: How Gender and Age Shape Receptivity. *Journal of Advertising Research*, 51(1), 258–275. DOI: 10.2501/JAR-51-1-258-275

Taylor, L., Fiore, A., Mendelsohn, G., & Cheshire, C. (2011). “Out of My League”: A Real-World Test of the Matching Hypothesis. *Personality and Social Psychology Bulletin*, 37(7), 942–954. DOI: 10.1177/0146167211409947 PMID: 21632966

Telefónica Tech helps B2B customers unlock the value of Big Data and the IoT with Tableau. (n.d.). Tableau. https://www.tableau.com/solutions/customer/telefonica-tech-helps-b2b-customers-unlock-value

Thakur, S., Sandhu, S., & Yehuwalashet, F. (2024). 16 E-Commerce and Trade. Handbook of Artificial Intelligence Applications for Industrial Sustainability: Concepts and Practical Examples

Th y gì qua b ng x p h ng 50 t báo, trang đi n t nhi u ngư i xem nh t Vi t Nam năm 2021? (n.d.). Https://Www.Qdnd.Vn. Retrieved March 23, 2022, from https://www.qdnd.vn/xa-hoi/cac-van-de/thay-gi-qua-bang-xep-hang-50-to-bao-trang-dien-tu-nhieu-nguoi-xem-nhat-viet-nam-nam-2021-674421

Thiel, C. E., McClean, S., Harvey, J., & Prince, N. (2023). Trouble with big brother: Counterproductive consequences of electronic monitoring through the erosion of leader-member social exchange. *Journal of Organizational Behavior*, 44(9), 1320–1339. DOI: 10.1002/job.2748

Thilagavathy, N., & Kumar, E. P. (2021). Artificial intelligence on digital marketing-An overview. *Nveo-Natural Volatiles & Essential Oils Journal| NVEO*, 9895-9908.

TikTok is the third largest worldwide social network behind Instagram and Facebook eMarketer Newsroom. (n.d.). Retrieved March 23, 2022, from https://www.emarketer.com/newsroom/index.php/tiktok-is-the-third-largest-worldwide-social-network-behind-instagram-and-facebook/

Todor, R. D. (2016). Marketing automation. *Bulletin of the Transilvania University of Brasov. Series V, Economic Sciences*, •••, 87–94.

Trieu, V. H. (2017). Getting value from Business Intelligence systems: A review and research agenda. *Decision Support Systems*, 93, 111–124. DOI: 10.1016/j.dss.2016.09.019

Truong, Y., McColl, R., & Kitchen, P. (2010). Practitioners' perceptions of advertising strategies for digital media. *International Journal of Advertising*, 29(5), 709–725. DOI: 10.2501/S0265048710201439

Tsimonis, G., & Dimitriadis, S. (2014). Brand strategies in social media. *Marketing Intelligence & Planning*, 32(3), 328–344. DOI: 10.1108/MIP-04-2013-0056

Turing, A. M. (1937). On Computable Numbers, with an Application to the Entscheidungsproblem. *Proceedings of the London Mathematical Society*, s2-42(1), 230–265. https://doi.org/DOI: 10.1112/plms/s2-42.1.230

Twilio. (2023). *The growth report 2023: The AI edition*.

Vale, L., & Fernandes, T. (2018). Social media and sports: Driving fan engagement with football clubs on Facebook. *Journal of Strategic Marketing*, 26(1), 37–55. DOI: 10.1080/0965254X.2017.1359655

Van Esch, P., & Stewart Black, J. (2021). Artificial intelligence (AI): Revolutionizing digital marketing. *Australasian Marketing Journal*, 29(3), 199–203. DOI: 10.1177/18393349211037684

Van Reijmersdal, E., Smit, E., & Neijens, P. (2010). How media factors affect audience responses to brand placement. *International Journal of Advertising*, 29(2), 279–301. DOI: 10.2501/S0265048710201154

Varikuti, M. (2023, May 6). *Can Machines Think?* ILLUMINATION. https://medium.com/illumination/can-machines-think-a36969b741fe

Veer, N., Pawar, P., & Kolte, A. (2019).. . *Effectiveness of Social Media Tools and It's Impact on Promotions.*, 8, 224–230.

Venkatraman, V., Dimoka, A., Pavlou, P. A., Vo, K., Hampton, W., Bollinger, B., Hershfield, H. E., Ishihara, M., & Winer, R. S. (2015). Predicting Advertising success beyond Traditional Measures: New Insights from Neurophysiological Methods and Market Response Modeling. *JMR, Journal of Marketing Research*, 52(4), 436–452. DOI: 10.1509/jmr.13.0593

Vernon, J. (2014). The power of YouTube ads. The ultimate guide to start running ads on YouTube. *MarketingHY*. https://marketinghy.com/2014/06/

Vidgen, R., Shaw, S., & Grant, D. B. (2017). Management Challenges in Creating Value from Business Analytics. *European Journal of Operational Research*, 261(2), 626–639. DOI: 10.1016/j.ejor.2017.02.023

Vietnamese top list of most online shoppers in SEA | Business | Vietnam+ (VietnamPlus). (n.d.). Retrieved March 23, 2022, from https://en.vietnamplus.vn/vietnamese-top-list-of-most-online-shoppers-in-sea/204780.vnp

Vlačić, B., Corbo, L., Costa, E., Silva, S., & Dabić, M. (2021). The evolving role of artificial intelligence in marketing: A review and research agenda. *Journal of Business Research*, 128, 187–203. DOI: 10.1016/j.jbusres.2021.01.055

Walsh, J. P., & Ungson, G. R. (1991). Organizational Memory. *Academy of Management Review*, 16(1), 57. DOI: 10.2307/258607

Wamba, S. F., Gunasekaran, A., Akter, S., Ren, S. J. F., Dubey, R., & Childe, S. J. (2017). Big data analytics and firm performance: Effects of dynamic capabilities. *Journal of Business Research*, 70, 356–365. DOI: 10.1016/j.jbusres.2016.08.009

Wang, C. (2011). Social Shopping Development and Perspectives. [IJVCSN]. *International Journal of Virtual Communities and Social Networking*, 3(2), 51–59. DOI: 10.4018/jvcsn.2011040103

Wang, H., & Lee, S. (2018). Consumer Perceptions of Influencer Marketing: A Qualitative Study in South Korea. *Journal of Consumer Behaviour*, 30(2), 211–228.

Wang, Q., Liu, C., & Chen, Z. (2019). AI-Driven Data Analysis in Digital Marketing. *International Journal of Business Analytics*, 6(3), 68–82.

Wang, T., & Bailey, R. L. (2023). Processing Peripherally Placed Advertising: The Effect of Thematic Ad-Content Congruence and Arousing Content on the Effectiveness of In-Video Overlay Advertising. *Journal of Interactive Advertising*, 23(3), 203–220. DOI: 10.1080/15252019.2023.2217810

Wang, Y., & Sun, S. (2010). Assessing beliefs, attitudes, and behavioral responses toward online advertising in three countries. *International Business Review*, 19(4), 333–344. DOI: 10.1016/j.ibusrev.2010.01.004

Wanless, L., Seifried, C., Bouchet, A., Valeant, A., & Naraine, M. L. (2022). The diffusion of natural language processing in professional sport. *Sport Management Review*, 25(3), 522–545. DOI: 10.1080/14413523.2021.1968174

Ware, C. (2012). *Information Visualization: Perception for Design.* Morgan Kaufmann.

Watson, H. J. (2014). Tutorial: Big data analytics: Concepts, technologies, and applications. *Communications of the Association for Information Systems*, 34(1), 65. DOI: 10.17705/1CAIS.03465

Weaver, A. (2023, April 4). *Generative AI in plain language: What it is, what's hype, and what's real.* Writer. https://writer.com/blog/generative-ai-defined-hype-vs-reality/

Web & Hubspot. (2023). *2023 AI trends for marketers.* Adnews Staff. (2022, July 25). *Heinz resumes Draw Ketchup campaign.* Adnews. https://www.adnews.com/42091

Wedel, M., & Kannan, P. K. (2016). Marketing analytics for data-rich environments. *Journal of Marketing*, 80(6), 97–121. DOI: 10.1509/jm.15.0413

White, C. (2023, October 4). Key differences between machine learning and generative AI in marketing. CMSWire.Com. https://www.cmswire.com/digital-experience/machine-learning-and-generative-ai-in-marketing-critical-differences/

Wixom, B. H., & Watson, H. J. (2001). An empirical investigation of the factors affecting data warehousing success. *Management Information Systems Quarterly*, 25(1), 17–41. DOI: 10.2307/3250957

Wolinsky, J. (2023, June 29). *What's coming next decade for AI in marketing?* CMSWire.Com. https://www.cmswire.com/digital-marketing/whats-coming-next-decade-for-ai-in-marketing/

World Market Watch LLC. (2024). *The CMO Survey.*

Wright-Isak, C., Faber, R. J., & Horner, L. R. (1997). Comprehensive Measurement of Advertising Effectiveness: Notes From the Marketplace. In *Measuring Advertising Effectiveness* (1st ed., Vol. 1, p. 10). Psychology Press.

Wu, D., Zhang, G., Liu, J., Shen, S., Yang, Z., Pan, Y., Zhao, X., Yang, S., Tian, Y., Zhao, H., Li, J., & Cai, L. (2022). Influence of particle properties and environmental factors on the performance of typical particle monitors and low-cost particle sensors in the market of China. *Atmospheric Environment*, 268, 118825. DOI: 10.1016/j.atmosenv.2021.118825

Wu, P. C. S., Yeh, G. Y.-Y., & Hsiao, C.-R. (2011). The effect of store image and service quality on brand image and purchase intention for private label brands. [AMJ]. *Australasian Marketing Journal*, 19(1), 30–39. DOI: 10.1016/j.ausmj.2010.11.001

Wu, Q., Yan, D., & Umair, M. (2023). Assessing the role of competitive intelligence and practices of dynamic capabilities in business accommodation of SMEs. *Economic Analysis and Policy*, 77, 1103–1114. Advance online publication. DOI: 10.1016/j.eap.2022.11.024

Wu, Y.. (2017). Impact of Influencer Marketing on Consumer Engagement: Evidence from China. *Journal of Interactive Advertising*, 18(2), 231–246.

Yaakop, A., Anuar, M. M., & Omar, K. (2013). Like It or Not: Issue of Credibility in Facebook Advertising. *Asian Social Science*, 9(3), 154–163. DOI: 10.5539/ass.v9n3p154

Yang, C., & Liu, Z. (2021). Application of computer vision in electronic commerce. *Journal of Physics: Conference Series*, 1992(2), 022134. DOI: 10.1088/1742-6596/1992/2/022134

Yang, L.. (2020). Impact of Influencer Marketing on Brand Positioning: Evidence from the United States. *Journal of Brand Management*, 35(4), 482–497.

Yang, Y., Habib, K., & Wood, M. O. (2023). Establishing best practices for E-commerce transport packaging waste management in Canada: A systematic review. *Journal of Cleaner Production*, 429, 139377. Advance online publication. DOI: 10.1016/j.jclepro.2023.139377

Yashveer Raghav, Y., Tipu, R. K., Bhakhar, R., Gupta, T., & Sharma, K. (2023). The future of digital marketing: Leveraging artificial intelligence for competitive strategies and tactics. In Teixeira, S., & Remondes, J. (Eds.), (pp. 249–274). Advances in Marketing, Customer Relationship Management, and E-Services. IGI Global., DOI: 10.4018/978-1-6684-9324-3.ch011

Yaveroglu, I., & Donthu, N. (2008). Advertising Repetition and Placement Issues in On-Line Environments. *Journal of Advertising*, 37(2), 31–44. DOI: 10.2753/JOA0091-3367370203

Yeo, S. F. (2020a). Effects of Social Media Advertising on Consumers'. *Online Purchase Intentions.*, 12(1), 18.

Yiu, L. D., Yeung, A. C., & Cheng, T. E. (2021). The impact of business intelligence systems on profitability and risks of firms. *International Journal of Production Research*, 59(13), 3951–3974. DOI: 10.1080/00207543.2020.1756506

Yiu, L. D., Yeung, A. C., & Jong, A. P. (2020). Business intelligence systems and operational capability: An empirical analysis of high-tech sectors. *Industrial Management & Data Systems*, 120(6), 1195–1215. DOI: 10.1108/IMDS-12-2019-0659

Yoon, S.-H., & Lee, S.-H. (2022). What Likeability Attributes Attract People to Watch Online Video Advertisements? *Electronics (Basel)*, 11(13), 1960. DOI: 10.3390/electronics11131960

Zanjani, S. H. A., Diamond, W. D., & Chan, K. (2011). Does Ad-Context Congruity Help Surfers and Information Seekers Remember Ads in Cluttered E-magazines? *Journal of Advertising*, 40(4), 67–84. DOI: 10.2753/JOA0091-3367400405

Zhang, J., & Mao, E. (2016). From Online Motivations to Ad Clicks and to Behavioral Intentions: An Empirical Study of Consumer Response to Social Media Advertising. *Psychology and Marketing*, 33(3), 155–164. DOI: 10.1002/mar.20862

Zhang, X.. (2018). Effectiveness of Influencer Marketing in the Healthcare Industry: Evidence from China. *Journal of Health Communication*, 25(3), 315–330.

Zhang, X., & Yuan, S.-M. (2018). An Eye Tracking Analysis for Video Advertising: Relationship Between Advertisement Elements and Effectiveness. *IEEE Access : Practical Innovations, Open Solutions*, 6, 10699–10707. DOI: 10.1109/ACCESS.2018.2802206

About the Contributors

Tran Minh Tung gains (his 1st Doctoral Degree) a Doctor of Business Administration (DBA Degree) in Marketing Management from University of Technology and Management (UITM), Poland and a Master of Science in Business Information Systems from Heilbronn University, German. He is currently Director FSB Danang - FPT School of Business and Technology (FSB) - FPT University cum Media and Business Lecturer. He has over 18 years of work experience and over 12 years in teaching and sharing at both over 40 Enterprises and over 22 Higher Educational Institutions in Vietnam. His research interests are in Social Media, PR, Marketing, Marketing in Higher Education, Innovation Teaching Methodology, Data Driven Marketing, Information Systems, Standards Based Curriculum, Experience Learning and Gamification in Education. Recently, he has completed and obtained (his 2nd and 3rd Doctoral Degree) EdD - Professional Doctorate in Educational Administration & Leadership and Doctor of Philosophy (Ph.D.) in Media and Communication from European International University, EIU-Paris, France, in 2023 which can assist him in his personal development plan (PDP) and professional career in current role in leading and administrating international higher education as well as teaching Media and Business.

***

Shivani Agarwal is an Associate Professor, Galgotias University, Greater Noida, India. She has earned her PhD from Indian Institute of Technology, Roorkee in Management. She has completed the executive programme in HR Analytics from IIM Ahmedabad. She has more than 13 years of experience in teaching and in handling various administrative positions. She also presented several research papers at national and international conferences. Dr. Agarwal has contributed chapters to different books published by Taylor and Francis, Springer and IGI Global. She has conducted and attended various workshops, FDPs and MDPs. She is the Book Series

Editor of Information Technology, Management & Operations Research Practices, CRC Press, Taylor & Francis Group, USA. She is a guest editor with IGI-Global, USA. Her research interests include Quality of Work life, Trust, Subjective well-being, knowledge management, Employer Branding innovation. She can be contacted at jindal.shivani24@gmail.com.

K. Balaji is an Assistant Professor in Business and Mangement, Christ University, Bangalore. He did Ph.D. from KLU Business School, KL University,Vijayawada. He is having 12 years of teaching experience. He has to his credit 23 Research Articles published in reputed National and International Journals. He has participated and presented more than 12 papers in both National and International Seminars/ Conferences and also attended more than 50 workshops/FDPS organized by various reputed organizations. He has also participated in more than 50 seminars / webinars organized by various reputed organizations. He has also attended in 6 Short Term Training programs.He has successfully conducted 3 webinars, one 5 day FDP and one International Conference on Reimaging marketing in New Normal. He is a ratified as Assistant Professor by both JNTUH, JNTU Anantapur and Sri Venkateswara University,Tirupati. His specialized areas include, Accounting and Financial management, Marketing Management, Retailing Management, Consumer Behavior studies, Entrepreneurship and Business Laws.

Deeksha Dwivedi is a Software Engineer at Leslie's, USA. She is a former Asst. Professor in the Department of Management, HRIT, Ghaziabad. She holds PhD in management. Her research focuses primarily on stress management, talent management, knowledge management and artificial Intelligence. Dr. Deeksha is author of more than 12+ research papers published in national and international journals. Her book "Stress Management in Software Industry: Indian context" is published in multiple languages. Her hobbies include hiking, gardening, traveling, and cooking.

Matthew A. Gilbert, MBA, is a lecturer of marketing at Coastal Carolina University, where he teaches courses in advertising, personal selling, and principles of marketing. His academic research focuses on artificial intelligence, marketing technology, the sharing economy, social media marketing, and sports marketing. A charismatic communicator, he has facilitated professional development workshops and delivered three TEDx Talks. He is a prolific writer who has published articles, book chapters, short stories, and textbooks. As a consultant, he crafts marketing content, creates business curricula, and composes professional communications. When asked why teaching is his tenure, he explains, "education empowers me to influence individuals and impact organizations while improving myself in the process."

Madhavi Sripathi is an Associate Professor and Mentor (AS&A) in the Department of Business and Management Studies at Seshadri Rao Gudlavalleru Engineering College, Andhra Pradesh. She holds a Ph.D in Marketing from Acharya Nagarjuna University, and successfully cleared the APSET in Management. Dr. Sripathi has served as the Principal Investigator for a UGC-funded Minor project and holds a patent. She is actively engaged in academia, serving as an editorial board member for journals like IJTPD, IJSSHR, and IJMCI, and as a reviewer for the International Journal of Bank marketing and Hindawi and Wiley Journals. With a remarkable 14 years of teaching experience, Dr. Sripathi has authored 33 research articles, published in various international and national journals along with three highly regarded textbooks titled "Health Economics for Hospital Administration", "Marketing Analytics", & "HR Metrics and Analytics", and delivered guest lectures on consumer rights and entrepreneurship as also presented her research findings at several conferences. She organized a number of SDPs. In addition to her scholarly pursuits, she is a member of the Hyderabad Management Association (HMA) and the Indian Academic Researchers Association (IARA).

Trinh Le Tan is a lecturer at FPT University, Vietnam. He graduated with a Doctor of Business Administration. The honorable Dean awarded him an outstanding Lecturer in three semesters (Summer 2021, Summer 2022, and Fall 2022). His industry and academic experience made him an excellent fit for the journal editorial board of the International Journal of Academe and Industry Research (ISSN:2719-0625). His research works involve a wide range of topics, including entrepreneurship, consumer behavior, organizational behavior, and green supply chains.

Index

A

B

C

D

E

www.ingramcontent.com/pod-product-compliance
Lightning Source LLC
LaVergne TN
LVHW081334300926
849161LV00008B/1975